FRATERNAL BROTHERHOOD

FRATERNAL BROTHERHOOD

The Story of Alpha Omega
Theta Fraternity Inc.

Frederick M. Gross

Library of Congress Control Number:		2009901840
ISBN:	Hardcover	978-1-4415-1563-6
	Softcover	978-1-4415-1562-9

To order additional copies of this book, contact:
Xlibris Corporation
1-888-795-4274
www.Xlibris.com
Orders@Xlibris.com
58023

CONTENTS

DEDICATION

Normally a book is dedicated to one person, but since Alpha Omega Theta Fraternity has sixty years of history, I felt there was more than one person worth mentioning.

As such, on behalf of the alumni of Alpha Omega Theta Fraternity, this book is dedicated to the four original founding members of Alpha Omega Theta: Ed Carroll, John Stefano, John Sposito, and Jerry something or other who left the fraternity a few short months after its founding. You should have stuck around, Jerry.

A special dedication goes to founding brother Ed Carroll who sadly, passed away in January 2008 and did not get a chance to see this book. Ed did get to attend the AOT Grand Chapter Reunion in 2007, and all of us from the combined Long Island chapters were honored to meet him. According to founding brother John Stefano, it was Ed Carroll who wrote all of AOT's documentation, including its earliest constitution and bylaws. He was, in essence, the author of Alpha Omega Theta.

Without a doubt, this book is also dedicated to Joe Brugnolotti, Al "Mickey" Percy, Billy Meyer, Jim Stack, and Chick Hackney for bringing AOT from Brooklyn to Valley Stream.

Additionally, I would like to mention every AOT brother who lost their lives serving their country. Their names are too numerous to list.

On a personal level, I want to share this dedication with my good friends Tommy Farndell and Danny Carmeinke. Tommy and Danny were both good friends of mine since junior high school, and both have passed away. Tommy's untimely passing was in his senior year of high school and hit us all hard in Oceanside AOT.

Tommy was my best friend in junior high, and we dogged for and were inducted into AOT together. I never would have made it into the frat without you, Tommy. I miss you, bro.

Danny was one hell of a guy. He was a lot of fun to hang out with. I can't think of any better way to put it. You are missed, Danny.

PROLOGUE

This book is a depiction of sixty years of history of Alpha Omega Theta Fraternity. Alpha Omega Theta was a high school fraternity that was founded in Brooklyn and had multiple chapters in Nassau County on Long Island, as well as in Middletown, Connecticut. This book was made possible by the many brothers of Alpha Omega Theta, who gave interviews and provided correspondence. The events depicted in this book are based on real events and real people. The names of the characters have been changed to protect the privacy of the real people they are based on, except in the instances of those who have given the author express permission to use their real names.

The events and stories told in this book are derived from various e-mail correspondences, one-on-one interviews, and my own memories. Some stories are dramatized in order to provide flow to the book.

Alpha Omega Theta Fraternity Inc. had a long and tumultuous run, from its humble beginning in Brooklyn in 1946 until the demise of the last high school chapter in 1996 to its resurgence in Canada in 2006. The fraternity went through many changes: from its founding in the 1940s, when it was formed as a social club; through the 1950s, when it was brought to Long Island and the chapters began functioning as athletic social clubs exclusively for top-performing athletes; and into the 1970s through the 1990s, when Alpha Omega Theta Fraternity, as well as other area fraternities, began to resemble street gangs with fancy Greek names.

Alpha Omega Theta Fraternity has had alumni from all walks of life: doctors, lawyers, businessmen, law enforcement officers, etc., and even some notable members, such as actor Steve Buscemi, Hollywood director Ted Demme, fitness guru Jeff "Body by Jake" Steinfeld, and Ron Atanasio, who played professional soccer for the New York Cosmos. AOT also has its fair share of heroes: FDNY Captain Terry Hatton, who lost his life at the World Trade Center on 9/11/2001; John Kedenburg, who died in Vietnam and was awarded the Congressional Medal of Honor; and many others too numerous to mention.

This book takes you on a long wild ride through the decades, from formal black-tie ballroom dances in Brooklyn to backyard keg parties on Long Island to all-out warfare with other fraternities.

This book was written by author Fred Gross, an alumnus of the Kappa Theta Chapter of Alpha Omega Theta from Oceanside, New York. Fred was inducted in to AOT at the age of fourteen in 1978. As the Webmaster of the fraternity Web site at alphaomegatheta.com, Fred Gross has accumulated an abundance of e-mails, stories, and anecdotes from members of various chapters, and he felt there was a story that needed to be told.

If you are a college-age man of good character and you are interested in carrying on the traditions of a proud brotherhood, visit our Web site at www. alphaomegatheta.com and contact us at webmaster@alphaomegatheta.com to charter a chapter of AOT at your school.

CHAPTER ONE

My Hell Night Part 1

Five long weeks I'd waited for this night, and now it was here. Five weeks of slow torture. There I sat, waiting for the start of my Hell Night. For those of you who don't know, Hell Night was the grand finale of dogging for a fraternity. *Dogging* was the slang term we used for pledging. This evening would no doubt be painful and humiliating.

Why would someone want to go through three to five weeks of humiliation and embarrassment for the privilege of joining a fraternity? I think there is no simple answer to that question; however, the allure of earning your "colors," of being able to walk into school wearing your fraternity sweater, to be able to give that sweater to a girlfriend to wear, is a very powerful enticement to a young man and very difficult to resist.

Fraternities were a time-honored tradition in Oceanside. Oceanside is a village in the county of Nassau in New York State. In fact, many of the towns surrounding Oceanside had fraternities and sororities as well. It was March 1978, and the fraternity I was about to join, which was called Alpha Omega Theta, had chapters in Baldwin, Rockville Centre, Freeport, and our main chapter in Valley Stream. That's powerful brotherhood and a lot of tradition. The opportunity to join a frat, to be a member of a brotherhood, and the respect that comes with it, well, that was too powerful to resist for a kid my age. My name is Fred Gross; at the time of my Hell Night, I was fourteen years old, and I was in the eighth grade. I was a student at Oceanside Junior High School.

There were other fraternities in both Oceanside High School and Oceanside Junior High School. Besides AOT, there was Omega Gamma Delta, whose colors were black and gold, and Alpha Sigma Phi, with their black and red. The fraternity I hoped to become a member of this evening, Alpha Omega Theta, had green and red. Very soon, I would find out just how two simple colors would impact my life. When you are in a fraternity, your colors are like a flag to be defended. With rival fraternities in the same school and town, as well as in the surrounding towns, you would be defending them often.

Looking back, I don't really think I knew exactly what I was getting into by dogging for and joining AOT. I just knew I wanted to wear colors, go to frat parties, and meet girls. I was young for joining a fraternity, but the minimum age-group requirement was eighth grade. Very few eighth graders would join a fraternity, especially when they had to dog for four or five weeks. I was determined to join AOT; my uncles had both been in Omega Gamma Delta, and I wanted to be a fraternity man too.

So there I was, fourteen years old, about to get ritually beaten by high school-age kids in Pete Wilhelm's basement. Pete Wilhelm was my next-door neighbor. I had known him all my life. In fact, our families both moved into Oceanside when the town was 95 percent woods. Pete was the one who asked me to dog for Alpha. Pete was three years older than me; he was well-known and respected in Oceanside High School, and he was my friend. When Pete asked me to dog for AOT, I was thrilled. I had no idea what dogging entailed, but I immediately accepted the invitation to interview with the fraternity. The interview was five weeks ago.

Obviously, I passed the interview and was permitted to dog. *Dogging* was the term that was used to describe a prospective new member. This neophyte was to become a servant, a pet, a "dog" to the entire fraternity for the amount of time imposed upon him as his dogging period. College fraternities call this *pledging*. But for us, the guy putting in his time, earning his frat colors, was a dog. A dog was low on the food chain. He tagged along with the fraternity, was obedient, and did what he was told. A dog's loyalty was absolute and unquestioning.

When you dogged for a fraternity, you wore the dogging attire. In respect to dogging for AOT, proper attire was a white collared shirt with a green tie and red suspenders. This was to be worn every day, everywhere that you went, except in the privacy of your own home. A dog, especially an Alpha dog, was to have a fresh-shaved crew cut and a clean-shaven face. A dog was expected to carry plenty of gum to go around and cigarettes as well. God help you if you didn't have enough of both for everyone when asked.

A dog was humble and never spoke unless spoken to. A dog followed orders given without question. There were some exceptions to that rule. A dog was not required to obey any order that violated his morals or sense of decency; however, it was not advisable to question orders given by a brother. This lead to demerits, which could lead to being blackballed. Once a guy was blackballed, he was gone. He was no longer considered worthy of the fraternity and was never again to be considered for membership in the brotherhood. Not ever. Nobody wanted to be blackballed. It was like being declared to be a piece of shit. Once people found out you were blackballed by a fraternity, you would be unwanted by the other fraternities. Nobody wanted a guy that wasn't good enough for the other frat. So a dog would tolerate just about anything to avoid being blackballed.

There were also sororities in Oceanside. They dogged girls for membership also. They didn't have beatings or paddling like the fraternities did. But they had a totally different way to torture and humiliate their dogs. Girls have their own special brand of cruelty. Sororities would strip their pledges down to panties and bras. They would cover them in mud, molasses, dog shit, just about anything slimy and offensive. They would make their pledges eat wet coffee grinds, mixed concoctions of various condiments—hot peppers, horseradish, and whatever they found in the refrigerator that day, just about any nasty, vomit-inducing slop.

In Oceanside, the different fraternities and sororities often paired off into partnerships. This was a big reason to want to join a frat—to meet sorority girls from your frat's sister sorority. Delta Pi Delta was AOT's sister sorority. Their colors were red and white. Tau Delta Gamma paired up with Omega Gamma Delta, and Tau's colors were blue and red. Alpha Nu Gamma was with Alpha Sigma Phi. ANT, as they were referred to, had gray and red. Over the years, there were quite a few fraternities and sororities that didn't have the longevity of the major players. Many unsuccessful fraternities and sororities closed up and were forgotten over the years.

I had been here for about ten minutes, and already I was scared shitless. The meeting hadn't officially started yet, but the early arrivals wasted no time having fun and games with the dog. And since I was the dog, that meant I had to do tricks, be obedient, and give in to whatever they wanted to do to me. It was my last night as a dog, so they wanted their last licks before it was over. I had been forced to stand at attention with hands at my sides, while Jim Nunley, one of the AOT brothers, practiced his spinning back kick, right to my stomach. He said he wanted to "break in" his new Frye boots. I doubled over, gasping for breath; they stood me up, and he went for practice kick number two. Next, I got grabbed by Joe Farella, a Nassau County champion wrestler. He put me in a full nelson, a headlock, a sleeper hold, and a painful abdominal stretch. Have you ever seen that stuff on Saturday-night wrestling? Trust me, it's not as fake as it looks. It's painful. I thought he would break my spine.

I had been slapped numerous times, backhanded, open-handed right across the face. And the meeting hadn't officially started; this was barely the beginning. Finally, John Jaeger entered the room. John was the president of AOT. Everyone quieted down as soon as he arrived.

John was a scary-looking guy. He was tall, muscular, and looked really serious all the time. His crew respected him, and he commanded the room with ease. With just the sight of him walking in the door, all talk stopped, and all eyes were on him. They were just getting ready to start the meeting. John Jaeger instructed John Borelli to take me to another room. John Borelli was my pledge master. He was the only one I was comfortable around. He was a nice guy and looked after me like I was a little brother. It was his job to keep me dogging and to prevent me from dropping out before completing my pledging period. I suppose he did a good job. I was still there, and I didn't drop out. I thought about dropping out many times, but I didn't.

John took me to the bottom of the stairway that led down into Pete Wilhelm's basement. He told me to wait there until someone came to get me. At the bottom of the stairs, there was a wall in front of me and two doors. To my right was the door leading to the bedroom Pete shared with his older brother Dave. Dave wasn't in a frat. To my left was the doorway to hell. On the other side of that closed door was Pete's father's workshop. Pete's dad was an architect, and he did his drafting in his basement. Passing through the work area and going left in an L shape was a semifinished playroom area. That was where the meeting was now convening.

I sat at the bottom of the stairs, nervous and scared. I wrung my hands, rubbed my face and forehead. I would have paced, but I was at the bottom of a stairwell—there was nowhere to pace. All I could do was sit there and wait. I could hear the noise and commotion from the meeting. They were loud, but I couldn't hear what was being said through the walls. Sounded like a party almost.

After a few minutes, it got quiet in there. Then I could hear footsteps, the sound of boots walking on hard concrete floor. The door opened, and I saw John Jaeger standing there, looking annoyed, maybe even a bit pissed. This was unusual, and I immediately knew something was wrong. It was the pledge master who was supposed to lead the dog into the meeting. For John Jaeger to personally come to see me, there had to be something wrong.

John looked me right in the eye and said that I had been a lousy dog. He went on to say that I had missed two meetings while I was dogging, and there had been complaints from some of the brotherhood that I was one of the worst dogs they had seen in years. Simply making it to Hell Night was no guarantee that you would be inducted. Hell Night was the last step, and it had to be completed successfully. John was very stern and serious; he told me that they would be voting on me again, and the outcome of this last vote would determine if I would be permitted to finish my Hell Night or get blackballed and be sent home.

Five long weeks of slow torture and humiliation, weekly meetings, beatings, and paddling; and now that I was down to the wire, my last night, my induction night, they were actually considering blackballing me and tossing me out the door. I couldn't believe this shit. I knew I missed two meetings, but there were reasonable explanations for that. As for me being a shitty dog, well, that was debatable. Perhaps I wasn't the most enthusiastic dog they ever had, but I did follow orders. I always wore my dogging attire, although I never did get a crew cut. Hey, it was 1978—everybody wore long hair. The goofiest thing a kid could do in 1978 was to get a head-shaved, military-style crew cut. They had allowed me to continue to dog without getting my head shaved, but it was now one of the reasons for my possible blackballing.

I couldn't believe I had gone this far, done all of these stupid embarrassing things. I willfully submitted myself to weekly beatings and paddling, and now it looked like it might all be for nothing. So I now had two possible scenarios. Best-case scenario was I'd pass the vote, Hell Night would commence, and I would catch the beating of my life to get inducted. Worst-case scenario: I'd get blackballed, sent home, and would look like a fool to the whole school when I showed up tomorrow with no colors and everyone knowing I was thrown out. That was a clear case of being screwed either way.

John turned and walked away, closing the door behind him. I heard the sound of his boots as he walked across the concrete floor back to the meeting room. I sat and thought, *How did I get myself into this? What was I thinking when I thought it would be cool to join a fraternity? How did this all begin? Where did this all begin?*

CHAPTER TWO

Where Did This All Begin?

Where did this all begin? The answer to that question goes back before my time of recollection, in fact, before my time of existence. The beginning of the story of Alpha Omega Theta Fraternity Inc. goes all the way back to 1946-October 16, 1946, to be exact. That is the birth date of Alpha Omega Theta Fraternity. That was the date that four young students at Brooklyn Manual Training High School in the Park Slope section of Brooklyn got together with an idea. They had the idea of strengthening their bonds of friendship by forming a brotherhood.

There were many fraternities and sororities at Brooklyn Manual Training High School. But these young men wanted something that was theirs. They wanted to build something unique instead of joining one of the existing fraternities. John Stefano was a sophomore, as was his best friend, Ed Carroll. John was approached by Ed one day before school ended and was asked to meet at Ed's house early that evening to discuss a matter of great importance. John's curiosity was piqued, but Ed would not discuss the reason for the gathering. He insisted that John be there and be on time. John spent a good part of the day wondering what Ed was so worked up about. John arrived at Ed Carroll's house around 7:00 PM. He walked in the door and went to the basement. Down in the basement, he found Ed together with two other friends of theirs—John Sposito and Jerry Percale. They seemed to have been waiting for him. Now that John was there, they could get down to business.

"So what's all this about? What are you guys up to?" John said as he took a seat at the basement bar beside Ed.

Ed Carroll looked John right in the eyes and said, "We are starting a fraternity."

John was a bit skeptical at first. "There are a dozen fraternities in school, Ed. Why would we want to start a new one?"

"Because ours is going to be different than the others, Jerry," said Ed.

There was confidence in Ed's voice, and John could sense how serious Ed was. But still, he pressed for more information from Ed. "OK, Ed, how are we going to be different?"

"Well, for one thing, John, we are not going to be restricted like the other fraternities. All the other frats are grouped up in cliques. There are Italian fraternities, Irish fraternities, sports fraternities. They have fraternities for every social and ethnic group."

Besides, Ed Carroll's girlfriend, Penny, whom he would marry later in life, had just started a new sorority called Delta Phi Delta, he explained; and she was encouraging Ed to get his friends together to form a fraternity they could pair up with.

John was intrigued, but still wanted to know more about this plan. "OK, Ed, give me an example. How are we going to start a new fraternity in a school that has eight or ten frats and convince others to join us instead of the existing fraternities at Brooklyn Manual High School?"

Jerry Percale spoke up. "We are going to start with a core group of close friends. It will be us to begin with. Then we will build on that."

The four of them would be making the core of this new fraternal brotherhood; they would be the founding fathers. They would form a brotherhood that strengthened the bonds of friendship by giving everyone a chance to get in. That didn't mean anyone could get in; it just meant that they were forming a club that would not restrict or segregate based on race, religion, or any other superficial reason.

Tonight was the night they would do something so extraordinary that it would last longer than any of them could ever imagine. It would spread far beyond the confines of the Park Slope section of Brooklyn, New York. Tonight was the birth of Alpha Omega Theta Fraternity. There was no turning back. The fraternity's motto was chosen with those exact sentiments. John Stefano was studying Latin in school at that time, and he had the stroke of genius to give AOT "the password" *Alea iacta est.*

Alea iacta est was what Julius Cesar said upon crossing the Rubicon, just before invading his homeland of Rome. *Alea iacta est* means "The die is cast" in English. And its meaning was interpreted to all of those in Alpha Omega Theta over the years and decades to mean that "once it has started, it will never end." The password of the fraternity was the core of its existence as a whole. To all of those who were members over the years, *Alea iacta est* was a powerful reminder of all who came before us, and the importance of passing the brotherhood on to the next generation. The brotherhood these young men formed on this night would indeed grow and spread.

Now that the brotherhood had a name and a motto, it needed a theme, a coat of arms, colors, and bylaws. Being mid-October, it was quite early for Christmas, but it was decided that since the Christmas season was right around the corner, the fraternity's colors would be green and red. After brainstorming into the night, they bounced ideas around for what the fraternity would stand for. Ed Carroll had the idea of basing the fraternity's ideals after medieval knighthood. The values of Alpha Omega Theta Fraternity would be the kind of values of a brotherhood of gallant knights. Noble characteristics such as bravery, gallantry, chivalry, integrity, valor, and many more bold personality traits would be required for membership. In fact, the pledging process would do for prospective members what military training does for new recruits. A new member would be expected to learn, earn, and posses all of those characteristics that would be required of a brother of Alpha Omega Theta.

Right after founding Alpha Omega Theta, Jerry Percale was chosen to be its first president. Jerry, as it turned out, was not as enthusiastic as the others, and he didn't stay in the fraternity for long. Within the first three months, he had left the fledgling brotherhood, and Ed Carroll was to become its second president. Ed played a huge part in the early development of AOT and its documentation. According to cofounding member John Stefano, Ed wrote all of the fraternity's bylaws, its constitution, and opening and closing prayers; just about everything else that was put down on paper was written in longhand by Ed Carroll. That is, everything except for the pledge's greeting. The pledge's greeting was what the pledges were required to say to an AOT brother every time he greeted them. The pledge's greeting was written by John Stefano, and the greeting was to be used by every chapter of AOT for decades to come.

The fraternity actually functioned without a coat of arms for most of its first year. The brothers did brainstorm ideas for a crest that would best represent their ideals as a brotherhood. After going through a book of various crests, they came upon one that had a knight's helmet and crossed swords. They all knew instantly that this was just the look they wanted. It represented strength and honor. This would go along with the medieval knighthood theme, and a coat of arms was designed. This would be affectionately referred to as the Shield by many AOT brothers in the years to come. The Shield was in fact shaped like a shield, with a knight's helmet sitting on top, turned to the left. It had two crossed swords behind it, so that you could see the handles at the top left and right and the points of the swords poking out the bottom left and right. Right through the middle of the shield were the fraternity's Greek symbols, from top to bottom; and of course, the shield was green and red. With green being the dominant color and red being the secondary color. Every part, every section, every line on the coat of arms had a meaning. There were thirty-five meanings in all, and new brothers would be required to know them and live them in every facet of their lives.

Bravery, gallantry, chivalry, integrity, valor, and all the other characteristics that would define each individual brother and the fraternity as a whole would be a way of life for these young men, and they would teach it to all who wished entry into the brotherhood. That—to be dubbed a Knight of Alpha Omega Theta Fraternity—would be an honor and a privilege only offered to those with the above qualities and good character. These things would all come to pass, but now was the hardest part. Now they had to take their ideas and their brotherhood into the world and convince others to join them.

This proved to be a very difficult task. As expected, many of their fellow students shunned them and their efforts. After all, there were plenty of well-established fraternities to choose from. Why would anyone want to join a brand-new one? Who would join a new fraternity that had only four members? And after Jerry Percale left the frat, they were down to only three. This was discouraging and disappointing, and to men of lesser quality and determination, it would have been a good reason to call it quits. But not this bunch; these three were men of quality, and quitting was not in the plan. Brave, gallant knights don't give up. They give it all they have and go down swinging their swords. The original AOT brothers went all out to demonstrate to everyone they were indeed a bona fide fraternal brotherhood. They went to the same local sporting goods store that other fraternities went to, to get their colors made. Friedman's Sporting Goods on Flatbush Avenue made colors for all the local fraternities and sororities. They ordered green-and-red sweaters and patches that had the AOT shield embroidered and sewn on to the right front pocket of the sweaters. They had fraternity pins made up. There were two types of pins: one for brothers and another for pledges. Although it would be a long while before Alpha Omega Theta Fraternity would get its first pledge.

The three original brothers would wear their colors often and with pride. They made sure they were seen everywhere in their sweaters—at school, around town, at John's Pizzeria on Seventh Avenue, everywhere they knew they would be seen. It took a long time before they found someone willing to pledge for their new fraternity. In fact, it seemed like most of the 1946-47 school year went by with no one showing any interest in joining this three-man fraternity. But these three original AOT brothers were persistent in their quest for new blood.

The year was 1946, just one year after World War II had ended. This generation of high school kids was the first one that would not have to go to fight the Germans or the Japanese. The world was at peace; the cold war had not started yet. The iron curtain had not been drawn across Europe; the Berlin Airlift hadn't happened yet. In 1946, the phrase "cold war" hadn't been coined yet, and the country was four years away from a very hot war in Korea. Yet these young men seemed to have the world by the balls. The future was bright, and we hadn't yet learned to fear and despise the Russians. The main goal of fraternities in the late 1940s was to have the biggest and grandest black-tie ball. All the fraternities and sororities threw these big ballroom affairs, and now the fledgling Alpha Omega Theta Fraternity wanted the respect and recognition of throwing a ballroom bash that would be a night to remember. Those wishes would come true as AOT would soon get a reputation for throwing the grandest parties in Brooklyn.

After pounding the pavement for almost a full year, the guys finally had their first pledge. They bent the rules somewhat to make a sweet deal to the pledge. After all, the fraternity's bylaws called for a three-week dogging period. That had been unrealistic since up to this point, no one wanted to pledge for a three-man fraternity. Then Charles Laemmle showed interest in joining AOT. He was offered a one-week dogging period, and he accepted. The AOT brothers took it easy on him for the whole week. They finally had a pledge, and no one wanted to see him drop out before the week was up. They made him perform tasks that were menial, but not very degrading, for a fraternity dog. He shined the brothers' shoes, carried their books, passed out pieces of bubble gum whenever he was asked by one of the brothers. He was made to sing silly songs in public. One such song went like this:

> Do my ears hang low?
> Do they wobble to and fro?
> Can you tie them in a knot?
> Can you tie them in a bow?
> Do my ears hang low?

By the pledging standards that would follow, in Brooklyn and in other chapters, Charles Laemmle had it easy for his one week of dogging. Saturday night came, and it was time for Charles Laemmle's Hell Night. Charles thought it would be as easy as the previous week of dogging had been. He was to find out how wrong he was.

Charles Laemmle was told to meet the brothers promptly at 7:00 PM in front of Brooklyn Manual Training High School. Charles was there fifteen minutes early and found all three AOT brothers already there waiting for him. The four of them walked down Fifth Street to Prospect Park. Spring was almost over, and summer was close. It was a warm night. None of them spoke much during the walk. John Stefano was carrying a duffel bag. Charles was afraid to ask what was in it.

They entered Prospect Park and went to a secluded wooded area. Charles was ordered to go to Prospect Lake and steal two boat oars. He was ordered to acquire the oars and return to the exact spot they were standing on within thirty minutes. The tone of their voices as they gave Charles his orders was stern and demanding. Charles could tell they meant business. This was not going to be as easy as the past week of dogging had been. This was Hell Night. But what the hell did they plan to do with boat oars?

Before sending Charles off on his mission, it was time to dress him up in his Hell Night attire. Charles was ordered to strip down to his underwear. Without question, he complied. From out of the duffel bag, John Stefano pulled out a woman's dress, stockings, and high-heeled shoes. Charles was stripped down to his underwear and was in a state of shock. They were in the middle of a dark park in a secluded area. He was scared for the first time since he began dogging. Despite his fear, he was determined to finish this thing, so he complied. He put on the dress, the stockings, the wig, and the heels, and then the three AOT brothers started smearing makeup all over Charles's face. There was no attempt to apply technique to the application, just smeared makeup—eye shadow, lipstick, and rouge.

By the time they were done with him, he looked like an ugly, drunken prostitute. Charles was humiliated, but there was nothing he could do. Now they sent him on his way. Charles was instructed to go to Prospect Lake, taking a popular footpath so as to be seen by as many people as possible. Charles walked the path and did see people who pointed and laughed at him. He was hideous- and ridiculous-looking. But he was on a mission and was determined to get those boat oars and return to the AOT brothers.

When he got to the boatyard, he found it gated and locked. Charles climbed the fence, leaving his high heels on the ground outside the fence, and jumped onto the ground in the yard where the rowboats were kept. These rowboats were for park patrons who wanted to spend a day at the lake and take a leisurely row around it. Charles made his way to the boats and found the oars were kept on them.

He threw the oars over the fence and climbed over. He grabbed the oars and the high heels that were on the ground beside the fence and took off running back to the spot where the AOT brothers were waiting. He passed a few people along the way. He looked totally crazed, and people got out of his way as he ran by, holding two boat oars under one arm and a pair of high heels in the other hand. He arrived back at the meeting spot and found them waiting for him. He was instructed to put the oars down and stand at attention. John Stefano reached into the duffel bag and pulled out a bandana. He used it to blindfold Charles. Charles was instructed to walk with the AOT brothers and to hold both oars and the duffel bag. Ed Carroll led the way, with Charles following and John Stefano behind him. John Sposito walked on the left of Charles to keep him boxed in and to make him walk with them. At first, they walked on the footpath for at least a quarter mile. Charles tried to determine where they were going by his sense of direction. But as soon as they went into a wooded area, he knew he was lost.

They walked for another fifteen or twenty minutes through trees and brush, and then the brothers stopped walking. Charles stopped with them; he had to. He was ordered to keep his blindfold on. John Stefano again reached into the duffel bag and pulled out a small saw. John Sposito placed one of the boat oars against a tree, with the paddle on the ground and the handle between two tree trunks split like a fork. Charles was brought over to the tree and was instructed to saw the boat oar in half. It was awkward to try to saw while wearing a blindfold, kneeling on the ground, and wearing high heels. He finished the first one, and Jerry Percale brought him the other to saw in half. He finished both oars and was both curious and afraid of why they wanted boat oars and what they intended to do.

Charles was stood up and brought to the tree. He was positioned to bend forward, holding himself up by leaning into the tree. The tree was Y shaped, with the tree trunk splitting into two thick branches spreading left and right. He leaned on the tree, one hand against each tree stalk. They had also taped his mouth shut with heavy-duty duct tape. They were in a public park after dark and didn't want anyone to hear screaming.

While Charles was off stealing the boat oars, the AOT brothers decided on the number of shots he would get when he returned. *Shots* was the term frat members used to refer to paddling a new member. All frats paddled new members. The number of shots was the number of times a pledge would get hit with whatever was being used for a paddle. An assortment of items could be used for a paddle. In my days in the Oceanside chapter, the most common paddle was a wooden baseball shaved down with a wood plane. We would shave about one-quarter to one-third of the bat off, leaving a nice, flat surface, and then paint and decorate the bat with the fraternity's colors, Greek letters, and emblems. Sometimes a two-by-four would be carved into a paddle. Just cut a length about four feet long, and then with some creative carving and whittling a handle long enough for two hands to grip, you had a custom-made paddle.

The paddle of choice this evening would become the paddle of choice for most of the future inductions by the Brooklyn chapter. Boat oars—simple, easy, and painful to get hit with. A boat oar cut roughly in half makes a perfect paddle. Sometimes holes would be drilled into the wide part of the oar to break down the wind resistance when swinging it.

Charles stood at the tree, bent over for what seemed an eternity. John Stefano and Ed Carroll grabbed the two paddles and stepped back about fifteen feet from Charles. They were ready to give him the first two of the twenty shots they decided he would get this evening. They rotated the paddles between two available brothers, and the other two brothers would hold Charles's hands to the branches of the tree from the other side of the tree to prevent him from dropping to the ground or breaking free.

Charles Laemmle screamed, but nobody was near the wooded area where they were paddling him. He writhed with pain, trying to break loose, but his arms were being pulled forward by two brothers, and he was pinned, being pulled forward in the Y shape of the tree. All three took their turns swinging the boat oars and holding Charles in place. They ran up on him, gaining as much momentum as a fifteen-foot sprint could give them. They swung those paddles as hard as they could. And there was absolutely no anger or hatred in this vicious assault. This was no different than he would have been treated if he had gotten inducted into another fraternity. This was the way fraternities inducted members.

The whole paddling took about two to three minutes to finish. It seemed a lot longer to Charles, but then again, he was the one getting paddled. The brother who had been holding his arm for the last two shots released him, and he fell to the ground instantly. They helped him up. They had him do fifteen or twenty deep knee bends to get the blood circulating in his legs. After a five-minute break, they began what would be the finishing touch of the inductee's Hell Night.

Charles was ordered to strip to his underwear again. Now they pulled more goodies from the duffel bag: a bottle of dark molasses, a small pillow, and a box of breakfast cereal. The brothers gathered around Charles and poured the molasses all over his head and smeared it all over his upper body. They ripped open the pillow and threw handfuls of feathers on him. He was being tarred and feathered with molasses. They threw handfuls of breakfast cereal on him for good measure. Charles was told to put the dress, stockings, and high heels back on.

They took Charles back over by the tree where he had been paddled, and he was ordered to face the tree, the same position he had been in while being paddled. He was told to count to one hundred using the Mississippi counting system. One Mississippi, two Mississippi, three Mississippi, right up to one hundred. He was warned not to cheat on his counting or he would get one hundred shots. He was told to remove his blindfold after counting to one hundred and to find his own way home. The last instructions he got was to show up at Ed Carroll's house tomorrow at 7:00 PM sharp. He was told to wear his best clothes; a jacket and a green necktie were a must. Charles was warned not to tell anyone what had transpired this evening.

This abandonment was something that would later come to be known as a Hell Night hell ride. This is where the pledge is taken far from home, very far from home, and abandoned, usually on a deserted dirt road in the middle of nowhere, with no money to get home and no idea of where he was being dropped off. Charles Laemmle was still in Prospect Park, but he was not sure exactly where. He had been taken to this spot blindfolded. He was also highly disoriented from the paddling, and the fear factor left him in a state of confusion.

The three AOT brothers took off running while Charles counted. They ran all the way to Ed Carroll's house. They sat on his front stoop, talking about the hazing they just put Charles Laemmle through. Ironically, they hoped he wasn't hurt too badly. They also hoped he would keep his mouth shut about what happened. They knew he would find his way home; they just didn't know how long it would take him to figure out what part of the park he was in. They wondered what people would think, seeing him walking home tarred and feathered and wearing women's clothing. Most importantly, they hoped Charles's parents wouldn't flip out if they saw him in this condition.

Charles staggered out of the park and went home as fast as he could. It took him about fifteen to twenty minutes to figure out where he was and plot a fast way home. He ran most of the way. When Charles got to his house, he quickly shed the dress and stockings; he left the high heels back in the park. Charles went straight to the bathroom and took a quick look in the mirror. He was horrified at how he looked. He really did appear tarred and feathered. Charles pulled off as much of the feathers as he could, and then he jumped into the shower to clean up. It took him at least a half hour to not only clean himself, but clean the mess of feathers out of the bathroom as well.

Charles took a look at his ass and was not surprised it was all black and blue. He wondered if it was worth it to be subjected to this kind of pain and humiliation. For better or worse, his Hell Night was over, and now he had to deal with the meeting tomorrow night at Ed Carroll's house.

The next day in school, not a word was said by any of the AOT brothers or Charles about what transpired last night. The school day was uneventful, and no one asked Charles about his status with AOT. Charles was anxious to get it over with already, and he wasn't sure what they had planned for him this evening. Whatever it was, it couldn't be too messy. After all, he was told to wear his best suit.

The meeting was scheduled for 7:00 PM, and Charles was early, arriving at 6:45 PM. He found the others were already there waiting for him. Charles was welcomed at the front door by Ed Carroll, who warmly greeted him with a firm handshake and invited him into the house. He was asked to sit on the living room sofa and wait to be called. The three brothers went down to the basement to start their meeting.

Ed Carroll, as president, called the meeting to order. The meeting began with a short nondenominational prayer. The first order of business was the induction of their new member, their first pledge. Ed banged a gavel on the table and said a final vote would be taken on the new pledge proposed for membership. According to the rules and bylaws established by Alpha Omega Theta Fraternity, a unanimous vote was required for admission into the brotherhood. If even one brother blackballed the new pledge, the new guy was out.

A formal vote was taken, with John Stefano walking around to each brother with a hat in his hand. Each brother had two marbles, one white, one black. Each brother would drop one marble into the hat. The marbles would then be dumped onto the table in full view for all to see. If there was even one black marble on the table, the pledge was blackballed and dismissed.

The vote was taken, the marbles collected from all three brothers and dumped onto the table. All the marbles were white. Charles had passed his last vote. This was merely a formality since they all were dying to induct their first new member. No one wanted to blackball Charles. But this method of voting was the way things would be done now and in all future inductions. Ed Carroll went to get Charles from the living room. He was brought into the meeting. All the brothers were wearing white collared shirts and neckties. He was brought to the table where the president and the vice president were sitting, President Ed Carroll to the right and Vice President John Stefano to the left.

"All rise," said Ed Carroll. "Mr. Laemmle, your membership in Alpha Omega Theta Fraternity has been voted on, and you have been accepted as a brother into this brotherhood."

"This is a great honor we have imparted upon you, and you should be honored by our recognition of your worthiness. Please remain standing while all brothers take their seats," John Stefano said. Ed Carroll lit four candles on the table. There were two green and two red ones. The lights were turned off so the room was candlelit only.

President Ed Carroll spoke. "Charles Laemmle, you are about to embark on an adventure with your new brothers into the brotherhood of Alpha Omega Theta Fraternity. This is a new fraternity, so there will be many challenges ahead. You are the first to be accepted into our brotherhood and, we are certain, will not be the last. We add your personal qualities to our own to make our brotherhood stronger. Alpha Omega Theta Fraternity was founded on the evening of October 16, 1946. The brotherhood of AOT was formed with four original founding members. We that you see here this evening are the three remaining founding members. The colors of this fraternity are green and red. You shall be seen wearing green and red as often as possible from this day forward. The password of this fraternity is a solemn secret and should never be repeated outside of the sanctity of a formal gathering of the brotherhood. The password of Alpha Omega Theta Fraternity is *Alea iacta est*. Repeat after me, Brother Laemmle."

"*Alea iacta est,*" replied Charles Laemmle.

"*Alea iacta est,* Brother Laemmle. This is a Latin phrase, and its English translation means 'The die is cast.' These are the words spoken by Julius Cesar when he crossed the Rubicon before invading Rome and proclaiming himself emperor. What 'The die is cast' means to us is that this thing of ours has begun and cannot be stopped. Once it has started, it will never end. Please repeat, Brother Laemmle."

"Once it has started, it will never end," stated Brother Laemmle.

"Each Greek letter in our name has a meaning, Brother Laemmle. Alpha, first. Omega, last. Theta, always. Repeat after me. First, last always."

Charles Laemmle repeated, "First, last, always."

"Brother Laemmle, you will now recite two oaths of brotherhood to bond you to us and us to you. Please repeat after me. I—state your name—hereby becoming a brother of Alpha Omega Theta Fraternity, do solemnly swear to uphold the laws and name of my fraternity. I promise to have respect for my officers and fellow brothers. So help me, God."

Charles Laemmle replied without hesitation, "I, Charles Laemmle, hereby becoming a brother of Alpha Omega Theta Fraternity, do solemnly swear to uphold the laws and name of my fraternity. I promise to have respect for my officers and fellow brothers. So help me, God."

"Brother Laemmle, you will now recite the second oath of brotherhood, and your initiation will be almost complete. Place your right hand over your heart and raise your left hand and repeat after me please. I—state your name—having been inducted into the Brotherhood of Alpha Omega Theta, do solemnly swear to abide by all rules and traditions set forth by this fraternity and will, to the best of my ability, uphold the constitution of Alpha Omega Theta.

"I will at no time commit any acts or deeds to hinder her name and will constantly strive to maintain the common cause of the Brotherhood, namely, 'to preserve the Union of Inspired Joyful Brotherhood,' the inspiration leading to the birth of this fraternity.

"I promise to have respect for my superior officers and my fellow brothers, and I will aid them whenever possible.

"I shall hold my fraternity before everything except my god, my family, and my country.

"So help me, God."

Charles Laemmle repeated the oath word for word, with conviction and pride. "I, Charles Laemmle, having been inducted into the Brotherhood of Alpha Omega Theta, do solemnly swear to abide by all rules and traditions set forth by this fraternity and will, to the best of my ability, uphold the constitution of Alpha Omega Theta.

"I will at no time commit any acts or deeds to hinder her name and will constantly strive to maintain the common cause of the Brotherhood, namely, 'to preserve the Union of Inspired Joyful Brotherhood,' the inspiration leading to the birth of this fraternity.

"I promise to have respect for my superior officers and my fellow brothers, and I will aid them whenever possible.

"I shall hold my fraternity before everything except my god, my family, and my country.

"So help me, God."

President Ed Carroll spoke. "Please remain standing and keep your hand on your heart, and I will now formally induct you into the brotherhood.

"I, Edward Carroll, by the power vested in me through the constitution of Alpha Omega Theta Fraternity Inc., do hereby induct you into the Brotherhood of Alpha Omega Theta, self-assured that you will strive to the best of your ability to uphold the constitution of said fraternity."

All three brothers began to applaud loudly. As the clapping and cheering died down, John Stefano stepped up to Charles Laemmle and extended his hand to shake. He reached out with his fingers curled inward toward the palm and his thumb in the opposite direction, as if to pick up a coffee cup. He grabbed Charles's hand, and the two gripped tightly. "This is the handshake of Alpha Omega Theta Fraternity. You are to always shake a brother's hand in this fashion, in public or private." This handshake would come to be affectionately known as the grip by Alpha brothers in the upcoming decades. Each of the three original brothers stepped up to Charles to give him the fraternity handshake.

"And now the final part of your induction. Brother Laemmle, step up to the chapter roster book and sign your name."

A registry book with blank lined pages was placed upon the table. The inscription at the top of the page read as follows: "October 16th 1946. We the Brothers of Alpha Omega Theta Fraternity do establish this, the Alpha Chapter in Park Slope, Brooklyn, with the majority of our membership recruited from Brooklyn Manual Training High School. It is our mission to spread our brotherhood all across New York and the world."

Directly below that inscription were the signatures of each of the four original brothers.

1. Jerry Percale—President
2. Ed Carroll—Vice President
3. John Sposito—Secretary
4. John Stefano—Treasurer

Right below their names was another inscription. It read as follows: "September 30th 1947. First Pledge Class Inducted." There was the number *1* with a blank space next to it waiting for a signature. Charles signed his name, and the room broke out into applause again. President Carroll now reached behind the table and brought out the same duffel bag that was taken along on Charles's Hell Night last evening. This time, he pulled out a brand-new Alpha sweater. It had a green body with red trim and a brand-new Alpha shield sewn on the right front pocket.

"Charles, please take off your formal jacket and don your new sweater."

Charles wasted no time in putting on his newly earned colors. After putting on his sweater, John Stefano pinned an Alpha pin on the lapel of Charles's sweater. Ed Carroll informed Charles of the induction fee he now owed the fraternity. The amount was $15. That was enough to cover $7 for the sweater and $2 for the fraternity pin and left a few dollars for the treasury. The brothers were lenient and gave Charles up to two weeks to pay up his induction fee, or risk additional fines. The ceremony was over, and the meeting was brought to a close with a short closing prayer.

The next day at school, it was noticed by everyone at Brooklyn Manual Training High School that AOT had a new member. Charles Laemmle proudly walked the halls of school with his brand-new green-and-red sweater. The frat of three was now four, and they had a newfound respect from their peers. There were half a dozen fraternities at Brooklyn Manual Training HS, and AOT was now a respected member of that Greek club scene. Their sister sorority, Delta Phi Delta, was also just getting started, but they were doing well with recruiting girls.

Now that they had broken the ice by dogging and inducting their first new member, the brothers were eager to get more dogs and make a big push to increase their size and numbers. All of them wasted no time in recruiting. They wore their sweaters often. The Alpha shield with its knight's helmet and crossed swords was a great-looking crest and quite enticing. They pitched the benefits of membership to all who were not yet affiliated with the other fraternities, especially the younger students. The freshmen were ripe for recruitment. It was early in the school year, and the freshmen of Brooklyn Manual Training HS had just come of age for fraternity membership. Most of the male students knew long before they got to high school that they would be joining a fraternity as soon as they were old enough to be recruited. The Alpha brothers pitched the virtues of being on the ground floor of a structure that was destined to go sky high.

They were successful beyond their hopes and aspirations. The freshmen were eager to join. They wanted to be involved with building a dynasty. They also recruited a few sophomores as well. The brothers had recruited five pledges to dog for the fraternity. This would be the first large pledge class for the fraternity. In fact, measured by future standards of the fraternity, five was a large number of pledges. They would, as a rule, never induct more than four or five at a time. Quality, not quantity, was the way AOT wanted it.

These dogs were given a two-week pledging period. The next group of pledges would be dogging six weeks, but this group was promised two weeks. The shorter dogging period made it easy to recruit this crew. And once the fraternity inducted these pledges, it would be that much easier to recruit more and make the next pledge class accept the standard pledging time frame of six to eight weeks.

Although they would only be dogging for two weeks, nothing else would be easy for this group of pledges, starting with their pledging attire, which was mandatory. Each dog had to show up at school wearing a green necktie and red suspenders. The necktie had to be tied and adjusted so that both ends were the exact same length. Failure to tie the tie perfectly would result in a hard, stinging slap in the face. They also had to wear a clean white collared shirt and black shoes shined daily. The AOT brothers really regimented their new pledge class. They had to show utmost respect at all times to their superiors in the fraternity. They were not permitted to speak unless spoken to. They were not permitted to make direct eye-to-eye contact unless being spoken to. There was a standard greeting that all dogs had to memorize and recite every time they approached or were approached by an Alpha brother.

An Alpha dog was expected to recite, without hesitation, "Greetings Mr. Stefano, most excelled brother of Alpha Omega Theta Fraternity. I am but a humble dog who most joyfully awaits your every command, sir."

In fact, the pledge greeting was written by John Stefano. Failure to say this at any time or to say it without feeling would result in a demerit and a hard smack in the face. Dogs of any fraternity did not want demerits. A certain number of demerits would result in an automatic blackball. In AOT, fifteen was the maximum number of allowable demerits. Fifteen demerits, and you were dismissed permanently.

This bunch of dogs was enthusiastic. The Alpha brothers often had them walk in single file, almost like marching, to and from school. Eyes forward, right hand on the shoulder of the dog in front of you. No talking. Sometimes the dogs were kept all together and dogged as a group by all four AOT brothers. Sometimes they were broken into smaller groups and taken in threes or fours by individual AOT brothers to do menial tasks like cleaning their bedrooms and doing their household chores. Mostly, the dogs were taken into public places and made to say and do silly and humiliating things.

A common prank was to have a dog get on a public bus with a broom and dustpan and sweep the whole bus from front to back, pick up the dust, and get off at the next stop, leaving the bus passengers bewildered. Also a favorite was penny racing: having the pledges compete pushing pennies down the sidewalk with their noses. The loser would get smacked by all brothers present. They could be ordered to stand at attention for a few hours, or even be forced to hold books up with both hands extended until someone was first to drop them. The loser, of course, was smacked in the face. There were also push-up competitions. But probably the nastiest hazing was when the dogs were instructed to stand in front of the window to Bickford's Cafeteria and eat live goldfish in full view of the lunchtime patrons. No doubt one of the earliest instances of American sushi consumption.

Any dog unfortunate enough to pledge during winter had to endure the AOT brothers using them for target practice to sharpen up their snowball-throwing skills. One of the favorite games to play with the dogs was to have them line up outside on a cold day and order them to recite the sentence "Puss without boots" and instruct them to say it perfectly. Incorrectness would require the dogs to remove one article of clothing. No matter how perfectly they tried to say it, they were always told they were wrong and had to remove an article of clothing. This continued until they were down to their underwear and shoes. Of course, the next logical item to remove were the shoes. Well, once the shoes, or "boots," were removed and the dog said "Puss without boots," they were finally told they had gotten it right. The trick to this exercise was to remove the shoes or boots first. By the time the dogs caught on, this game was no longer useful. But all dogs fell for it at least once.

Shortly after inducting the brother from the second pledge class of Brooklyn AOT, the brothers inducted their first honorary brother. John Cangin was a good friend to most of the senior Alpha members, and especially the officers. John Cangin was afflicted with cerebral palsy and could not be expected to undergo the hazing and paddling. But the brothers had decided unanimously that they wanted John Cangin in the fraternity. John was inducted with a ceremony and no paddling. John would become one of the most loyal AOT brothers. He was dedicated and participated in everything fraternity related. One of his great contributions was to affect every chapter of Alpha Omega Theta for years and decades to come.

By 1948, Alpha Omega Theta Fraternity had grown into its own and was highly respected in the neighborhood and at Brooklyn Manual Training High School. They had grown in size to twenty-five members, and there was no shortage of guys wanting to join. By this time, AOT was more selective and would take only four or five dogs at a time per pledging period.

John Stefano's father was so impressed with the brotherhood his son helped build that he made a suggestion that would have a profound effect on the future of the fraternity. He suggested that they incorporate. The idea was intriguing. They were all still high school kids and were all too young to sign legal documents to form a corporation. John Stefano brought up the idea of incorporating the fraternity at the next meeting. It was discussed, and the idea was unanimously approved. The problem was that none of the members were old enough to sign legal documents required to form a corporation. It was during this topic being discussed that Brother John Cangin stood up and said, "I can get the fraternity chartered." The brothers knew John was serious and asked him how he would go about doing this.

John Cangin said that his father had the legal contacts to get the ball rolling and that all they needed were a few more adults to sign the charter of incorporation on behalf of them. John Cangin got his father and uncle to sign the document, John Stefano got his father to sign, Brother Billy Meyer got his father to sign; additionally, a few other adults known to the brothers also signed the documents, and the rest is history.

They went to 110 East Forty-second Street to see New York attorney Irving Rollins to file the application for corporate status. A corporate charter was typed, and seven adult representatives of the AOT brothers signed and notarized them. In March of 1948, the brothers of Alpha Omega Theta transformed their fraternity into a legal, not-for-profit corporation. On March 19, 1948, seven adult family members of the fraternity signed and notarized the certificate of incorporation.

The signers of the AOT corporate charter were as follows:

Anthony Stefano
Frank Cangin
Edwin Cangin
John J. Murphy Sr.
Charles H. Meyer
Frank M. Sullivan
Frank Sciara

These were fathers and uncles of the Alpha brothers. They signed the legal documents to legitimize their kids' endeavor. On March 24, 1948, the Honorable Justice Julius Miller signed the certificate of incorporation, and Alpha Omega Theta Fraternity Inc. was born.

On March 23, 1948, Irving R. Rollins, the lawyer representing Alpha Omega Theta, was sworn before notary Marc Hermelin, and his statement notarized.

On March 24, 1948, the application for corporate status by Alpha Omega Theta Fraternity was approved for filing by Judge Julius Miller, justice of the Supreme Court of the State of New York.

On March 25, 1948, the charter of incorporation was filed with the New York State Department of State, and the legal corporate entity known as Alpha Omega Theta Fraternity Inc. was born. The Alpha Chapter of Alpha Omega Theta was established as an adult fraternal brotherhood. The Alpha Chapter was founded at and operated out of Brooklyn Manual Training High School, but the documents of incorporation state that an undisclosed address in New York City was chosen as the location of the fraternity's headquarters.

As popular notion and consensus, future generations of Alpha brothers would come to recognize 1948 as the year of the fraternity's founding. In fact, the fraternity was founded in 1946, but was legally incorporated as a not-for-profit corporation in 1948. Nevertheless, 1948 is regarded as the year of AOT's birth.

On April 30, 1949, the first Alpha Omega Theta Spring Dance was held at Astor Caterers. Brother Charles Laemmle had been assigned the task of finding a venue and securing the party room for the night.

After the room rental was secured, the brothers discussed who would be the honored "sweetheart" of the ball. AOT brother Frank Natale was madly in love with a young lady named Connie Iaricci and wanted to impress her, so the AOT brothers chose her to be the first AOT sweetheart. Later in life, Frank would marry Connie.

The fraternity assigned responsibility to various brothers to hire a band, print and sell tickets, establish a journal, sell advertising space in the journal to raise money for the party. Responsibility was also delegated to work the door and the dance floor. The party would be a night to remember and was first of a series of annual sweetheart dances held by Alpha Omega Theta Fraternity.

By the early 1950s, AOT had grown considerably and was on par with, if not superior to, the other fraternities at Brooklyn Manual Training High School. Brother Joe Brugnolotti recalls some of the details of Brooklyn Alpha's growth during this time.

"I became a member on February 27, 1950. The membership wasn't very large, but we had some good pledge classes that brought us up to the numbers of the other frats at school. What launched us was incorporating the swim club into AOT. That took place in 1951, I believe. They were approximately fifteen in number. It was at this point that the popularity of AOT took off. We won every election for years to come. They were school elections: senior class president, student council president, boys' exec, Mr. Manual, etc. We went from approximately thirty to forty-five members in school. This was a large number for one frat. If I recall, there were about six frats, three male Hi-Y (YMCA) clubs with Greek names, and eleven sororities. The swim team had a brief indoctrination and a Hell Night."

Joe also shares his recollections of Brooklyn AOT's expansion into Valley Stream and Connecticut.

"Chick gives himself too little credit for the Long Island chapters. At the same time as Valley Stream started, we started the Connecticut chapter. Later, we launched the Epsilon Chapter from graduates of our locals, plus some members from the workforce. It went belly-up when I went into the navy, the summer of 1955. The Connecticut chapter was made up of relatives. We went to Long Island and had Hell Night. I don't remember the specifics, and I remember nothing of Connecticut Hell Night. I remember that you were slapped in the face when you were declared a pledge. Hitting was a minimum with the exception of a few brothers. They would have a fake argument and slap the pledge. We had an inductee ceremony for both Valley Stream and Connecticut in Brooklyn with a reception to follow."

And this was Joe's reflection on the poor communication between the chapters in the 1950s.

"The communications were minimal. I remember going to Valley Stream for a beach party. Our car broke down, and Chick's father had to drive the girls back home. I think we got the car fixed the next day. We all went to Connecticut for a Grand Council meeting and to attend a dance that the chapter was having. Also, many of the members of the chapter attended a dance at the Livingston Manor that the Epsilon Chapter had. I believe that was the last year, if not close to it. I was just helping the Brooklyn boys get hooked up with Long Island. Someone had sent me a postcard naming the Long Island chapters, and I thought it might help them with a sense of belonging to productive chapters."

And this was just the beginning. Over the next sixty years, there would be two chapters in Connecticut, multiple chapters on Long Island, and even two chapters in Canada. When the four founding members came together with the idea of starting a fraternal brotherhood, they had no idea what they had created, how far it would spread, and how many years it would run. First, last, always. Once it has started, it will never end.

Three founding AOT brothers on the right and
John Cangin on the left

Group picture of Brooklyn AOT, 1955

Brooklyn AOT brothers

Brooklyn AOT pledges on Hell Night

CHAPTER THREE

Chick Hackney

In the autumn of 1951, Anthony Hackney was an eighth grader in junior high school in the Park Slope section of Brooklyn. Anthony wanted to join a fraternity, and he was particularly interested in AOT. Alpha had a reputation for being one of the best fraternities at Brooklyn Manual Training High School. Their pledge classes were like military recruits. They were regimented and disciplined, and usually, 90 to 95 percent of any given pledge class would complete dogging and make it to induction night. Pledges who couldn't take it, the ones who had enough, could drop out at any time. Of course, their reputation would be tarnished to the other fraternities, but most of the other frats and sororities at Brooklyn Manual Training High School rarely inducted more than 60 to 70 percent of their dogs; the rest dropped out. Alpha took fewer pledges. As a rule, they were particular and choosy about who and how many were invited to dog in any pledge class. AOT was interested in quality, not quantity.

Anthony recalls being asked to join Alpha Omega Theta. "I was brought in by some fellows in my neighborhood. One of them, Gene Gamble, was the current president of that chapter, and Russ Gerbino. They were good-quality guys."

Anthony was eager to get asked to pledge for AOT. He had been hearing stories about their reputation and their parties since he was a kid. Now he wanted in; he wasn't interested in the other fraternities. His wish came true when he was approached by the two older AOT brothers. They were all wearing green-and-red sweaters with the fraternity crest sewn on the pocket. They looked respectable and distinguished. They had the look and attitude that all the kids in the neighborhood wanted to have.

Anthony had played it cool and 100 percent correct. He showed interest in AOT, but he didn't pester or kiss up to anyone. A few placed words to the right people, and word got back to the AOT brothers that Anthony Hackney would make a good recruit. The two senior AOT brothers who approached Anthony were people he knew personally. "I knew them well from my old neighborhood (Third Street and Sixth Avenue), and my parents also knew them from the neighborhood."

They went up to Anthony and asked him if he was interested in pledging for a fraternity; they informed him that AOT was about to start their fall pledge class and asked if he would be interested in dogging for AOT. Anthony still played it cool and said he might be interested but he wanted to go home and discuss it with his parents first. It was a good answer, they thought. He didn't jump at the chance, although he wanted to, yet he showed a definite interest. He was thrilled, but didn't let it show in his expression while they spoke. The AOT brothers told Anthony they would meet him in the same location tomorrow.

The next day, Anthony was waiting at that same spot a few minutes early. The same four AOT brothers showed up and asked if Anthony was still interested in dogging for Alpha. Anthony told them that he had discussed it with his parents and they were OK with him pledging for Alpha. The AOT brothers told Anthony that a meeting to hold interviews for prospective pledges would be held that upcoming Friday evening. He was given written directions and a letter of invitation to present at the meeting. They told Anthony to be prompt and on time at 7:00 PM. He was also told to wear his best clothes.

Anthony showed up fifteen minutes early and found four other pledges already waiting. All together, there were five pledges. There were supposed to be six, but one didn't show up. That's an automatic blackball and disqualification from ever being considered for membership in Alpha Omega Theta again. All five of them were nervous. They all heard stories about what happens when you go down to a fraternity; now they were about to find out that most of what they heard was true.

The pledges were kept together outside of the house where the meeting was being held. The pledge master stayed outside with them. It was his job. The prospective pledges were brought in one at a time to be interviewed by the fraternity brothers. As a formality, each one was asked to produce the letter of invitation to the president upon entering the room. Each one was interviewed and brought back outside and told to wait to be called back in. While they waited outside, they were told not to talk, especially not to each other. It was not permitted to ask about the kinds of questions that were being asked or what else had transpired during the interview.

The interview process was mostly a formality and a touch of mental manipulation. By virtue of the fact that each one of them was chosen to pledge and had a letter inviting them to interview, it was a fair assumption that they were liked by the fraternity. But the interview would be used to rattle the pledge to see how easy it was to make him nervous and afraid. The questions were a mixture of straightforward and nonsensical. Who are you? Why are you here? Who invited you? Why should we let you in? What can you do for us? Weren't you blackballed by Omega Gamma Delta last month?

After the interviews were over, each pledge was voted on. The time-honored method of each brother dropping one marble into a hat was the way they voted on each pledge. All white marbles were required to pass the interview. One black marble, and that guy would be sent home, blackballed. This was a good group of recruits; they all passed the interview. They were brought back into the meeting all together. They were told by the chapter president that their applications to pledge had been accepted and that they had all passed their interviews. They were informed by the chapter president that the length of this pledge class's dogging period would be six weeks.

Now the pledge master walked up and down the line the pledges formed. He placed a green necktie around the neck of each pledge and stated firmly, "You are now a pledge of Alpha Omega Theta," and followed it with a sharp, bruising slap across the face. Each was given a small bronze pin that had the fraternity's Greek letters on it. This was their pledge pin, and they were to wear it every hour of the day, except when sleeping. The pledge pin was to be worn on the right collar of a clean, pressed white shirt. The pledge uniform, in addition to the pin, was the green necktie they were given by the pledge master on top of a white shirt. The necktie was to be adjusted so that both ends were the exact same length. If the tie was off even a fraction of an inch, it would constitute a serious infraction. Alpha brothers often checked the dogs' ties to ensure proper technique in tying it; if the two ends failed to line up perfectly, and often it did, the pledge could expect a hard smack in the face. They were to wear dressy slacks and black shoes, which were to be shined daily.

Usually, the pledge master would assign pledge names to new recruits, but Anthony had been called by his nickname, Chick, since infancy, and the name stuck with him all of his life. The AOT brothers continued to refer to him by the name Chick. One of the other pledges was give the name Smile Fast. And he was expected to smile fast whenever he was approached by an Alpha brother. If he didn't smile fast enough, he got a hard smack in the face.

Each pledge was given a "dog book." This book would be carried at all times and handed over to any AOT brother who wished to write in it. The dog book was used to keep track of merits earned and demerits assigned for bad behavior.

Chick recalled his early days as an AOT pledge. "I was still attending junior high school and was fourteen years old. The hazing was pretty physical. The slapping contests were stupid and served no purpose. I remember not being able to hear for a week out of one ear."

The pledge class Chick was in was outstanding, and all but one of them was inducted. Chick really didn't like the hazing. It was pretty severe. They were given an order to fall in and snap to attention, and the slowest one got a hard slap across the face. The punishment for failing any task was a slap in the face or, sometimes, a punch in the stomach. No one was exempt. All the dogs got a fairly equal amount of physical abuse, although some got it worse. There were physical challenges, such as one where all the dogs lined up at attention, and they would all be forced to hold up stacks of books above their head with two hands. The first one to drop the books would get a kick to the ribs or a slap to the face. Chick hated these contests, but he had his eyes on the prize at all times—the coveted green-and-red sweater. He was determined to earn that sweater. Chick's reasoning for wanting to gain admission into AOT: "AOT was top draw."

Chick's pledge class ran through fall into winter. And with that came the inevitable target practice the dogs would be used for when it snowed. Hell Night was indeed hellish for Chick and the other dogs. They endured all the usual hazing rituals. They all got slapped around and paddled. They had to steal boat oars from Prospect Lake in Prospect Park, which were used as paddles for their Hell Night. They were made up and dressed up as clowns, prostitutes, blackface, and many other ridiculous getups. They got dropped off in various locations in Brooklyn after their paddling was done. They were dropped off in groups of two and three.

The next evening, all five were inducted into Alpha Omega Theta Fraternity wearing their best suits. Each was given a sweater and a fraternity pin. The fraternity pin was different from the pledge pin. The pledge pin was brass and had AOT's Greek letters on it. The fraternity pin was shaped like the Alpha shield with the knight's helmet and crossed swords. It was green and red. Alpha brothers wore the fraternity pin on the lapel of their sweaters. And now Anthony "Chick" Hackney had his. This was a proud moment for Chick; he worked for this, and he knew failure was never an option.

The parties were everything Chick had heard about them. They were black-tie affairs. Most Alpha brothers attended them in tuxedos, although a tux was not required, and some brothers and attendees wore their best suit instead. They would hire swing jazz bands to play and charge admission to enter the affair. They were referred to as the Annual Spring Dance. They spent months preparing for the annual dances, and they always were thrown in honor of one of the Alpha brothers' girlfriends, who would be referred to as the Sweetheart of Alpha Omega Theta for that evening.

Some of Chick's fondest memories of Brooklyn AOT were the fancy ballroom parties they threw in some of the fanciest places in the city. Chick remembers those parties.

"The fraternity had it together. They conducted huge dance parties (semiformal), which took place at some of New York's finer hotels (Hotel Taft comes to mind). Journals were put together, and many, many ads were sold by everyone on a competitive basis. There was enough money to pay for the best bands, the entire dance, etc., etc. These were incredible dance parties, which were attended by adults, as well as brothers, etc. (plus, other adults like my parents). My dad belonged to a men's club in Brooklyn who saw how AOT put on a successful bash, and they adopted some of our techniques."

The parties were held in some of the fanciest places in the city. These affairs were so well planned that they would have two live bands alternating throughout the night. One band would play swing music, and the other would play cha-cha. The AOT brothers would not only finance these parties with selling advertising in the party journal they passed out to guests, but they would usually make more than they needed to pay for the party and actually make money for the treasury between the advertising and charging admission to enter the party. On May 7, 1954, the Annual Spring Dance was held at the Taft Hotel on Seventh Avenue in New York City. This was the last Alpha party Chick would be attending with the brothers of Brooklyn AOT. Shortly after the party, there was one more fraternity-related event that Chick would be involved in.

Joe Brugnolotti had three cousins who were all brothers living in Middletown, Connecticut, and the Alpha brothers were going up to Connecticut to start a new chapter of AOT in Middletown. They went up in two carloads to induct the first members of a chapter to be formed outside of Brooklyn, New York. Joe's three cousins were the Zelinski brothers—Steve, Donald, and Robert. They were the first members that Joe Brugnolotti recruited, and they in turn recruited five friends from Middletown High School to be the charter members.

The Middletown chapter was christened and designated the Gamma Chapter. They were the third after the Alpha and Beta chapters in Brooklyn. Joe Brugnolotti was related to the Zelinskis by marriage. They were barely third cousins and hardly ever saw each other. But over the summer, Joe had visited the Zelinskis and pitched the three brothers the idea of starting a chapter of Alpha Omega Theta Fraternity.

Chick had just gone along for the ride and really didn't participate in the induction ceremony. The AOT brothers were happy he came along. They wanted to look impressive to the new recruits in Middletown, and the more who came along, the batter the ceremony looked. This induction was much different than any other Chick had been involved in, including his own. There was no hazing or paddling. Nobody wanted to jinx the ceremony by scaring these new guys. The AOT brothers assumed the new guys knew nothing about the hazing rituals from the Brooklyn fraternities. In actuality, they did. There were a few other fraternities in and around Middletown. But the Brooklyn AOT brothers made it easy anyway.

They had a simple candlelit ceremony and told the recruits the history of the fraternity, gave them the crest and a book of fraternity documents, and wished them luck with the future for the newly established Gamma Chapter. Middletown Alpha in Connecticut was a seed that was planted and left to grow on its own. Very little info about the status or growth of Connecticut AOT made its way back to New York. The Gamma Chapter of Middletown, Connecticut, was destined to have a long, successful, and proud run. But they were mostly an island unto themselves. There would be some interaction and adventures between the New York and Connecticut chapters of AOT. But for now, Chick's main concern was his family's impending move from Brooklyn to Long Island. This induction and launching of a new chapter was to be the last active participation Chick Hackney would have as a member of the Alpha Chapter of Alpha Omega Theta fraternity.

Chick's family had made a decision to move out of Brooklyn. They had purchased a new house at 73 Fritchie Place in Valley Stream, Long Island. They wanted a suburban environment and a quieter life that Brooklyn didn't have to offer.

Chick was about to start his junior year of high school, and he would be going to a new school, leaving all of his fraternity brothers behind. He hated the thought of leaving Brooklyn since he still loved Alpha Omega Theta. Chick had three great years with the fraternity, and now it was all over.

Or was it?

CHAPTER FOUR

Delta Chapter

From the day Chick Hackney told his fraternity brothers that he was moving to Valley Stream, Long Island, they were imploring him to recruit charter members and start a new chapter in his new school. Chick was skeptical about that idea and was more concerned about fitting in at a new high school, and even making friends there. What were the chances that a new kid from Brooklyn would walk in to Valley Stream Central High School and start a chapter of a Brooklyn fraternity there? Pretty slim chance, Chick thought.

The AOT fraternity in Brooklyn was on the decline. They were inducting fewer new members, and senior brothers who had already graduated from Brooklyn Manual Training High School were still active in AOT in an attempt to keep it alive. These senior brothers were instrumental in encouraging Chick Hackney to make a serious effort to plant the AOT flag in Valley Stream Central High School. These senior brothers were Joseph Brugnolotti, Al "Mickey" Percy, Jim Stack, and Bill Meyer. The aforementioned were especially excited about the prospects of spreading the brotherhood to a new town, and they worked really hard to push Chick to recruit charter members. Joe Brugnolotti would not take no for an answer. Chick knew they had only the best intentions. He was mostly worried about not finding students in his new school who would be interested, and thereby disappointing everyone in Brooklyn.

As luck would have it, there was a series of events that took place after Anthony "Chick" Hackney started his junior year in Valley Stream Central High School, which would facilitate the chartering of a new chapter of AOT there. Chick was surprised to find only one fraternity existing in Valley Stream Central High School. He was also surprised to find that it was a fraternity that also had a chapter at Brooklyn Manual Training High School. The fraternity was

Omega Gamma Delta, whose colors were black and gold. Chick was surprised to find a familiar organization, although he shouldn't have been.

Omega Gamma Delta was one of the largest high school fraternities in the tristate area. In fact, they had active chapters in at least five states. At this time, they were expanding in Long Island quickly. The Valley Stream Central chapter of Omega had been at Valley Stream Central High School since 1938. The Valley Stream Central chapter of Omega had originally been an independent fraternity called Sigma Lambda Alpha, until the founder of that fraternity, a guy named Tom Ward, decided to flip his entire fraternity and join the much-larger statewide fraternal organization called Omega Gamma Delta.

Omega Gamma Delta—the Alpha Psi Chapter, as they had been chartered—had been the only show in town at Valley Stream for eighteen years. Although there were multiple sororities, nobody ever had the nerve to try to start another fraternity and challenge Omega's grip over the Valley Stream social scene. This would soon change.

Chick began his junior year at Valley Stream Central High School, and he wore his Alpha sweater often. The Omegas in Valley Stream Central High School didn't recognize the green-and-red sweater. They may have figured it was a fraternity or some kind of club, but they didn't know exactly what it was. They also weren't going to pay much attention to a new kid wearing a club sweater from another school. He was a new guy, and he was the only one wearing that kind of sweater. Omega Gamma Delta was the be-all and end-all of social clubs at Valley Stream Central High School. But not everyone was so awestruck by them.

Shortly after beginning school, Chick made the acquaintance of another junior named Jerry Smith. Jerry noticed Chick's sweater, and he knew it represented a fraternity from out of town. Jerry saw Chick wearing the AOT sweater a few times and finally, one day, decided to break the ice and start a conversation. Jerry asked Chick what kind of sweater he was wearing. Chick responded that it was his fraternity sweater.

"What fraternity has those colors?" asked Jerry.

"My fraternity is AOT," replied Chick.

"AOT? What's AOT?" asked Jerry.

"AOT is Alpha Omega Theta Fraternity," Chick replied. "It's the best fraternity in Park Slope, Brooklyn."

Jerry changed the subject by asking if they had Omega Gamma Delta in Brooklyn also. Chick told him that they did have an Omega chapter in Brooklyn Manual Training High School.

"Why does Omega have chapters in both schools and AOT is only in Brooklyn?" Jerry asked.

"I don't know. I guess they need guys to take it to other towns to start new chapters," Chick replied.

"Well, you're new in town, and you're a member of AOT," Jerry said. "Why don't you start a chapter? We really do need an alternative to Omega Gamma Delta here in Valley Stream."

"Well, that sounds great, Jerry. I found my first recruit. But it's going to take more than just the two of us to launch a chapter," Chick said.

"How many do you think we will need to get started, Chick?" Jerry said.

"Well, I would think we would need at least five people in total, Jerry," Chick said.

"I know of at least that many who may want to start a fraternity to give Valley Stream high school students a better alternative, and those guys may have friends as well, Chick. When can we get this thing going?" Jerry said.

"Well, you get your guys together, and I will get my Brooklyn frat brothers together," Jerry said.

"So what else happens when you pledge?" Jerry asked.

Chick thought it was over. Why would Jerry or anyone else want to pledge and get paddled by guys from Brooklyn? He hesitated to tell Jerry about the paddling and physical abuse that went with pledging a fraternity.

Jerry laughed. "Don't worry, Chick, I have been around Omega guys for years. I know what fraternities do to pledges. Everybody knows what fraternities do to pledges. The question is how will we be treated as the original charter members? If we have a good crowd to start it up, will they go easier on us?" Jerry said.

"Well, that's a good question. I don't really know how it will go, but I can find out," Chick said.

"OK, how long will it take to find out?" Jerry asked.

"How long till you know how many guys will be in?" Chick replied.

"Let's give it a week. I will talk to all my friends, you tell your frat brothers you have a bunch of recruits and see what kind of initiation they will give us," Jerry said.

The next few days, Jerry told all his close friends about what he and Chick had been planning. The response was better than either of them thought. Jerry and Chick made a great team. Jerry got them on the hook, and Chick reeled them in. Jerry would get their interest by telling them he knew this new guy from Brooklyn and he and Jerry were planning to start a chapter of a Brooklyn fraternity here in Valley Stream. It was a quality frat that had history and foundation in Brooklyn. There was no shortage of guys in Valley Stream who wanted something other than Omega to join. But they wanted assurance that it was for real, that they would really have backing from a solid fraternal brotherhood.

Joe Brugnolotti, Mickey Percy, Billy Meyer, and Jim Stack from the Brooklyn chapter were constantly pushing Chick to recruit members for a new chapter in Valley Stream. They saw in Chick and in the village of Valley Stream a great opportunity to carry on the name of Alpha Omega Theta into an untapped territory.

Chick recalls the encouragement he got from them. "They were persistent, persistent, persistent, and persistent about pushing me into getting a chapter started in Valley Stream."

Despite his massive contribution to building a successful new chapter, Chick has been modest and has always credited Joe Brugnolotti with being the driving force in the formation of Valley Stream AOT. Chick also credits Mickey Percy, Jim Stack, and Billy Meyer for being instrumental in the chartering of Valley Stream AOT; however, in Chick's own words, Joe Brugnolotti was the George Washington of Long Island AOT.

Once they met Chick, they were all for it. Chick looked good in his green-and-red sweater, and the guys were impressed with him and his confidence. Chick really talked up the benefits of AOT membership. He looked like he didn't have a care or even a second thought about Omega Gamma Delta or what they might think of nonaffiliated students starting an AOT chapter in Valley Stream Central. The guys that Jerry recruited were interested, and they wanted to do it. But they also wanted to meet these mystery Alpha brothers from Brooklyn.

The young men who would make up the charter membership of Valley Stream Central Alpha Omega Theta were an impressive bunch. They were all athletes—football players, soccer players, baseball players, basketball players, and especially wrestlers. Many of them were on the Valley Stream Central High School wrestling team.

That was the edge they had over Omega. Few Omega members were on the wrestling team. The wrestling team was to become the AOT clique. In fact, it was through intercounty wrestling that Alpha Omega Theta Fraternity would spread throughout Nassau County, Long Island. Jerry had recruited many members of the Valley Stream Central High School wrestling team, and Chick had them eating out of the palm of his hand. Everybody was gung ho for this. The next step was to organize a meeting with the Brooklyn AOT brothers.

Chick also insists on giving a large share of credit to his good friend of more than fifty years, Jerry Smith, for recruiting charter members to the new AOT chapter.

"Jerry and I played football together, where I got to know many of the guys during my very first days at Valley Stream Central. Jerry, being a natural leader in many ways, was a big supporter and recruiter in starting the new chapter. He pushed hard to make it happen."

Now that there was a good-sized crew to work with, Chick made contact with his AOT brothers in Brooklyn. He contacted Joe Brugnolotti and told him that he had charter members. He let Joe know there were nine interested recruits. With Chick, that would make a chapter of ten members. Joe was impressed. Ten charter members in a new town where that frat's name wasn't known was great work. Joe assured Chick that he would let the others know that this thing looked like it was a go.

Chick and Joe Brugnolotti arranged the first meeting with the Valley Stream recruits and the AOT Brooklyn brothers. They met the next Saturday afternoon at Chick's house. Joe Brugnolotti wasted no time putting together a small crew of AOT brothers to drive out to Valley Stream to meet these potential charter members. The first trip they made, Joe brought Mickey Percy, Billy Meyer, and Jim Stack to meet Chick's friends. They were all excited about getting the first chapter started outside of Brooklyn, but they didn't want to seem too eager.

They had no idea that Chick's recruits felt the same way. They really wanted an alternative to Omega Gamma Delta, but they didn't want the Brooklyn AOT guys to think they were not good enough for Omega and were therefore settling on AOT as an alternative. Although Omega Gamma Delta had been the only show in town for quite some time, the new AOT recruits had little care for what the Omegas thought of their efforts to found a new fraternity in Valley Stream Central.

Chick's take on the relationship between early AOT and Omega Gamma Delta: "We didn't care what Omega thought. We were our own proud group that grew in a hurry. We were the student-athlete leaders who were considered good, clean-cut kids. We played sports with many of the Omega members, who, till this day, are still friends. There never really was any competition between AOT and Omega. We played many sports together, and to this day, I have some very dear friends from Omega. If AOT were there before 1954, when many of the student athletes decided to pledge Omega, I believe that most of them would have pledged AOT. This is my personal belief. Anyway, we didn't get started until 1954, and Omega was there many years before that. We were proud of who and what we were and always kept our noses clean. Most of the athletes at the time were good-quality, clean-cut kids."

Jerry and Chick brought eight other young men besides themselves to the meeting. Joe, Mickey, and Jim arrived around 2:00 PM, and they were very impressed with the turnout. There was a great feeling at the meeting in everyone. They had planned on it being a thirty- to forty-five-minute meeting, but it ran two and a half hours. The recruits had lots of questions about AOT. Where it started, when it started, how many chapters were there, what would be expected of them as charter members, etc., etc.

The AOT brothers wanted to know a little about the Valley Stream recruits as well. What interested them in AOT, why they didn't join Omega, what they would do to bring AOT a good name and reputation in Valley Stream. The AOT recruits had a lot of things going for them at this point. They already had strong bonds of friendship, they all played different sports together at Central, they all pretty much had ignored Omega, and they all were 100 percent ready to start a new chapter of Alpha Omega Theta fraternity. They told Joe, Mickey, and Jim that they could even have more recruits for the next meeting, but the AOT brothers suggested they keep it between the original group of ten to launch the new chapter, and then they could recruit their first pledge class later on.

This first meeting was to satisfy everybody's curiosity. Participants on both sides wanted to meet each other and ask questions. Everybody had a great feeling about it. They agreed to meet again the following Saturday for a formal induction. At the next meeting, AOT would bring more brothers from Brooklyn to formally launch the Valley Stream Central chapter. This would be the second chapter founded outside of Brooklyn and the fourth chapter of the fraternity since 1946.

The following Saturday, they set the induction ceremony to take place at Chick's house. This was the talk of the school that week. There was a real buzz going around Valley Stream Central High School. The soon-to-be Alphas showed their commitment and sense of brotherhood right from the very beginning. They stuck together, they had each other's backs, and they refused to consider dropping the formation of the new AOT chapter.

The Alpha brothers in Brooklyn had a meeting Friday evening to discuss the induction ceremony that would take place the next day in Valley Stream. After much debate, it was decided not to haze the Valley Stream charter members. The consensus was that since they were starting a chapter in uncharted territory, and these outstanding young men were agreeing to build the foundation from the ground up, their induction should be a ceremony and not paddling. They chose who would make the trip to Valley Stream for the induction. The catalysts who made this all happen were Joe Brugnolotti, Billy Meyer, and Mickey Percy, so they were chosen to preside over the induction. In addition to them, chapter president Pat Fucci, chapter secretary Jim Borgia, Jim Stack, Bill Meyer, and Jack Brierley would attend the chartering ceremony.

The Brooklyn AOT brothers showed up at Chick Hackney's house promptly at 2:00 PM on Saturday. All of the Valley Stream recruits were wearing collared shirts and ties. In addition to Chick Hackney and Jerry Smith, the following charter members were inducted: Mark Everett, Bobby Marsh, George Smith, Fred Gifford, Dick Moray, Mel Mayer, Rich Caste, and John Cisco. This was the crew that Chick and Jerry put together. These were the charter members of the first Long Island chapter of Alpha Omega Theta Fraternity Inc. Little did they know on this day that they were planting a seed, and that it would indeed grow. The fraternal brotherhood they started would spread far and wide and in a very short time.

They held the induction ceremony in Chick's basement. The lights were turned off, and candles were lit. Joe Brugnolotti ran the meeting and told the new recruits the history of Alpha Omega Theta Fraternity Inc. He passed on to them the meanings of the Alpha shield and the Latin and English versions of the fraternity password.

The new chapter was christened and designated Delta Chapter. They were given a leather valise filled with official fraternity documents. Among the items they were given were their official charter signed by the officers of the Brooklyn chapter, their documented procedures for running meetings and inducting pledges, as well as blank ledgers and registry books to begin their own treasury books, meeting-minutes recordings, and a registry for keeping track of member rosters. They were also given empty photo albums to begin documenting the history and exploits of the chapter. Pictures were taken of the ceremony and the celebratory dinner they had later that evening to give them their first pages in the Delta Chapter's photo album history books.

Lastly, each new member was given a brand-new green-and-red fraternity sweater with an Alpha patch on the right front pocket. After being sworn in as brothers of Alpha Omega Theta Fraternity Inc., each new charter member was handed his sweater and given the Alpha handshake by each of the Brooklyn brothers. Each new brother signed the Delta Chapter's roster book under the heading "First Brothers Inducted," and registered the time and date of their induction into AOT.

Elections were held immediately after inductions were finished. The first officers were elected to run the first class of Alpha Omega Theta Fraternity in Valley Stream Central High School. The following Delta Chapter brothers were chosen to be the first officers:

Anthony "Chick" Hackney—President
Jerry Smith—Vice President
Mark Everett—Treasurer
Fred Gifford—Secretary

The following brothers were the first charter members of Delta Chapter:

Bobby Marsh
George Smith
Dick Moray
Mel Mayer
Rich Caste
John Cisco

The brothers from the Brooklyn chapter presented treasurer Mark Everett with $25 in cash to give Delta Chapter's treasury a head start. The closing ceremony took place; all the men in the room applauded intensely. All the brothers went to Brooklyn for a celebratory dinner. A great time was had by one and all. It was a great day and an evening that would be long remembered by all who took part.

All ten newly chartered Alpha brothers showed up in school Monday morning wearing their brand-new green-and-red AOT sweaters. They made a big splash on their first day as chartered members of AOT. Their classmates were quite impressed. They were approached by everyone. Everybody wanted to shake their hands and congratulate them.

This was a bold new undertaking, and the whole school seemed to be buzzing about it. There were multiple sororities in Valley Stream Central High School, and now they had a new fraternity to fraternize with. They all wanted to partner up with the new fraternity called AOT. The Alpha brothers wasted no time in making their mark in Valley Stream Central. They were respected and admired instantly, and they carried themselves with pride.

Within two weeks, they already had a long list of potential new pledges. There were plenty of guys who wanted to join a fraternity. A few of the recruits had been contemplating pledging for Omega and quickly changed their mind and accepted the invitation to interview with AOT. The buzz around the new chapter of AOT was all good, and Chick recalled how easy it was to recruit their first pledge class of the Delta Chapter of AOT.

"The first pledge class knew that we would be successful just by looking at the original members and knowing that we were hell-bent on being a great organization and had Joe B. and other Brooklyn brothers behind us to back it up. We may have been just starting in Valley Stream, but we started with substance, as well as support. (Thanks to Joe B., Mickey Percy, Billy Meyer, etc.)."

The Delta Chapter brothers had formal stationery printed for all their needs. The recruits invited to interview were given a formal letter of invitation. It was an impressive-looking invitation, printed with red ink on green paper. The letterhead had the fraternity name on top written in fancy-scripted lettering. In proud, bold letters, the letterhead said, "Alpha Omega Theta Fraternity Inc., Delta Chapter," and the Alpha shield was printed on the upper-left corner of the page. The invitation to interview addressed the recruit, and at the bottom, it was signed by both the chapter president and secretary. A jacket and tie was required for the interview, and an RSVP was requested.

In addition to the interview letters, they had fancy membership cards printed, and Fred Gifford, the chapter secretary, used the letterhead to create numerous official fraternity documents. The traditions, bylaws, procedures, and meeting minutes were typed on the chapter's official letterhead.

The first pledge class of Valley Stream Central AOT had ten recruits. They were all exceptional athletes and students. Beginning with this first pledge class, a precedent was set to require all pledges to be on an athletic team and a student with an A academic average. This crew was an outstanding bunch. They all became Alpha dogs and began pledging one week after the interview letters were handed out.

The pledging process took a new shape in Valley Stream. Pledges were to be referred to as dogs at all times. While pledging, they were not to be addressed by first name. When they were spoken to, they were given orders such as "Dog, be at the flagpole tomorrow morning at seven thirty, have a cup of coffee and a buttered roll for me, and don't be late."

After some discussion, it was agreed that there would be no physical hazing with the new chapter. Chick Hackney had taken vicious beatings when he dogged for Brooklyn Alpha. He had actually lost hearing in one of his ears for almost a month from the constant slapping he endured, and he intensely hated bullying tactics that usually went along with physical hazing; so he decided to abolish the face-slapping, the punching, the paddling, and other abuse. This was a noble idea, but it did not last long after the departure of Chick and his class of 1956. Delta Chapter would soon take to hazing and paddling pledges soon after Chick and his crew moved on.

The dogs had to wear green ties and red suspenders at all times. The new practice of "brick carrying" became a new form of punishment for demerits. A dog that was issued a demerit was required to carry a brick around all day at school and continue carrying it while dogging after school until he went home. One demerit, and the dog carried one brick; two demerits, he carried two bricks. It was a tough regimen. In the opinion of Chick, this was tougher on the dogs and a better method for the fraternity to demand strict discipline, as opposed to always slapping the dogs around.

The dogs hated brick-carrying, but they respected it. The Omegas were amazed at the way the Alphas carried themselves and demanded strict obedience from their dogs. This crew of dogs was motivated. They wanted to successfully complete their pledge period, and in fact, all of them did. They were not given a free pass to get in. They were given a three-week pledging period, which became the usual standard in most Long Island chapters in the years to follow.

The dogs were required to carry the books of Alpha brothers, in addition to their own, and any bricks they had to carry from demerits. They had to report to the Alpha brothers in the early-morning hours before school. Usually, they met in the park behind Valley Stream Central High School. The dogs were required to bring hot coffee and buttered rolls for the Alpha brothers to have before school. They had to show team spirit, especially if they were in a crowd, such as the front of the school. They had various chants and also had to sing the fraternity song on demand. The song became known as "The Alpha Song" and was sung to the tune of "The Stein Song."

The whole crew of dogs was exceptional; they all completed their three-week pledging period and were inducted. The dogs were put into cars and taken to Valley Stream State Park. Once they had arrived at the park, they were taken blindfolded deep into the park. Each dog was stripped to his underwear and then abandoned in the park to find his way home. They were told they had to compete to get back to the meeting first. This became a traditional mind game played on dogs on their Hell Night over the years. Many chapters would tell the dogs that they were being voted on again for membership after the hazing, or they were dropped off miles from home and told to get back to the meeting in less than an hour or be blackballed. There were various other forms of mental torture that were used on dogs when they were close to the end of their initiation to make them think they might not get in.

This race between the inductees back to the meeting was one of the more tame examples, but the dogs did the hundred-yard dash to get back to the meeting before the other dogs. The AOT brothers were waiting for them back at the meeting, and to everyone's relief, they were told there would be no blackballing of anyone. The dogs were told to be at the meeting to be held in two days dressed in slacks, black shoes, pressed white collared shirt, and a black tie. There would no more dogging up to the induction ceremony. No AOT brothers would give any of them orders, and the inductees were no longer obligated to wear pledging attire. They were not considered members yet, and the two days was a cooling-off period for the AOT brothers and the pledges.

The meeting was held at Chick Hackney's house Sunday evening. All ten dogs were inducted. They were a mix of seniors, juniors, and sophomores. This helped the new chapter of Alpha Omega Theta form a strong foundation in Valley Stream. The seniors who started the chapter and some of the ones just being inducted would not have more than the remainder of this school year to run with the fraternity. But the juniors and sophomores being inducted ensured that the Delta Chapter of AOT planted the seeds into the 1958 school year and would guarantee a good run for at least the next two years. Although the Delta Chapter was destined to have the longest run of any AOT chapter, these first years were important foundation-building time. These young men were pioneers; they were blazing a trail and establishing rituals and traditions that would last for decades.

During the induction ritual, the inductees were brought in all together. They were led into the room by the pledge master and the sergeant at arms. They were brought to a table that had two candles seated in candleholders that looked like World War I bombs—the kinds of bombs that pilots flying single-engine planes dropped by hand. The president, Chick Hackney, sat in the center of the rectangular table; Vice President Jerry Smith sat at his right side, and Secretary Fred Gifford sat on his left side. The two candles on the table and a few other candles around the room were the only light.

President Chick Hackney made a little speech about how well they all had done as dogs and how they all passed their trial by fire, culminating in their Hell Night. Chick proceeded to read the inductees the history of Alpha Omega Theta Fraternity Inc. from the books and documents they had been given by the Brooklyn brothers at the founding of Delta Chapter a month before. The ideals and standards of the brotherhood were imparted upon them. They were told that from this day forward, every man who was a member of AOT was their brother for life. This included brothers from the past and brothers-to-be in the future. There would always be a special bond between Alpha brothers, regardless of year, decade, or chapter.

The inductees were informed of the password, *Alea iacta est*, "The die is cast." Once it's started, it will never end. The importance of honoring the password and motto of the fraternity was explained to them. They were told that they were building an organization that would long endure if they took it seriously and not as a passing phase. These new members were responsible for cementing the foundation that future brothers would build on.

The inductees were given copies of the fraternity crest, known as the shield, to keep. They were told of the shield's many meanings and its correlation with the honor and virtue of knighthood. They were made to recite the oath of brotherhood one at a time as each was sworn in. Lastly, President Chick Hackney recited a formal induction, thereby declaring these young men to be brothers in the fraternal brotherhood of Alpha Omega Theta Fraternity Inc. Each newly inducted brother signed his name in the Delta Chapter roster book under the heading "Second Brothers Inducted," recording the time and date of the ceremony and induction.

The newly inducted brothers were each handed a new green-and-red-sweater, and they were shown the fraternity handshake, known as the grip. President Chick Hackney and Vice President Jerry Smith walked up the line; Chick shook hands with each new member with the fraternity grip, and Jerry handed each man his sweater, followed by a firm fraternity handshake. The treasurer, Mark Everett, now stepped up and informed the new brothers that they each had an induction fee to pay to the fraternity.

The Delta Chapter of Alpha Omega Theta Fraternity Inc. now numbered twenty members. In addition to that, they were already recruiting for the next pledge class. Alpha was looking good on Valley Stream Central High School campus. They were the cream of the crop. They were high-average students,

—

varsity lettermen, and popular with the many sororities in school. The Omegas were not happy about this, but they were powerless to do anything about it. The Alphas, to their credit, treated the Omegas like they didn't matter in the least. As far as the AOT brothers were concerned, there was no contest, no rivalry. There were now two distinct choices of fraternal brotherhood for Valley Stream Central High School. The Alphas were top performers in all aspects of school life; they demanded excellence from their pledges and members. Exclusion based on religion or race was banned by the fraternity's bylaws. There would be no excluding friends and good recruit prospects because of religion or race. These ideals and bylaws were passed on and ingrained in the other Long Island chapters as well.

Although AOT was founded as a nonsegregated and nonrestricted fraternal organization with higher ideals than most of their rivals, it was never sanctioned by any of the school systems where it operated. Chick's thoughts on AOT's relationship with the school system: "We started without permission and didn't give it a thought. I believe we were all members of one of the varsity teams or another. Football, wrestling, basketball, baseball, track. Each and every one of us played in sports, and each and every one of us promoted a very proud image to the school, coaches, and the community. I'd like to think that we were not arrogant but were very proud of AOT and the green and red."

Six weeks after the first pledge class was inducted, Delta Chapter was now ready to hold their second pledge class. Once again, they had a pledge class of ten recruits. This pledge class was very important. The Alpha brothers had definite plans on expansion, and this pledge class was very important toward that plan. Very shortly, in the midpoint of the 1955-56 school year, two new high schools were scheduled to open in Valley Stream. In addition to Valley Stream Central, there would now be North and South high schools in Valley Stream as well.

With that happening, there would be two new high schools in Valley Stream that would be ripe for planting the AOT flag and recruiting new members for new chapters. It was already a fact that some of the Alpha members currently attending Valley Stream Central High School would be going to the new North and South high schools, due to redistricting, as soon as they opened in January of 1956.

Alpha Omega Theta already had a substantial number of members who would be going to Valley Stream South High School. Although there would be only a few AOT members scheduled to attend Valley Stream North High School, there was no cause to worry about that. There would be plenty of time to recruit new members in Valley Stream North. Omega Gamma Delta was also trying to position their prospects for establishing new chapters after the new high schools opened. A new chapter in Valley Stream South High School was assured through a splintering of the Delta Chapter and established members proclaiming a new chapter in South High School. But even before that would happen, there was a very real prospect for establishing a new chapter with brand-new recruits in another town.

The town was eighteen miles away from Valley Stream. It was an incorporated village called Freeport. This had been in the works for at least the past six weeks. The Delta Chapter brothers were, in fact, very psyched about starting the second chapter on Long Island. They were more enthusiastic for launching a chapter in Freeport than they were about the new chapter at Valley Stream South. After all, the new chapter at South was assured by virtue of the fact that some of the Delta Chapter brothers would be going to school there in January. A new chapter would be formed there by default. But Freeport was another story. This was the first occurrence of the Delta Chapter AOT brothers starting a new chapter by recruiting charter members in another town. Good things were happening. The first push at expansion was about to happen.

The second pledge class was outstanding in every aspect of the AOT requirements. All ten of them passed their pledging period and were inducted as brothers of Alpha Omega Theta Fraternity. Many of these ten new recruits would be going to Valley Stream South High School, so they helped assure the launching of a second chapter in Valley Stream, New York. Their initiation was the same as that of the prior pledge class. They attended a meeting in the basement of Chick's house. They were stripped down to their underwear and dropped off in Valley Stream State Park. Again, these inductees were warned to find their way back to Chick's house in less than an hour or face failure to be inducted.

They were successful in getting back to Chick's house on time and were all inducted into the Delta Chapter a few days later. They earned their colors, their sweaters. Now that this pledge class was over, it was time to plan for the future, new chapters, expansion.

Alpha Omega Theta was about to have a growth spurt in the next two or three years to come. Chick had some hand in the chartering of the Freeport chapter, but most of the new chapters to be founded came into existence after Chick graduated high school. Jerry Smith and Fred Gifford were instrumental in recruiting Rocky Clarke, who would become a charter member of Freeport AOT and who would in turn have a big influence on the growth of new AOT chapters. Chick recalls, "Many chapters sprang up throughout Long Island. Freeport was an early one. My contact with AOT after 1956 was minimal, to say the least. Jerry Smith and Fred Gifford were more instrumental in ongoing achievements after high school. The guys who graduated Central in 1957 and later carried on with the LI growth. I attended school in Florida and sort of lost touch after a while."

Valley Stream Central first AOT class of 1956

Valley Stream Central AOT class of 1957

Valley Stream Central AOT class of 1959

Valley Stream Central AOT class of 1962

CHAPTER FIVE

Expansion

Freeport AOT—Zeta Chapter

The Alpha brothers from Valley Stream Central had been working on establishing a new chapter in the village of Freeport for the past two months. They had gotten to know a bunch of guys from Freeport through inter-high school wrestling. Most of the AOT members in Valley Stream Central were on the Central High School wrestling team. They developed a close relationship with members of the Freeport High School wrestling team.

There were no fraternities at all in Freeport High School, although there were three sororities. The potential recruits from Freeport had a lot in common with the AOT brothers from Valley Stream. They all wrestled, they were all good students, all upstanding members of their school's social scene.

The first students from Freeport High School to be approached were Rocky Clarke, Don Hamilton, Ed Strickland, and Joseph Bateman. They were recruited by Jerry and George Smith. There was a real comfortable friendship established among these guys. Rocky and Don were very much into the idea of starting a fraternity. They had toyed with the idea of starting their own and briefly considered Omega, but after being taken to Brooklyn to meet some of the members of Brooklyn AOT, they were sold on starting an Alpha chapter in Freeport. Rocky and Don later recruited two more charter members to start the chapter; they were Peter Fawcet and Paul Samuel.

Rocky Clarke recalls the early contacts between Valley Stream and Freeport.

"The first contact came through wrestling. Freeport only started a wrestling team when I was a freshman. That would have been 1953-54. Since it was the first team, several of us freshmen wrestled varsity for all four years. We got pretty friendly socially with the guys from VS Central, Jerry and George Smith, Dick and Charlie Moray, Mark Everett, Arnie Argenti, Fred Gifford, John Cisco, etc. The best I can remember, they talked to us about AOT and invited us to a meeting. I think some of the original Brooklyn brothers were there. We were convinced and agreed to start a chapter. I believe the only contact between Valley Stream and Freeport came through us on the wrestling teams. It was up to us to recruit the other charter brothers. Four of our six first members were wrestlers. I remember that we didn't have to go through Hell Week, but the Central guys did administer a Hell Night. They blindfolded me, drove me to Connecticut, and dumped me on a back road somewhere."

Once they had made up their mind to go forward, there was no turning back. In fact, out of the six charter members recruited to form the Freeport chapter of AOT, four of them were on the Freeport High School wrestling team; the other two were on the Freeport High School football team. All six of them were inseparable, all having been close friends since grammar school. In 1956, athletes and jock types were highly respected on Freeport High School campus by peers, teachers, and administrators, so there was literally no opposition to what they were planning.

A game of hurry-up and wait ensued, similar to the way the Delta Chapter in Valley Stream was chartered by Brooklyn Alpha. Nobody wanted to seem too eager, even though they all were. The Freeport guys didn't want to seem like they had no better prospects and therefore wanted to start an AOT chapter right away. And the Valley Stream Alpha brothers didn't want to seem like they were in a hurry to launch new chapters although they were indeed eager for this to happen as soon as possible. Most of the chapter members had been gathered within the first two or three weeks of recruiting, but they all played the waiting game. There were meetings to discuss the new chapter, held in Freeport, Valley Stream, and one gathering in Brooklyn to get the blessing from the mother chapter. The Brooklyn meeting went well, and it was the final hurdle to establishing a chapter in Freeport.

Once a sufficient amount of time had passed and everyone could save face, a date was set to induct the Freeport recruits as charter members of a new chapter. There would be no pledging since they were charter members; however, they would have to endure Hell Night.

On March 10, 1956, fifteen members of the Delta Chapter of AOT came to Freeport in four carloads. They met at the Freeport Speedway with the six charter members they would be inducting. The Freeport Speedway was also sometimes known as Freeport Stadium. It was a quarter-mile-diameter racetrack. There had been stock car races at Freeport Raceway since 1933. It was a popular spot not only in Freeport but on all of Long Island. Freeport Raceway was situated on the edge of Freeport, right between the Meadowbrook Parkway on the east side and the swampy marshland on the south side of the stadium. The swamp behind the stadium was a perfect spot for a late-Friday-night hazing.

The stadium was closed, and the Alpha brothers and inductees had to climb a fence to get to the swamp behind the stadium. The Freeport inductees got a fairly easy Hell Night induction by the standards that would follow in the upcoming years and decades. They were stripped to their underwear, covered in molasses and Rice Crispies, and then were dressed in strange outfits like dresses and shoved blindfolded into the trunks of cars for a long ride.

There was no physical hazing as Rocky Clarke recalled. "No beating and no paddling, a lot of mutual respect because we were friends and peers. We wouldn't have put up with that anyway. There would have been a rumble. We were green wrestlers, but seasoned street brawlers, and we didn't take shit from anyone. They did some other stuff on Hell Night, weird outfits, I think."

The real Hell Night hell ride would be in the boondocks of Connecticut. There were four cars all together—two inductees each in two cars, and one inductee each in the remaining two. They were dropped off in four different locations. They were all dropped off in remote, wooded areas far from the nearest public phone. Rocky Clarke was one of the unlucky ones to be dropped off alone. He was left on the side of the road in Stratford, Connecticut, covered in molasses and cornflakes, wearing a dress, with no money to make a call even if he could find a phone. Rocky was picked up hitchhiking by Connecticut state troopers on Merritt Parkway. He was obviously a mess, and they were not going to leave him looking like that walking down the parkway. He was taken into custody. Rocky spent the night in jail in Connecticut, and his mother picked him up the next morning.

A meeting was arranged for next week in Freeport for the formal induction. The meeting would be held at newly inducted Freeport brother Paul Samuel's house. On March 15, 1956, at 7:45 PM, the first meeting of the Freeport chapter was opened at Paul Samuel's house. All six Freeport brothers were present, as well as five brothers from the Valley Stream Delta Chapter.

The Freeport chapter was officially designated the Epsilon Chapter of Alpha Omega Theta Fraternity Inc. Elections were held, and the first officer class of Epsilon Chapter was sworn in as follows:

> Don Hamilton—President
> Paul Samuel—Vice President
> Rocky Clarke—Secretary
> Peter Fawcet—Treasurer
> Ed Strickland—Corresponding Secretary
> Joseph Bateman—Dog Master

The brothers from Delta Chapter presented Epsilon Chapter's new treasurer Peter Fawcet with $25 as the first deposit into the Freeport AOT treasury. The brothers of the newly christened Epsilon Chapter took control of the meeting and voted on and passed chapter bylaws in respect to dress code, dues payment, fines for violations, absences and tardiness, and induction fees for new members.

Epsilon president Don Hamilton and secretary Rocky Clarke were elected and chosen to be the Epsilon Chapter's representatives to the Grand Council of Alpha Omega Theta Fraternity. It was agreed the next meeting would be held at Don Hamilton's house next week on March 21, 1956, at 6:45 PM. The first meeting of Freeport AOT, Epsilon Chapter was adjourned at 9:10 PM.

The second meeting was held as scheduled at Don Hamilton's house; all six brothers were present. The first week of AOT in Freeport High School was a resounding success. There was a large number of Freeport High School students who wanted to join AOT already. A list of twelve names was brought up for possible interviews to become the first dogs of Freeport Alpha. After voting on the interview candidates, another measure was voted on for all six AOT brothers to meet with Freeport High School principal Mr. Southard to discuss the new fraternity, its place in the social structure of Freeport High School, and the pledging boundaries that would be permitted in school. Lastly, plans were discussed to hold the first Freeport Alpha Dance at the VFW Hall in Freeport.

A special meeting was scheduled for April 7, 1956, a Saturday night, at Paul Samuel's house. All of the prospective interviewees whose names were brought up would be interviewed at the next meeting. This meeting was adjourned at 8:20 PM.

The interview meeting began promptly at 8:00 PM. Of the fourteen names brought up at the last meeting, ten showed up to be interviewed. Out of the ten interviews, nine of them passed unanimously. One was voted down unanimously. The four who didn't show up for their interview were permanently blackballed from Alpha Omega Theta, Epsilon Chapter. It was voted on and determined that the pledging period would be for three weeks.

On Friday, April 28, 1956, Hell Night took place for the six dogs still remaining out of the original eight. One of them had dropped out after the first week of dogging, and the other was blackballed and disqualified from membership for not displaying proper attitude with the brotherhood. All six dogs were taken on the Hell Night hell rides. They were dropped off in remote areas thirty to forty miles from Freeport and left to find their own way home.

On the next night, Saturday, April 29, 1956, the six dogs were inducted into Alpha Omega Theta Fraternity. The rules of chapter meetings and bylaws were explained to the new inductees, as were the meanings of the fraternity's crest, the fraternity password, and the fraternity handshake. A motion was made to make Rocky Clarke sergeant at arms. The motion passed unanimously. Rocky now held two offices and titles. Corresponding secretary Ed Strickland announced the Freeport chapter's name and designation were changing.

Word didn't travel as fast in the 1950s, but word finally got to the Brooklyn chapter about the Freeport chapter's chartering. Generally, they were thrilled at the news of another chapter being founded; however, the chapter designation of Epsilon was already taken. The brothers in Valley Stream assumed Epsilon was the next logical chapter designation when they chartered and named the Freeport chapter so, but they didn't know that the older, inactive brothers from the Brooklyn Alpha Chapter of AOT had formed an alumni chapter and had chosen Epsilon as the designation. Hence, the new and permanent name for the Freeport chapter was to be Alpha Omega Theta Fraternity Inc., Zeta Chapter.

With that, a long-running tradition had been born in Freeport, and it was named AOT. The Freeport brothers worked hard on collecting money for advertising the dance program for the Zeta Chapter's first formal dance, which was held at the VFW Memorial Hall in Freeport. The brothers sold advertising space to all the popular merchants in town. The method was perfected by the Brooklyn brothers during the years they too had annual dances and earned money to pay for their dances by selling ad space to local merchants in the dance program, which would be given to the party attendees. They would charge advertisers $1 for a quarter of a page, $2 for a half page, and $5 for a full-page ad. Other chapters and sororities would often buy ads, and in Brooklyn, it was common for other fraternities to buy ads as well.

Parties like this were a formal-dress affair. Jackets and ties were required of the guys, and girls wore formal party dresses. There would be a live band, food, and drink, but no alcohol would be served at all. Someone might spike the punch, as was a usual practice in the 1950s, but no official serving of alcohol took place at these parties.

The members of Freeport Alpha's Zeta Chapter were among the top students in Freeport High School. They were top athletes and A-average students. They had reputations that were impeccable in school and around town. This was one of the reasons they were so successful so quickly in establishing Alpha Omega Theta Fraternity in Freeport. They received no resistance from the principal, the school system in general, or from the students or parents of students who would dog for the fraternity. As individuals, they had great reputations; as a group they combined their reputations and made AOT a great success from day one.

This party was highly anticipated at Freeport High School. They had a growing list of guys who wanted to get into AOT. The brothers discussed holding another pledge class before school closed in June. But they decided to make them all wait. The brothers wanted to put all their effort into the upcoming party. So the next pledge class would have to wait until late June, although they had a list of eager would-be pledges.

As expected, the dance was a success, and it fueled the further growth of the Freeport chapter. The next pledge class was held in September of the 1956-57 school year. Elections were held over the summer, and Don Hamilton was reelected to serve as president, as was Vice President Paul Samuel and Secretary / Sergeant at Arms Rocky Clarke. They were all founding charter members of Freeport Alpha, but they were juniors when they started the fraternity the previous year. Since AOT was a democratic organization, they held open elections, and all three of them were reelected. The new treasurer was Pat Hiller.

The 1957 school year was a year of explosive growth for the Freeport chapter of AOT. They held three pledge classes and tripled the size of the chapter.

Oceanside AOT—Kappa Theta Chapter

In September of 1957, Alpha Omega Theta Fraternity came to Oceanside, New York. Two chapters of AOT had already been established on Long Island—in Valley Stream and Freeport—and now the Oceanside chapter was to become the third chapter on Long Island, founded a year before the Baldwin chapter and shortly after the Freeport chapter.

Unlike in Freeport and Baldwin, where there were no established fraternities to compete with, Oceanside had a chapter of Omega Gamma Delta, which had been in existence since 1940. Just like in Valley Stream, the Omegas strutted around like they owned the town and the school. Just like in Valley Stream, Omega Gamma Delta was the only fraternity in town. A common thread in most Omega chapters at that time was that they were a restricted organization. In the words of early Oceanside AOT alumnus Gary Schwartzberg, "At that time, Omega only took 'Christians,' and the school was 'ripe' (i.e. football and other sports players) for another fraternity. Most of us fit into that category (I was varsity football and baseball)." Gary was one of the first inductees from the first pledge class of Oceanside AOT in 1958.

Although Oceanside had only one fraternity prior to the founding of AOT, they did have a lot of so-called athletic social clubs. These athletic social clubs were a 1950s version of street gangs. They had colorful names such as the Counts, the Gents, the Emeralds, the Morticians, the Dukes, and the Squires. And that is just naming a few that existed over the years. The Squires were associated with the local Knights of Columbus chapter. Students who were too young to join the Knights of Columbus would become members of the Squires. All the athletic social clubs were greaser types, with black leather jackets that had their club name stitched on the back.

Opposite from that greaser culture was Omega Gamma Delta, which represented outstanding students and athletes in Oceanside. There was a much-higher standard to join Omega, but there was an ugly side to that exclusivity. Just as in the Valley Stream Omega chapter, the Oceanside chapter was segregated and restricted. Omega Gamma Delta was a white-Christians-only fraternity. And to many of Oceanside's nonaffiliated outstanding students and athletes, it was good reason not to consider joining Omega.

Many of Oceanside's top athletes were not affiliated and would not join Omega. These outstanding students were Christian and Jewish, and some were Hispanic; although the Hispanic students were Christian, they would not be considered for membership in Omega Gamma Delta. Through contact with the officers of the Valley Stream chapter, these nonaffiliated Oceanside students were recruited to form a chapter of AOT in Oceanside. According to founding charter member Jack Barlow, the Valley Stream AOT members put the charter members of Oceanside chapter in contact with Freeport AOT alumnus Rocky Clarke. Rocky had graduated the year before, and he was living with his girlfriend in an apartment in Massapequa. Rocky had been secretary of Freeport AOT and had expert typing skills, so he handled the issuing of the charter to the new Oceanside crew. Jack Barlow thought that Rocky was the Grand Poobah of AOT, considering the high level of respect the Valley Stream brothers displayed to him at the time. It was the last official act that Rocky would perform as a member and officer of Alpha Omega Theta Fraternity.

This had been in the works since early in the 1957-58 school year. The previous Valley Stream officers from the class of 1957—President Dick Moray and Treasurer Duncan Sikes and Secretary Bobby Playa of Valley Stream AOT—had been working with some of the Oceanside students to recruit charter members. But there was great difficulty getting started in Oceanside. Omega Gamma Delta had been the only show in town since 1940, and the school administration wanted to keep it that way. The school administration at that time did not have an aversion to fraternities like they would in decades to come. In 1957, the school administration regarded Omega as being representative of the best and brightest in the school, and they wanted to maintain that aura of exclusivity. The Oceanside chapter of Omega didn't want competition coming into the school either, so there was real aversion to starting up AOT in Oceanside from more than one angle.

Because of the aversion by the administration and the Omegas, this whole plan was kept hush-hush for as long as possible. The first four guys to agree to become charter members began recruiting others even before they were inducted into AOT. When they had enough charter members to launch a chapter, they went to Valley Stream, and the first four members from Oceanside were inducted by Valley Stream AOT with a Hell Night—only ceremony as soon as school started in September. The first four Oceanside students to get inducted were Alan Theo, who was to become Oceanside Alpha's first president, and Frank Santillo, who was to become the first vice president, as well as sophomores Jack Barlow and Barry Wolf. They were given a Hell Night induction in Valley Stream. Their induction was not as rough as usual, and for good reason: they had promised to produce a large number of additional charter members to induct right after they got inducted. They received a paddling and no Hell Night hell ride.

Previously, the charter membership had varied between six to ten members among Valley Stream, Freeport, and, later, Baldwin Alpha; but Oceanside AOT was about to make a huge splash in Oceanside High School. The chapter had not been officially declared and chartered with only four members, but these four had recruited fifteen additional students who were definitely interested and couldn't wait to get started. This first group of inductees was not pledged and was regarded as original charter members, along with the other four.

Before the first week of school, the Omegas already knew what was up. They wasted no time in trying to put a stop to it. Not only did the Omegas not want a rival fraternity in Oceanside, they also didn't want to compete for recruits with AOT. The vice president of Omega, Art Wrigby, approached several key recruits for the charter class of AOT and offered them a proposition. It was proposed at the last Omega meeting that if the key charter members for AOT would switch over to Omega Gamma Delta, they would let them all in with an honorary induction and no pledging.

"Interesting proposition," said Jack Barlow. Jack was one of the younger recruits. He was a sophomore in Oceanside High School. "But what about Gene Gellman and Gary Schwartzman and my good friend Barry Wolf? Are they also invited to join Omega with a no-pledging induction?"

"Listen, guys, you know I can't promise that. That's just not going to happen," Art Wrigby said. "Don't turn down a chance to get a fast-track induction to the best high school fraternity around just because of your Jewish friends. Let it go, they'll understand."

"Nope," said Jack Barlow. "If my friends aren't welcome in your fraternity, then neither am I. I don't turn my back on my friends. We are going to start a chapter of AOT in Oceanside."

"You heard the man, Art," said Frank Santillo. "This is a done deal. Jack, Barry Wolf, Alan Theo, and I are already in AOT, and this coming Thursday night, we plan to induct a charter class of members to start up in Oceanside. Tell your Omega brothers to get used to it. We are here to stay."

"Who are your charter members?" asked Art Wrigby.

"Sorry, Art, we are not sharing that info with you. We don't want any of our recruits being persuaded to go over to Omega. You'll see who we have the day after the induction when they all show up in school wearing their AOT sweaters, and you will be surprised at who we got," said Frank Santillo.

"He and his Omega buddies are gonna shit their pants when they see who we got," said Jack.

Art Wrigby was annoyed with the results of the conversation. He couldn't understand why these guys would turn down a chance to get a fast-track induction into Omega Gamma Delta in favor of starting a chapter of a new fraternity like AOT. He didn't get it; he didn't understand the fact that Omega's restrictive practices were offensive to most of the AOT recruits, offensive to the Jewish students who were banned from joining, and offensive to the Christian AOT recruits who shared a bond of friendship with their Jewish friends that went all the way back to grammar school. These guys refused to join a club that wouldn't also accept their friends. This honorable principle was right in tune with that of the founding four members of AOT in 1946, who would not join other fraternities that wouldn't have their friend John Cangin, who had cerebral palsy.

There was a common thread of honor and a true sense of brotherhood in the lineage of AOT from the founding brothers right up to the new Long Island chapters, even though no one really knew that. At this point in time, there was very little communication with the Brooklyn chapter.

That Thursday night, a meeting was held in Frank Santillo's house on Woods Avenue. It was in the detached garage that the induction took place. Just as planned, fifteen students from Oceanside High School showed up for the induction as charter members of Oceanside AOT. Fifteen members of Valley Stream AOT came to the meeting to induct the largest charter member class of any new chapter up to date.

Frank's garage, detached from the house, was jam-packed. Since there were so many members to induct, it was decided that this bunch would not be taken on a Hell Night hell ride. There were too many inductees to take them all on long rides, fifty miles into nowhere. Instead, in addition to the mandatory paddling, these charter members were subjected to a new form of hazing. These inductees were brought face-to-face with each Valley Stream member of AOT and were slapped open hand across the face. This was a hazing tradition that would continue for decades and was called being "taken around the room."

Although the original Alpha chapter in Brooklyn did routinely slap pledges, both during inductions and while pledging on a daily basis, this was the first time the Long Island chapters had commenced using open and closed fists on inductees. After this induction, all chapters of Alpha would take inductees around the room on their Hell Night. As time went by, the intensity of this physical induction ritual would worsen, and pledges would eventually run the Hell Line gauntlet.

On this evening, the hazing was brief to keep the induction ceremony rolling along so that it wouldn't take all night. After all the charter members were paddled, they began the formal part of the induction ceremony. The new Oceanside brothers were told the history of Alpha Omega Theta Fraternity. They were told of AOT's founding in Brooklyn, New York, and its incorporation in 1948 and its movement into Long Island. The president of Oceanside Alpha, Alan Theo, was handed a folder with printed materials for Oceanside Alpha to keep as the first official documents of the chapter. Among them was a document titled The Principles of Kappa Theta, which was the actual charter drawn up by Rocky Clarke to be presented to the newly christened Kappa Theta Chapter of Alpha Omega Theta in Oceanside, New York; also, the oath of brotherhood and the oaths of officers; a standard letter of invitation to interview for new recruits; a letter of suspension, which was given to chapter brothers who were to be suspended for various forms of misconduct; "The Alpha Song," to sing the praises of the founding members; the opening and closing prayers to open and close meetings; and a few other odds and ends. The only thing not enclosed in the folder was a constitution. That was something that did not exist at this time, but interchapter discussion regarding collaboration on a constitution binding all Long Island chapters would take place shortly after the founding of the chapters in Baldwin and Rockville Centre in the upcoming year.

Each inductee was administered the oath of brotherhood, and the newly elected officers were administered the oath of office. Each new member paid a $10 induction fee to the new Kappa Theta Chapter treasury. That covered the $6 charge for an AOT sweater and $4 to put into the treasury. All the new Alpha brothers from Oceanside were given the Alpha grip by all the Valley Stream brothers, and they all signed a sheet of paper affirming the oath of brotherhood. The paper was on brand-new stationery, which had been printed up green paper with red lettering and had the AOT shield in the upper left corner and had "Kappa Theta Chapter" written under "Alpha Omega Theta Fraternity Inc." The paper with the original charter members' names was entered into the chapter's books for permanent archiving, along with a written description of the events of the evening.

The next day, nineteen students showed up in Oceanside High School wearing green-and-red sweaters. To say the Omegas were shocked would be a gross understatement. Not only did AOT charter and declare a new chapter in Oceanside High School, they also robbed Omega Gamma Delta of most of the top-tier athletic-affiliated students whom they were planning to recruit that same month. Suddenly there was a new order in Oceanside High School, and the Omega's aura of exclusivity was burst permanently. The students the Alphas had recruited and inducted were all football players, soccer players, lacrosse players, wrestlers, as well as team captains. These were the caliber of students the Omegas always went for each September, but this year, the pickings were slim for recruitment into Omega Gamma Delta.

The Oceanside chapter wasted no time in recruiting their first pledge class. There was a real buzz going around about AOT, and there was big interest among the juniors and sophomores to join. The first pledge class started with fifteen dogs. There were four juniors, nine sophomores, and even two freshmen. Pledging freshmen was not routine in the early days of the Long Island chapters. But sometimes exceptions were made. In this case, the two freshmen were Chip Hawkins and Jim Stapleton. In 1957-58, freshmen still attended Oceanside Junior High School on Castleton Court, about a mile away from Oceanside High School. The junior high was popularly called Merle because the side entryways and the district administration offices were on Merle Avenue.

Chip and Jim were both on the junior high wrestling team and were well respected. Jim was big for his age, very strong, and stood eye to eye with most juniors and seniors. Chip was his best friend. Although it was Jim who was asked to pledge, Jim said he would be willing if his friend Chip was invited too. One day, representatives went to Merle to talk to and recruit Jim and Chip. They spoke with chapter president Alan Theo and pledge master Tony DiStanza.

The Alpha guys wanted to start planting seeds among the younger students at the junior high on Merle Avenue. They were sure Chip and Jim were top-shelf, high-quality recruits, and they would spread the word among the freshman class about AOT so that there would be a big pledge class next September when the freshmen became sophomores and moved over to Oceanside High School. They were right. Oceanside Alpha's classes of 1960 and 1961 had big rosters of AOT members and had some of the most respected students in school. And as per the strict requirements, all members were players of at least one school sport or athletic team. The Alphas were highly respected right from the start of the Oceanside chapter.

The first pledge class of the Kappa Theta Chapter dogged for a period of three weeks. Jim Stapleton and Chip Hawkins didn't get dogged during the school day much because they were attending the junior high and there were no AOT members in Oceanside Junior High at the time. Occasionally, Alpha brothers would go to the junior high to dog them, but mostly, they did their dogging after school, when they were required to go over to the high school as soon as classes at the junior high let out for the day.

It didn't take long for word to spread around the junior high school that Chip and Jim were dogging for Alpha. There was a strong, positive buzz about this new fraternity; everybody wanted in. After Chip and Jim got inducted, there would be many more from this class getting into AOT in the next pledge class and the one after that.

This pledge class was introduced to the concept of merits and demerits. For each demerit they were issued by an Alpha brother, they would receive one shot with a paddle at the next meeting. So five demerits meant five shots, seven demerits meant seven shots, and so on. Dogs were issued demerits for not following orders or for performing a task badly or coming in last place in a push-up contest. And that's just a few examples. If an Alpha brother took to disliking a particular dog, that dog may find himself getting a disproportionate number of demerits to the other dogs.

A dog could work off demerits by earning merits. In 1957, the rate of exchange was twenty-five merits would wipe out one demerit. In later years, future dogs would need fifty to one hundred merits to wipe out one demerit. During this pledge class, Chip and Jim would average four to seven demerits each and, subsequently, four to seven shots at each meeting as a result. The paddling's at the meetings would of course wipe out all demerits, and the dogs would start the next pledge week with a clean slate.

In addition to the paddling, dogs were required to carry a brick for each demerit as well. Although Alpha was a new fraternity in Oceanside, they were not giving the first pledges an easy ride. Because the chapter got off to a big start with such a large charter membership, they were already competing against Omega Gamma Delta in a way that embarrassed and annoyed the Omegas to no end. Because of the successful launch of the new chapter, there was no shortage of students who wanted to get into AOT. As a result, the first pledge class had a rough ride to their induction, and this would set the standards for future pledge classes in Oceanside Alpha.

Hell Night was truly hellish for this first pledge class of Oceanside AOT. They all got a severe beating, for starters. They all were stripped down to their underwear and had them filled with molasses, bananas, eggs, and cornflakes. They put their pants back on, and they all got paddled. All received twelve shots with one-inch-thick planks of wood cut into the shape of a paddle. The paddles had holes drilled in them to allow airflow, more speed, and velocity when swinging them.

In later years, around 2004, the time of the first Oceanside AOT reunion, Chip Hawkins reminisced about his Hell Night induction, and he had this to say. "Society and the school administration had little effect on the dogging process. So if you don't mind my telling you that if you hadn't been hit by Bob Petrocelli [1959-60] bearing a 'screamer,' you hadn't been hit. A 'screamer' was a six-by-twenty-four-inch oak paddle with one-and-a-half-inch holes closely drilled in it to cut down wind resistance. Its trajectory was from across the room with two full three-hundred-sixty-degree turns incorporated to gain full momentum. The scrotum was released and unprotected due to the grabbing of both ankles with both hands to maximize the stretching of the skin across the buttocks. I was hit by Bob Petrocelli in spite of other brothers pleading with him not to hit me too hard. He had reputation for really beating on guys. I was ninety-nine pounds when I graduated, so you can imagine how small I was as a freshman. Anyway, Bob started running at me from about twenty feet away and turned two circles to gain momentum and speed and really nailed me. I wanted to cry so bad, but he warned me if I did, he would only hit me again."

Later on, after the beating and paddling, Chip was chosen for a bizarre hazing ritual that the others didn't have to submit to. Chip was forced to lie down on his back faceup. They filled his mouth with water and instructed him not to swallow or spit it out. They dropped a live goldfish in his mouth. They all got a good laugh watching him being used as a living fish bowl, but the real kicker came when someone dropped an Alka-Seltzer tablet into his mouth as well. He was under strict penalty of getting twelve more paddle shots from Bob Petrocelli if he spat out the foamy water and fish before the fish died. Needless to say, he kept his throat closed tight and didn't spit out the foamy mess until he was told to, which was after the goldfish stopped flopping around in his mouth full of Alka-Seltzer.

About his Hell Night hell ride, Chip had this to say: "Jim and I were in the same car for the ride out to nowhere. We were warned not to have any money on us, or we would be taken out of state. I took a chance and taped twenty cents to my left foot on the bottom. We were dropped off on one of the north/south parkways, I believe east of the Meadowbrook. We were a mess, the parkways were unlit, and no one would pick us up. We hitched for about an hour, walking as we went. Finally came to a gas station [all-nighter] and scared the shit out of the guy in attendance. I called my mother, and she came to pick us up."

This was the grand finale for the first pledge class of Oceanside's Kappa Theta Chapter of Alpha Omega Theta. This was the beginning of one of the biggest AOT chapters on Long Island, a chapter that had one of the longest runs in existence. The subsequent classes of 1959, 1960, and 1961 had huge AOT rosters and highly respected membership. Each of these classes had the top-tier athletes and team captains as members. Omega Gamma Delta really had to catch up during these years.

Chip Hawkins was a proud Greenie, as Alpha members preferred to be called, although he hated the obscure reference to being in "the Christmas Club." He and Jim Stapleton remained close friends during their time in high school and in AOT. In the winter of their senior year, they attended an Alpha keg party that nearly ended in disaster.

The party seemed to be going OK; there was plenty of drinking, and after catching what seemed like a nice buzz, Chip stepped outside with his girlfriend for a make-out session in the back of his car. They were just getting busy and steamed up the windows and all when they heard loud voices outside the car.

Something didn't sound right, and because the windows were so steamed up, they couldn't see what was going on. So Chip stepped out of the car to see what was going on.

Chip saw a huge muscular, V-shaped guy on top of another guy on the ground, pummeling him. There was no mistaking that V shape; it was Chip's best friend, Jim Stapleton, beating the shit out of someone. Chip rushed over to stop the guy's friends from jumping Jim from behind. Not that Jim needed help. Jim Stapleton was a Nassau County wrestling champ. He was one tough dude, and he didn't lose matches, or street fights.

Within seconds, all hell broke loose. Dozens of Alpha brothers flooded out of the house into the street to surround and pound these three unfortunate party crashers who had come all the way from Queens thinking Long Islanders were punks and that they would have no trouble taking over the party.

It turned out that Jim Stapleton had escorted these three out of the house, with a warning not to try coming back, when one of them pulled a knife and stabbed him three times in the chest. Lucky for Jim none of the stab wounds were deep enough to hit vital organs, and he was not seriously injured despite being very bloody. Even with three stab wounds, Jim was still able to ground and pound the guy who stabbed him, beating his face to a bloody pulp.

Right after the Alphas swarmed the party crashers, the Nassau County police showed up; no doubt, neighbors had called in the disturbance. In the confusion that ensued after the cops arrived, while the Alphas were explaining the situation to the cops, the party crashers had slipped away and took off running through neighborhood yards.

The cops closed off the area with a few squad cars and eventually cornered the Queens party crashers in a nearby schoolyard. They had to take Jim to the hospital for treatment, and after catching the guys from Queens, the cops brought them to the hospital so Jim could identify who stabbed him.

"Which one of these guys stabbed you?" the cop asked, and Jimmy just laughed and said, "The guy with the beat-up face." It looked like hamburger from the pounding he had received from Jim.

Even though the three Queens party crashers had been jumped and worked over pretty bad by the Alpha brothers, the cops considered the guys from Queens to be trespassing and in the wrong neighborhood. Oceanside, much like most of Long Island's communities in the '50s and '60s, was close knit. In today's climate, everybody would have been arrested for rioting or gang activity. But in 1961, the outsiders got a ride to the station house, and later that evening, they went to the Nassau County Jail.

Oceanside Alpha was founded as an alternative to Omega Gamma Delta, which was a jock fraternity restricted to Christians only. Although AOT was founded as a nonsegregated fraternity, it was still exclusionary as well, accepting top athletes only. The formation of AOT in Oceanside showed that there was an alternative to Omega Gamma Delta, and that the school "athletic social clubs," which were 1950s-style gangs, were declining and fading out with the growth of Greek-letter fraternities.

A year after AOT was formed in Oceanside, other new fraternities also popped up as alternatives to not only Omega but to Alpha as well. The third fraternity formed in Oceanside was Alpha Theta Gamma, popularly known as Alpha Theta. Their colors were black and white. They soon had chapters in Rockville Centre and Freeport. The next one was Sigma Lambda Rho, which was the total opposite of Omega. Sigma Lambda Rho was founded as a strictly Jewish fraternity, but that restriction didn't last long. Their colors were purple and white.

Baldwin AOT—Sigma Chapter

By 1958, the Zeta Chapter of Freeport had established themselves as a class act. Their presence in Freeport as the only fraternity at that time was built on the respect of their peers and the school administration. Now they were about to establish a new chapter in neighboring Baldwin. Baldwin was the next town next to Freeport, and the close proximity resulted in students in the two communities making acquaintances with each other.

One such cross-town friendship was about to facilitate the founding of a new chapter of AOT. Baldwin High School senior Pete Martin was by chance dating a girl from Freeport High School whose brother was in Freeport AOT. Pete was invited to form a chapter in Baldwin if he could gather enough charter members.

Baldwin High School had no fraternities at that time, and the field was wide open, so the idea seemed great. Pete asked around among his friends and did get positive feedback, but no definite agreement from anyone other than Frank Genaro, Jimmy Sneed, and John Burn. All were on the Baldwin High School football team. There were others who were genuinely interested, but they wanted to see if Pete would go through with it first. Sometimes people need a push, and seeing Pete, Frank, Jimmy, and John get initiated first would encourage them to follow.

Since there were only four of them, certainly not enough to charter a new chapter, the four of them would have to dog for Freeport Alpha. They were not offered a one-night induction given to charter members since they didn't have enough members to charter a chapter. The usual pledging period was three weeks. They weren't entitled to start the Baldwin chapter with just a Hell Night induction with only four charter members. Their four names had been brought up for membership and passed. The four Baldwin students were invited to come and interview at the next meeting in Freeport. Since they were going to be the foundation for starting a new chapter, they were given a two-week pledging period.

Word got around Baldwin High School pretty quickly that these four were planning on becoming members of AOT and would soon be establishing a chapter in Baldwin. The school administration in Baldwin High School did not take this news well. Their response was total opposition to a fraternity being established in Baldwin High School, even if the members were outstanding students and athletes. Attempts were made to dissuade the four of them from joining Alpha. None of them showed any sign of wavering on their intent to pledge for Alpha Omega Theta Fraternity.

A few days before the interview meeting in Freeport, John Burn suddenly changed his mind and declined to attend the interview. It seemed that Baldwin High School gym teacher George Craig had called John Burn's mother and convinced her to keep her son out of it. John Burn was captain of the Baldwin High School football team, and George Craig was the coach. He had considerable leverage over the players on his team and convinced John's mother that the fraternity would be bad for his academic and athletic future. The school administration in Baldwin really wanted to put a stop to these young men starting a fraternity, but there was no turning back. A day after John Burn announced he was not going to join AOT, Jimmy Sneed also informed Pete Martin that his parents also had been contacted by George Craig and had refused to let him pledge for the fraternity.

Jimmy Sneed and John Burn dropped out before they even got started, but Pete Martin and Frank Genaro attended the interview with AOT in Freeport and passed the vote. They began dogging the next day. Since there was no active chapter of AOT in Baldwin, there was no one to dog them during school hours. Occasionally, a few Freeport brothers would show up at Baldwin High School during lunch break or immediately after school. But mostly during the two-week pledging period, the two dogs from Baldwin High School were not pledged until they went to Freeport after school.

The two dogs were required to wear pledging attire during the school day even though there were no AOT brothers in Baldwin. The attire was a green bow tie and red suspenders; shined black shoes; cleaned, pressed slacks, and a white collared shirt. They had to have a fresh-shaved crew cut at all times.

Pete and Frank were both determined to complete their two-week pledging period. They began dogging during the first week of school in September of 1958. They were excited about forming a chapter of AOT in Baldwin. They had some difficult hazing rituals to endure in the process. Among them was the usual requirement to carry a cigar box containing plenty of cigarettes and gum to give to the Freeport AOT brothers and a couple of tins of shoeshine polish and a brush to be able to polish a brother's shoes on demand. In addition to that, both dogs from Baldwin were required to shave their genital pubic hair and keep it in an empty Marlboro cigarette box, which was to be kept with them at all times. Another fun activity was a drill called "air raid." When any AOT brother shouted "air raid," the dogs were required to hit the ground in a crouching position, head between knees, and hands clasped behind the neck. This was done whenever and wherever they were, regardless of who was watching or how many bystanders were present. They could be ordered to do an air raid in a crowded shopping center with bewildered shoppers not knowing what the hell they were doing.

There was also the unforgettable homemade electric chair. As crazy as it sounds, the Freeport AOT brothers rigged up a wooden chair with a six-volt lantern battery and a switch. Both dogs had to sit in the chair and get zapped whenever they didn't perform their dogging requirements up to par, or simply when they wanted a good laugh at the expense of Pete and Frank, strapped in and jumping and jerking in the rigged-up electric chair. As hazing practice goes, this one was one of the harshest rituals and wasn't used again after these two dogs finished pledging.

The two-week pledging period went by, and it was time for Hell Night. The two pledges from Baldwin were brought to the Freeport Speedway on Merrick Road in Freeport. The dogs were taken behind the stadium to the swamp in back. It was there that they were forced to catch killies and eat them live. Killies are small minnow-type fish, which are plentiful in the waters around Long Island. Pete and Frank gagged on every live killie they ate. Pete was so disgusted by the live flopping fish in his mouth that he started biting them in half before washing them down with creek water—two pieces of flopping fish being washed down with nasty, salty creek water. It was enough to make them vomit although they didn't actually upchuck; they just gagged and spat out a few of the live killies.

After the live-fish appetizer, it was time for the entrée. Both Baldwin dogs were treated to cans of Puss 'n Boots cat food. The stuff was smelly, greasy, and extremely disgusting. But they ate it until they cleaned the cans of every nasty morsel.

When dinnertime was over, the dogs had to get paddled. Although physical hazing had been banned by the Valley Stream chapter under President Chick Hackney, that time had come to an end. These two dogs from Baldwin were among the first to take a paddling since the Long Island chapters were formed. The number of shots was heavily debated by the Freeport brothers and officers. The differing ideas on how many shots were sufficient led to a split in the ranks of Freeport brothers. This in turn led to loud arguments and a shoving match between Bob Farnswell and Joe Carlucci. Freeport chapter president Richard

Bateman, younger brother of Joseph Bateman, one of the founding members, took control of the situation and separated the arguing factions. President Bateman suggested ten shots should be the standard number of paddle shots at this and future inductions. He put it to a vote, and it passed. Some wanted to give as many as twenty-five shots, and others wanted to limit the liability by keeping the number of shots at five or six. Ten shots was a compromise, and everybody was willing to accept it. Ten shots became the usual standard for inductees in many other chapters in the upcoming years.

Each dog was given their ten shots with flat planks of wood with handles drilled out. They looked similar to cricket bats. After the paddling, they were tarred and feathered using blackstrap molasses, cornflakes, and pillow feathers. Then they were stuffed into the truck of a car and taken on a long ride. The ride ended at George W. Childs State Park in Pennsylvania. This location was close to the intersecting points between New York, New Jersey, and Pennsylvania.

It was there at the entrance of the closed state park that they were dropped off, abandoned in the middle of nowhere with no idea how to get home. The only hint at which way to go was the direction the car the Freeport brothers went when they left. Pete and Frank started walking and walked all the way to Port Jervis, New York. There they stopped to rest and got some food with $5 that Freeport AOT brother Jeff Cronin had slipped them on the sly to help them on their way.

After eating, they got directions from one of the waitresses at the coffee shop. She was quite bewildered at the look of them, but she knew they had been through a hazing ordeal. Their options were to either cut through New Jersey via High Point, or take the New York Thruway. They chose to take the thruway. It was 1:00 AM when they started their trek over a small mountain range to take a shortcut to the thruway. It was an all-night hike, and they finally reached the New York Thruway at dawn.

When they got to the thruway, they started hitchhiking. Most people got one look at them and kept on driving. They looked pretty nasty with dried black molasses, cornflakes, and pillow feathers all over them, even though they had spent most of the trek pulling the stuff off in clumps.

Finally a car pulled over. There was a young guy in his early twenties riding with his girlfriend. She urged him to pass them by and not give them a ride. He felt bad for them. He asked them what had happened to them. They explained that they had been through a fraternity initiation and now they were finding their way home. In fact, they had an obligation to be at the meeting that afternoon—on time, cleaned up, and presentable, or risk being blackballed for failing their Hell Night task.

Against his girlfriend's wishes, the driver offered them a ride. She complained the whole time Pete and Frank were in the car about the nasty way they smelled. He took them to the Bronx, where they could now catch a subway to Jamaica Station. They spent the $5 Jeff Cronin had given them on food, but Pete's mother had sewn $10 into his jeans, and they used that for subway fare to make their way to Jamaica; and from there, they took a bus all the way back to Baldwin.

They made it home around noon on Sunday, and they attended the induction ceremony meeting that evening. Peter Martin and Frank Genaro were both inducted as members of Alpha Omega Theta Fraternity and were sworn in as president and vice president of the newly chartered Sigma Chapter of Baldwin, New York. Although there were only two of them, they would work together with the Freeport chapter to pledge and induct their first new members of Baldwin Alpha.

Monday morning, Pete Martin and Frank Genaro went to school proudly wearing their green-and-red AOT sweaters with the fraternity crest sewn on the right front pocket. They were an immediate attraction to their fellow students at Baldwin High School. Everybody seemed to want to congratulate them. Many had inquired about how they could join AOT.

This also caught the attention of the school administration, namely the principal of the high school. He was not at all happy about this new Greek-letter fraternity establishing a presence in his school. For the time being, he did not take any action or confront Pete and Frank about wearing sweaters, and the first pledge class of Baldwin Alpha was allowed to wear pledging attire, that being a green bow tie and red suspenders and carrying a dogging box, which was a shoe box or a cigar box.

Additionally, they were able to use the latest hazing routine, called brick carrying, on their new dogs,. Brick carrying happened whenever a dog got a demerit. He had to carry a brick with him all day long. If he got another demerit, then he carried two bricks all day long. Some dogs would need a knapsack to carry a half-dozen bricks around with them. Freeport Alpha was already using this procedure, and now they were practicing brick carrying in Baldwin as well.

At any rate, AOT was a smash hit at Baldwin High School, and they recruited four eager dogs within the first few days of school after their Hell Night. Jim Sneed, who was one of the two guys who declined to be interviewed by Freeport Alpha after the football coach interfered, decided to go for it and dog for the new Baldwin Sigma Chapter. Two other pledges were Baldwin High School seniors Tom Redding and Ray Garibaldi; the fourth pledge was a junior named Ralph Vernon. Ralph would actually become the second president of Baldwin Alpha in his senior year.

Pete and Frank were pleased to bring in three seniors whom they were friends with, but they also understood that they needed to recruit more juniors if the chapter was to become successful. Without a substantial number of juniors to fill the ranks, there would be no one to pass the fraternity on to in the next year. There was no real shortage of juniors who wanted to join; in fact, there were sophomores who wanted in as well. But for the first pledge class, Pete and Frank decided to keep it small and mostly seniors. They wanted more seniors to fill the as-yet-unfilled offices of treasurer and secretary, as well as to create a hierarchy.

The first pledge class of Baldwin Alpha was dogged during school hours and was subjected to air raids and other silly hazing techniques. Brick carrying was particularly tough on them, and they had to carry the bricks to Freeport after school. Since the Baldwin chapter had only two official members, Freeport Alpha dogged the new Baldwin pledges and paddled them at weekly meetings in Freeport until they were inducted.

After the four pledges' induction, Baldwin Alpha now had six active members and, as such, qualified to conduct themselves independently as a chapter. Within a few weeks after induction of the four dogs, Baldwin Alpha was ready for their second pledge class. This pledge class had eight dogs made up of juniors and sophomores. One notable thing happened during this pledge class. Chauncey Benton, the principal of Baldwin High School, was now thoroughly pissed at the sight of six fraternity members wearing sweaters every day and eight additional students pledging and creating disturbances in and around the school daily.

Mr. Benton called Pete Martin to his office and informed him that there would now be a permanent ban on wearing fraternity sweaters on school grounds. Additionally, pledging attire, brick carrying, and dogging the pledges was also banned on school grounds.

This would be the final word on fraternities in Baldwin High School for the next thirty-somewhat years. Officially, Baldwin High School banned fraternities and all fraternity activities including wearing colors and pledging dogs on school grounds. But this did not stop the growth of Alpha Omega Theta, nor did it stop formation and growth of other fraternities from the late 1950s to the late 1980s.

The irrelevancy of the fraternity ban in Baldwin High School manifested itself immediately when AOT began recruiting new pledges in large numbers. The Sigma Chapter of AOT grew from two members to roughly twenty members within the 1958-59 school year. In fact, late in the school year, around May of 1959, several Baldwin High School students, who technically lived in North Freeport but attended Baldwin High School because they lived in the Baldwin school district, started a chapter of Omega Gamma Delta. Perhaps because they were Freeport residents, the AOT brothers from the Baldwin side of the district line never invited them to join AOT, so they hooked up with Omega. The rivalry between AOT and Omega would follow Alpha Omega Theta in almost every town that had an AOT chapter.

The senior Baldwin AOT brothers recruited six new pledges from the junior class of 1960. Since dogging was not allowed in school, the dogs had to meet at the strip mall beside Baldwin High School before and after school to pledge. The school, classrooms, and athletic events were considered neutral territory. No pledging during practice or during a game or in class at all. But once they were off school grounds, they were subjected to air raids, push-up contests, and other pledging rituals.

Baldwin AOT member Jim Wood from the class of 1960 shares his recollections on the dogging and induction experience of his time. "I believe the Baldwin Class of 1960 was the first AOT pledge class after Martin and others founded the chapter (most of them were '59). It was still new to the high school, so there was plenty of disdain to go around from teachers and administrators in respect to wearing the colors.

"Pledging was silent inside school and during all athletic events, but hazing occurred at a strip mall next to the high school before and after class. I believe it was Ray Catapano who was tasked during Hell Week to bring in a pound of toenails. We all were placed at attention in front of a store, and one by one were asked to produce whatever each had been charged to find. There were the usual things—a jockstrap, a bra, condom, etc. When Catapano was asked, he reached into a paper bag and took out a short plank of wood into which he had 'toed' a pound of eight-penny nails. We all lost it. He's a funny guy."

Later that night, the dogs were taken blindfolded on a ride out to Centereach, which is forty miles from Baldwin. They were taken in twos in separate cars. Once they got to Centereach, they were tarred and feathered with molasses and pillow feathers.

Jim Wood recalls his hell ride. "Hell Night consisted of a blindfolded car ride out on the island. We went in twos. When the car stopped, we were taken out of the car (it must have been October as I remember the smell of cut hay) and stood next to each other still blindfolded. Then warm molasses was poured over us, followed by two or three bags of feathers. We were told to count to one thousand, after which we could remove the blindfold, but we waited only until the sound of the car was gone."

The dogs were ordered to count to one thousand before removing the blindfolds, but as soon as the sound of the car leaving the area faded, they removed their blindfolds and started walking in the direction of the sound of the cars. They were dropped off in the middle of a huge potato field. Back in the late 1950s to the early '60s, most of Long Island was potato fields, especially Suffolk County. Pledge Jim Wood had a $5 bill sewn into the seam of his jeans, which was undetected by the Alpha brothers. Ray Catapano had no money on him at all. The penalty for getting caught with money would have been severe.

Jim and Ray started walking in the same direction they heard the car drive off to. After about a half hour of walking, they finally came to an actual paved road. They started hitchhiking. Car after car would slow down, look at them tarred and feathered, and drive away fast. Until finally a Suffolk County police car saw them and stopped. The officer laughed hysterically at them, knowing that they had just been through a hazing ritual. He took pity on them and gave them a ride to the local precinct and allowed them to wash up, gave them hot coffee and doughnuts, and called their parents to come get them. They both made it home around midnight. Others were not so lucky. Some inductees were unlucky enough to walk twenty miles or more before getting picked up by someone.

The Baldwin High School AOT pledges from the graduating class of 1960 remained very close over the next nearly fifty years. They had all the foundations of a real and true brotherhood. They grew up together, went to the same schools all their life up until high school. They joined Alpha Omega Theta together; the bonds of brotherhood ran deep and followed them all their lives. Although adulthood took them in different directions—such as college, the military, and settling with families in different parts of the country—whenever they got together at reunions or events they had in common, they continued their conversations as if they last saw each other yesterday.

The brothers of Baldwin's Sigma Chapter of AOT were all athletes. They didn't all play the same sport, but they showed up in the stands to cheer each other at all the games and events. Being committed to athletics meant staying in great physical shape, which meant not too much partying. Although they did have parties and the drinking age was eighteen at the time, they didn't serve beer or alcohol at the few parties they did have. Their parties were also inclusive, meaning they invited students who were not AOT members, as well as Omega members. The parties they did throw were big house parties, and they were the envy of Baldwin High School.

In the summers, the Baldwin AOT members frequented Jones Beach's West End. To this day, Baldwin alumni still meet at Jones Beach for an all-class reunion/picnic. Back in 1960, Jones Beach State Park used to allow beer consumption on the beach. The Alpha brothers did partake in consuming beer on the beach during the athletic off-season. One summer day, a hearse drove onto the beach. Several men got out wearing tuxedos and black bathing suits under them. They proceeded to the middle of the sand, set up a blanket and umbrella. They sang a few creepy songs and then dug up a coffin they had buried the night before. When they opened the coffin, it was filled with beer.

To quote Jim Wood, "Ah, that was quite an afternoon."

Rockville Centre—Mu Nu Chapter

Rockville Centre was the town next to Oceanside. In 1958, the newly chartered Kappa Theta Chapter from Oceanside began recruiting students from Southside High School in neighboring Rockville Centre. Students from Oceanside and Rockville Centre had always been closely acquainted. The district lines were drawn as such so that some students who lived in Rockville Centre actually went to Oceanside High School. Many students from Oceanside had friends in Rockville Centre. It was natural for Oceanside AOT to quickly recruit charter members in Southside High School.

As it was in the other schools and towns, the members recruited were all top-performing athletes and scholastically had no lower than a B-plus average. With ten charter members, the Rockville Centre chapter was formed and duly chartered the Mu Nu Chapter of Alpha Omega Theta Fraternity. Once again, an AOT chapter was formed in a school and town that had no fraternities. Alpha would be the first to fraternize in Southside High School, but soon after, within a few years, a chapter of Omega Gamma Delta would be formed in Rockville Centre as well. It seemed like Omega refused to be outdone and almost always managed to form chapters in towns that had AOT chapters.

Rockville Centre Alpha was to become a unique chapter of AOT. Although all chapters were somewhat unique with their own customs and bylaws, Rockville Centre's Mu Nu Chapter would become quite philanthropic.

Many chapters would do community service at times, but Mu Nu AOT set a very high bar when it came to charitable donations and good deeds. They regularly participated in CARE and sponsored poor children in impoverished parts of the world. They would send money to support children, with the whole chapter sharing sponsorship, and would receive letters written by the children and their grateful families. The letters would be read out loud at chapter meetings.

In 1966, a local community newspaper reported that a local Little League team had lost their sponsor due to the sponsoring business closing. The Little League team would lose their place on the season's roster without a sponsor. The brothers from Mu Nu AOT, led by chapter president Richard Edlin, decided to take up the cause for this Little League team. They held a raffle and a carnival for local children and used the money to sponsor the team.

Not surprisingly, the Little League team was renamed AOT, and their team uniforms were green and red. Also, team AOT became league champions that year and a few more times in the next ten years of being sponsored by Alpha Omega Theta Fraternity, Mu Nu Chapter. Rockville Centre Alpha was a bunch of respected, civic-minded young men. Many of them had parents on the school board or in the Rockville Centre village government. They seemed to always be getting good articles written about them, and the school administration never banned the wearing of fraternity colors because of their outstanding conduct.

The Mu Nu Chapter set a fine example that most of the other chapters could not emulate.

Uniondale AOT—1959 Unknown Chapter Designation

Oceanside Alpha brother Jim Stapleton had a cousin who lived in Uniondale, which was three towns away from Oceanside. Jim's cousin was named Bill Simon. Bill had been to Oceanside and met all the Alpha brothers. He liked the idea of a brotherhood and the connection to multiple chapters in other towns.

In the summer of 1959, Jim Stapleton had proposed his cousin Bill and five of his friends from Uniondale for membership. They were brought to a meeting in Oceanside and were inducted. Since they were to be charter members, they were not required to dog and were inducted with a Hell Night ceremony. Bill's friend Mike Bullock was elected to be president of the Uniondale chapter, and Bill was its first vice president; Richard Gruen was chosen as first sergeant at arms, and Carmine Prencepio was elected as secretary. Carmine had cousins in Oceanside named Lou and Phil Gerardi, who would also become Alpha members in later years.

The Hell Night was severe, and these six charter members were given a good beating and paddling. They were also taken out on Long Island and dropped off in Riverhead. The next day, they were formally inducted as brothers of Alpha Omega Theta Fraternity, given sweaters, and had their charter drafted by Oceanside AOT and were officially recognized by Valley Stream AOT, which had earned the unofficial role of Grand Chapter by virtue of the fact that they were the first chapter on Long Island.

The Uniondale chapter had a long run up until 1978. Their chapter name and designation is unknown and lost in time.

Garden City AOT—1964 Unknown Chapter Designation

Garden City was in close proximity to all of the Long Island towns that had Alpha chapters. The history of the Garden City chapter is murky. It is probable that either Oceanside or Rockville Centre started the Garden City chapter. Without actually knowing, it is the best assumption to say that Rockville Centre spread AOT to Garden City. Rockville Centre was the closest town to Garden City, being right next door.

In 1964, Garden City had a chapter of the Gents, which was founded in Oceanside as a "social club" and a fraternity that was unaffiliated with any of the multichapter Greek-letter fraternities in the South Nassau area at the time.

This single-chapter fraternity called Kappa Gamma Theta had existed only in Garden City for about five years until 1963. In the 1964 school year, Kappa Gamma Theta disappeared, and Alpha Omega Theta emerged in their place.

Again, without firsthand knowledge from early Garden City AOT brothers, we can only surmise that the entire chapter of Kappa Gamma Theta flipped and became affiliated with the multiple chapters of Alpha Omega Theta that were in most of the surrounding towns. This is the best explanation as to why they just disappeared at the same time AOT emerged.

Garden City Alpha, just like Uniondale Alpha, did not run as long as the other chapters. It is difficult to find actual members from those two chapters around today who have definite knowledge of the founding of those two chapters, or the closing of them.

What is known about Garden City Alpha is that, as usual, they were outstanding students and athletes. Omega Gamma Delta never managed to form a chapter in Garden City, so when the Gents faded out, the Alphas were the school's cream of the crop.

Similar to the Rockville Centre chapter, the Garden City bunch had the utmost respect from the school administration. Some of the high schools allowed fraternities to purchase a booster page similar to an advertisement in the school's yearbook. Some schools did not allow this, but Garden City was the only school to print the student's fraternal affiliation under his picture in the yearbook. It would say something similar to

>John Smith
>Football Captain, Soccer, Lacrosse, Alpha Omega Theta Fraternity

It was through researching all the Garden City yearbooks from 1957 to 1974 that I was able to determine the demise of Kappa Gamma Theta in 1963 and the immediate rise of Alpha Omega Theta in 1964.

Amityville AOT—Unknown

Although little is known about the life and times of the Uniondale and Garden City Alpha chapters, nothing is known of the Alpha Omega Theta chapter from Amityville, New York, except that they did in fact exist. From the earliest days of the Amityville chapter, they were considered reclusive and antisocial toward the other AOT chapters. They never participated in interchapter functions or sent representatives to Grand Council meetings. The year of their formation, year of their demise, and their chapter designation are unknown.

Freeport AOT party invitation, 1956

AOT pin

Oceanside AOT at the original Nathan's circa 1970

Group picture of Middletown AOT class of 1969

CHAPTER SIX

The Grand Council

As soon as the first Long Island chapter was founded in Valley Stream in 1955, the idea of forming an interchapter AOT Grand Council was put forth. The Grand Council was to be a governing body to oversee the growth of new chapters and the development of existing chapters. The Grand Council was to be the supreme authority of Alpha Omega Theta Fraternity, and the head of the Grand Council was given the title of grand chancellor. This was the equivalent of being president of all the chapters.

The first grand chancellor was Fred Gifford of the Valley Stream Central chapter. Fred was secretary of his chapter, but he was supreme leader, Grand Poobah, of Alpha Omega Theta Fraternity with the role and title of grand chancellor. The chartering of Freeport Alpha brought new membership to the Grand Council, but communication with Brooklyn Alpha was scarce, and rarely were there Grand Council meetings attended by Brooklyn Alpha. And by this time, the chapter in Middletown, Connecticut, had already become a lost tribe, completely disconnected from the Long Island chapters and the mother chapter in Brooklyn. It wouldn't be until 1968 that Middleton AOT would reconnect with the Long Island chapters.

By the end of 1956, the whole idea of the Grand Council petered out. There were only two chapters, Valley Stream Central and Freeport, in 1956, on Long Island. Brooklyn and Middletown were pretty much out of the picture by then. By 1958, Alpha Omega Theta had seen the addition of new chapters in Valley Stream South, Oceanside, Baldwin, and Rockville Centre. By 1959, Uniondale would also join the fold. A new interest in reconvening the Grand Council was brewing. The need to draft a binding constitution to define the fraternity as a whole and create a foundation for future growth was apparent. Each chapter

—

sent representatives to the Grand Council, and the meetings became known as GC meetings.

The representatives from Valley Stream Central, Valley Stream South, Oceanside, Freeport, Baldwin, and Rockville Centre began collaborating on the constitution of Long Island chapters in the fall of 1958. This was not an easy task, and it took almost five months to complete a constitution that was acceptable to all the representatives from all the chapters.

Freeport chapter members Richard Bateman and Gary Suttman, who were president and vice president, respectively, played an active role in the writing of the fraternity's new constitution. Meetings were held regularly at Gary Suttman's house, and his mother would often serve food to the fraternity brothers. Baldwin president Peter Martin and his vice president, Frank Genaro, also played a big part during the weekly writing sessions, as did the presidents and vice presidents of all the chapters that sent delegates to the Grand Council meetings.

The Grand Council meetings were almost always on Sundays. There was an existing constitution, which had been written in Brooklyn and passed on to Valley Stream when they formed a chapter in 1955; but the earlier constitution was inadequate to unite multiple chapters, so it was decided by a consensus of the delegates that they would revise the constitution. The Grand Council used the older constitution as a reference and a template.

The writing sessions were usually at Freeport brother Gary Suttman's house, but one Sunday, the meeting took place at Baldwin chapter president Peter Martin's house. After a two- or three-hour marathon writing session, the Alpha brothers went to Baldwin High School for a quick game of softball.

What they didn't know was that two members of Brooklyn Alpha were hoping to attend that Grand Council meeting. One of them was Bobby Baher, who was the current and most likely the last president of Brooklyn Alpha, and the other was Joe Brugnolotti. Joe had been a driving force behind the formation of the Valley Stream chapter three years earlier. Although it was Chick Hackney who recruited members and led the new chapter, Joe was the guy who pushed Chick to follow through with chartering the first Long Island chapter. Joe still occasionally spoke to Chick, and although Chick had graduated and gone off to college, Joe managed to get contact info for the current Valley Stream chapter leadership. Someone in the Valley Stream chapter had sent Joe a postcard with a list of all the active Long Island chapters of AOT. Through his contact with Valley Stream AOT, Joe learned the location of the upcoming meeting in Baldwin, which was at Peter Martin's house.

Joe brought Bobby Baher to meet the Long Island chapter delegates in hope that Brooklyn would take a seat on the Grand Council. Bobby had asked Joe about the Long Island chapters and wanted to meet them. Long Island Alpha was obviously growing in leaps and bounds, but Brooklyn Alpha was at the end of its run. Membership was declining. Older members who had been holding the Brooklyn chapter together had begun drifting apart. Some went into the military, others went to college, and some got married and had no time to run with a Greek-letter club anymore.

Bobby Baher was still a high school student in Brooklyn Manual Training High School and was proud to be in AOT, and even prouder to be its president. He wanted some of the good fortune that Long Island Alpha was experiencing to hopefully rub off on the Brooklyn chapter. He wanted to witness and learn how they organized and expanded and perhaps bring those techniques back to Brooklyn. He was, in fact, hoping for reunification between Long Island Alpha and the mother chapter in Brooklyn. Brooklyn Alpha had tried to expand within Brooklyn, with limited success. They had managed to start a Beta Chapter in Brooklyn Technical High School in the 1950s, but the Beta Chapter never really became independent of the Alpha Chapter at Brooklyn Manual Training High School. In contrast, the Long Island experiment was a huge success, and Bobby Baher wanted to be involved with them.

Unfortunately, this was not to be. By the time they arrived at Peter Martin's house, the meeting had adjourned, and the brothers had gone to Baldwin High School for a quick game of pickup softball. By the time Joe and Bobby had gotten to the high school, the game was over as well, and the Alpha brothers were already leaving.

Peter Martin was curious about the Brooklyn guys. He and a few others did stay and chatted with Joe and Bobby. Pete Martin could not help noticing that Joe Brugnolotti was a few years past high school age. He found it somewhat unusual for a guy almost thirty years old to be still involved with a high school fraternity. This gave Pete and some of the other AOT brothers the impression that Brooklyn AOT was an adult men's fraternal club, more like the Elks, rather than a high school organization. This may have led to an aversion to hook up with the Brooklyn chapter by the Long Island Alpha brothers. That and the fact that in 1959 communication was not so easy, prior to cell phones and e-mail; exchanging contact info didn't usually lead to long-distance communication.

Sadly, by 1960, the original Alpha Chapter of Alpha Omega Theta Fraternity disbanded the Brooklyn chapter. Lack of enthusiasm and a changing environment in the Brooklyn neighborhoods where AOT ran contributed to the demise of not only AOT but the other fraternities at Brooklyn Manual Training High School, which would change its name to John Jay High School in 1960. Bobby Baher was to be the last president of AOT in Brooklyn. Former treasurer Joe Brugnolotti recalled getting a letter in the mail while he was in the navy, informing him that the chapter had closed, and since his name was on the chapter bank account, he needed to go close the account. Since he was already stationed, the money went uncollected.

In January 1959, the new constitution of Alpha Omega Theta was completed and circulated to the Long Island chapters. The constitution was a bold document for a bunch of high school kids to write. It was far reaching and attempted to unite the individual chapters under the banner of the new Grand Council. The constitution would detail the offices and duties of officers of the Grand Council. The higher officers were to be called the grand chancellor and vice chancellor. Lower offices were created for a record keeper and a correspondent, to maintain detailed records of each chapter and to establish and maintain communication with all the AOT chapters. An obscure office was created, called gabble editor, to establish a fraternity publication, which may or may not have ever seen publication.

The constitution also established the Grand Council as the supreme legislative body of Alpha Omega Theta Fraternity and declared its bylaws would supersede those of all individual chapters. A process was devised for convening a court to hear arguments and mediate issues between chapters, as well as to hear appeals of any brother who felt he did not receive justice in his chapter's court. Decisions made by the Grand Council were final and beyond appeal.

Methods for nominating and impeaching Grand Council officers were also established. A system was established of each chapter sending three delegates to the Grand Council, leaving the method of choosing their delegates up to each individual chapter. Methods for electing Grand Council officers from the convened delegates were established.

Each chapter was given the right to establish their own bylaws unique to their respective chapter, providing that no bylaw would be passed in direct conflict with the constitution and laws of the Grand Council. However, the constitution of Long Island chapters did establish standards and practices for the nomination and election of individual chapter officers. It also provided standards for chapter courts and established the GC court as being the last arbiter in any dispute passed beyond said chapter's court and into the jurisdiction of the GC court.

In the new constitution, individual chapters were required by fraternity law to recruit enough new members to maintain a respectable number of brothers at all times. Additionally, each chapter had an obligation, by fraternity law, to always seek new charter members in other towns to establish new chapters. A standard method for pledging new recruits was established. A minimum dogging period of two weeks was established, binding to all chapters.

All in all, it was a great effort by the delegates of the combined chapters on Long Island to draft and ratify a constitution; unfortunately, not long after circulating the constitution to the chapters, the Grand Council stopped meeting. Most likely, the GC officers graduated and moved on, and when the new school year convened in 1960, no effort was made to keep the Grand Council together. There was a six-year gap until the Grand Council was reconvened in April 1966.

An attempt was made to reconvene the Grand Council, and on April 24, 1966, Valley Stream Delta Chapter secretary Al Oderno sent out correspondence to the other chapters, inviting each one to send representatives to the first Grand Council meeting since 1959. On May 28, 1966, a meeting was convened with representatives of the Valley Stream Delta Chapter, the Oceanside Kappa Theta Chapter, the Freeport Zeta Chapter, and the Rockville Centre Mu Nu Chapter being present.

Items discussed at the first Grand Council meeting since 1960 were standard copies of the official Alpha shield being distributed to all chapters, revival of the Alpha newsletter, mandatory usage of the Latin pronunciation of the Alpha password as opposed to the English pronunciation, organization of interchapter softball teams, creation of permanent records of the rosters of all Alpha chapters on Long Island, standardizing pledging regulations, an increase in dues and induction fees to include money for the Grand Chapter, and calling for elections of Grand Council officers at the next GC meeting.

The second reconvened Grand Council meeting took place on June 23, 1966, in Freeport. Chapters in attendance were Baldwin, Freeport, Garden City, Oceanside, Rockville Centre, and Valley Stream.

The main topic of discussion was the formation of a Grand Council treasury and a Grand Council—hosted multichapter Alpha party. The Casino Pool in Freeport was rented, and the party was set for August 13, 1966. All chapters were required to sell tickets to the party in order to pay for it.

The Garden City and Rockville Centre chapters proposed bringing candidates from Seaford and Westbury to the next GC meeting so they could start chapters in those two towns.

The third GC meeting was held in Rockville Centre on August 3, 1966. Attending chapters were Baldwin, Freeport, Garden City, Oceanside, Rockville Centre, Valley Stream, and Uniondale.

Ticket money was to be collected from all chapters, but Garden City was the only chapter that brought a substantial amount of money to the meeting.

The first newsletter was distributed to all chapters by the Valley Stream chapter, and all chapter secretaries were now required to contact the Valley Stream chapter secretary on a monthly basis to provide news of their chapter and updated roster lists.

The representatives were reminded of their chapter's behavior at the upcoming party, which was to include two bands and four bouncers. Tickets to the affair were to cost $3.50 per couple, with a total cost of $330 for the whole thing.

Copies of the GC constitution and standard pledging rules were distributed to all chapters. Grand Council officer elections were set for the next GC meeting to be held in Baldwin.

At the fourth GC meeting in Baldwin, held on August 31, 1966, the first elections of Grand Council officers since 1959 took place. Rockville Centre chapter president Richard Edlin was unanimously nominated for the office of grand chancellor. Richard was uncomfortable with there being no opposing candidates, so he nominated Baldwin chapter president Gene Mallary. In the secret ballot election that followed, Gene Mallary won, and Richard Edlin was to become vice chancellor.

Very shortly after the party and the summer vacation that followed, the GC was to become disjointed in 1967, with Oceanside, Rockville Centre, and Baldwin holding joint meetings together and the other chapters keeping to themselves once again. The close proximity of those three towns caused those three chapters stick together.

In 1968, one last attempt was made to unite all the Alpha chapters on Long Island. An Alpha brother who was to become legendary in the Oceanside chapter and among the other chapters was elected president of Oceanside Alpha. The brother was Billy Weitzman.

The turmoil was beginning to erupt between Oceanside Alpha and Oceanside Omega, as well as racial tension in Freeport, which was becoming more racially mixed, led to the final meetings of the Grand Council of Alpha Omega Theta Fraternity. No attempt was ever made again after this to convene the Grand Council of Alpha Omega Theta Fraternity.

Billy Weitzman was known to be one tough son of a gun, and no one could beat him in a one-on-one fight. He was unanimously chosen to be grand chancellor, but he turned it down. At this time, Billy had his hands full with tension that was reaching the boiling point with Omega Gamma Delta in Oceanside, and he couldn't give the Grand Council his undivided attention. Garden City chapter president Jerome Grady was then chosen to be grand chancellor, and Billy Weitzman became vice chancellor.

The Grand Council did meet regularly throughout 1968, and the tensions in Oceanside with Omega Gamma Delta and the racial tensions in Freeport were usually the topic of the meetings. Although Garden City didn't have rival fraternities or racial issues, Jerome Grady, Garden City AOT president, did a great job of running the Grand Council and was well respected by the brothers of all the AOT chapters. However, the tightness of the combined chapters was at its high point in 1968 and was not to be carried over into subsequent years.

In 1970, the Grand Council was reconvened under the leadership of Valley Stream AOT president Rich Morgyle. Rich's older brother Tom had been AOT president in Valley Stream two years earlier and had been a member of the Grand Council at that time. When Rich was elected president of AOT in Valley Stream, he started up the Grand Council again after a brief hiatus. The Grand Council meetings were always held in the Cue Club in Rockville Centre. The Cue Club was the location that Rockville Centre AOT had held their chapter meetings for years, and possibly decades. Rockville Centre AOT had such a great reputation in their town that they were given full use of the private room in the back of the Cue Club to hold meetings; and when the GC convened, a large room was needed, and the Cue Club was the perfect place. During the year, each chapter was always updated about the other chapters' parties, and they frequently attended each other's parties. During this year, the Rockville Centre chapter held a dance at the Holiday Inn on Sunrise Highway in Rockville Centre, and all the chapters were invited to attend. After the dance, they all went around the corner to a hole-in-the-wall bar called Ryan's to drink the rest of night.

The end of the 1970 class year was the end of the Grand Council of Alpha Omega Theta. There were no chapter presidents like Billy Weitzman or Rich Morgyle who had the ambition to maintain a large organization in addition to their own chapter. In the years that followed, there would sometimes be joint meetings with two or more chapters of AOT, but never to the extent of the Grand Council.

CHAPTER SEVEN

The Legend of Billy Weitzman

All chapters of all fraternities have had presidents whose exploits are legendary. In Oceanside Alpha, the reign of President Billy Weitzman was indeed legendary and talked about for years, and even decades, after.

Billy Weitzman's presidency was a wild ride, and everybody wanted to get on board. Billy Weitzman had gotten into Alpha in September of his sophomore year. He had been in the Counts and the Squires when he was in junior high school. The social clubs were fading out by the late 1960s, and the real social scene in Oceanside belonged to the fraternities. The Counts, the Morticians, the Emeralds, the Dukes, and the Outlaws had all gone extinct. The Gents and the Squires were still around, but barely hanging on. The Squires were a junior club to the Knights of Columbus, so they still had backing. The Gents had more than one chapter in their heyday, and the Oceanside chapter would eventually become an Island Park club in 1970, when the students from Island Park stopped attending Oceanside High School.

In the mid-1960s, the greaser's look and attitude was going out of style. With that, the whole athletic social club scene was going extinct. The collegian social scene brought on by the fraternities became a way of life in Oceanside with the disintegration of the social clubs.

From the beginning of the two major fraternity's chapters in Oceanside—Omega Gamma Delta founded in 1940 and Alpha Omega Theta founded in 1957—the fraternities were the upper crust of the school's student body. To be in a fraternity, you had to be an athlete on a school team and a good student. Any lower than an 85 average, and you would not be eligible for membership in either fraternity. By contrast, the social clubs attracted greasers and beatniks. Black leather jackets with DA haircuts were the usual look for social club members.

The large assortment of clubs in Oceanside High School was an indication of how many students at Oceanside High School could not or would not join the fraternities.

Billy Weitzman was inducted into the Counts when he was in Oceanside Junior High School. He was in eighth grade when he was asked to dog for the Counts in 1964. None of the fraternities recruited in the junior high in 1964, and the social clubs started to recruit there in an attempt to keep their thing alive.

Billy Weitzman was a quiet kid when he was in seventh grade and not prone to conflict or confrontation. On the first day of school, when he started the eighth grade, there was another kid named John Kunkel, who had been left back, in a few of his classes. So he was repeating the eighth grade. John Kunkel was bullying the smaller younger eighth graders, and Billy was getting pushed around by him as well.

Billy was a skinny kid with a Jewish last name although he was half Italian on his mother's side. This may have led Kunkel to think Billy was an easy target for bullying. He was wrong.

By the end of the first week of school, Billy was getting to his breaking point. He had enough and wasn't taking Kunkel's shit anymore. When Billy was walking into English class, Kunkel smacked him in the back of the head as he walked by. Billy snapped, lost his temper, and turned to Kunkel and pushed him hard. When Kunkel lunged at Billy to retaliate, Billy grabbed him in a choke hold and took him to the floor. The teacher tried to break his grip, but Billy refused to let Kunkel go. Other teachers in nearby classes had to get involved, and soon there were three or four teachers pulling Billy away from John Kunkel. Billy's face was red with anger, and Kunkel's was turning purple from lack of oxygen. The teachers managed to pull Kunkel away from Billy, and at that moment, the social stature of both of these kids changed.

John Kunkel was not so feared anymore, and Billy became a hero to his peers. He proved his toughness, and he beat down a bully who had been harassing many of the eighth graders. Billy also caught the attention of the older kids, some of whom were looking for up-and-coming recruits for the social clubs.

Billy was recruited by the Counts. He was told he would dog for two weeks. Dogging for fraternities was longer than two weeks, but the social clubs were looking to get people in faster. They took it easy on him during his dogging period until his Hell Night. On his Hell Night, they took Billy on a ride to Jones Beach, which is on the southwestern part of Long Island. There he caught a severe beating and paddling. He was then stripped to his underwear, doused in blackened used motor oil, and then made to drop and roll on the sand. He was left there with no money and made to walk home alone covered with used motor oil and beach sand covering him from head to toe. When Billy got home, he washed up and got himself cleaned up. When he went into the kitchen to get something to eat, his mother screamed in shock. Billy was black and blue from the paddling from his buttocks to the backs of his knees. It took two weeks for the bruises to fade out.

Billy was excited and enthusiastic about being a Count. He now could wear colors. The Counts' colors were black and red, and they had tee shirts that had a skull and crossbones on it. Billy was hardcore member and never missed a meeting. He was proud to be a Count, and he wore his colors often. What Billy didn't know at that time was that the Counts, as well as the other clubs, were fading out fast. Each week, fewer members showed up for meetings. Eventually, the president of the Counts stopped coming to meetings as well.

The older members in the high school were moving on, and they gave up on recruiting new blood to carry on after they were gone. The fraternities were growing, and newer fraternities had come onto the scene at Oceanside High School, like Sigma Lambda Rho, whose colors were purple and white. But as for the Counts, by the end of Billy Weitzman's eighth-grade year, there were almost none left. Infighting and arguments led to most of the membership walking away from the club. When Billy started his ninth-grade year, the club folded. They attempted to hold meetings after school started in September, but only a handful of younger junior high members showed up. They didn't have the organizational skills to keep it together, so that was it. The Counts were gone from Oceanside until a brief revival in 1981.

Billy was quickly asked to join the Squires. As soon as he was no longer affiliated with the Counts, the Squires asked him to join. He was told there would be no dogging and only minor paddling with a paddleball racquet. They were right about the initiation; it was so easy it was a joke. And Billy wasn't very impressed with the Squires at all after getting into the club. There was no hazing and five whacks at the most with a thin paddleball racquet. And after getting into the Squires, he was totally bored with the meetings and the lack of purpose or structure. Midway through the ninth grade, he quit the Squires and took a break from clubs.

Billy knew he was destined to join another club or fraternity. He was not content to be an independent. He knew everybody who was anybody belonged to a major club or fraternity in Oceanside High School, and he was determined to find the right organization before beginning his sophomore year. Before the end of his freshman year, Billy was approached by the Gents to join.

The Gents were still going strong and didn't appear to be shrinking or fading out like the other clubs. But Billy had a feeling that the day of the social clubs was nearing an end. Besides that, the Gents mostly had their membership roster from Island Park. Up until 1970, neighboring town Island Park students, who were called Parkers by Oceanside students, went to Oceanside High School. After 1970, the Island Parkers were bused to West Hempstead High School.

With the Gents' members being mostly from Island Park, Billy didn't see any good reason for joining them, so he turned them down. When the Island Parkers switched from Oceanside High School to West Hempstead High School, the Gents had permanently left Oceanside. The only thing left to decide for Billy was which fraternity to join and how to get that fraternity to invite him for an interview.

Little did he know that the fraternities in Oceanside High School were already interested in him, and they were watching him, just waiting for him to enter the high school in his sophomore year. Sigma Lambda Rho, purple and white, had approached Billy, as well as Alpha Theta Gamma, black and white. Both had tried to recruit him at the end of his freshman year in late June, but Billy decided to wait until he entered the high school next September before deciding which one of them he would go into. As it were, Billy would not be joining either of those two fraternities anyway.

Sigma Lambda Rho and Alpha Theta Gamma were both minor players in the fraternity scene at Oceanside High School, and Billy had decided against joining either one of them over the summer vacation. That left two choices of fraternal brotherhoods to choose from. One was Alpha Omega Theta, and the other was Omega Gamma Delta. Billy didn't know many people in either one of these two fraternities. What he did know was that Omega was a restricted fraternity and they didn't invite or induct Jews. Although Billy was only half Jewish on his father's side, he had a Jewish name, which was a guarantee that they would not invite him to pledge. Even half Jews who had Christian names were excluded from Omega. On his first day of school in his sophomore year, Billy was surrounded by four Omegas. They were led by Thomas Dapolero. Dapolero was a junior and was also a hardcore Omega man. Dapolero did most of the talking, and the others stood there looking menacing in their black-and-gold sweaters. Everything Billy had thought and believed about the fraternity process for recruitment had gone out the window with that bullying.

Thomas Dapolero proceeded to tell Billy that Omega had chosen him for membership despite his Jewish name and that he should be grateful to them for that. Billy was the first Jew to be allowed into Omega, they told him. They said they were doing him a favor by overlooking his heritage because he had a reputation for being tough.

Billy was not happy at all and felt disgusted with himself for not telling all four of them to fuck off. He felt like he let himself down by being bullied and not challenging them. He really was intimidated by the tightness of the Omegas and felt helpless to stand up to them alone. When he went home, Billy was quiet and slightly depressed. It was noticeable to his father, who pulled him aside and asked him what was wrong. Billy confided in his dad about being surrounded by the Omegas, being harassed, and letting them get away with it. Billy's dad was firm and didn't hold his hand or wipe his nose for him. Mr. Weitzman lectured Billy on the importance of standing up for himself, even if it meant catching a beating. "Never let yourself get punked out, Billy," was what Mr. Weitzman told him.

The next day at school, the same guys approached Billy and harassed him again,; they handed him a letter inviting him to the next Omega meeting for an interview—in full view of the whole lobby of students. They were loud about it, and they weren't simply inviting him so much as they were telling him to be there and trying to forcefully recruit him. After the Omegas walked away, Billy stood there holding the envelope they had put into his hand and stared at it for at least a minute. He was in another world in that moment, contemplating what his father had told him, what the Omegas had told him, what he thought his options were.

At that moment, Billy was approached by George Agunkis. George was the president of Alpha Omega Theta, and he was stepping up to Billy to introduce himself. George had witnessed the whole spectacle of how the Omegas tried to intimidate Billy. It was as if George could read Billy's mind at that moment. He knew Billy was contemplating going along with it and joining Omega.

"You'll be a punk and a loser if you join that snotty, restricted fraternity," were the first words George said to Billy. It was like a cold slap in the face, and it instantly brought Billy out of his funk.

"There's dozens of them and only one of me," Billy replied to George.

"They don't respect you, Billy," said George. "They want you in because they think you're tough, but they also want to break you, break your spirit before letting you in. They want to put you in your place and make sure you stay there so they can control you and make you their boy."

"I wanted to tell them to fuck off and take their shit fraternity with them," said Billy.

"Well, here is your chance, Billy. AOT has been watching you since last year, and we want you in our fraternity. We're not gonna bully you or intimidate you or try to make you look bad in front of people. The choice is yours, and nobody is gonna harass you for turning us down, but we will turn our backs on you if you go with them," said George.

"I want to join, I want to be in AOT," said Billy.

"Then there is one thing you have to do to prove yourself to us," said George.

"What do I have to do?" said Billy.

"You have to go up to those Omegas, especially Dapolero, and tell them to their faces you want nothing to do with them or their fraternity. Turn them down face-to-face," said George.

"Done deal," said Billy. "By the end of the day, it will be done."

"Come and see me after you tell them to fuck off, and I will have your invite-to-interview-for-AOT letter for you," said George.

True to his word, Billy showed up in the school lobby after the last class of the day. He had been seething all day just thinking about how much he hated the Omegas, and especially Dapolero. He wanted to punch out Dapolero, but he was smart about it and played it just right. Billy walked right up to Dapolero, in full view of his Omega buddies and everyone else in the school lobby, practically nose to nose; Billy pulled out the envelope containing the letter inviting him to interview with Omega. He opened the envelope and pulled out the letter. It was obvious to everyone it was an Omega letter because it was on gold/yellow paper with black print. Billy looked Dapolero right in the eye, pulled out a cigarette lighter, and lit the letter on fire.

"Take your scumbag fraternity and shove it up your ass," Billy said to Dapolero in a firm voice that everybody within earshot heard. Even people too far away to hear what was said knew what had happened. It was not every day that someone being invited to interview with Omega Gamma Delta burned their invitation. In fact, it never happened, until now. Billy held the burning letter by the corner, looking Dapolero in the eye the whole time, until there was nothing left of the letter except the small corner he held between his thumb and forefinger. When the letter had burned away, Billy let go of the unburned corner and let it drop at Dapolero's feet.

Dapolero was stunned, and he couldn't believe what had just happened. Billy waited for Dapolero to break eye contact before he turned on his heels and walked away. He then walked a straight line to the Alpha bench. That was the section of the lobby that the Alphas claimed as their ground. All eyes were on Billy as he went over to the AOT guys, and as he approached the Alpha bench, George Agunkis stood up and handed Billy an envelope. Everyone saw, and everyone knew Billy had just been invited to interview for AOT, including the Omega guys. This was taken as a terrible insult by the Omegas, a slight not to be forgotten, and it was the beginning of a vicious rivalry. There was always a rivalry of sorts between the Alphas and the Omegas, but things were about to turn up to high gear.

Billy went to the AOT meeting that week expecting to begin pledging. Instead, he was inducted in what would be known as an honorary induction. An honorary induction was when a proposed member was inducted in one evening without dogging for the usual eight to ten weeks. In the 1960s, honorary induction was reserved for students of high stature whose membership was highly sought after by the fraternity. In later years, honorary inductions would take on a whole new definition. Billy was inducted in one night with a paddling of ten shots and no beating or a Hell Night.

What Billy wasn't quite aware of at the time of his induction was that in the ebb and flow between the Alphas and the Omegas, the Alphas were currently in the ebb status. That is to say that with the Alphas and Omegas being the top two fraternities in Oceanside, there were times that the Alphas were top-shelf and times that the Omegas were the first choice of freshmen and sophomores. When AOT was founded in OHS in 1957, they took a lot of wind out of Omega Gamma Delta's sails. That status of being the cream of the crop stuck from the founding of the Oceanside chapter in 1957 right through the highly respected AOT classes of 1960 and 1961; shortly after that, little by little, the Omegas regained ground and respectability. They had reestablished themselves as the top-shelf fraternity in Oceanside High School, and most students coming into the school would make Omega their first choice on their wish list. Those who didn't make the cut would go into AOT. A few guys had dogged for AOT, and right before getting inducted into AOT, they were asked to dog for Omega and subsequently started dogging all over again for Omega. Some AOT members had left to join Omega as well.

George Agunkis had just taken over as president of AOT, and he wanted to turn the tide back in AOT's favor insofar as the school's pecking order was concerned. Some of the guys George had dogged with when he pledged years earlier had jumped ship and dogged for Omega right on the eve of their AOT induction. He had also seen some of the AOT membership defect to Omega, and he wanted a new order to be established this year.

George saw in Billy the means to establish that new order. Billy was young and a sophomore, but there was something about him that told George he had to have him in AOT. Billy had been in two social clubs and had many friends from them in his age-group. George saw an opportunity through Billy to bring in plenty of new blood. This hunch paid off in a big way. Billy did bring in friends from the Counts and the Squires, and the first one he got in was his cousin Bobby Weitzman. Bobby was a large robust kid, and his nickname was Beefy Bob, or just Beefer. No one dared to call Beefer fat to his face. Just like his cousin Billy, Beefer took no shit and was not afraid to throwdown with anyone who challenged him or disrespected him.

Beefer didn't get the honorary induction that Billy got, nor did most of the former Counts and Squires that Billy proposed for membership. They all had to dog but were given two- or three-week pledging periods, although the usual pledging period had been eight to ten weeks up to that time.

Within the first two months of school starting, Billy had gotten his closest friends into Alpha. In addition to his cousin Beefer, Mike Sutherland, Charlie and Angelo Termani, Tony Sorrento, Jim Maryland, and Donnie Bloom all pledged and were inducted into AOT. These guys would form the core of what would later be Billy's officers during his presidency. Throughout the rest of the school year, AOT continued to induct new members at regular pledging intervals, which were one pledge class per season. Students from the sophomore class were beginning to choose AOT first.

By the end of Billy's sophomore year, AOT had inducted fifteen new members from Billy's sophomore class. That gave AOT a great jump start in their move to become the top fraternity in Oceanside High School. By the beginning of Billy's junior year, the shit would really hit the fan with the Omegas.

The first week of school in 1967 came, and all the fraternities were looking to recruit from the sophomores who came into the high school. As usual, they all passed out letters inviting prospective pledges to come down to interview. Additionally, the Alphas had planned a big house party to bring in the new school year and to entice students to want to pledge for Alpha. The fraternity that throws the best parties always gets the best new members. The Omegas were already spreading word that they intended to crash the Alpha party. A successful party crash would steal the thunder from the Alphas, and the Omegas would gain pledges who would turn Alpha down in favor of Omega.

One morning in the school lobby, everyone was hanging out, and the Omegas started talking about how they would crash the Alpha party and turn it into an Omega party. They were being loud and arrogant about it and were deliberately talking shit within earshot of the Alphas. The loudest of the Omegas was Thomas Dapolero. He was bragging about how he would lead the Omegas right into the Alpha party and take over. Dapolero was now a senior and an officer in Omega Gamma Delta. Billy Weitzman stepped up and proclaimed loudly that he would personally beat the shit out of any Omega guys who dared to try to crash the Alpha party set for that upcoming Saturday night. Dapolero shot Billy a dirty look as if to say, "Yeah right." Dapolero still hated Billy for turning down membership in Omega and for burning the letter in front of everyone. Billy also still hated Thomas Dapolero for being a representation and embodiment of a fraternity that he thought was arrogant.

Saturday night came, and the party was held at AOT brother Angelo Santori's house in the basement. The Alpha party was open to potential pledges and all girls from the school. However, the party was closed to all other fraternities and their members. Other fraternity members showing up wearing their colors would be the biggest insult and a direct challenge. And that was exactly what happened. About an hour after the party started, ten or twelve Omegas showed up at Angelo's house wearing Omega sweaters. They demanded entry and pushed the two AOT bouncers who were watching the door. While they were demanding entry into the house, one of the girls who saw them trying to crash the party ran down to the basement and started screaming, "Billy, Billy, the Omega guys are here, and they are coming in."

Billy's blood boiled. He warned them not to come to this party. He was serious, and they didn't respect him or his fraternity. Billy was as mad as he was that day that he grabbed John Kunkel in a choke hold, probably even madder. Billy put down his beer and ran up the stairs out of the basement. When he got to the front door, he found the two Alphas bravely trying to keep the Omegas out. By this time, a few other Alphas had gathered at the front door and were trying to convince the Omegas to leave. Billy brushed right past the Alphas and punched the first Omega guy he saw right in the mouth. That guy was Thomas Dapolero. Dapolero was always the leader, always the biggest mouth, and for that he got knocked out with one punch.

After Dapolero collapsed, his Omega brothers rushed to help him up, but he was totally out of it, and they had to carry him with his arms across their shoulders. Billy was pissed, and the adrenaline was still pumping. He stepped right up to the other Omegas and told them to get the fuck out of there. He challenged any one of them who wanted to throw down with him as well since he had just knocked out their Omega brother. Everybody could see Billy was pissed, and they had just witnessed their friend getting knocked out with one punch. Nobody challenged Billy, and they left carrying Thomas Dapolero.

When the party continued, Billy was the man of honor. Everyone wanted to have a beer with him. All the girls wanted to dance with him; in fact, many of the girls at that party started scheming how to become his girlfriend. Billy was an instant celebrity among his fraternity brothers. And when word got around school about what had happened, everyone wanted to pledge for Alpha. The first pledge class inducted twelve new members in early fall.

Billy was now getting a reputation for being a tough guy, and with that came challenges, particularly from the Omegas. They wanted Billy's head for embarrassing them again and for busting Thomas Dapolero in the mouth. It seemed like Billy was getting into a fistfight at least once every other week. Billy was quickly getting a rep for being an unbeatable street fighter. All of his opponents were getting knocked out with one or two punches. Most would crumble like a crashed cigarette pack after one punch to the face, but a few who fell too slowly were unlucky enough to get hit twice. Nobody could take getting punched out by Billy, and the Omegas hated him for it. The school year was young, and it was Billy's junior year, but there was already talk of electing Billy to be the next AOT president.

Although Billy wasn't an officer or a senior yet, the fraternity was growing in leaps and bounds, and it was growing around him. Billy was a winner, and he was making the Omegas look like a bunch of douche bags. By the end of his junior year, Billy had fought with most of Omega's senior class and kicked each and every one of their asses. Alpha Omega Theta was growing and had regained their place as the top frat in Oceanside. As expected, Billy was unanimously elected president of the Oceanside chapter of AOT when elections were held in May of 1967.

The shit really hit the fan in 1968 when Billy became AOT president. AOT was growing faster than ever before. Everyone wanted to be in Alpha.

The tradition of holding only two or three pledge classes per year had gone out the window that year when, under Billy's leadership, AOT began inducting new members on a fairly regular basis. Honorary inductions, which had been few and far between, were taking place at two or three times per month. The manner of inducting honoraries changed drastically. Prior to this time, honoraries got paddled maybe five to seven times, and that was their induction. Billy changed the honorary induction to a full-blown Hell Night hazing with a beating, paddling, and dousing with kitchen condiments. This would become the manner in which older students in the high school would get inducted into Oceanside AOT up until the chapter's dissolution. Younger students were still required to pledge the fraternity and dog for three to five weeks. But the tradition of keeping the fraternity exclusive and limiting the number of members to no more than forty had come to an end.

This was alarming to the Omegas since there was an unspoken rule with AOT and Omega that kept fraternities' membership rosters at between thirty to forty members, to always maintain the aura of exclusivity about them. Under Billy Weitzman's leadership, Oceanside AOT had grown to seventy-five members. And they were not at all shy about letting the whole school know who owned the town. Undeniably, AOT was the biggest, the strongest, and the best fraternity in Oceanside in 1968; and their president, Billy Weitzman, was the king of Oceanside. There was nothing the Omegas could do about it either. And they were not at all happy about it.

As the school year progressed, the Alphas ran almost like a cult. Everyone in AOT respected Billy Weitzman, including the other AOT chapters, and nearly everyone in Omega despised him but didn't want to fight him. Billy's fights were known to be quick and over with one or two punches to the face. Nobody could take his punch without going down, and the ease with which Billy knocked out his opponents made the fights routine, uneventful, and downright unfair to the poor slob who had no chance to fight back.

The anger within Omega was brewing and festering as the year progressed. Billy was untouchable one-on-one, and AOT had grown so much that none of the other fraternities would challenge their superiority in Oceanside. The other Alpha chapters looked up to Billy as the de facto leader of AOT as a whole. Billy was offered the office of grand chancellor in the Grand Council in 1968 but turned it down. He did serve as vice chancellor.

Halfway through the school year, the trouble with Omega finally came to a full boil. The Omega vice president, Mike Pumo, had resigned his office and quit Omega, then joined AOT. This infuriated the Omegas. The Omegas were tired of Billy making them look bad. They decided they wanted to take him down a notch. The Omegas knew AOT had a Grand Council and that Billy was respected and looked up to by all the AOT chapters. But a move planned and executed at the right time would not give the other AOT chapters time to step in and stand together with Billy and Oceanside AOT.

In 1968, Nathan's was the place to hang out in Oceanside. All fraternities hung out there, but in 1968, it was undeniably AOT territory. As long as the other fraternities knew their place, there was no trouble. Even frats from out of town came to Nathan's to hang out. As long as they didn't step on any AOT toes, they were cool to be there.

One Friday night, 150 Omega members from all the surrounding towns' chapters had gathered in Nathan's parking lot. Their purpose was to chase out the Alphas from Nathan's and hunt down Billy Weitzman. The gathering seemed sudden and spontaneous, but it was planned well in advance. Word got to Billy that combined members of all the local Omega chapters were all over Long Beach Road, as well as at Nathan's, looking for him. Billy drove by Nathan's in the passenger seat of AOT vice president Mike Sutherland's car. Billy peeked out the window as he ducked his head, trying not to be seen as they passed by, and he was both impressed with the show of strength by the Omegas, and he was nervous about the potential for this to turn out bloody if there was a confrontation. Billy had made sure the Omegas knew Oceanside was his town, and his leadership of AOT was almost cult-like, but this invasion showed that Omega had enough and were both willing and able to call in large numbers of troops to fight.

In the words of Alpha Sigma Phi president of 1968 Scott Ossner, "Oceanside was under martial law and was turned into an armed camp by the combined chapters of Omega Gamma Delta. The Omegas hated Billy Weitzman so much because he ruled Oceanside and nobody in Omega could challenge him. For that, they sent 150 guys from all the other towns that had Omega chapters to take him down."

Billy told all of his guys to stay away from Nathan's that night and to avoid being seen wearing colors on any main drags or hangouts. He could have called out the other AOT chapters to come down to Oceanside the next night as a show of force, but he decided against it. Instead, Billy decided to take the problem right to the source: the president of Omega in Oceanside.

Billy went over to the Omega president and asked for a private meeting. The two of them took a walk, and Billy told him that since he was the source of anger among the Omegas, he was willing to fight any Omega guy one-on-one and accept the results of the fight as being the end of the whole thing. Since it was already known that nobody in Oceanside could beat him in a fight and none would step up to his challenge, he offered to take on the toughest guy from any Omega chapter one-on-one. Billy also informed them that if they refused his challenge, he would consider the matter over and done with, and if the out-of-town Omega guys came back looking for trouble, he would not hesitate to call in all the local Alpha chapters to deal with them, and to even invade the towns of neighboring Omegas if the shit hit the fan again. No one ever took Billy up on his one-on-one challenge, and the out-of-town Omegas never came back to Nathan's during Billy's remaining months as president of AOT.

The whole thing seemed to fizzle out in an anticlimax in regard to the AOT and Omega rivalry in 1968. There were few, if any, problems between the Alphas and the Omegas in Oceanside after that. But the seeds for all new problems were being planted by Billy.

In the midst of all the struggles between AOT and Omega, a new player had entered the fraternity game in Oceanside. That player was Alpha Sigma Phi. The founder of Phi in Oceanside was a sophomore named Scott Ossner. Scott, just like other sophomores, was intrigued with fraternities and the respect that came with being a member of a fraternity. Scott saw fraternity guys wearing their sweaters in school; they looked cool. He also noticed that fraternity guys routinely let their girlfriends wear their frat sweaters. This was the key, the Rosetta stone, the whole reason to join a fraternity—to give your sweater to a girl to wear. In short, joining a frat brought a member into a whole new social circle that meant getting a chance at meeting the prettiest and most popular girls in school. That was the reason to join a frat—to meet girls, plain and simple.

When the tap on the shoulder and letter of invitation didn't come to Scott Ossner, midway through the school year, he decided to "put out feelers," to use his own words, to see if he could gain the attention of any of the school's fraternities. Since fraternities were still jocks-and-athletes-only clubs, which Scott was not, none of the frats expressed interest in pledging Scott. A chance encounter at Scott's job as an orderly at the Mercy Hospital in Hempstead would change that and have a reverberating effect for years and decades.

Scott was finishing his shift at the hospital and was in the locker room putting his street clothes on when he noticed one of the other orderlies putting on a fraternity sweater. From a distance, it looked like an Alpha sweater. Scott asked if he was an AOT member. His coworker gave him a sneer and said no.

"We don't have AOT in Hempstead. We have Alpha Sigma Phi," was what he told Scott. Scott realized the sweater was black and red, not green and red. Scott was immediately interested and asked if there was a chance of starting a Phi chapter in Oceanside. Once it was determined that Scott had six or seven guys to start with, the Hempstead Phi chapter approved forming a chapter in Oceanside. Within a few years, the Hempstead chapter of Phi would fade out, and the Oceanside chapter would become the largest and most powerful Phi chapter in Nassau County. But for now, the upward climb for Oceanside Phi would be slow and difficult.

When Scott discussed the terms of chartering a chapter with the Phi members from Hempstead, he was surprised to find they would not have to dog. "They will dog you for us," was what Scott was told.

"Who are they?" Scott asked.

"The other Oceanside fraternities, especially AOT. They will dog you for us when you show up in their school wearing our colors," he was told.

And they were right. As soon as Alpha Sigma Phi launched in Oceanside, the shit hit the fan. The guys Scott Ossner put together to form the charter class of Phi were not the usual fraternity-member material. The other fraternities were all athletic clubs, and the founding members of Phi in Oceanside were the equivalent of 1980s stoners. They were the pot-smoking beatniks of Oceanside High School, and they were all sophomores.

The first day they all showed up in school wearing black-and-red sweaters, it didn't take long for Billy Weitzman to scope one of them out. Billy stopped in mid-conversation and did a beeline right up to the half-stoned-out kid in the Phi sweater and demanded to know why he was wearing that sweater. The kid told him it was a Phi sweater. Billy told him, "Take it off, and don't wear that sweater in this school or anywhere in this town again. Those colors look too close to mine. From a distance, it looks like an AOT sweater, and you better tell your friends to put that shit away and forget about it."

The new fraternity was instantly harassed and ridiculed by all the other existing fraternities in Oceanside, especially AOT. Billy was adamant that no one in AOT was to tolerate the wearing of Phi colors in Oceanside.

In the words of Scott Ossner, the early existence of Phi members in 1968 was like this: "The early Phi guys' uniform consisted of sneakers to run for their lives when being chased down by AOT guys. Also, we wore black leather jackets for protection when diving through bushes and leather gloves for climbing fences to escape getting jumped. For our first two years, we could not wear Phi colors in school or anywhere in Oceanside. Billy Weitzman was the man in charge of the social scene in Oceanside, and he decreed no Phi colors could be worn."

And that was the humble beginning of one of Nassau County's biggest Alpha Sigma Phi fraternity chapters. They were literally an underground organization for their first two years. In fact, many Phi members in later years mistakenly believed that 1970 was the founding year of Oceanside's Alpha Sigma Phi. That was because the first two years were virtually forgotten. But Scott Ossner was a very intelligent and well-organized man. He had plans for Phi and was not going to let it disappear so quickly. But 1968 was Billy Weitzman's year, and Phi barely registered as a blip on Billy's radar screen. The hard time Billy and his AOT crew gave to Phi would leave a grudge that would last for so long that no one even remembered what it was about in the first place.

Toward the end of the year, as Billy's presidency was winding down, Billy had given the Alpha brothers of Oceanside a new purpose. That was to seek out members of the Brooklyn AOT chapter. Billy had taken good care of the Alpha books that were in his care as president. He had taken all the ditto sheets, which contained the signatures of all the brothers inducted into the Oceanside chapter since its founding in 1957, and he assigned his secretary the task of transcribing all of their names into a master roster book. The ditto sheets were getting crinkled and damaged, and Billy knew they wouldn't last long, so he had the idea of putting all the names of brothers inducted into a book in the chronological order of the dates they were inducted. From that point forward, all new brothers would sign "the book" upon induction into Oceanside AOT. At the same time, a new green briefcase was purchased to keep all the chapter's documents in. The book and the suitcase stayed with us up until the end of the Oceanside chapter.

Billy also took the time to read through all the documents in the Oceanside books. He had a great sense of curiosity about the beginnings of the fraternity. The documents in the Oceanside books said that the fraternity was founded in Brooklyn in 1948. Nothing else was said about the founding chapter. Billy decided to take his crew on weekend excursions into Brooklyn to search for members of Brooklyn AOT. This was like looking for a needle in a haystack. Brooklyn is a big place, and since the documents didn't say what section of Brooklyn or what high school AOT came from, it was hit-or-miss to go looking. But that is what Billy and his crew did. For three or four weekends in a row, they got into cars, drove to different parts of Brooklyn, and then walked around wearing AOT jackets, hoping they would be recognized by someone. After about a month of these weekend road trips, they finally gave up on finding the lost tribe of Brooklyn AOT. Little did they know that the Brooklyn chapter had folded about eight years earlier.

The documents in the Oceanside books spoke of Connecticut chapters as well. Although the documents referring to Brooklyn were vague, these documents stated the Connecticut chapter was in Middletown, and thus gave them a definite place to look for AOT-affiliated brothers. One Saturday, they drove up to Middletown, Connecticut, from Oceanside in two carloads. When they arrived, they walked into the first luncheonette they saw and ordered lunch, played pinball, and dropped dimes in the jukebox. Within fifteen minutes of their arrival at the luncheonette, about five guys walked into the establishment, and there was instant recognition by all in the room.

The style of the jackets was different, but each group of guys instantly recognized the others as AOT brothers. The Oceanside Alpha jackets were varsity-style solid green jackets with a red stripe around the shoulder and armpit. The fraternity name was sewn on the back of the jackets in Old English lettering. The jackets worn by the brothers of the Middletown AOT chapter were solid green jackets with the name of the fraternity embroidered on the back in scripted lettering.

This was a joyous occasion, with more members of Middletown AOT coming to the luncheonette after word spread about the Long Island AOT members coming up. Billy and his crew were made to feel welcome and at home by the Middletown brothers. They actually stayed the night in Middletown and went to a bonfire keg party that Saturday night. The Middletown AOT brothers took the Oceanside guys on midnight rides in the back of a pickup truck through winding roads and cornfields. Such a good time was had by everyone that they made an attempt to reestablish communication between Long Island and Middletown AOT chapters.

Billy had set out to locate lost chapters of AOT. Although he was unsuccessful in finding Brooklyn AOT, he did reconnect Long Island AOT to their long-lost brothers in Connecticut, if only for a moment. The following year, Middletown AOT members would visit Oceanside and were taken by the Oceanside members to meet Valley Stream AOT members. The Middletown brothers spent the weekend. There would be more road trips to Middletown by Oceanside AOT members in 1969 and 1970; sadly, there was not much communication after that.

The end of the school year brought the end of the Billy Weitzman presidency. Billy's end-of-year party started a tradition in the Oceanside chapter that took place almost every year. We called it the Senior Dinner. That was a dinner organized by junior members of the frat to celebrate the past year and thank the outgoing seniors. The outgoing officers were usually given plaques or some award at the dinner.

Billy's Senior Dinner took place at a popular pizzeria/restaurant in Oceanside called Joe Terzo's, which was in the same spot that Alias Smith and Jones stands today on Woods Avenue. This party was for fraternity members only. No invites and no girlfriends.

As it were, one of the junior members brought a Super 8 video camera to the party and captured about twelve minutes of the event. Billy can be seen walking in, wearing a suit and tie and smoking a cigar. He is also seen giving the Alpha grip to other members at his table. As the camera pans around the party room, you can see the strong sense of pride and brotherhood in the room. There are smiles and Alpha handshakes all around. Nearly everyone in the room is videotaped wearing Alpha sweaters and thin black ties. The newly elected officers can be seen stepping up to the outgoing officers for a formal passing of the guard to the next Alpha class.

Although the video is short and silent, except for a sound track that was added, it is a real window into fraternity life in 1968. The video can be seen on the official AOT Web site at alphaomegatheta.com.

After graduation, Billy joined the army before being drafted. He served in Vietnam with honor and distinction. Billy built on the leadership skills he learned as president of AOT to become squad leader in Vietnam, and after returning home, he rose through the ranks of the Carpenters Union to become union president in the 1980s and 1990s past 2000. I count Billy as one of my good and close personal friends, and I am honored to have his friendship.

Billy Weitzman on the right and Jerry Bracco on the
left at the AOT reunion in 2007

Billy Weitzman on the left and Joe "Spooky" Furino on the right at
Bracco's Clam Bar in Freeport

ALPHA OMEGA THETA FRATERNITY

Garden City AOT group picture, class of 1968

Freeport AOT group picture, class of 1967

CHAPTER EIGHT

AOT in the Seventies

By the beginning of the 1970s, the next stage of AOT's existence was beginning to unfold. By 1970, Alpha Sigma Phi had grown in size and stature in Oceanside. They had also planted chapters in West Hempstead, Island Park, and Rockville Centre, in addition to their first chapter in Valley Stream North. In the words of Oceanside AOT president from 1977 Phil Gerardi, "When Phi came into the picture, that was the beginning of the end of the fraternity system. That's when fraternities became gang-like." This profound statement was in reference to the changing attitude of fraternities toward each other and the public's attitude toward fraternities after Phi came into the picture. Alpha Sigma Phi was an extremely violent clique that was indeed more like a gang than a traditional Greek-letter fraternal brotherhood, and their addition to the fraternity system profoundly affected the stature and reputations of all the other fraternities.

Phil's statement about Phi was true, but all fraternities had their share of bad behavior and excess. AOT had settled into the major chapters in Valley Stream, Freeport, Oceanside, Baldwin, and Rockville Centre. The larger chapters were Valley Stream, Oceanside, and Baldwin; the smaller ones were in Freeport, Garden City, Uniondale, and Rockville Centre. The chapter in Amityville had faded out in the early seventies, and the Garden City and Uniondale chapters had folded by 1978. The chapter in Middletown, Connecticut, had a long run up until the 1980s, but was totally disconnected from the Long Island chapters. The remaining chapters held their own during the seventies, and there would be many backyard keg parties, road trips, brawls, and even a few charitable events from time to time. The AOT Grand Council no longer met, but the individual chapters were still thriving and passing down the traditions year after year.

For the most part, AOT and Omega were still jock fraternities throughout most of the seventies. Alpha Sigma Phi was a throwback to the greaser era, and in Freeport, a new fraternity had come into the scene called Delta Gamma Rho. Delta Gamma Rho, known as Delta for short, was founded in Freeport from a breakaway faction in Freeport AOT, and their colors were black and green. The formation of Delta Gamma Rho in Freeport actually caused the Freeport AOT chapter to briefly fold in 1977 and then reappear in 1980, when the older brothers of the guys who restarted it in 1980 had given them documents and colors to reestablish the Freeport chapter. This didn't sit well with Freeport Delta, and there were quite a few fights between the two during the late seventies and into the early eighties. Delta soon had a second chapter in Baldwin and later tried to found a chapter in Oceanside, but it was short-lived. The Oceanside students who lived on the Baldwin border had joined Baldwin Delta, and when there were about fifteen to twenty of them, they tried to branch out and form an Oceanside chapter of Delta Gamma Rho in 1977. This didn't go over well with Alpha Sigma Phi in Oceanside, and the fighting started immediately, with Phi firing the first shots and demanding the dissolution of the Oceanside chapter of Delta Gamma Rho or all the Delta members would be fair game for jumping's and their colors forcibly taken from them. Delta Gamma Rho was similar to Phi with the street punk, troublemaker attitude being a prerequisite for membership. This conflict wasn't a case of dog and cat, which will eventually find a way to coexist. These were two vicious dogs that could not be in the same town together. One had to go, and Phi was already well established in Oceanside. So Delta in Oceanside folded within a few months of harassment, jumping's, and fraternity colors being pulled off their members' backs. Later, the members of Delta were absorbed into AOT and Omega.

The relationship between AOT and Omega had settled into a quiet rivalry, with little friction between the two for most of the decade. AOT and Omega chapters in all the various towns would regularly and routinely play softball and football against each other and would also attend each other's parties. The real animosity was growing now between AOT and Alpha Sigma Phi in all the towns where the two coexisted. In Freeport and Baldwin, the trouble was usually with Delta Gamma Rho and sometimes with Phi. This animosity manifested itself in fights and all-out brawls that grew more intense, violent, and even deadly as time moved on. Garden City was a tranquil sea of quiet. There were no other fraternities in Garden City, and there were no fights in Garden City, either. The Alpha chapter there prided itself in having the cream-of-the-crop students, all of whom had prospects for good futures and came from good, influential families. They didn't need or want the kind of trouble that was brewing with Phi, which probably led to the dissolution of Garden City AOT between 1977 and '78.

—

Garden City was too upscale and highbrow for the kind of brawls and rumbles that were brewing up in the other communities of South Nassau.

Uniondale also had no other fraternities; however, Uniondale was rapidly changing, with the racial makeup of the town becoming predominantly African American. Situated between Roosevelt and Hempstead, which both had a majority of blacks, Uniondale was quickly succumbing to white flight as large numbers of blacks were moving into Uniondale from the city. And with the influx of blacks from the five boroughs came the street gangs from the city as well. The situation was volatile, and there were fights and violent confrontations. The AOT members had lived in Uniondale most of their lives and felt like their territory was being taken from them. AOT had a long tradition in Uniondale since 1959, and they wanted to preserve their brotherhood and traditions. There were quite a few all-out brawls between the Alphas and a gang known as the Godfathers, which had its membership derived from Uniondale and Hempstead. These fights culminated in gunplay, when the Godfathers started carrying and bringing guns to the rumbles with AOT.

By 1978, white flight was nearly complete as the town was now mostly black, and the few whites who remained in Uniondale sent their kids to private schools as they planned their eventual departure from Uniondale as well. The Alphas in Uniondale were fighting a battle they could not win in the end. No one wanted to get shot for a street corner or a tee shirt with a fraternity emblem on it, so Uniondale AOT disbanded in 1978. For the Alpha chapters that remained viable and strong during the seventies, it was a very different way of life than in the fifties and early sixties. The doo-wop dances of the fifties gave way to the phenomenon of the seventies known as the keg party. All AOT chapters had keg parties, usually charging party guests per person to enter and get all they could drink. These parties usually happened in someone's backyard, most likely when their parents were not home. A band would be hired, sometimes a teen band from school and sometimes a professional band, if the fraternity could afford it. It always ended with cops breaking it up and dozens of drunken teens puking on the neighbors' lawns. Every once in a while, a party room was rented at a local firehouse. But usually, the firehouse would refuse to rent out the room or would cancel the party when they learned it was going to be a frat party.

It was common for AOT chapters to go on road trips. Usual activities like ski trips or camping happened frequently. Valley Stream Alpha had annual ski trips. They would plan the outing with an event organizer and charter a bus to take the fraternity upstate. Sometimes they needed two or three buses, depending on how many wanted to go. The drinking would usually start as soon as the bus left the parking lot bright and early at 6:00 AM. The rest of the weekend, drunken teens would stumble and fall all over the ski slopes.

Valley Stream AOT brother Anthony Ratobala had some recollections of dogging and fraternity life in Valley Stream in the late 1960s and into the early 1970s.

"There were three degrees in the pledging process. You had to be a freshman to pledge, but most pledges were sophomores. First, you were invited to a smoker, then an interview. During all interviews and degrees, the dog was on his knees facing the officers in a dark room with candles.

"Example of questions asked at interview: What's more important than the frat? Answer, religion, family, country, and school.

"What does fraternity mean to you? Answer, brotherhood.

"Pledges always had to tell a joke. Pledging was four weeks. First degree was the start of pledging. You were welcomed to pledge by the president and the officers. You were then introduced to all the officers, starting with the president on down. The last guys to welcome you were the pledge masters. The last pledge master shook your hand and then slapped your face as hard as he could, and then you were thrown into a room with the rest of the pledges. After the first week, they let you know if you were still a dog, then you were required to get a crew cut. That was the worst part of pledging circa 1968."

Brother Anthony Ratobala's recollections of pledging attire and the second degree of pledging in Valley Stream AOT are as follows: "The dog attire was a white shirt, red suspenders, green bow tie, crew cut, shoeshine brush and polish, and dog book. There was often competition between Alpha and Omega pledges. My brush and suspenders were stolen from an Omega pledge. We often wrestled the Omega pledges. Second degree began two weeks into pledging. The dogs had to eat whatever a brother gave them. Always a live goldfish and whatever the brother concocted in his kitchen. Dogs were also shot with shaving cream and whip cream. Rumor had it that Kenny Lewerson and Al Tonellson pissed in their concoction, so I did my best to avoid them. Dennis Shaka gave medicine that induced vomiting, which was kind of redundant. After the first fifteen minutes, most of us were puking anyhow. I specifically recall regurgitating the entire way home wearing shaving cream and whip cream from head to toe, while Tom Buck and Larry Penaro did their best to comfort me. I always had a weak stomach, but never barfed that much in my entire life."

And Brother Anthony Ratobala recalls third degree and his Hell Night.

"Third degree was Hell Night. All dogs dressed as a female, had to bring a gift for a specific brother. Mine was Jimi Hendrix's *Are You Experienced* album for Paul Gold. Then you had to take twenty shots while dressed in a dress. You were then taken somewhere blindfolded and had to make your way back home. Myself and fellow dogs Rich Buck and Bob Virgo were driven by Rich Mancelli, Kenny Lewerson, and Ira Irdman to Rocky Point. When we arrived, I was numb from having to bend completely over the entire ride in the backseat of Mancelli's Chevy Impala. Lewerson and Irdman were nuts, difficult guys for a dog.

"Mancelli, who later became vice president, was completely sane and an easy guy to pledge for, but Irdman and Lewerson must have influenced him, or maybe there was a full moon, because Mancelli seemed as crazy as Irdman and Lewerson. When we arrived at Rocky Point (I later learned the town of Mancelli's summer home), they tied Rich Buck to a tree branch the same way a hunter would tie a deer, bound his hands to his ankles, and tied the ankles to a tree limb, with Richie upside down. They then placed me on the ground and tied Virgo to me. They accurately viewed Virgo as a wiseass. When they left, they each kicked Virgo in the ass hard enough for me to feel each and every kick. Maybe that doesn't sound too bad, but the pain was exacerbated by his ass being black and blue with blood blisters from the shots. After Hell Night, I wasn't comfortable sitting for two weeks, a sensation only a dog can empathize with.

"After untying ourselves, Virgo and I untied Buck. We made our way out of the woods to the nearest highway and hitchhiked, dressed as women, to the town of Rocky Point. We met a guy around our age closing up a Wetson's hamburger joint who let us use his phone and fed us. Buck called his dad, who knew the area. He picked us up, and I believe we were home before Mancelli.

"My friends who pledged were taken to Robert Moses State Park by Rex Johns, another nut, but not difficult to a pledge. About five or six went to Robert Moses State Park in Rex's station wagon. After Hell Night, you were inducted a few weeks later, where you were required to say the Greek alphabet before a match blew out or was blown out.

"The thing I always remembered about induction was the dog was dressed in a white shirt and tie, but when he was told to raise his right hand, at least one brother said, 'Your right hand,' to further unnerve the inductee. Sometimes they would scare a pledge and those pledges awaiting induction, who couldn't get through the Greek alphabet, by returning him to the waiting room."

Lastly, Brother Anthony Ratobala remembers attending his first meetings as a full brother of Alpha Omega Theta.

"I was inducted in October 1968. The first interview for new pledges I attended as a brother was January 1969 at Eric Mussaka's house. It was on the day the Jets won their only Super Bowl against the Baltimore Colts. Imagine having a fraternity function on the day of the Super Bowl in 2008. I remember Rich Prenza, who later played tight end for Duke, screaming the score and game updates as we interviewed perspective dogs. After pledging and induction, there was always an induction party for brothers only."

Of the many skiing trips Valley Stream AOT went on, Anthony Ratobala remembers the first one.

"Craig Soburg's administration had just concluded in late winter 1970. Rich Morgyle's administration began with the announcement that there would be an Alpha ski trip. I believe the only guy who had ever skied before was Stan

Wolman. I believe the trip was organized by Rich Morgyle himself. Rich was the second Morgyle to be president. His brother Tom was president 1968, and his younger brother Ralph would also become president in 1973.

"There were only about twenty-five who went on the first Alpha ski trip, all guys and all brothers except for about two guys. We caught the bus Saturday at five AM at Valley Stream Central High School. Everyone had begun drinking beer prior to departure. I think Kevin and Dennis Farr arrived at the bus loaded, perhaps from the night before. At that age in 1970, no one thought it was odd for a bunch of underage teenagers to consume beer at five AM. It certainly didn't appear odd to any of us. Indeed, it was almost normal. If you tried it today, the chaperones would all be arrested, and Peak Ski Tours shut down forever.

"Both Farr's were great guys, but as different as Oscar and Felix. Dennis reserved and polite. Kevin wild and brash. Kevin continued imbibing beer the entire ride up and actually filled an entire six-pack, using empty beer cans to piss in. We all relieved ourselves similarly. As I mentioned, there were tour chaperones. These people were really into skiing and thought we were there to get instructions from them. All most of us wanted to do was drink. One guy with a beard was immediately christened Daddy-O by Anthony Zarro. He kept trying to get us to stop drinking the entire way up. He eventually settled for us keeping the beer cans down. I specifically remember him saying, 'Keep the cans down, or I get it up the ass," a saying we repeated the entire weekend and then some.

"When we got to Davos Mountain, we all tried skiing. We weren't dressed in anything other than Alpha jackets. We must have looked like a bunch of green-and-red kamikazes. At least that's how most of us skied. After skiing, we were taken by bus to the Laurels Hotel in Catskill, New York. We again commenced drinking in our respective rooms, with Daddy-O attempting to stop the drinking. That instigated the first of many pillow fights. During one such altercation, three or four pillows broke, and the entire hall floor was covered with feathers. Security was summoned, and Morgyle and Kevin Morrison had to quell the riot and mollify security. In the end, security couldn't determine how many pillows we had destroyed. They were going to charge us $5 for each pillow but didn't know how many to bill us. Tom Decker was given the task of counting all the pillows, allotting one for each bed. After Decker counted all the pillows, there were two extra, so he boldly informed security that they owed us $10, payable immediately.

"After dinner, most of us with ID made our way to the lounge, where we harassed the entertainment and drank cocktails. We eventually wound up in the indoor pool, which some guy closed by vomiting.

"The last night, Daddy-O was abruptly awoken by a pail of water. No one skied Sunday. We arrived home and needed a week to recover. The trip was so popular that Warren Rubel organized the 1971 Alpha ski trip, and approximately

150 people went on four buses. The second trip was good, but nothing was as good as the first Alpha ski trip of 1970."

Valley Stream AOT was not the only Alpha chapter up to mischief. In the winter of 1974, Baldwin Alpha Omega Theta planned a trip to the Paramount in the Catskills. They booked the hotel under the name Baldwin High School Boys Choir. They knew they couldn't book rooms for Alpha Omega Theta Fraternity, hence the subterfuge in the name used for the rental. The entire trip consisted of getting drunk in the hotel rooms and trashing the place. The local cops in the Catskills put the whole Alpha contingent under house arrest and would not let them leave their rooms. The Catskills police contacted the First Precinct in Baldwin to determine whom they had in custody, and then Nassau County police visited the homes of all the Baldwin AOT members who were being held in the Catskills to collect money from their parents to pay for the damages. After payment for damages was made to the Paramount, the Alpha members were then released without charges.

Baldwin AOT at that time hung out during the day at the Chat N Nibble Coffee Shop in the shopping center adjacent to Baldwin High School. At night, the Burger King on Grand Avenue was the hangout. Baldwin AOT typically held their Hell Night inductions at Robert Moses State Park and would abandon the pledges there.

When pledges were first interviewed, it would take three blackballs to kill the pledge's possibility of dogging for the fraternity. Pledges were brought in blindfolded and forced to kneel at a table where the officers sat. On the table was an Alpha tee shirt. The pledges were told that they would get an automatic induction with no pledging, paddling, or hazing of any kind if they had balls enough to grab the tee shirt off the table and make a break for the exit. Pledges who didn't try were deemed to be gutless and mostly got blackballed; those who did make a grab for the tee shirt would get a massive pounding by the whole fraternity in an all-on-one. If someone was lucky enough to make it to the door with the tee, there was always one of the frat's biggest guys blocking the path and throwing the poor pledge back into the room to catch a beating. No one ever made it out the door with the tee shirt.

As usual, pledges were required to carry at all times a shoe or cigar box filled with bubble gum, cigarettes, shoe polish, and their pledge book. Obviously, dogs had to dispense gum and cigarettes and shine shoes upon demand. Dogs had been trained to respond to commands such as "air raid," where they would instantly hit the ground crouching in a cannonball position, and "fleas," where the dog would have to drop to the floor on his back and start scratching his whole body like crazy. For carrying out these commands, they would get merits or demerits in their pledge books. The merits never amounted to much, but the demerits could get a guy blackballed.

Pledges had to show up at the Chat N Nibble Coffee Shop in the early morning before school for pledging. At Christmastime, the Baldwin AOT brothers would dress up their dogs like Santa Claus and bring them to the Green Acres Shopping Mall in Valley Stream, forcing them to stand around ringing a bell in front of a big kettle. The money went toward a Christmas keg party.

Baldwin AOT brother Paul McLaughlin, alumnus 1974, recalled, "On Hell Nights, all the brothers and pledges would meet in the parking lot where the Baldwin Historical Society now stands. We would pile into cars and drive to some remote spot, where the pledges were pelted with eggs, covered in molasses, paddled, and then abandoned. You were inducted at the next meeting and given the password, told its meaning, and shown the secret handshake."

Paul McLaughlin also reminisced about his experiences with another fraternity rite of passage, jumping. The term *jumping* is fairly self-explanatory. Jumping happened when a fraternity member or members were attacked and beaten, essentially "jumped" by another fraternity whose members outnumbered them at that given moment. Standing on a busy street corner or in a public place like Nathan's in Oceanside or Burger King in Baldwin wearing colors was usually a precursor to getting jumped by another fraternity. In many cases, the guys doing the jumping would strip the guys catching the beating of their fraternity colors.

Many times, jumping's took place across town lines. Guys from a rival frat from another town would go cruising into the neighboring town and look for guys wearing fraternity colors. They would usually only jump guys who were alone or in relatively small numbers. As it were, Paul McLaughlin was jumped in Baldwin at the corner of Sunrise Highway and Grand Avenue, which was only a block and a half from the AOT hangout at Burger King on Grand Avenue. The perpetrators were an obscure fraternity from Valley Stream Central High School called Kappa Delta Nu. Known as Kappa for short, it had only two chapters in Valley Stream Central and South, although they had chapters in all Valley Stream high schools in Central, North, and South in the 1950s. Later years had seen the dissolution of two Kappa chapters, and this fraternity had never branched out of Valley Stream.

Paul McLaughlin was on his way to Burger King when he was intercepted by a carload of Kappa members from Valley Stream Central. They roughed him up pretty bad and took his colors, which was a varsity-style jacket that had the fraternity name on the back. Those jackets were pretty expensive even in the early seventies, so losing one was not only humiliating but also an expensive loss that may need to be explained to your parents.

After getting jumped, Paul ran to Burger King to rally his frat brothers. As luck would have it, the lot was filled with Baldwin AOT and Omega members. The Alphas and Omegas had been becoming pretty intertwined in most towns they coexisted in and certainly stood together in the face of out-of-towners infringing on their territory and jumping their friends.

Then either out of luck or stupidity, depending on which way you look at it, the carload of Kappa's drove right into the Burger King parking lot right into the middle of all the Alphas and Omegas. Paul instantly recognized the car and pointed them out to his friends. The car was immediately surrounded, and the Baldwin fraternity members tried to pull the Kappa's out of their car. The car sped out of the parking lot onto Grand Avenue with guys hanging off the station wagon as they tore off down the road. A Nassau County cop car quickly saw the commotion and pulled the car over a few blocks away.

The cops quickly surmised the Valley Stream Kappa's were cruising Baldwin looking for trouble and they found it. The cops retrieved Paul's Alpha jacket and returned it to him. Paul was asked if he wanted to press charges, but he declined. Instead, Paul told the cops that his brother was a Rockville Centre cop, and he asked them to pile a shitload of tickets on these guys, which they did.

The following week, the Baldwin Alphas attended an AOT meeting in Valley Stream to get the lowdown on these guys from Kappa and plot some revenge. The brothers from Valley Stream AOT knew who the Kappa's were just by the description of the station wagon they were driving. The Valley Stream Alphas assured their Baldwin counterparts that they would take care of the Kappa's. Apparently, they did because the Kappa's never came back into Baldwin again.

Paul McLaughlin recalled that the Valley Stream chapter was really big; they were tight and well organized. The Valley Stream Alphas referred to themselves as the Grand Chapter. The following week, some Valley Stream Alphas attended a Baldwin meeting, and they brought Alpha pins with them to sell to the Baldwin guys. Nobody in Baldwin AOT had Alpha pins, so they were a big hit at the meeting.

Paul had some interesting memories of Baldwin Alpha parties of the early 1970s.

"We threw lots of backyard keg parties, $2 for all the beer you could drink, and literally hundreds of kids would show up and get tanked. These parties always ended up getting raided by the cops. Thinking of it now, it seems crazy. We were all underage, some of us only in ninth grade, and all drunk, puking in the streets and trawling for equally drunk girls to take advantage of."

In Oceanside, the relationship between AOT and Phi became increasingly volatile during the 1970s. When the Oceanside Phi chapter was founded in 1968, the fraternity was largely regarded as a joke by AOT and Omega. Their inability to attract quality members during their first two years led to their decision to recruit heavily from the junior high school.

Junior-high recruitment was virtually unheard of in the fifties and sixties. On some rare occasion, a freshman might be considered if he was a legacy member with an older brother, but apart from that, junior high kids had to wait until they were sophomores to join a major fraternity in Oceanside. Phi president Scott Ossner's idea to recruit heavily among the eighth and ninth graders was sneered at by the other fraternities from 1968 to 1970. But by 1971, the reality hit the Alphas and the Omegas that Scott Ossner had a brilliant plan for the future of Phi. Every September, when school would start, it was like Fall Rush was for college fraternities. All the eager sophomores would wait to be tapped for membership in the fraternities. But in 1971, there was a big change in that ritual. Phi had been recruiting pretty heavily for the past two or three years, and in 1971, a shitload of new sophomores came into the school wearing Phi sweaters. Phi had shown interest in them when they were younger than the requirements for other fraternities, recruited them, and developed them into loyal members of Alpha Sigma Phi. As far as new member recruitment, the pickings were slim for all the other fraternities in 1971 and 1972.

It was tough to get sophomores to join AOT or Omega when all their friends were already in Phi. And that status quo had a leveling effect on the fraternity system in Oceanside. By 1975, Roger Ossner, Scott's younger brother, became president of Phi. Roger had a mean temper and was known for being a tough street fighter. Both Scott and Roger were black belts in karate and taught it as well. Roger took extra pride in Phi, and the growth under him was explosive. They continued recruiting heavily in the junior high and within the high school as well. Within a short time, AOT and Omega had to begin recruiting eighth and ninth graders to keep up with Phi and prevent their pool of future recruits from being all taken up by Phi.

Roger had no liking or respect for the other fraternities and wanted to demonstrate Phi's power and dominance in Oceanside. Phi had developed a real snake-and-mongoose—type relationship with AOT. Phi never had many fights with Omega, but there was bad blood between Phi and AOT, going back to Billy Weitzman's decree that Phi was not allowed to wear colors in Oceanside because the sweaters looked like AOT sweaters from a distance. The fact that Phi had to exist underground for their first two years had left a lasting hatred for AOT among the Phi guys.

This sudden growth of Phi to almost eighty members in the mid-1970s caused an informal alliance between AOT and Omega in Oceanside. The two frats had little or no problems with each other during the seventies. They regularly had football and softball games together, and the two fraternities' rank and file maintained close friendships on individual levels. Phi's attitude was gang-like and fiercely territorial. Throughout the latter half of the seventies, fights between AOT and Phi were common, and struggles for dominance of maintaining Nathan's as a territorial hangout were common as well.

Although Phi was becoming very successful in recruiting members, they were attracting guys with a greaser / street punk attitude, while AOT and Omega were still attracting athletes. All of the Oceanside AOT presidents during most of the seventies were top athletes in Oceanside High School.

One of the top athletes in 1971 was Rudy Lamonica. Rudy was an extremely gifted soccer player. He had a bright future ahead of him, with the probability of playing pro soccer somewhere in Europe or South America. Soccer had never been popular in the USA, and there were no pro soccer leagues at the time in the United States. Rudy had gotten such a name for himself that Brazilian soccer great Pelé had come to meet Rudy. Rudy's soccer jersey signed by Pelé has been proudly displayed outside of the OHS gymnasium in a glass case for years. Rudy had been afflicted by leukemia in his senior year and, sadly, died of the disease. A soccer tournament was named for him called the Annual Rudy Lamonica Memorial Indoor Tournament; it is the oldest indoor youth soccer tournament in the USA.

By the mid-1970s, Oceanside AOT was beginning to rebound and maintain respectable numbers in their roster. In 1974, one such recruit was Phil Gerardi. Phil was a thirteen-year-old in eighth grade, and he was a legacy member. Phil's older brother Lou Gerardi was an alumnus from 1969, and Phil's cousin Carmine Prencepio was a charter member of Uniondale AOT in 1959. Phil's brother Lou was called "half an ear" because he had gotten half his ear bitten off in a fight when he was in high school.

Phil had actually been asked into Omega Gamma Delta before he was asked into AOT. He had been given a letter of invitation by the Omegas, and for a thirteen-year-old kid, it was something to feel proud about. He brought the letter home and showed it to his brother Lou and another AOT alumnus, Gary Theo, the class of 1969 treasurer and president, respectively. Phil was all excited about being given a letter by one of the major fraternities in school.

He said to them, "Look, guys, I got a letter from Omega Gamma Delta."

They said, "Oh yeah? Let us see that."

Then before his eyes, Lou and Gary tore the letter up into pieces.

Phil said, "What the fuck, man? What are you doing?"

His brother Lou said, "You're not going into Omega. Your whole family was in Alpha."

A few weeks later, Phil was asked into Alpha. Phil was taken on as a pledge with the dogging period being five weeks. When he started out, there were eleven dogs all together. By the end of the second week, half of them had dropped out already. At the end of the fifth week, when the remaining dogs expected to be inducted, the pledging period was extended another week. It was usual for fraternities to extend the dogs' pledging period. This would always cause most of the dogs to drop out, but that was a way of only inducting the pledges who were serious about joining.

Phil recalled one humorous anecdote from when he was dogging. His pledge master had called him and told him that Brother Jake Miraz had signed him out for the day, which meant Phil had to go with Jake Miraz for the day and do whatever he was told. Jake Miraz was working at the pizzeria, at what used to be the old Times Square Store in Oceanside. Phil was told to meet Brother Miraz at the pizzeria at the time of the finish of his shift. Phil showed up, as told to, at the time he was supposed to be there. As usual, he was in full dogging uniform: a green bow tie, red suspenders, a fresh white shirt, pressed slacks, and black shoes. When Phil entered the pizzeria, Brother Miraz made eye contact and motioned for Phil to stand off to the side and wait while he continued pressing pizza dough into pies. All of a sudden, in front of a packed pizzeria, Brother Miraz starts singing, "It was raining hard in Frisco." And he was singing the song as loud as you can imagine. He was a curiosity to the patrons at first, but he kept on singing louder and louder.

According to Phil, "He was singing just like he was on stage. Then all of a sudden, he jumps on top of the counter. The manager comes out screaming at him, 'What the hell are you doing?' And he says, 'Shut your mouth, I'm singing a song.' And he keeps singing the song. Everybody in the pizzeria was laughing, and finally, the manager says, 'Get down off the counter. You're fired.' Then Miraz throws the dough at his manager and says, 'Nobody fires me, see. Fuck you, I quit.'"

As he walked out from behind the counter, he turned to Phil and said, "You, you're with me. Come on, let's go." And Jake Miraz, the guy who was just singing show tunes to a crowd of pizzeria patrons, walked out the door with a thirteen-year-old kid wearing a green bow tie and red suspenders in tow. It was comical, to say the least. It turned out that Jake had wanted to quit the whole time, but this was how he planned to make his exit from his job making pizza pies all along.

By the end of the sixth week, all the other dogs had dropped out, and Phil was the last one. In fact, Phil was at the end of his rope as well. He had had enough and wanted to drop out, but he thought his older brother Lou would kick his ass for dropping, so he continued. At the meeting on the sixth week, they told Phil he would be dogging another two weeks. Phil left the meeting disappointed, totally exhausted from pledging, and ready to quit dogging.

Usually at the end of a meeting, the dog or dogs would be dismissed first and told to go home while the brothers closed the meeting. Phil was walking home from the meeting, thinking about how he could tell his brother that he wanted to drop out, when a car pulled up to him. It was late and dark out; Phil didn't recognize the car, but when older guys wearing frat sweaters demanded that he approach their vehicle, he figured they were Alpha guys from the meeting. It was common for them to harass dogs all the way home after a meeting, so Phil figured it was the AOT guys about to haze him.

When Phil walked up to the car, he first realized that he didn't recognize any of their faces, and then he noticed the sweaters were purple and white. These guys were Sigma Lambda Rho. They had spotted Phil walking down the street sporting a crew cut, a green bow tie, and red suspenders, and they knew he was an Alpha dog. As soon as Phil was close enough to grab, they pulled him in through the passenger window and roughed him up pretty good. They took him on a joyride, beat him up, and then threw him out of the car a few blocks away and left him lying on the street.

Phil returned to the Alpha meeting all beat up and bruised. They saw Phil had been beaten up, and they asked him what happened. Phil told them he was jumped by guys in purple-and-white sweaters. The Alpha guys pulled Phil into the car and took him to Nathan's on Long Beach Road. They pointed out some guys in purple-and-white sweaters and asked Phil if they were the guys. They were, Phil told them. Almost instantly, these Sigma Lambda Rho guys were surrounded by angry, pissed-off AOT guys.

Nobody abused AOT pledges; only AOT abused AOT pledges. These guys were beaten to within an inch of their lives, and they all had their colors taken by the AOT brothers. They were also told to tell the rest of their friends that there would be no more purple and white in Oceanside. With that incident, the Sigma Lambda Rho fraternity ended in Oceanside. Some of AOT's toughest guys were in that car with Phil when they went to Nathan's that night. If not for the jumping incident, Phil was ready to drop out, but now he saw how they stood up for him, how they avenged his jumping, and Phil got his first taste of what brotherhood was all about. After that incident, Phil was resolute to finish his pledging and earn his colors. He finished out the last two weeks of dogging without a second thought of quitting or dropping out.

Phil Gerardi would be getting the traditional Hell Night in what would be one of the last times that would be done in Oceanside. Phil got the full treatment with a beating and paddling at the meeting; and then he was driven out to Quogue far out east in Suffolk County, given a send-off paddle shot, and then he was abandoned on a dark road in his underwear with no money. Well, supposedly with no money. Phil was instructed that he had to be back in Oceanside at Nathan's in four hours, or he was blackballed.

Phil's aunt, knowing he would be abandoned with no money, suggested sewing a dollar bill into a secret seam in his underwear. It was risky because if the AOT brothers discovered it, Phil could have been taken farther away, like Upstate New York or Connecticut. But no one noticed the hand-sewn seam or the dollar bill in Phil's underwear. After Phil was dropped off, the first thing he had to do was to find some clothes. He found a house with a clothesline, but it only had women's clothing hanging on it. That was all Phil could find in the immediate area, so he took a sundress and ran off with it. He started walking, and after about a four- or five-mile walk, he finally hitched a ride with a young driver. Phil explained the reason he was hitchhiking wearing a sundress was that he was pledging a fraternity and he had to be back in Oceanside by a certain time. Phil got lucky, and the guy drove him as far west as Massapequa, dropping him off in front of the All-American Hamburger stand on Merrick Road. It was there that Phil got change of the dollar bill his aunt had sewn into the seam of his underwear, and he called home for a ride. About twenty minutes later, Phil's uncle Jerry picked him up and took him to Nathan's in Oceanside. Phil had made it back in time; he was given a few more welcome-home shots with shaved-down baseball bats, and then was told he would be inducted at the next meeting. The next week at the meeting, Phil became a full brother of Alpha Omega Theta at the young age of thirteen.

Phil reflected on the first brew-up he went to as a full member of AOT. Despite his mother imploring him to not go to the party, he went anyway. She told him that he was too young for a party attended by high school kids. It was held at Brian Suliven's house. Brian Suliven was known for having great basement parties and brew-ups. He had his whole basement painted in fluorescent paint. There was an Alpha shield painted on the wall. The whole place was lit up with fluorescent black lights, strobes, and even a smoke machine. There was loud music, people drinking, dancing, and smoking weed. It was a surreal scene for a thirteen-year-old to walk into. Phil described it as total debauchery, just like the party scenes in the movie *Animal House*.

Oceanside AOT would also hold dances in rented halls. It was at this time that they were just beginning to rent party rooms, and one by one, the fraternity became unwelcome at every hall-rental place in town. There were rarely any real damages, but the rowdiness, the teen drinking, and vomiting all over the place were enough to cause every place they threw a party to tell them "Don't come back."

Phil remembers one party at a place called the Knights of Pythias in Oceanside. It was a large hall; there was live music, and the party was open to non-brothers if they paid to get in. Guys would bring their girlfriends, and they danced. The party drew close to two hundred guests, including AOT brothers. The place had a lower level below the dance floor. Phil was passed-out drunk under the stairwell, and he was woken up by beer dripping on his face. It appeared that the dance floor was saturated with beer from a time-honored dance called the Alpha Gator. Traditionally, new members would be "gatored" at their first party after joining the fraternity. This entailed all the Alpha brothers gathering around the new guys in a circle and shaking up beer bottles or cans and spraying them down until they were soaked. Phil had already been gatored earlier, and others were gatored after him. When Phil awoke to find beer dripping not only down the stairs, but through the wooden dance floor, he also noticed the floor above him was buckling up and down from the force and weight of all the people on the dance floor above. It actually looked like it was about to collapse.

The destroyed dance floor wasn't the only damage that night. Some of the AOT members had broken into a locked room that must have been a chamber for the Knights of Pythias rituals. They found a casket with a skeleton inside of it. It was most likely not a real skeleton, but it looked real enough. At about the same time, Phil Gerardi and AOT president of 1976 John Bouman were trying to placate a neighbor who was complaining about the noise and rowdiness. At that magic moment, younger AOT brothers John Jaeger and Jimmy Nunley dragged the casket to an open window and threw it out. The thing landed right in this guy's front yard with the top opened and the skeleton exposed. The homeowner was infuriated.

Phil Gerardi reflected on that moment. "What else could we say to the guy after that? A casket with a skeleton in it comes flying out and landed on his lawn. There wasn't anything else we could say to him after that."

Phil recalled another funny story from an AOT party in 1975. Some of the AOT brothers had a contest going to see who could bring the ugliest girl to the party. A side bet was made, and a pool of money was collected from all who were in the contest. Many of the AOT brothers had asked ugly girls to accompany them to the party. None had told the girls that they were in a contest, but each hoped to win the pot. As the party progressed, it looked as though brothers Mike Ciaffalo, who was also known as Snitchy by the AOT brothers, and Jeff Lane were in a dead heat to win the prize when brother John Trip showed up with the prize-winning date. John had climbed the fence at Camp DeBaun on Atlantic Avenue and stolen a goat from the petting zoo. John's date, the goat, was a unanimous winner. The AOT brothers kept the goat as a mascot for the duration of the party and returned it to Camp DeBaun before the night was over. A typical fraternity prank involving a farm animal.

Phil shared his thoughts on Alpha Sigma Phi and AOT's relationship with them.

"Phi guys were always a pain in the ass. You could never trust them. They would never do anything if there was a fair fight. If they had you outnumbered, they would start shit. Roger Ossner was Phi president in 1975, the same year Bobby Smits was president of AOT. Roger didn't mess with guys himself. He was an interesting guy, and he always sent his minions to do his dirty work. I always got along with him, but I always suspected that he sent his guys to mess with me and my guys."

Phil spoke in more detail about the constant problems with Phi during his time in AOT. For a few years, from around 1972 to 1974, Phi was huge, and both AOT and Omega had gotten smaller. There was always ebb and flow among the fraternities when it came to size superiority, and Phi's massive recruitment drive in the junior high schools from 1969 onward had swelled their ranks. By 1976, AOT had caught up and was as big, if not bigger, than Phi was at the time.

In Phil's words, "We had beefed up mightily, and we couldn't wait for them to start trouble. I can honestly say I don't ever remember an Alpha guy starting a fight with those guys. They always started the shit. I wouldn't say it if it weren't true. Alpha guys only went after them if it was in retaliation, if the Phi guy did something."

Phil recalled one Phi member who had been trouble to him.

"In my days, I must have had at least twenty-five to thirty fights, and I never lost one except for one time, and that barely counted. I was at Nathan's, and I was in tenth grade, and I literally woke up on the street. Two AOT guys, Larry Fleishman and Sam Herenson, had picked me up and asked me what happened. I didn't know what happened. Then somebody later told me that this guy Kurt Westingburg, a Phi guy, coldcocked me. I was just standing there, I had no idea. I woke up, and I didn't even remember getting hit. That was the only time I was ever beat.

"The guy was in Oceanside Phi, but he lived in Island Park, so you could never find the guy. He was a real troublemaker. He was a big guy. A lot of guys were afraid of him. He looked older than he was. So he knocked me out when I was in tenth grade, and I never forgot it.

"So what happened is that when I was a senior, I became president, and the summer before senior year, we had an end-of-the-year brew-up. All of a sudden, Bubba Howe comes flying into the brew-up, and he tells me that Kurt Westingburg is at Nathan's with a whole shitload of Phi guys, and he is talking shit about kicking my ass, so I say, 'Let's go.'

"There were a lot of guys at the AOT brew-up, I'd say about thirty guys. We all piled into cars and went to Nathan's, and sure enough, there were about forty Phi guys there. They were all waiting there for us, and this was gonna be some fight. So Kurt is there, and I couldn't wait to get at this guy. I had been waiting a long time, and there he was. The reason he wanted to come after me is that I had been elected president of Alpha, and he had just been elected president of Phi, and he was saying, 'The first thing I'm gonna do is kick the shit out of Gerardi, and we're gonna wipe out Alpha.'

"So I get out of the car and go over to him and say, 'You wanted to see me?' And he says, 'Yeah I wanted to talk to you about what's going on between Alpha and Phi.' And as I go up to him, he puts his arm around me as if we are gonna talk, and I see him clench his left arm that was around my neck and then try to hook me with his right fist. This time I see it coming. I block it with my left, I hit him in his jaw, and he had a glass jaw. The guy dropped to his knees, and I hit him, I'd say about thirty times. I beat this guy within an inch of his life until both my arms were heavy. I was talking to him as I hit him, telling him, 'I have been waiting two fucking years for this,' and I'm hitting him as hard as I can, and he was just taking every punch.

"The Phi guys were completely stunned. A couple of the other Phi guys got their asses kicked also. Those Phi guys were so shocked that I kicked his ass. It was supposed to be a complete mismatch. They thought I was gonna be dead in two minutes. But he got his ass kicked, and they threw him out of office after that. Later, they elected Santos Gonzalez to be Phi president, and I kicked his ass three weeks later at Nathan's, and that was that. We didn't have a problem with Phi for the rest of the year. Our problems with them were over. They knew better. They were just a bunch of thugs."

Phil also remembered AOT's relationship with Omega Gamma Delta in Oceanside.

"Every Halloween, we would have the famous Alpha/Omega egg fight. The whole town was the boundary, and we went looking for each other. It was always a good time. We had a few guys come over to AOT from Omega. Omega had become a very withered fraternity by 1976. They were becoming smaller and smaller. A lot of their guys were coming over to us.

"This one guy had come over to Alpha from Omega, and he was petrified to come because Alpha was a tremendous fraternity by this time, but he was friends with a lot of guys in Alpha, and they brought him over. In those days, if you came over from another fraternity, you only had to take a few shots to get in. I think it was six shots. So he comes in wearing white carpenter pants. When he came down the stairs, I don't think he knew how big Alpha really was, and he saw there was close to eighty guys in the room that night.

"After he was brought into the room, I was standing next to John Trip, and I asked him, 'Did you fart?' And he said, 'No, I thought it was you.' Now they bend the guy over to get his six shots, and it turned out he shit his pants. He was so scared when he came into that room, and then they started paddling him, and his white pants turned brown. It was shocking. The guy was so scared he shit himself. That could have been the end of his reputation, but the guys were cool about it, and nobody told anyone about it. They all laughed about it, but if you tell this story, don't print the guy's name. It's not fair to the guy."

Phil told the story of the time he and his crew stole the Omega banner from an Omega party. One night, they went to an Omega Gamma Delta party. It was the summer after Phil's sophomore year, going into his junior year. It was Phil, Bill Andronimo, Van Potts, Matt Keller, and Jimmy Condon. They paid at the door to get in, and they quickly noticed a huge Omega banner hanging on the fence. Then they hatched a scheme to steal the Omega banner from the party. Van Potts was looking at this banner, which was hanging on the fence kind of away from the rest of the party. He started telling the other AOT guys that he could just walk up and take it and no one would notice before he could run off with it.

So they were getting bored at the party and ready to leave. They were hanging around near the banner still drinking beers, and Van Potts kept saying that he was going to take the Omega banner when they left the party. Phil was trying to talk Van out of it, trying to convince him they would have to fight their way out of the party if he took the banner. And besides that, there were no problems with Omega at that time, and AOT president Bob Smits would be pissed if they started shit with Omega.

When they realized Van Potts was serious and had every intention of making a grab for the Omega banner, they decided to try to come up with a plan to get out of there in one piece with the Omega banner in their possession. They knew they were going to have to run for it; there was just no way that they were walking out of there with the Omega banner without getting chased. They plotted a diversion to get all the Omega guys away from the banner so it could be easily grabbed, which was supposed to enable Van Potts to grab the banner off the fence it was hanging from. When the diversion didn't draw enough people away, they decided that the best they could do was to try to slow the crowd that would no doubt be chasing Van down the street.

The diversion was only moderately successful, with only a few guys going over to see what the commotion was about. Van decided to make a grab for the banner anyway. As soon as he put his hands on it, he was seen, and that caused the commotion to come to full boil. It was instant reaction, with the whole crowd of Omega guys chasing Van Potts as he ran down the street with the Omega banner under his arm. The alternate phase of the plan didn't pan out well, either, when the crowd that chased Van just plowed right through Bill Andronimo and Jimmy Condon, who had thought they could hold the crowd back long enough for Van to make a clean getaway; they couldn't.

The last attempted roadblock were Matt Keller and Phil Gerardi, who waited on the street, standing on the roof of a car with the intent to do a flying tackle on top of the stampede of Omegas that were chasing Van Potts. Phil did his Superman impression and missed everyone, falling facedown on the concrete, and everyone just trampled and ran past him.

It didn't take long for them to realize Phil and Matt were in on it, and the two of them were surrounded by the pissed-off Omegas. Billy wound up in a fistfight with one of Omega's senior members and kicked his ass. It was an event that would lead to all of these guys getting a reputation for wild antics and for not backing away from a fight even when outnumbered. In the end, Van did escape with the banner, and AOT president Bob Smits was pissed at them for starting the incident. Van had to give the banner back and apologize for taking it. But the story of when they stole the Omega banner right from their own party was one that Phil would tell many times over the years. As funny as it seemed at the time, it actually caused a diplomatic incident between AOT and Omega.

Phil would become president of Oceanside AOT in the class of 1977. Phil had to be creative when throwing parties in his time as president. AOT already had a reputation for trashing party rooms and were not welcome to rent any decent places for a party. Phil and his crew had started renting adjoining rooms at the Holiday Inn in Rockville Centre. They would get the oldest-looking AOT brothers to rent two or three rooms that had connecting doorways, and they would turn them into a big party room with a tremendous brew-up.

Phil recalled, "We had to get creative like that because we were running out of halls. We had wrecked so many halls. In those days, they couldn't do anything to teens that wrecked the place, but they wouldn't let us come back."

Phil shared his thought on Oceanside AOT's relationship with other Alpha chapters.

"Valley Stream Alpha and Oceanside Alpha always got along great, but Oceanside Alpha and Baldwin Alpha didn't get along well at all. Here is a perfect example. We went into Baldwin Burger King once, and a lot of Baldwin Omega guys jumped on our car. There were three of us, and there were at least twelve of them. They were all over the car, and there was a whole pack of Baldwin Alpha guys there, and they didn't lift a finger to help us out. We had to push and shove our way out of there. It was uncomfortable with Baldwin Alpha. They didn't give a shit if we got jumped since we were from Oceanside. With any other chapters, we got along OK. Freeport were good guys. Rockville Centre were good guys. My best friend, Greg Colarossi, was from Rockville Centre Alpha."

Fraternity life in the 1970s wasn't all about brawls and drinking, although it played a big part in the social scene. However, as rare an occurrence as it was, we did do some charitable things. When I was fourteen years old and a new AOT member in the spring of 1978, we played a marathon softball tournament on the baseball field behind the gym at Oceanside High School. The event was planned in the closing weeks of President John Jaeger's class. The softball game was played to collect money for muscular dystrophy.

Each member of the Oceanside chapter was required to collect $20 from sponsors. We were each given a sponsor sheet, and we were supposed to collect $2 from each sponsor until we had collected $20. I went door-to-door, and I remember it was not too bad collecting. I had no difficulty collecting my share of sponsors. Some people did question me about the time and date of the games, and I always told them they were invited to come over to the high school and watch us play; in fact, we were told to invite each person who sponsored us to watch the games. The whole thing was on the up-and-up. We got permission from the high school to use the field for the day, and they were supposed to have the field lights turned on for us after dark.

It was a beautiful sunny spring day, and we had a great turnout. Most of the active members of the Oceanside chapter were there at some time in that day. Guys came and went all throughout the day, but we had enough guys there to have two teams playing consecutively all day long. We had planned to play game after game all day long from 11:00 AM until 11:00 PM. I remember people from the Muscular Dystrophy Association came down mid-afternoon to bring us sodas. They brought us about a dozen cases of cheap RC sodas, and they were piss warm, but we drank them anyway. I actually don't recall anybody bringing beer that day. That was probably because we knew the Muscular Dystrophy Association people would be coming to watch us, and we didn't want to look like thugs. I remember President John Jaeger giving them the money we had collected at the same time they dropped off the sodas for us. I don't think they stayed long to watch us play, though.

I was never a good athlete, but that day was a lot of fun. I stayed the whole day and played almost every game. We actually didn't get to play until 11:00 PM as planned. The field lights never came on like we had been told they would, so we had to call it a day around 8:00 PM, when it got too dark to see the ball. But we did have fun, and it was one of those rare occasions when the fraternity actually gave back to the community. And because it was such a good cause, it was easy for us to collect the money.

On other occasions, when the fraternity needed money for a not-so-good cause—namely, our treasury—we would raffle off a "basket of cheer." A basket of cheer was a gift basket filled with bottles of various liquors. Each brother would be given $20 worth of raffle booklets, selling one raffle for $1. These raffles were always a pain in the ass to sell because nobody ever won the basket. People were wise to that, and usually, most AOT brothers would just pull $20 out of their own pockets to pay for the raffle tickets they were responsible to sell because they couldn't sell the tickets, and the fraternity required brothers to come up with the money whether they sold the raffles or not.

For me, the closing act on Oceanside AOT in the 1970s was the big brawl in front of Oceanside High School at the end of the 1979 school year. Tom Shriver was AOT president that year, and he was actually expelled from school as a result of the rumble. The fight was between AOT and Phi, as usual. It involved about twenty or so members in a free-for-all right under the portico in front of the school. The whole thing began when AOT members found an AOT tee shirt partially burned in the back of the school; and in retaliation, they tore a Phi shirt to pieces in front of a bunch of Phi members, and that sparked the brawl. Once the fight broke out, AOT and Phi members were bolting out of their classes to jump into the fight. According to witnesses, the AOT members kicked ass that day, with only one AOT member suffering an injury. This brawl was the beginning of the end of AOT and the other fraternities in Oceanside. The school administration took a zero-tolerance approach to fraternity violence after this, and the whole fraternity system became a house of cards by the mid-1980s.

Oceanside AOT group picture in front of Oceanside High School

Valley Stream Central AOT at Anti Drug Parade, 1970

Oceanside AOT at Memorial Day Parade, 1978

Valley Stream Central AOT younger brothers circa 1971

Oceanside AOT brew-up in front of Oceanside High School

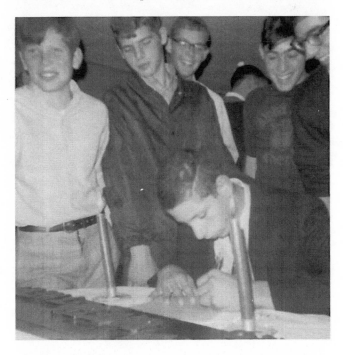

Valley Stream AOT induction ceremony circa 1972

Oceanside AOT, 1978

CHAPTER NINE

How Did I Get Here?

It was March of 1978 when I was inducted into Alpha Omega Theta Fraternity. However, there was a long chain of events that led to my joining AOT. My earliest recollections of fraternities were when I was a young kid, around seven or eight years old. My two uncles were in Omega Gamma Delta Fraternity. I remember when my younger uncle Greg was dogging for Omega and his older brother, my uncle Jim, was dogging Greg at home day and night. I remember when I was a kid, I liked the Omega tee shirts with the skull and crossbones on top of the shield. I had lived in Manhattan for a few years when I was in grammar school, and I remember a street gang called the Black Spades, who used to congregate in the park where we played after school.

A few years later, when I began the seventh grade, I was most excited about going into junior high school because that was when fraternity membership began. I recall seeing dozens of girls all wearing colored ribbons in their hair, signifying they were dogging for the various sororities. Girls dogging for Tau Delta Gamma wore blue-and-red ribbons, and girls wearing red-and-white ribbons were dogging for Delta Pi Delta. Most of these girls who began pledging were all in seventh grade. I couldn't help but notice that nobody in my class had begun dogging for any fraternity yet.

I was in math class talking to my friend Mel, and I asked him if he knew anyone who was dogging for a fraternity yet. He replied that fraternities didn't start recruiting until the eighth grade. We were both disappointed, but we figured we would get asked when it was our time. The seventh grade was tough enough on a kid without a fraternity anyway. Just trying to adjust to a new school, rotating classes every forty-two minutes, getting pushed around by bigger, older kids was enough to deal with. I settled in and made new friends during the seventh grade, some who would be my friends all through high school.

By the beginning of eighth grade, I was changing and becoming an adolescent typical of the late 1970s. I wanted to have cool friends and be seen with the right crowd. My best friend at the time was Tommy Farnswell. His real name was George, George Thomas Farnswell, but he had always been called Tommy. Throughout my seventh- and eighth-grade years, Tommy and I were inseparable. Tommy lived one block away from me, and we had been friends since were kids playing hide-and-go-seek in our neighbors' backyards.

Right at the beginning of the school year, Tommy had become friends with some older kids in the high school. I don't how he met them, but their names were Gerard Rosello, Brad Gaynor, Jimmy Benedict, and Pat Giron. All were high school juniors, except for Pat Giron, who was in ninth grade—the same as Tommy, although Pat went to Catholic school and not Oceanside Junior High like us.

I instantly thought these guys were cool. They all wore leather bomber jackets and Frye boots. They strutted around Atlantic Avenue like they owned it, and when we hung with them, it was like we owned the street too. Sometimes on Saturday nights, Jimmy Benedict would "borrow" his mother's car, and we would go cruising around town. In addition to the good feeling I got from being with a cool crowd, I was also introduced to something that would be a big part of my life for many years. These guys turned Tommy and me on to smoking marihuana for the first time.

As soon as I felt what it was like to get high, I was totally into it, and I smoked almost every day for many years. I would become what was considered a stoner through all of junior high and high school. Weed was pretty cheap back then. We would all chip in a few dollars and get a dime bag, which would get us about six to eight joints, depending on how fat they were rolled. In 1978, Oceanside still had plenty of vacant lots and abandoned houses, so we never had a problem finding a place to hang out and smoke. I remember on Long Beach Road, where there is now a Party City, there used to be a vacant lot right next to the Oceanside Veterinarian Hospital. Inside that lot there was a four-foot ditch someone had dug. We would jump into it, and our heads would be below the level of the spotlights the cops would shine back and forth from their cars when they passed by. We would just stay still, and the lights would go right over our heads.

We also found a lot on Atlantic Avenue that was pretty large and went way back from the street. We actually built a small shack toward the back of that lot so we would have some kind of shelter in the cold winter. It was perfect because there were no residential neighbors on either side of the lot, and the commercial property on the left and right was not in use, so no one ever noticed

—

us going back there. The place soon became a popular spot, and we actually had to expand and add a room to it. It was all built with plywood that was found or pilfered, old two-by-fours, and the foundation was built on skids. We carpeted the floor, put insulation in the walls, and we would leave our smoking gear there until other people started using "the shack," as we called it, and we didn't want our stuff stolen.

These guys also introduced me to shoplifting, which I never liked and never let become a habit. But at that time, they insisted that we go to the local A&P Supermarket and steal Sternos to keep warm. Despite all the insulation and the doubled-up plywood, it was still freezing in that shack in the dead of winter, and Sternos used for keeping trays of food warm made just enough heat to warm up the shack. So when we had to, if we had no money, we would steal Sternos from the local A&P.

After a while, the luster of hanging with these guys began to wear off. They started treating Tom and me like little kids to be pushed around. When we walked down the street and we passed tall bushes or hedges, these assholes would suddenly scream "football" and start pushing us into the bushes. It may have been humorous once or twice; I assure you, it became downright painful, and I would go home with scratches all over my body and face.

One night, when we were in the shack, there was some conversation going back and forth. I was too stoned to remember what it was about, but I remember Jimmy Benedict getting pissed at me for some reason, and he threw something at me that bounced off my knee. I thought it was a cigarette lighter, but all the other guys started saying, "Holy shit, Jimmy, you stabbed him." I was smiling and laughing; I didn't feel a thing. I told them that he didn't throw a knife; it was a cigarette lighter or an ashtray. I wasn't hurt. But they brought a flashlight over to my knee, and I had an eighth-of-an-inch slice in my pant leg right on the center of my knee. I rolled up my pant leg to check it, and there was a small stab wound that was oozing blood and went to the bone.

Jimmy became panicked and begged me not to press charges. The other guys were busting his balls and telling him that I could claim attempted murder if I wanted to. Jimmy was almost in tears, and he started putting pressure on my knee to stop the bleeding, and he was telling me to walk around to keep my knee active.

I was really stoned out beyond belief, and I didn't feel a thing. I thought they all were making a big deal out of nothing. I told Jimmy to forget about it since I wasn't hurt anyway. Later that night, I was walking home with Tommy, and he was telling me that what Jimmy did was asinine and reckless. Tommy insisted that Jimmy picked up a folding knife and deliberately threw it at me, and that it was pure luck that it didn't hit me in a vital part of my body. I was still thinking it was not such a big deal and told Tom to forget the whole thing.

After all, our entire walk home was almost two miles, and my knee felt fine as we walked.

The next morning, I woke up still fuzzy from being stoned the night before, and I stepped onto the floor. As soon as my full body weight was on my right leg, I collapsed onto my bedroom floor. It all came back to me at that moment, and I remembered Jimmy throwing that knife at me. I sat on my bedroom floor and looked at my knee; it was still oozing blood, and I could see the stab went right to the knee bone. At that moment, I was pissed and realized Jimmy and those other guys were assholes, and I needed new friends.

By this time, Tommy and I had been hanging out with these guys for about three or four months; we had been drawn into their circle of friends. It wasn't so easy to get away from them. Shortly after the knife-throwing incident, they started pressuring Tommy and me into something else. All of these guys were members of the Squires. They had explained to me that the Squires were connected to the local Knights of Columbus, and as such, they were allowed to wear their jackets in school. Fraternities were not allowed to wear jackets with emblems or fraternity names on them in school in Oceanside. I remember they wore blue Windbreaker jackets with the word *Squires* on the back in yellow lettering. I thought they were dumb-looking jackets, and I had no desire to own one, much less be seen wearing one.

Because the Squires were connected to the Knights of Columbus, they were, in effect, a strictly Catholic organization. Gerard Rosello and Jimmy Benedict started asking me a lot of questions about my religious affiliation. I told them my mother was Catholic and my father was Jewish and that I myself had no affiliation or membership in any church or temple. They started pressuring me to get baptized into the Catholic Church and become a member of St. Anthony's Church in Oceanside so that I would be eligible to join the Squires.

I had no problem with religion, but not just so that I could join some half-assed club. Joining a church and accepting Jesus was both serious and personal, and it turned me off to these assholes and their shitty club the Squires, for which they were pushing me to get baptized just to become a member of. I knew I had no intention of going along but didn't know how to get out of it. By this time, these guys had become bullies, and Tommy and I could not confront them or break away from them; we were younger and smaller than they were. Tommy and I spoke about it, and he told me that he had no intention of joining the Squires even though he already was eligible.

Tommy said, "I am already a member of St. Anthony's, and I would never join the Squires. They suck, they are a stupid club, and we will be goofed on if we are seen wearing those Windbreaker jackets."

"Well, how are we supposed to get out of this?" I said to Tommy.

"Well, I spoke to Pete Wilhelm a few days ago, and he asked me to dog for Alpha Omega Theta," Tommy said.

Pete Wilhelm was my next-door neighbor, and I had known him all my life. Pete was a junior in Oceanside High School and was well respected.

"And you know what?" Tommy said. "Pete is gonna ask you to dog too."

"Really?" I said. "I can't believe it that Pete would ask us to go down to Alpha."

"He wants both of us to dog for AOT together. We have to figure out how to get away from these assholes and their bullshit club. The Squires are so gay, and I would never want to be seen wearing a Squires jacket," Tommy said.

"Well, I am going to start hanging out with my friend Ed Oren. Ed likes AOT, he told me he thought AOT was the best fraternity to get into. Do you think Pete would ask him to dog with us also?" I said.

"I think we should try to get ourselves in first and worry about getting our friends in after we are members," Tommy said.

The next Friday night, instead of hanging out with Gerard Rosello and the others, I invited Ed Oren to sleep over my house. In the eighth grade, sleepovers were common and really were an excuse to stay up all night, smoke some weed, and talk about which girls in school we thought were pretty or about the sexiest TV actresses. In 1978, *Charlie's Angels* was one of the biggest shows on TV, so horny young teens like us talked a lot about Farrah Fawcett, Kate Jackson, and Jaclyn Smith.

But on this night, we also talked about fraternities. I asked Ed which fraternity he thought was the best to dog for, which one would he prefer to get into? He said Alpha was the best, and that was when I told him that my next-door neighbor Pete Wilhelm had asked me to dog for AOT.

"You were asked to pledge for Alpha?" Ed said. Ed was impressed and asked if he could dog too. I told him that I couldn't ask Pete on his behalf, but I assured Ed that if I got in, I would get him in soon thereafter.

After we smoked some pot, we decided to take a walk over to Nathan's to play some video games in the game room. I knew that if I ran into Gerard, Jimmy, and the others, they would be pissed that I ditched them on a Friday night; but I was sure they wouldn't be at Nathan's. I had been hanging with them for months, and we never went to Nathan's. But as luck would have it, they showed up. All of them—Gerard, Jimmy, Brad, and Pat—and even my friend Tommy was with them as well. When they saw me hanging out with Ed, they took off after us; Ed and I took off in another direction.

Over the next few days, each of those guys were calling my house and demanding I return to their little group. I must admit I was intimidated and afraid of them. They were telling me they were going to come to my house and drag me out if I didn't go back to hanging out with them. Well, they did come to my house, and they were banging on my front door, demanding I come out. I was contemplating calling the cops when I looked out my front window and I saw Pete Wilhelm walk into my front yard. I opened my front door and stepped outside, and I couldn't believe what I saw. There were four of them and only Pete, but Pete humbled all of them. Pete demanded to know what the hell they were doing ganging up on me in front of my own house. They started apologizing and insisting that there was no problem. Pete said there must be a problem for four of them to come all the way across town to gang up on me.

Pete suggested a one-on-one fight with me and Pat Giron since he was the youngest of them. I said I was ready to fight him if Pete kept the others from jumping in. Pat Giron refused to fight, so Pete told them to take a walk and never come back around our neighborhood. They apologized and skulked away, embarrassed and humiliated.

As soon as they were gone, Pete looked at me and said, "I told you those guys were assholes. Are you ready to get in with a good crowd and join a real fraternity?"

"Yes, I'm ready. What do I do? When do I begin?" I said.

"I am going to propose your name for membership at the next meeting, and Tommy Farnswell too. They will vote on you, and if you pass the vote with nobody voting you down, you will be invited to come to the next meeting for an interview," Pete said.

"So if I get voted down I don't get to dog?" I asked.

"Don't worry, you are in eighth grade. The youngest AOT members at this time are in tenth grade. Nobody knows you, so nobody is going to down you. You will go to the interview, and you will probably be asked to dog for the fraternity after the interview."

I spoke with Tommy later that night and told him what happened, and we were both thrilled to be getting a chance to dog for AOT and were relieved to be rid of Gerard Rosello, Brad Gaynor, Jimmy Benedict, and Pat Giron. We wondered what to expect when we went to the interview. We had no idea of what was expected of us when we were to begin dogging.

A few days after that, Pete told us that our names had been brought up at the last meeting and we were invited to come and interview with Alpha Omega Theta Fraternity at the next meeting. Pete gave us a briefing prior to attending the meeting. Besides Tommy and I, there would be three other dogs from Boardman Junior High School. There would also be two honorary inductions that night. We were told to wear slacks and shoes, plus collared shirts and ties to the meeting. Pete arranged for Tommy and me to get a ride to the meeting, which took place on Woods Place just off Woods Avenue.

It was winter, and there was snow on the ground although it wasn't snowing out. There were three other potential dogs from Boardman Junior High. They were Mike Apice and Andy Moran, who were in the eighth grade, and Anthony LaPaglia, who was in the ninth grade. There were two sophomores who were there for an honorary induction, which meant they would be getting in with just one night of beating and paddling if they passed their interviews, and we would be pledging for however long they told us we had to.

They put all of us in the driveway and told us to stay put and not to talk while they got the meeting started. I must admit I was totally ignorant to what was about to happen. I was only fourteen years old and had never gone down to a fraternity before. Even though they told us to not talk, we still chattered a little bit. The two honoraries that night were John Corano and Chuck Shawn. They started talking, and it came up in the conversation that if anyone was caught padding their pants to lessen the effects of paddling, they would be paddled bare-assed. John Corano said that he was wearing long johns, thermal underwear.

"You don't think they will consider long johns to be padding, do you?" John said.

"I wouldn't chance it," Chuck replied. "Lose them while you have the chance."

In a matter of ten seconds, John Corano had stripped down to his underwear, in the freezing cold of winter, right there in the driveway. He took the long johns, crumpled them up in a bunch, and stuffed them into the bushes running along the driveway. He then got dressed just as fast. He looked at all of us and asked that nobody tell what he had just done.

We were brought down to the basement one at a time to be interviewed. We were warned not to tell the others any of the interview questions or what went down during our interviews. They took the dogs first. I don't remember in which order we were interviewed, but I do remember my turn. I was walked into the side entrance of the house and walked down the stairs into the basement. I practically shit my pants when I walked into the room. There were about forty or more guys crammed into that basement, and it was dimly lit with candles.

These guys looked mean and serious. They were all in high school, and none were as young as me. They brought me to the center of the room, and the president of the chapter stepped up to me. The president of Oceanside Alpha in 1978 was John Jaeger. He was tall, slightly built, and had some acne or pockmarks on his face. He was stern and serious, and the mood was definitely scary.

"State your name to the fraternity," John Jaeger said to me.

"Fred Gross," I replied.

"John Jaeger, president," he said as he extended his hand to shake mine.

"Greg Bushemi, vice president. Bubba Howe, sergeant at arms," they said as each officer stepped up to shake my hand.

I was then told to sit on a small stool in the center of the room. I was then told by John Jaeger that each Alpha brother would now introduce themselves to me and I was required to remember all of their names. They started on the right side of the room, and all of the guys present started saying their names, and they went around the room in a clockwise movement as the names were rattled off in my direction. They mumbled and slurred their words as they spoke, and they threw in nonsense names like *Mickey Mouse, Jimi Hendrix, Mick Jagger*, and other stupid names. Obviously, I could not learn all their names in ten seconds, but John Jaeger seemed agitated and angry when I could not point to any brother in the room and remember his name. They repeated the process of the brothers rattling off their names two or three more times until I was sufficiently scared shitless.

When we got past the introductions, they started the interview. I was asked various questions by the AOT brothers, such as the following:

"Why did you come down to Alpha?"

"What can you do for us?"

"Can you host fraternity meetings at your house?"

"Can you have keg parties at your house?"

"Are you willing to defend the Alpha colors if you have to?"

"Do you know anyone in this room?"

"Why should we let you in our fraternity?"

I remember vividly one guy behind me, whom I could not see, grabbing a handful of my shoulder-length hair and saying, "Hey, Frampton, are you gonna get a crew cut?" Crew cuts were supposed to be a requirement when dogging for a fraternity. But it was the late 1970s, and everyone had long hair. A crew cut was definitely not in style at that time, and I was probably more afraid of cutting my hair than of catching a beating from the fraternity.

There were lots of other questions, and many of them were nonsense questions designed to rattle the person being interviewed. They were very effective. As I said before, I was only a little nervous when I arrived at the meeting, totally oblivious as to what the fraternity pledging experience was all about. And now I was scared shitless. They brought me back up to the driveway, told me not to talk about the interview, and grabbed the next pledge to be interviewed. They told me they would vote on me and would let me know if I had passed or was downed.

All the interviewees had been talking before the interviews, but after they started taking us in one by one, we all stopped talking completely. I guess seeing the look on the face of the guy just interviewed told the rest of them not to ask. They finished with the dogs' interviews first to get us out of the way so they could enjoy their time beating on the honorary inductees. They brought us back in one by one to tell us we had passed the interview and that we would start dogging the next day. I was told to report to the high school every day no later than 3:00 PM and to call my pledge master every night. I was paddled five times with a shaved-down baseball bat, and then I was told to go straight home. The paddling hurt more than I had expected. It was really painful to have a shaved-down baseball bat swung full force against the ass. For some dumb reason, I thought the paddling would be with paddleball racquets or something like that. I had no clue they would use shaved-down baseball bats.

All the dogs had gotten five shots; on the first night, dogs were usually given no more than five shots, but the number of shots and the severity of the physical hazing would increase each week at each meeting. We were then introduced to John Belatti, who was to be our pledge master during our dogging period. We were told that for the next four weeks, we would be dogging and that we were required to wear a collared shirt and tie to school each day. We were all told to run home because when the meeting adjourned, they would be driving around looking for us, and they would dog us if they saw us going home. Tommy and I lived close to each other, so we went the same way home. The other three dogs went in other directions. As luck had it, a car did pull up to us while we were walking, and it had Alpha guys in it. We were lucky they didn't dog us and actually offered us a ride home. In the car were both John Corano and Chuck Shawn, and both of them were wearing AOT sweaters. I must admit I was a bit jealous since I was told we would be dogging four weeks before we could get in the fraternity, and they got in after only one night of hazing.

The next day, Tommy and I went to school wearing ties, and it didn't take long for everyone to realize we were dogging for AOT. Since there were no Alpha members in the junior high school, we were on our own. There were about twenty members of Alpha Sigma Phi in Oceanside Junior High and about fifteen Omega Gamma Delta members. On our first day, we were more of a curiosity to everyone for being the only Alpha dogs in the school. Everyone asked me what frat I was dogging for, and then they would ask, "Why Alpha? There's nobody in AOT in this school."

The first-day feeling-out period was the last one I got from the other fraternity members in the junior high. The second day was when the bullshit started, and the third day was when the shit hit the fan.

My first day dogging was eventful in the fact that it was the first time I got drunk. It was Friday, and I went to the high school at 3:00 PM, as I was told to, and I found the only Alpha brother there waiting for me was my pledge master, John Belatti. He told me I would be going with him for the day, so I followed. We walked the back way out of the high school down a long, L-shaped blacktop path to what we called "the footbridge." It was a small wooden bridge that connected Arch Street and Arrow Street over a small creek. As we walked, John asked me if I had brothers or sisters he might know. I told him no, but I had uncles who went to Oceanside High School. When I told him who they were, he knew them from playing soccer. So I had scored a small brownie point. He asked me what bands I liked, and I told him I was into the Who, Jethro Tull, and Aerosmith. He stopped walking for a second and said, "You like Aerosmith? They are my favorite band. You're cool by me, related to the Volpes, and you listen to Aerosmith."

We walked all the way to his house, which was about a mile and a half from the school. When we got to his house, he told me to take a seat at his kitchen table, which I did. He brought a deck of cards and a bottle of whiskey, two shot glasses, and put them on the table. He asked me if I knew how to play poker. I said no, I didn't. He said he would teach me. We would be playing for shots of whiskey; loser of the hand took a shot. Before we started, he gave me a pair of green-and-red suspenders and told me I had to wear them with my shirt and tie every day until I finished dogging. I put on the suspenders.

We played the first hand, and I won, so John took a shot. I also won the second hand. It was the last hand I would win that night. I don't know how many hands we played, but we played until it got dark out. I was floating and feeling nice. I thought I was in control of my physical state. I would find out later what happens to a fourteen-year-old kid who drinks half a bottle of whisky.

I don't remember anything that we talked about while playing poker except that I told John I had to be home at a specific time. Not because I had a curfew, but because I had a double date with two girls from Boardman Junior High and my friend Tommy. We had met these girls at Times Square Store, which used to be in the location where Kohl's Department Store now sits. Back in our teen years, Times Square Store—or TSS, as it was called—was the place to hang out and meet other teens, especially girls. Shortly before we started dogging for AOT, Tommy and I had met two girls named Elise Kohn and Helene Goldstein. Helen was called Beanie by her friends. Beanie was going with Tommy, and Elise was my girlfriend, if you can call it that. The most we ever did with those girls was to sit on a couch and kiss them; sometimes we would spend all day at someone's house just making out, with marathon french-kissing sessions. Anyway, we were expecting the two girls to meet us at my house to hang out. We had only been going steady for a few days, and I wanted to look cool; so I told them it was totally cool to hang at my house and smoke pot in my bedroom, which actually was totally true. I smoked weed in my room all through my teen years. My house was a usual hangout all through junior high and high school because no one bothered us when we smoked pot and played music in my room.

The date was on a Friday night. The next order of business was that I was supposed to be able to get some pot to smoke that night. I had checked all over school that day with my usual sources and was unsuccessful in scoring any weed. Failure to deliver the smoke, as I had promised I could, would have been embarrassing; and we would have wound up sitting in my room with nothing to talk about and trying to break the ice. Weed was an amazing icebreaker, and I was eager to get some for this gathering.

I don't remember much about the marathon poker tournament John and I played that evening; it was all a blur. But I do remember asking him if he could get me some pot. I told him that Tommy and I had a date with two girls whom we wanted to impress, and I was supposed to cop some weed but could not find any. John told me that he was expecting Bubba Howe, the AOT sergeant at arms, to arrive at his house any minute. I remember him saying they were going to the Oak Beach Inn, or OBI, as it was called, that night. He said Bubba always had weed, and he would ask him to sell me some.

I remember when Bubba arrived; Bubba was called Bubba for a reason. He was a huge guy—tall and stocky, very intimidating, and not the kind of guy people wanted to get into a fight with. John asked Bubba to sell me some weed, and I remember Bubba saying that he didn't have enough to sell. But John pressed him and explained that the Alpha dogs had a hot date with two young chicks and we wanted to impress them. Bubba said OK and offered to sell me $10 worth. It was perfect, just enough to roll four of five joints to smoke with the girls. After he sold me the weed, they said they had to go. I don't remember if I asked them for a ride or if they knew I was too drunk to make it home walking, but I wound up getting in the car with them. All I remember was getting dropped off in front of my house and those guys speeding away right after they shoved me out the car door. It was likely they knew there would be trouble when I came home shitfaced, and they split the scene and drove away from my house really fast.

As I walked up my front walkway, I saw that Tommy was waiting there with Elise and Beanie. They had been waiting about thirty or forty minutes. I was late, but obviously, since I was dogging, I couldn't leave until dismissed. As soon as I walked up to them, they saw I was staggering drunk. Tommy asked me what had happened, and I told him I had been doing shots of whiskey with John Belatti. I tried to act like it was cool and everything was OK, but the whiskey was starting to hit me hard.

I told them I had scored the weed and invited them up to my room to hang out. I could hear Elise whispering to Beanie, "Look at the condition he's in. He's gonna pass out as soon as he sits down." I was embarrassed, but I pretended not to hear it. I figured that once we got to my room, put on some good tunes, and lit up a joint, it would all work out. It didn't.

I was sure they would like my room. My family wasn't well-off, and I didn't have any fancy or nice furniture, but I was pretty proud of the way I had set up my room. I had two car seats that Pete Wilhelm's brother Dave had given to me and an army footlocker, which I had found and put in between the two car seats like a coffee table to roll joints on. I had always asked every person that came into my room to sign the footlocker. It was covered with all the names and graffiti from all my friends and acquaintances. Every person who came into my room signed that footlocker, and everybody seemed to like to look at all the graffiti to see who had signed before them. I actually wish I still had that footlocker. What nostalgia if I could look at that now.

I also had a morbid sense of humor and style. I liked creepy stuff, and I had a GI Joe doll hanging from a noose with a hood over his head from the center of my ceiling. I also had placed pieces of netting in the four corners of my room, and I had put rubber spiders in them to make the room look infested. I also had black light posters on all my walls of demons and dragons and shit like that. I kept a black light on whenever people were hanging in my room. It was trippy. All my friends liked hanging in my room; it was cool-looking and a cool place to pass a joint or a bong around.

The girls seemed to like my room, and I remember rolling a joint and passing it around. Tommy and Beanie were sitting on the two car seats, and Elise and I sat next to each other on my bed. After taking one or two tokes off the joint, the room began to spin, and I could no longer keep my head up. I passed out right next to her. I remember being semiconscious, and I could hear them talking. Elise was sitting right next to my hand, and I could hear Beanie say something about me touching Elise's ass. Come to think of it, I probably was copping a feel under the guise of being passed out, but I really was out of it and couldn't move. They just hung out, smoking more weed while I was passed out until I woke up and ran for the bathroom, projectile-vomiting in the hallway before I got to the toilet.

I barfed my brains out and dry-heaved a few times as well. I went back to my room and lay down on my bed again, this time to pass out for the night. I remember hearing my aunt Valerie come into my room and ask what had happened to me. Tommy told her I had been drinking prior to coming home, and she told them all they had to leave at that point.

Such a well-planned night had turned into a total fucking disaster. It was a total cluster fuck and not at all like I had planned. I remember being really embarrassed the next time I saw Elise. We continued dating for about two months. Shortly after my getting inducted into Alpha, we stopped seeing each other, as did Tommy and Beanie.

I did get into some trouble for coming home drunk, but I was able to blame the fraternity for making me play drinking games, so I didn't get grounded as I remember. I almost never got grounded when I was a teen. I also experienced my first hangover that weekend, and I stayed in the whole weekend recovering.

On Monday morning, I went to school wearing my tie and the suspenders that John had given me. Wearing a tie was not fashionable in 1978 for a teen, but I really liked the green-and-red suspenders. Well, first thing in the morning, before classes started, I was approached at my locker by several members of Alpha Sigma Phi. The trouble was about to begin. Anthony Aiello, who was the toughest guy in the eighth grade and the de facto leader of the Phi guys in the eighth grade, had brought his two cronies, Phil Stone and Don McCartney, to surround me and intimidate me. They were definitely mean guys, especially Anthony Aiello. He was actually expelled from school in the eighth grade for bullying half the school. He was practically a full-grown man at the age of fourteen. He was almost six feet tall, and teachers didn't want to break up his fights. A lot of people who joined Phi did so to stay on Aiello's good side. He had a small cult thing going on around him at that time.

I would have many problems with Anthony Aiello over the years, and this was the beginning. Anthony asked me why I was dogging for Alpha Omega Theta, and I said I was invited by my friend and neighbor. He told me that since there was no AOT in Oceanside Junior High, I was barking up the wrong tree for trying. He let me know that there was nobody in school to back me up and that I was in hostile territory with a combined total of thirty-five or so members of Alpha Sigma Phi and Omega Gamma Delta all around me all day long in school.

I was basically told, not asked, to drop from dogging for AOT and to show up at the Phi meeting that same night to be inducted into Phi. The big attraction to Alpha Sigma Phi for all the junior high teens was that Phi didn't take dogs or pledges. Kids in the eighth, ninth, and sometimes even seventh grade were inducted into Phi with a one-night induction. So they had a large number of members in both Oceanside Junior High and Boardman Junior High. I was warned by Aiello that this was my only chance to drop out of AOT and join Phi, or there would be trouble.

These guys were scary, and I was intimidated, but I was warned by the Alpha brothers that Phi would harass me and threaten me to quit pledging AOT. They had told me that I was to tell them as soon as anyone in Phi bothered me and that they would come down to the junior high to back me up. One of my problems was that I was both stubborn and prideful. I was too stubborn to let Aiello and his cronies make me quit dogging, much less join Phi. I always knew, even at a young age, that Alpha Sigma Phi was a degenerate fraternity, and there was no way I would go down to Phi, not even under threat. Additionally, I was too proud to go ask the AOT guys to get the Phi guys off my back. I figured I would ride it out, and it would blow over in a day or two when they saw I was not dropping out of dogging. Well, on both accounts, I would bring a shit storm onto myself.

Obviously, I didn't go to the Phi meeting that night, and I didn't tell the Alpha brothers that I was being threatened and harassed by Phi when I showed up at the high school for dogging that day. The next day at school, there was an eerie silence from the Phi and Omega members in school. They seemed to be oblivious of me, and I really thought the whole thing was forgotten. I was very wrong.

Eric Haber was one of my best friends in junior high. We sat next to each other in homeroom for three years; our lockers were right next to each other. Eric was my fly on the wall when it came to what was going down with Phi. He was friends with most of them, but he was best friends with me. Eric came to me early in the day, maybe after third or fourth period, and told me that Phi and Omega had planned to jump me and beat the shit out of me when I walked past Farmer Joel's on Oceanside Road on my way to go dog at the high school. Their plan was to wait for me there in the parking lot and wait for me to walk by. Eric was serious, and he was afraid for me. He told me those guys were really pissed that I was trying to bring AOT back into the junior high, and even more pissed that I didn't drop dogging when they told me to.

I knew he was telling me the truth, and the only way I could avoid this was to either cut ninth period and leave early or take a long walk down Merle Avenue to Long Beach Road, and then go around in a big circle to avoid Farmer Joel's. The better and easier plan was to cut ninth period. I had planned to do just that, but I got caught trying to leave school by a hall monitor and was forced to go to class. Now I was screwed. Whether I liked it or not, I had to take the long roundabout path to the high school. And since the Alpha brothers expected that I would be at the high school no later than 3:00 PM, it was virtually impossible to take such an out-of-the-way route and get there on time when my classes dismissed at 2:35 PM. Nevertheless, I took off in the direction of Long Beach Road and figured if I ran as fast as I could, I might make it to the high school by 3:00 PM and still avoid Farmer Joel's.

I got to the high school at 3:10 PM, and the lobby was mostly empty. The only AOT guys there waiting for me were Rich Silver and Ron Mayer. They didn't say a thing about me being late, and I didn't tell them why I was late. Again, my pride would not allow me to tell them I was having trouble and to ask for help. Little did I know that help had already been sent.

I found out the next day in homeroom from Eric Haber what had happened at Farmer Joel's. It seemed that word about the Phi/Omega plan to jump me had made its way to the high school, and the Alpha brothers got wind of it. They sent two carloads of Alpha guys to Farmer Joel's around 2:30 PM to catch the crowd of Phi's and Omega's waiting for me. Eric had witnessed it, and as he described it, there were about thirty guys waiting to jump me in Farmer Joel's parking lot. Can you imagine thirty of the school's toughest Phi and Omega guys all waiting to jump one skinny, 140-pound fourteen-year-old eighth grader? What a tough bunch of guys, huh? A bunch of bullies and scumbags was what they really were.

Then all of a sudden, two cars pulled into Farmer Joel's, and eight guys got out. They were Alphas wearing green-and-red sweaters, and they waded right into the crowd, looking for the biggest, toughest-looking guy there. As I heard from more than one person who witnessed it, they grabbed a guy named Mario Romeo by the lapels of his Phi sweater and slammed him up against a car and told him that he and all his fraternity brothers would be getting visits from AOT every day after school if anyone else fucked with the Alpha dogs. As they walked away, another Phi guy named Buddy Washington mouthed off, and an Alpha guy backhanded him in the mouth. It silenced the whole crowd of Phi and Omega guys. They thought they were so tough; thirty of them, and they didn't have the balls to stand up to eight Alpha members from the high school. There was a large crowd from the junior high that had gathered to watch this whole thing. They expected to see me get the ever-loving shit kicked out of me, and instead, they saw eight guys in green-and-red sweaters bitch-slap and manhandle thirty combined members of Phi and Omega. The Phi and Omega guys were humbled that day, and the junior high crowd saw the true quality of Alpha Omega Theta. The bullshit and the problems I had with Phi stopped that day and for the duration of my dogging. Although the shit would stir up again many more times before I finished junior high.

With the temporary hands-off attitude Phi had taken toward me, the only thing now for me to concentrate on was dogging for Alpha and getting through the next four weeks. Dogging was nothing like I imagined. It was worse. They called it dogging for a reason, and that reason was that you were literally treated like a dog during the pledging period. You had to go with them everywhere and always stay a few steps behind them while walking. You had to do everything they told you to do without question. You couldn't speak until spoken to. You had to be humble at all times and always address an Alpha brother with the standard greeting. I remember it like it was yesterday.

"Greetings, Mr. Smith, most excelled brother of Alpha Omega Theta Fraternity. I am but a humble dog who most joyfully awaits your every command, sir."

Yep, I had to say that all the time to every Alpha brother who approached me. I also had to carry plenty of gum for everyone at all times. They had me doing crazy stuff like faking convulsions on the floor of the high school lobby. I was always being sent to grub up cigarettes for Alpha brothers. But the most embarrassing and difficult of the dogging tasks was when they would tell me to go up to girls and pinch their asses or grab their tits. There was one girl named Doreen, who was the girlfriend of Alpha brother Ron Mayer. The other AOT guys would always make me try to grab both her tits with both hands. She would get so pissed, and I always got my face slapped, and Ron would get really pissed and say, "Stop trying to grab my girlfriend's tits." As if I had a choice in the matter. I had to do whatever I was told by an Alpha brother, even when it pissed off another Alpha brother. And trust me, that was a big part of dogging: being made to piss off other Alpha brothers so they would get mad and dog me harder.

When being given multiple orders from multiple brothers, a dog was required to fulfill the first order given first, then the second, then the third, and so on. Sometimes there would be six or seven guys all telling me to do stuff at the same time, and if I couldn't decipher which orders went in which order, I would catch hell from all of them. My first day of dogging was spent drinking and getting to know my pledge master, as well as Bubba Howe. I thought dogging would be a breeze. I was wrong about that. My second day of dogging was my first day getting the full fraternity pledge experience, running around the high school lobby making an ass of myself for the amusement of the Alpha brothers.

Another daily ritual of dogging was when the pledge master would set up the dog's schedule for whom he would go with each day. They were like piranha, all wanting the dog for the day. It was humiliating; the pledge master would tell me I had to go with these guys today, and they owned me for the day. Whatever they said, I had to do it. And each day, I would be going with different AOT brothers. If I was lucky, I would only be doing menial tasks like cleaning someone's room or doing dishes.

On my second day of dogging, I was sent to go with Rich Silver, Ron Mayer, Steve Gold, and Guy Schiavone. I was taken to Rich Silver's house. When I got there, Rich Silver poured glasses of soda for all the brothers, and Steve Gold said, "Don't forget our pledge. Get him something also."

I thought, *Nice guys offering me a drink. This won't be so bad.*

"You want us to get you something cold and refreshing?" Steve Gold said.

"Sure," I said. "Thank you."

What they gave me wasn't soda, and it sure wasn't refreshing. I don't even think it was edible. They had taken every condiment in the refrigerator: ketchup, mustard, mayonnaise, hot sauce, soy sauce, relish, horseradish, eggs, and God knows what else. I can't tell you how bad it smelled and tasted; I can't even tell you what color it was. I think they created a new color in the spectrum that day. But I can tell you it was lumpy, chunky, it had texture, and it smelled really bad. I think the smell was worse than the taste.

"Drink up, dog," Steve Gold said as he put the glass of smelly mud in front of me.

"You're kidding me, right?" I said.

Steve stepped up to me nose to nose. "Do I look like I am kidding with you, dog?" Steve said in a tone that was extremely annoyed.

I looked at all of them looking at me, and I realized this was my first really tough test. Refusal to drink it would have led to me getting demerits, and too many demerits got a pledge dismissed.

"I'm not fucking around with you. Drink it, dog," Steve said.

At that moment, Guy Schiavone came up to me and put his hand on my shoulder and said, "I know it looks nasty, and it is, but I dogged for this fraternity, and I had to drink the same shit, and I survived it. If you want to get into AOT, you are going to be given plenty of nasty shit to eat and drink before your four weeks of dogging is over. Just to show you that it isn't so bad, save the last of it for me, and I will swig it down too."

Somehow, Guy made it seem not so bad, and I picked up the glass. The guys were all staring at me; Guy told me to just down it really fast, so I did. I turned the glass up and started swallowing in big chugs. It was as nasty as it looked and smelled. Guy was good for his word; he grabbed the glass from me before I finished it, and he downed the last of it.

"You see? Not so bad. Piece of cake," Guy said.

Steve Gold was annoyed with Guy for drinking some of the concoction, but I was glad he did. This group of guys was the one that took me dogging probably 75 percent of the time. Other Alpha brothers would request to take a dog for the day from the pledge master, but these guys delighted in abusing and torturing me. I was always being told to bother and harass people, especially girls; I was constantly being given vile, nasty shit to eat and drink. One time, they had all gotten McDonald's, and while they ate Mickey Dees, they gave me a Gaines-Burger to munch on. For those who don't remember, Gaines-Burgers were dog treats that were shaped like hamburgers. It was the nastiest thing I ever ate. It was dry and tasted like dirt. They didn't even give me a drink to wash it down with. I also was forced to chew aluminum foil. If you have never tried that, don't. If you have metal fillings, which most people do, chewing aluminum foil is like plugging your teeth into a light socket.

On the first day of dogging, two of the dogs from Boardman Junior High had dropped out already. Andy Moran and Mike Apice had been threatened by Phi members in Boardman Junior High and decided dogging for AOT was not for them. Anthony LaPaglia dogged for the first week until he had his fill of hazing.

After our first week of dogging, our second meeting as Alpha pledges was held at my next-door neighbor Pete Wilhelm's house. I was more afraid at the second meeting than at the first one. Before the meeting, Anthony LaPaglia came to my house so we could go to the meeting together. We got there, and Tommy Farnswell was already there. The brothers were gathering, and the meeting had not started yet. They started messing with us beforehand.

In a moment I will never forget, a guy named Paul Barbaro came into the meeting, and instantly, all the guys started chanting, "Headbutt, headbutt, headbutt." Paul Barbaro smiled and looked at the three of us standing next to each other. He stepped up to us and said, "Which one has the hardest head?" He extended the middle knuckle on his right hand as if he was going to knock on a door; instead, he knocked on each of our heads and then suddenly grabbed Anthony LaPaglia, who was standing in the middle. He said, "You have a hard head." He grabbed Anthony by the tie he was wearing and pulled him two steps forward; he then grabbed Anthony by his ears and headbutted him right between the eyes.

The sound was scary. It sounded like a coconut being smashed with a baseball bat. It was a hollow-crack kind of sound. I was standing right next to Anthony, and his eyes rolled up into his head, and he dropped to the floor. He had to be picked up because he could not stand back up on his own power. Anthony was delirious and out of it for the rest of the night. After the meeting started, they started taking us "around the room." Going around the room was when they took the pledges around to each fraternity brother, and each Alpha brother got one free shot to hit the pledge. We were slapped, backhanded, punched in the chest and stomach.

We all were getting the shit beaten out of us, but I saw the look on Anthony's face, and he looked barely conscious. He was barely able to keep his head upright. After the beatings, they paddled us. This time we were given seven shots each. We were again told to run home as fast as we could because they would be looking for us after the meeting. I lived right next door, and Tommy lived one block away, so we knew we would get home before the meeting let out. But Anthony lived a few miles away, and the only way he could go home was to go straight down Waukena Avenue. I offered to let Anthony stay at my house until the meeting let out, but he decided he would run for it and try to get home before the meeting let out.

The next day, when Tommy and I showed up for dogging, Anthony wasn't there. We were told he had dropped out of pledging, and now it was only Tommy and I. I spoke to Pete Wilhelm later that night and found out that Anthony suffered a mild concussion from the headbutting, and he could not continue dogging. Tommy and I continued to dog, and we spoke to each other almost every night to give each other support. Whenever one of us was thinking of dropping out, the other would talk him out of it.

Most of the time, we were dogged separately; we went with different Alpha brothers. But one Saturday afternoon, we were both taken to Bubba Howe's apartment in Freeport. We were told to clean the kitchen, do the dishes, and clean the bathroom. The bathroom was so nasty it looked like it hadn't been cleaned in years. The bathtub had dirt caked onto it, and we needed Brillo pads with scouring powder to get it clean. It took us hours to clean the place; it was really filthy. After we finished cleaning, we were brought into the living room to hang out. They had a really long bong they were smoking pot out of. It was so long that it had to be lit by a second person. The bowl to the thing was four feet away from the person smoking the bong. Tom and I were each given a hit off the bong. Since the chamber was so long, the one hit each got us both stoned out really good.

The rest of the time I dogged, it was the usual stuff: carrying lots of gum and stating the greeting to all Alpha brothers, running around doing stupid shit in crowded areas, and going to the meetings each week. There was one time I was taken to Ron Mayer's house by Ron and Rich Silver, and they drew my face up to look like Alice Cooper with permanent magic marker. I went home, and the stuff would not wash off. After showering, I saw that the permanent black marker didn't even lighten up, so I found a jar of Pond's face cream that my grandmother used, and I smeared it all over my face from forehead to chin. I let it sit for a half hour, and when I washed it off, the sink was filled with black goo. It was effective in getting the stuff off, much to my relief.

The third meeting we were supposed to attend was missed by both Tommy and me. I could not find out where it was being held, and I called everyone I knew. Back then, nobody had cell phones or answering machines, so if you called someone and they were not home, that was that. So they seemed annoyed we missed a meeting, but it wasn't held against us at the time.

Finally, our induction night had come. I was in school that day, nervous about it, but relieved it was almost over. Around lunchtime, I started getting a headache and felt dizzy, so I went to the school nurse. All I wanted was a cold compress or an aspirin. But the nurse said I had a fever and had to be sent home. I didn't want to be sent home because I had my Hell Night that evening to go to. I was sure if I was sent home sick, I would not be able to go. By the time I was taken home, my fever had gotten worse, and I was bedridden. My temperature was close to 104, and I was delirious. The meeting was at 7:30 PM, and around 6:30 PM, my friend Tommy came to my house to see if I was ready for the induction night. He saw I was sick in bed, and he told me he would tell them I had no choice but to stay home.

My aunt Valerie gave me an alcohol rub to lower the fever, and I remember how ice-cold the alcohol was against my burning-hot chest. I went to sleep for a few hours, and when I woke up, my fever had gone down a lot.

When I awoke, my aunt Valerie came into my room and told me my friend Tommy had come back and wanted to see me. I told her to let him in. I was still a little feverish, but the high temperature had broken, so I was able to sit up in bed and talk. Tommy came into my room, and he was wearing an Alpha sweater. I will never forget how disappointed I was that I didn't get my sweater that night. All because I got a fucking fever and had to stay in bed.

Tommy told me that his induction was so easy. He was almost laughing because he couldn't believe how fast it had gone by. He told me he was taken once around the room, and then he got ten shots with paddles. He said the ten shots went by in ten or twelve seconds, and it was over really fast. I always hated the paddling more than the beating, and hearing that they ran through it really fast set my mind at ease. At least the worst part of it would not take so long when it was my turn.

I asked Tommy what they said about me not being there for induction night, and he said they didn't make a big deal out of it. They told him to tell me my dogging would be extended another week until the next meeting. It sucked to have to dog another week while the guy I started dogging with had already gotten his colors; but the meeting I missed was on a Thursday, and the next meeting was set for Monday, so I really had to dog Friday, Saturday, and Monday. The last days of my dogging were the same shit—acting like a fool in public—except this time, my friend and former fellow dog Tommy was now a brother and was allowed to dog me as well.

I finally finished my pledging, five weeks of dogging—well, really four and a half. And now it was Monday night, and I was ready for my induction. I was scared, but I kept thinking of Tommy saying the whole thing would be over in a flash. I remember getting ready to go, putting on my shirt and tie, and going downstairs into my kitchen. My grandmother was there drinking coffee with her nephew, my second cousin Sal. Sal asked me what I was wearing a tie for, and I told him I was on my way to a fraternity meeting to get inducted. Sal tried to talk me out of it. He was telling me I would be sorry if I joined a group that was more like a gang than a brotherhood. I was a teenager and full of my own ideas on life, friendship, and peer pressure, and I figured, *What did he know?* I just put in nearly five weeks of dogging with weekly beatings and paddling's. There was no way I was going to just drop the whole idea now just because he thought it sounded stupid.

I straightened my tie, asked them to wish me luck, and walked out the door and went straight to Pete Wilhelm's house.

Oceanside AOT in front of Oceanside High School, 1978

Fred Gross in 1980.

Oceanside AOT brew-up, 1978

CHAPTER TEN

My Hell Night Part 2 and Beyond

I arrived at Pete Wilhelm's house early for the meeting; as I recall, I left off in chapter 1 with me sitting at the bottom of the stairs next to the room where the meeting was taking place. I had shown up at the meeting expecting it to be quick and easy, like Tommy Farnswell had said. But instead, I found that they were having second thoughts on inducting me.

It seemed that my missing two meetings, one of which was supposed to be my induction night, did not sit well with some of the Alpha brothers. Additionally, I failed to get the required crew cut. In fact, I never even cut my shoulder-length hair the entire time I dogged. There were a few Alpha brothers complaining that I had been a shitty dog. So these guys were voting on me again to decide if I would get blackballed. They may have been playing with my head, but I was really worried that they were going to send me home with no colors. I couldn't believe it.

After about twenty minutes of waiting there at the bottom of the stairwell, finally my pledge master, John Belatti, came for me. He didn't say anything except to motion me to come with him. He brought me into the center of the room, and the place was silent enough to hear a pin drop. John Jaeger came up to me and told me that they had voted and decided to allow me to be inducted but that I had to make up for the missed meetings. I didn't know exactly what that meant, but I would soon find out.

Then John said, "Take him around the room." And then Bubba Howe pinned my arms behind me in a "castle doors" position. For those who don't know what that is, castle doors position is when someone behind you pulls both of your arms back and locks them against his chest with his forearm and then grabs the back of your hair with his free hand or tucks his other free arm under your chin. Since I had long hair, he grabbed a fistful of it to control the position of my head. So with my arms pinned behind my back and my head immobilized, I was taken around the room in a clockwise movement. I was brought to each Alpha brother one at a time, and they got to take a free shot at me. Slaps to the face, backhands to the face, punches to the chest, kicks to the stomach; they hit me every which way, except they weren't allowed to kick the balls. Thank God for that, or I may not have ever fathered my children.

I had gone around the room starting at the twelve o'clock position and had gone all the way around and was back at the twelve o'clock position. I thought the beating was over, but no. Bubba kept me walking in a clockwise motion, and he was giving each guy in the room another shot at me. I couldn't believe that I was going around again. I was a fourteen-year-old kid who weighed no more than 140 pounds soaking wet, but these guys had no mercy for me at all. They used me for target practice. By the end of the second trip around the room, I could no longer hear anything except loud ringing in my ears. I saw people's mouths moving but could not hear them. Now to my shock, Bubba was taking me for a third trip around the room; I would have panicked except for the fact that I was delirious. Halfway through my third trip around the room, I lost the ability to keep my own head up, and my head was dangling from my neck. Bubba had to really pull my hair to position my head for each face slap and backhand. After the Alpha brothers had all gotten their slaps and kicks at me three times going around the room, the officers took their turns, and they gave as many slaps, punches, and kicks each as they wanted to give. Officers were allowed unlimited strikes.

Finally, the beating stopped after the third time around the room and the officers getting their piece of me. I was exhausted; my face was numb, my ribs hurt, my stomach hurt, my ears were still ringing. I was out on my feet. It was like walking in a dream. Now it was time for the paddling—but first, a little fun with food. They poured molasses down the back of my pants, and they gave me a raw egg and told me to put it between my butt cheeks, which I did. Now they took me to the end of the room and bent me over, head facing the wall and butt facing the room. They always positioned a guy on the longest side of the room so they could get the most forward momentum when they ran at you with the paddles. I was really scared now because the paddling was the worst part of it to me. Nothing hurt more than getting hit with a shaved-down baseball bat swung at your ass by a guy running full speed across a long basement.

But I thought about how Tommy told me that the paddling was rapid-fire and over in a few seconds. They bent me over; they had one guy fold over me and pin my two arms to my chest so I could not move them or stand upright. Then another guy lay facedown on the floor and hugged both of my ankles so I could not move my legs. They told me to put my tie in my mouth and bite down.

Then the paddling began. It was extremely painful. I felt each and every one of those shots as they swung baseball bats, axe handles, and two-by-fours at my ass and lower legs. That was the part that really hurt the most. Some guys took pleasure in striking you low and nailing the fleshy part of the leg below the ass and above the knees. Thigh shots, they were called, and a shaved baseball bat to the thighs was an instrument of torture.

I lost count after three shots; that's how much pain I was in. It seemed to go on forever, and I was starting to squirm. The guy lying on the floor holding my legs saw I was starting to freak out, and he yelled up to me, "It's almost over, Freddy." He had to yell because a room full of fraternity brothers swinging paddles at a pledge does tend to make a lot of noise.

I looked down at him since he was lying on the ground, and I asked him, "How many more shots?"

He replied, "Only ten more." I said, "What? I was only supposed to get ten shots." He laughed, and I knew I was screwed at that point. These guys were not going to stop until they had their fill.

Finally, they stopped, and the whole room rushed toward me. At first, I thought they were all going to gang up and do an Apache Line on me, but I realized they were now all patting me on the back and congratulating me. I heard John Jaeger say, "Someone put some colors on this guy." My friend Tommy stepped up and took off his sweater and helped me to put it on. Pete Wilhelm handed me an Alpha jacket as well.

John Jaeger was the first to give me the Alpha grip, the fraternity handshake. The Alpha handshake was four fingers curled toward the palm and the thumb curled around the four fingers. It was like two hooks hooking together. He told me this was to be used whenever greeting another Alpha brother. He also told me that whatever happened behind closed doors at an Alpha meeting stayed behind closed doors and never left the room. Everyone was shaking my hand with the Alpha grip and congratulating me.

After the meeting, some guys were telling me that they had never seen anyone get as many paddle shots as I had gotten. I asked how many I had been given, and nobody knew. They only knew that since I had missed two meetings, and for other infractions during pledging, I was to be taken around the room three times and given a paddle shot from each guy in the room, and the officers paddled me twice each. By my estimate, there were about forty guys in the room that night, and with officers going twice, I think I caught something like forty-five to fifty shots that night. I never saw anything like that happen again to anyone inducted after me.

I hung around Pete's basement until most of the guys were gone. I thanked Pete for bringing me down to AOT, and he told me to let him know if anyone gave me trouble at the junior high when I started wearing AOT colors to school.

I went home, and I went straight to the bathroom to shower and get cleaned up. I took off my underwear, and they were black from the molasses, and they were filled with eggshells. There was no point in even washing them. I just threw them away. I had eggshells embedded in my ass cheeks also. I looked at my ass in the mirror, and it was black and blue from the top of my butt to the backs of my knees. I could see the striped lines in the shape of baseball bats all over my legs. My face was bright red all over from being slapped so many times, and I had bruises on my ribs also from all the punches.

I got cleaned up, put on a pair of gym shorts, and went into the kitchen to get something to eat. I conversed with my grandmother and my cousin Sal, who was still at my house. As I turned to leave the room, my grandmother gasped and screamed, "Jesus, what did you let them do to you?"

"Its just part of the induction, Grandma, its no big deal," I said.

"So you let those guys do that to you just so you could join their club?" my cousin Sal said.

"It's not just a club, Sal. It's a fraternity," I said.

"You don't have to tell me, I know all about that shit. We had gangs when I was a kid no different than your fraternity. We beat the shit out of each other just like these guys did to you," Sal said.

"Well, the next time it won't be me getting beat," I said.

"So you get to join in on the next poor slob who is dumb enough to join your fraternity. I'm sure you and your new friends will have lots of fun together," Sal said.

"They're a bunch of animals. Why would you want to get into something like that?" my grandmother said.

"Your two sons Greg and Jimmy were both in Omega Gamma Delta. This is not new to you," I said to my grandmother.

"Yeah, well I didn't like it then, and I don't like it now," my grandmother said.

With that, I went up to my room, smoked a few hits of weed from a bong, and went to sleep.

The next day, I put on my AOT sweater and went to school. It's a funny thing after you get into a fraternity. Half the people congratulate you, and the other half kick you in the ass. Everybody knows you were paddled the night before, and they take some bizarre pleasure in kicking you in the ass. No one from Phi bothered me when I came to school wearing my colors. My friend Tommy and I were the only two Alpha guys in the school up against thirty-five to forty fraternity members from the other two fraternities.

The first day I was in AOT, I went to the high school after school to hang with the Alpha brothers as a full member of the brotherhood myself. They joked with me that I was coming to dog some more. Steve Gold came up to me and gave me the Alpha grip, and he said, "Sorry I was so rough on you when you dogged, but I am moving to Florida at the end of the year, and you are probably the last pledge I will get a chance to dog." I remember that all my dislike for Steve disappeared when he extended his hand to me. I really hated him when I dogged because he was the guy who always made me eat dog food and drink nasty shit. Although Steve never really hit me at the meetings, he got off on making the dogs squirm. He asked me to try to get him another dog before he moved in the summer. I told him I would try.

The following week after I was inducted into AOT, we were told that Rockville Centre AOT was having a party, and Oceanside AOT was invited. It was my first fraternity party, and they let us in for free. Tommy and I both got a ride there since neither of us had the means to get there on our own. It was a usual backyard keg party. There was a band playing and all the tap beer we could drink. I didn't get too drunk that night, but what I remember most about it was Tommy and I walking all the way to Hempstead, thinking we were heading back to Oceanside. When we got to Long Beach Road, we had no sense of direction, and we were not sure which way to go, so we just started walking, thinking we would find something familiar. Well, we walked until we saw a building that said "Hempstead Fire Department" on it, and we turned and walked all the way back. It was about a five-mile walk to Hempstead, then all the way back to Oceanside.

As good as the party in Rockville Centre was, it was just a warm-up for the next one. One week later, my next-door neighbor Pete Wilhelm had a party in his backyard while his parents were away. The place was packed shoulder to shoulder with people. The band was really loud, and the police came several times because of the noise. Never mind that the place was filled with high school teens drinking their brains out, the cops were mostly concerned with neighbors complaining about the loud music. The house next to Pete's was vacant, and it had a steady stream of guys going back there to piss and puke. Because Tommy and I were the newest members, we were on beer-distribution detail for the first hour. We just kept cracking open disgusting bottles of Schmidt's beer and passing them out. By the end of the night, there were people having sex in almost every bedroom of Pete's house.

Pete told me he spent days cleaning up his yard after that party. There was broken glass all over the backyard grass, and he was raking it up for a long time after that. It was such debauchery that the cops actually wanted to fine Pete's father when he came home the next day. I myself did get totally shitfaced drunk that night and had to be carried home with both my arms over the shoulders of two friends who brought me to my house. If they hadn't brought me home, I would have passed out in Pete's backyard that night.

Now that I had been to two frat parties, I was beginning to feel like a full-fledged brother; and after getting into a fraternity, the first thing to do was to get your friends in as well. I had a lot of friends when I was in the eighth grade, and I started asking them to join AOT. I found that Alpha Sigma Phi was growing fast among eighth graders due to Anthony Aiello's pressuring guys to join Phi, and there was a personality-cult thing going on around him. He was the toughest guy in the eighth grade; he was a vicious bully, and everyone wanted to stay off his bad side. In one fell swoop, almost all of my junior high buddies were going down to the next Phi meeting to get inducted. The only one of my friends who was already in Phi was Leo Black. Leo had gotten into Phi while I was dogging for AOT.

I tried to talk to my friend Eric Haber and convince him to come down to AOT instead. He said that he knew AOT was a better fraternity, but he was going down to Phi because he didn't have to dog for Phi. Alpha Sigma Phi did not take dogs, and guys in the junior high were always inducted with a one-night induction. That was another reason Phi had grown so much in the junior high school. All the guys who wanted to join a fraternity and didn't have the patience or the determination to pledge for one joined Phi because it was quick and easier to get in.

Eric also said he didn't want any of the problems I had with Phi when I dogged. We were best friends, and we sat next to each other in homeroom and had side-by-side lockers for three years, but Eric knew I alone could not keep Phi from harassing him if he pledged for AOT. He wanted to be in a fraternity, he wanted to get in with minimum hazing, and getting into Anthony Aiello's crew was something he saw as a good move socially.

I got the same story from Glenn Kreuz, Danny Carmeikle, and Pat Wynn. Ed Oren was still interested in joining AOT, but he wanted to wait until there were a few more guys to dog with him.

That night, Phi had inductions, and they inducted around eight to ten new members from the junior high school. I came to school in the morning, and I expected to see my friend Eric Haber wearing a Phi sweater; he wasn't. I asked Eric, "Did you get into Phi last night?"

"No, but I got my ass kicked by them," Eric said.

"What happened?" I asked.

"I got the shit beat out of me, and then they told me to go home. They said I was blackballed," Eric said.

I was shocked. I couldn't believe that Phi administered the beating and paddling first and then voted on the guy they just assaulted after the beating. I asked if any of our other friends were blackballed as well. He told me that Danny Carmeikle was also downed after getting beat up and paddled. I went looking for Danny and found him at his locker. When he turned to me, I was in shock at what I saw. Danny's upper lip was swollen so bad it was protruding longer than his nose. I asked Danny what happened, and he also said they beat the shit out of him first and then voted him out. I didn't know prior to this that Phi routinely voted on new members after beating them. Although it didn't surprise me, I thought Phi was a poor excuse for a brotherhood. Respectable fraternities like AOT, and even Omega, voted on their new members first and dismissed the ones who didn't make it before starting the hazing. We never beat anyone and sent them home without gaining membership. The small exception was with pledges, but it was up to the pledge to continue dogging or drop out.

I tried to convince Eric to come down to AOT, but he was through with fraternities after what happened to him. Danny Carmeikle would later become an AOT member, but not until high school. He would try again to get into Phi before junior high was finished, and it went worse for him the next time. Danny was talked into going down to Phi again a month later. He was promised he would not be blackballed this time. What they did was to tell Danny he had to dog for one week. Phi never took dogs, and they did that to Danny to fuck with him some more. They had him dog for two weeks before he knew they weren't going to let him join. Anthony Aiello had said, "Carmeikle will be dogging for us for the rest of his life."

A big part of my eighth-grade year was spent hanging out with my friends from the junior high, smoking pot, and drinking beers. I spent a lot of time with Eric Haber, Danny Carmeikle, Glenn Kreuz, Leo Black, Pat Wynn, and a few others. We hung out a lot in Baldwin at the Loft Lake Pond and by the railroad tracks in Baldwin. We were just beginning to drink beer, and believe it or not, we always managed to get some. We would stand in front of 7-Eleven and ask strangers to buy us beer. Sometimes it would take a long time, but we usually managed to get beer. At that age, drinking beer was not easy, and since we usually bought Schmidt's because it was the cheapest beer on the planet, we suffered from the horrible taste; and sometimes we would toss the unfinished beers that we could not stomach.

Even though Leo, Pat, and Glenn were in Phi and I was in Alpha, we had no problems. We were all friends before we were in fraternities, and being in different fraternities was not going to cause us to be enemies. I knew Phi was pushing Leo, Pat, and Glenn to turn their backs on me. They were supposed to become my enemies, but they had good character and were all too good for Alpha Sigma Phi. All three refused to turn their backs on a friend. In fact, by the end of junior high, all three would be out of Phi. Like I said, they were too good for that fraternity.

We got into all kinds of mischief at the lake and at the railroad tracks. There was a sewer pipe at the back end of the lake, and it had a large steel bar grating to cover it. We were able to climb under it and go into the sewer pipe. Why would we go into a sewer to hang out? Because it was out of sight, and no one would bother us while we drank beer and smoked weed. One time, a

Phi guy named Billy Summersby had made a lifelike dummy by taking pants and a shirt and then stuffing them with dry leaves; then he got a mannequin's head and put it on top and placed the dummy facedown in the sewer. We were hanging out; there were about six or seven of us, and we were all in on the joke except for one guy named Kenny Grimes. Billy Summersby was telling Kenny that we killed this guy and that he had to swear himself to secrecy, or we wouldn't let him out of the sewer. The poor kid was in tears, begging to be let out. It was so dark in there that with only candlelight, the dummy actually looked like a real dead body.

When we went to hang out by the train tracks, we did shit that could have gotten us killed. I remember Danny Carmeikle telling us he could make explosions by throwing metal on the train tracks. He called it arc welding. When he threw a steel rod under the wood that protected the third rail, it would touch the metal third rail and then fall to touch the train track. The contact would cause an electrical explosion. Danny got creative and bolder and was throwing bigger things on the tracks. Once he threw a bike frame, and after it exploded, there was only shredded metal left on the track.

One day, Danny's luck ran out. He had found a large pole; it was heavy, and he kept trying to get it to touch the second and third rails at the same time, but it kept missing. It took aiming to get it to go under the wood and fall down onto the train track. It had to be thrown like a javelin. Because this steel pipe was about four feet long and five inches in diameter, it weighed a ton. He kept missing the mark, so he kept moving closer to the tracks when he threw the pipe. Finally, he got so frustrated that he stepped right up to the third rail with the pipe and dropped it right onto the third rail. As soon as the pipe touched the second and third rails at the same time, it exploded in Danny's face. And because the pipe was so thick and heavy, it blasted itself upward and fell back onto the second rail and exploded again and then a third time; all three explosions happened in about ten seconds' time.

It was the first explosion that got Danny right in the face. He started running around, covering his eyes with his hands, screaming, "Ai, ai, ai." At first, it was comical, and Danny created his own nickname because for years, we would call him Ai Ai Danny. But when he started to say he was blinded and could not see, we all got scared. We got Danny to settle down, and when we looked at his eyes, he no longer had any white part in them. It was all blood red around the pupils. Danny told us he was only seeing white, and his vision didn't return for about a half hour. He was lucky he didn't permanently blind himself. But he did get a new nickname out of the experience.

As the school year progressed, I started hanging out with friends who were closer to my home. I started hanging out on a daily basis with Ed Oren, Scott Cole, Michael Lipsky, and Brian David. I knew all of them from school, especially Ed Oren, who had been a good friend since the first day of seventh grade. I lived far enough to get bused to school, but I had an aversion to riding the school bus. I preferred to walk, and since all these guys also walked, we used to meet along the way and walk to school together. We always smoked pot on the way to school. Somebody always had some.

I started working on these guys to get them to pledge for AOT. I knew Ed wanted to dog, but I had to work on the others. Mike Lipsky was totally against joining any fraternity, and he never did join any. Brian David was set on getting into Omega because his father had been in Omega. Scott Cole was open to the idea of dogging for AOT, but he wanted Brian David to dog with him, so I put the moves on Brian. I convinced him that it was unlikely he would be asked into Omega if no one had asked him yet. I convinced him that it wasn't as important to join his father's fraternity as it was to get in the same fraternity with the rest of his friends. I finally got him to agree to dog for AOT.

I also had some interesting and fun adventures with these guys. Although it was mostly Mike Lipsky, Scott Cole, and I who hung out after school. We were always looking for cool places to hang out where we could smoke pot; as I said before, there were no shortages of vacant lots and abandoned houses in Oceanside in 1978. At the location where the Sands Shopping Center currently stands on the corner of Mott Street and Long Beach Road, there used to be a huge lot that had some auto body shops in the far end; and right on the corner of Mott Street and Long Beach Road, there was an abandoned Victorian-style house.

In the lot, there was a huge tank; it was about twenty feet long and about eight feet high. There was a circular opening on top of it, and that was the only way in. There were two long, heavy poles leaning up against the tank, and we had to shimmy up the two poles with our hands and feet like a bunch of monkeys.

Oh, and another thing: this lot had three mean, vicious junkyard German shepherd dogs that lived there. In order to get into the tank, we had to outsmart the dogs every time we wanted to go in. About twenty feet away from the tank was a small hill about six or seven feet high. We would all run up the hill, and then two of us would start throwing rocks at the dogs to keep them at bay. While we did that, one of us would make a mad dash for the tank and shimmy up the poles to get in. After one guy was in, we would do the same routine again and again until we were all in the tank. Once inside, we hung out there for hours smoking weed. Usually, by the time we were ready to leave, the dogs had gotten tired of barking at the tank and had gone away. I don't remember ever seeing them when we left the tank, only when we went in.

It was pretty crazy to be playing around, taunting vicious dogs that were trained to kill just so we could climb into some big tank and smoke weed. But we did that every day after school for more than a month until one day, we found the tank had been removed. After that we started using the abandoned Victorian house on the corner. It was condemned and falling apart. Once again, we were doing dangerous shit just to find a spot to hang out where no one would bother us for getting stoned. That house was a rickety shack just waiting to collapse. One time, when we went into the house, it was winter, and it was freezing out. We could not get warm, so we made a crude stove to make a fire. Yeah, inside the rickety, dried-up tinderbox of a house, we laid out bricks in a square shape and then doubled up with another layer of bricks. We thought we had used enough layers of bricks to prevent embers from falling through the cracks, but we were wrong.

We left the abandoned house after finishing smoking weed and thinking that we had extinguished the fire. The next day, when we went to the house, we found it had burned to the ground. There was almost nothing left. We had a similar thing happen to us a block away from there, also on Mott Street. There was a row of abandoned cabana-styled condominiums. They had been abandoned for quite some time. We went inside one to get out of the cold wind. I remember when we were finished with the joint we were smoking, my friend Mike dropped the roach on the ground. We were looking for it, but he said, "Fuck it, it's just a small roach. It'll go out by itself."

Once again, the next day, the whole row of cabanas was burned to the ground. I said, "Jeez, guys, we gotta stop burning shit down." Anyway, I am sure the owners of those two run-down properties made out on the insurance money.

It was now getting close to the end of the year. Tommy and I had gone to our first Senior Dinner that year. This was a tradition in Oceanside AOT. At the end of the school year, the juniors would organize a dinner to honor the outgoing seniors and inaugurate the juniors who had just been elected to hold office in the upcoming school year. The Senior Dinner was held at McQuade's in Rockville Centre that year. I believe that we were charged $15 per person to attend. The seniors didn't have to pay this fee, and it was up to the Senior Dinner committee to collect enough from the brotherhood to have enough to pay for the seniors' plates. It was a cool thing to go to. They hung the Alpha banner on the wall of the party room we had rented out, and they awarded plaques to all of the outgoing officers. I remember feeling like I was part of something really cool that day.

Every year, in the first week of May, we would have ninth-grade honoraries. That would allow ninth graders to get an honorary induction without dogging. This was done to help get a few new guys inducted to the fraternity so we would have members coming over to the high school from the junior high at the beginning of the next school year. I had actually gotten a decent group together for the interviews. I had recruited Scott Cole and Brian David to dog, and I had recruited a young seventh grader from Boardman Junior High named Andy Caylen. They didn't allow seventh graders to dog, but since it was the end of the year and since Andy was a big, husky kid, they allowed him to pledge the fraternity. My friend Ed Oren was in trouble with his parents again, and he would be missing this dogging period. In addition to the dogs, I had recruited Steve Schiavone, who was Guy Schiavone's younger brother. Guy actually didn't want his younger brother getting into the fraternity. He thought his brother was too skinny to tolerate the beating. I was a skinny kid, and I had done it. I brought up Steve Schiavone's name for membership since his brother Guy wasn't going to do it. I also had brought up the names of Steve Zimmer and Steve Rod. Steve Zimmer was Steve Schiavone's best friend, so they went into this together. Steve Rod was a guy I met in the schoolyard during recess. He wanted to get into AOT, so I proposed his name for membership.

The meeting took place, and there were a lot of guys there to interview with the fraternity. As usual, we interviewed the dogs first, gave them their five paddle shots, and sent them home with instructions on how to begin the pledging process. After the dogs were sent home, we began interviewing and, later, administering beatings to the ninth-grade honoraries. A big mistake we made that night was to take the guys who had just caught their beatings and put them back together with the guys waiting to get beat. This caused a panic in three guys who were waiting their turn—the same three guys I had brought down to the fraternity. Steve Schiavone, Steve Zimmer, and Steve Rod all ran for it as soon as no one was watching them. They bolted down Oceanside Road away from the meeting. A few guys got in a car and went looking for them and brought them back to the meeting.

The three of them were all brought in together and made to explain why they ran away. Steve Schiavone said that when he saw Eddie Bane with a bloody nose and mouth, he worried about the thousands of dollars in braces he had in his mouth. Steve Rod made the same claim; Steve Zimmer had no braces in his mouth, and he just ran because the others ran. They were told they would be voted on again since they had run off; the fraternity had reevaluated their status.

It was decided that they were all blackballed, and they were told that if they had told us about the expensive braces, we could have modified the induction with no strikes to the mouth being permitted. But since they ran away—and, in the case of Steve Schiavone, also embarrassed his older brother Guy, who was in the fraternity—they had lost respect from the brotherhood and were no longer welcome to join. The other two ninth graders who came down that night, Ed Bane and Paul Sorvino, were inducted that night. Both of them were legacy members with older brothers who had been in the fraternity.

The next day at school, both Scott Cole and Brian David came up to me at my locker. Both were not wearing ties and collared shirts as they were supposed to. I asked why they didn't have ties on. They told me they had decided not to dog for AOT after all. Brian David had his heart set on joining Omega Gamma Delta because it was his father's fraternity, and Scott Cole refused to dog alone, so they both dropped out before even dogging one day. Andy Caylen, the seventh grader from Boardman Junior High, had showed up at the high school for dogging as scheduled.

The Alpha brothers took a liking to Andy right away. Andy was a good kid. I had become good friends with him the previous summer. My friend and neighbor Joel Sokoloff had moved from my neighborhood into Andy's neighborhood. Strangely enough, Joel would later join Freeport AOT even though he lived in Oceanside. I went over to that side of town a lot because Joel told me the streets were freshly paved in his neighborhood and they were perfect for skateboarding. I went everywhere on my skateboard; I was always looking for smooth streets to ride on. I met Andy on Joel's new block, and Andy introduced me to his neighbor Robyn Schreiber, who would become my girlfriend during my ninth-grade year.

Andy did great while dogging. He was quick to do everything they told him. He had been given a three-week pledge period, which was one week shorter than mine. Andy had gone through all three weeks, and at the end, just a day before he was to be inducted, his father made him drop out of dogging. I tried to convince Andy to come back into it later, but he said his father was pissed off and didn't want him in the fraternity. It was such a waste to complete the dogging period and then drop out on the last day.

So none of the four dogs I had brought down to the fraternity made it in, but Ed Oren told me he wanted to dog and would even dog alone and over the summer if he had to. I brought Ed down to a meeting in late June after school had ended. Sometimes meetings would be adjourned for the summer, but since we had a dog, meetings were held during the month of July.

Ed Oren was also a great dog. He had a funny personality and a great sense of humor, so not much would embarrass him. I felt bad that Ed gave up most of his summer to dog for AOT, but it was his choice.

When I dogged, I was left alone during school because there were no AOT guys in the school to dog me, and I would go to the high school at 3:00 PM to dog, and they were obligated to send me home by 6:00 PM. So I really got dogged about three hours a day. For Ed, since it was summer, he had to meet whomever he was dogging for early in the morning, and they kept him all day until nighttime. For him, it was a long summer, and he spent most of it being taken to Roosevelt Field Shopping Mall to bother strangers. He also was made to grub money off of strangers, and he was amazingly good at it. Sometimes he would collect up to $20 or more, and he had to give it to the Alpha guys who were dogging him. I believe they also made him sell fake pot—tea and oregano rolled into joints. Ed spent most of the time dogging for Rich Silver, Steve Gold, Ron Mayer, and Guy Schiavone just like I did. Those guys really enjoyed abusing pledges, and they were good at coming up with really strange shit to make us do.

Ed was getting tired of dogging such long hours every day, and he asked why I hadn't asked to have him for a day; so I did, just to give him a break. I had him come to my house, and I told him to cut my grass, and then we would just hang out the rest of the day smoking weed. He was actually insulted that I made him cut my grass. He thought that because we were friends, I shouldn't have made him do anything at all. I didn't get it; he knew he was dogging for a fraternity, and in that circumstance, the whole point of hazing is that it's your friends who haze you. Fraternities form bonds of brotherhood, but with my own best friend, the fraternity was beginning to create hard feelings between us.

Ed was also mad at me for not going to the meetings when he was dogging. It was summer, and I was probably out drinking beer at Loft's Lake in Baldwin. I wasn't abandoning him, but he was supposed to cope with dogging on his own, and my being at the meetings wasn't going to make things easier for him. I promised him I would go to his induction night. Because it was summer and most of the brothers were away, there were a small number of brothers attending the meetings.

On Ed's induction night, there were no more than fifteen to twenty brothers attending. He was given one walk around the room to get hit by each member and then ten paddle shots. Since there was a small number of guys attending the meeting, the president, Tommy Shriver, said everybody had to hit him when he was taken around. No one was allowed to give him a pass. I had not intended to hit Ed. In fact, during most of my years in AOT, I rarely hit inductees. But they said everyone had to take their shot at him, and Tom Shriver even looked at me and said, "I know he is your friend, but you have to hit him when he comes around." So when they brought Ed in front of me, I slapped him in the face, but I didn't hit him as hard as I could. After he got in the fraternity, he was insulted that I had hit him.

Besides Ed dogging for AOT, I had a great summer. We drank beer and smoked weed all summer long at Loft's Lake. I had gotten a summer job cutting grass with a landscaper that my friend Eric Haber got for me. I was getting paid $120 a week, and in 1978, that was plenty of money for a fourteen-year-old kid. I had weed in my pocket and drank beer at the lake almost every night. By that time, I had altered a copy of my birth certificate to say I was eighteen years old. It was a sloppy job and was easily recognizable as a fake, but I was able to buy beer at the beer distributor and at the 7-Eleven near the lake on Merrick Road.

Another extraordinary thing happened that summer. I finally got laid. Yes, I finally got my first piece. It wasn't under the most respectable circumstances of boy-meets-girl, though. It was actually me and two of my friends and one girl.

Here is how it went down. In the middle of July, on a hot summer day, I was walking down Rockville Centre Parkway in Oceanside with my friends Leo Black, Michael Lipsky, Matt Povinsky, and this guy named Kenny Grimes. As we got to the intersection on Oceanside Road, this girl from the neighborhood named Dawn Finkelstein came running up to us. She was clutching a bottle of vodka, which was nearly empty, and she was swigging from the bottle. At first, the guys were telling her to get lost. She was being very silly since she was drunk off her ass, and she kept hugging all of us and kissing us too. We crossed the street and went into the schoolyard of Oceanside School #5. By the time we got there, Dawn had finished the vodka and tossed the bottle. I never saw anyone able to swig from a bottle like that, and she was only thirteen at that time. She was already a hardcore alcoholic and drank hard liquor like a pro. I was just getting accustomed to the taste of beer at the age of fourteen, which is how old I was when this happened.

We went to the side of the schoolyard, and Leo was pulling Dawn's tube top down, exposing her tiny tits. She was just giggling and pulling it back up. Leo and Mike had pulled her tube top down three or four times, and each time, she would say "Stop" in a giggly, drunken way. I finally said to Leo that I thought the only reason she was stopping us was that we were outside in a public place. She really wasn't getting angry or upset, just embarrassed. I suggested that we take her to Leo's house. We had built a shack in Leo's backyard, and it was very cool to hang out there and smoke pot. But this was different. Leo said that if his mom or sister or anyone else saw us taking Dawn into the shed in his backyard, there would be a bad scene. That was when Michael Lipsky said we could take her to his house.

Michael's family went away on vacation for a few weeks, but because Michael had to go to summer school, he couldn't go with them. His parents didn't trust him to be in the house alone, so he had to stay at his grandparents' house until his family returned. Fortunately for us, Michael was very devious, and he had left one basement window unlocked so that he could get into his house when he wanted to. We did go to Leo's house briefly just so we could get our bicycles. We then rode to Michael Lipsky's house, which was right next to Oceanside School #4. I remember that I was the lucky one who got to have Dawn on the back of my bike. And I do mean lucky. None of those other idiots wanted to give her a ride. The whole ride over to Michael's house, she had her arms around my waist and was massaging my crotch. I knew that she was aware of what we were planning, and she had no objections at all. She was just as eager as we were.

We got to Michael's house and waited in the driveway while he climbed into the basement window. He came to the side door and let us in. When we got inside, she told us she was losing her buzz and asked if Michael had any alcoholic drinks to give her. There was no liquor in the house, but Mike grabbed a sixteen-ounce Budweiser tallboy can from the fridge. She opened it, turned her head back, tilted the can upright, and finished the whole thing in one long gulp, which took her about ten seconds. Like I said, she was a pro drinker.

We went upstairs into Mike's room, and he insisted that since it was his house, he should get to be with her first. No problem with that. Mike took her into his brother's room and got busy. Now the rest of us were sitting in Mike's room, talking about who would go next. Leo and I were arguing over it, and Matt said we should just flip a coin. Leo won the coin flip, and he was supposed to go next.

When Mike came back, he was smiling from ear to ear. He said, "She's all yours, whoever is going next."

I said, "Leo, you're up, bro."

Leo froze, stood there for a minute, looked at me, and said, "No, Freddy, you go next. I'll wait."

I said, "You sure you want to give up your turn? You won the coin toss."

"Yeah, I'll go after you," he said.

At this point, we could hear Dawn in the next room calling me. I said to Leo, "I'll gladly take your turn, bro. I am not at all shy or embarrassed about it."

As I was walking out of Mike's room, Mike leaned over to me and said, "Ask her for a blow job, she will give you head if you ask her. She blew me, and then I screwed her. She will do the same for you if you ask her to."

I went into Mike's brother John's room, and Dawn was naked on top of the sheets. There was no air-conditioning, and the place was sweltering hot. I was dripping with sweat. She was smiling and had her arms out, inviting me to come to her. I got undressed and got in bed with her. Just like Mike had said, I asked her for a blow job, and she did it. Then she climbed on top and rode me; I didn't even have to ask. It was definitely not bad for my first time. It was as awesome as I had imagined. After we finished, she asked me to send in Leo. I went back to Mike's room and told Leo she was asking for him.

"She wants you, Leo. You got no excuse to not go in there now," I said to Leo.

Leo went in the room with her and did it with her. When he came back to Mike's bedroom, he told Matt Povinsky that she was asking for him now. Matt just flat out said no, he was not going to do it. He kept saying that we were all going to get in trouble for this. We tried to convince him that there was nothing wrong with this. Even though she was intoxicated, she knew what was going on and was making her own choices. We weren't abusing a girl who was passed out or forcing her to do anything. We were all having a good time, and Matt was killing the mood. He still refused.

Now Kenny Grimes was saying he wanted to go. Leo told him that she had specifically said she didn't want Grimes touching her and she wasn't going to do anything with him. He got all upset and said he was taking his turn and we had no right to stop him. We told him that he could go into the room with her just to see if she would let him, but if she said no, he had to leave. He went in the room, and she was heard saying, "You're not touching me, you slimy animal." After that, we heard her yell at him to get the fuck off of her. We all burst into the room, and she was hitting him with both fists in his face and kicking her feet at him at the same time. He had his pants down to his knees and tried to climb on top of her. We all grabbed him and pulled him out of the room; he caught a few punches to the stomach along the way as we took him to the end of the hallway and shoved him down the stairs. When he was on the ground floor again, he pulled his pants up, and then Mike shoved him out the side door into the driveway, telling him to get the fuck out of there.

He got on his bike and yelled that he was going to tell everyone what we did with Dawn. We went back upstairs to see if Dawn was willing to go for another round with us, but the mood was killed. She had lost her buzz and wanted to be taken home. We all left Mike's house, and once again, it was up to me to give her a ride. Nobody else offered to give her a ride; and they all just drove away on their bikes. This time she was still hugging my hips but was not grabbing my cock again. She was starting to nod off, and it was hard to keep the bike steady with her wavering from side to side. I stopped at the creek on Waukena Avenue, just north of the Red Store. We also had a shack in the swampy area next to the bridge that ran over the creek. We hung out there a few minutes and then left again. As we were walking out of the weeds, we saw Derek Timothy, who would become an Alpha brother the next year, riding his bike in the other direction. I introduced them to each other, and they wound up being a couple the next school year. After that, I put Dawn back on the back of my bike and let her ride all the way back to her house.

We had all sworn that we would not tell anyone what happened that day, not only to protect Dawn's reputation, but so we wouldn't have every dumb ass in the school asking about it. But Kenny Grimes was true to his word, and he told everyone about it. We always denied it whenever anyone asked, but people knew something happened. People were talking about it the day after it happened. I know it was not something I wanted to tell anyone about back then. But all happened, just like I told it.

When school started in September, Ed Oren and I were the only two Alpha guys in the school. This year the shit would come to a boil with Alpha Sigma Phi. Anthony Aiello had been expelled the year before and was not in school anymore, but he still came to hang around on school grounds almost every day. I had problems with Anthony Aiello that year, as well as with another degenerate criminal in training named Billy Sandoval. Billy Sandoval was a sadist and a bad seed, plain and simple. He wasn't just a bully but a cruel and disgusting individual. Billy had an older brother named John and a younger brother named Joey, who was almost as bad as he was, but Billy was the worst of the three. I wound up being in the same shop class as he was, and one day, the guy tapped me on the shoulder; and when I turned around, he hit me in the jaw with a hammer. I don't know why my jaw didn't break, but I walked out of the class and went to the guidance office to ask to be switched into a study hall instead. I didn't want to be in the same room with that guy. They told me that once I dropped shop, I could not go back. I took the study hall. A month later, Billy Sandoval had dropped shop or was kicked out, I never knew which, and now I was stuck with him again in my study hall.

Shortly after high school, Billy Sandoval would be convicted of the abduction, rape, and murder of one of his neighbors. So when I say that he was a bad seed, I really mean this guy was rotten to the core, and I knew that even back in ninth grade. Billy's older brother John and younger brother Joey were not much better than him either. All of the Sandoval brothers had a reputation for assaulting people when their backs were turned, swinging weapons or ganging up two or three on one person. If you had a problem with one Sandoval, then you had problems with all of them. And all three of them were in Alpha Sigma Phi.

Early in the school year, we started dogging two legacy pledges. They were Paul Len and John Kane. Both of them had older brothers who had been in AOT, and both of them were eighth graders. Ed Oren and I had lunch different periods, and each of us had one of the dogs during our lunch breaks. I had Paul Len and Ed had John Kane.

Paul was a nice kid; he was a little shy, and he wanted to be in the same fraternity as his brother. When I had dogged, I was lucky to not have anyone in AOT in the school with me, or I would have been dogged all day long. I always felt bad for the Omega dogs because they were catching shit all day long from the Omega brothers. I decided to give Paul a break. I was not the kind of guy to have my fun humiliating someone in front of people. I knew he would get plenty of that from the other Alpha brothers, so I gave Paul just two rules to follow when he dogged for me during school hours. First was he was required to take his lunch with me and stay at my side during recess in the schoolyard. The second rule was he was required to bring me one pack of watermelon Bubble Yum every day, which he would give to me during recess. Back then, I smoked pot almost every day, and during recess, it was always smoke time for me. Paul didn't smoke, but the watermelon gum he gave me every day helped me to cover the smoke breath I had before going back to class.

Paul was a good guy about it, and he always had my gum for me without fail. I always filled his dogging book with merits, and I never hit the guy at meetings while he was being dogged. Ed, on the other hand, did dog John Kane during his lunch break. Paul and John began dogging together, and they were the only two dogs. Both of them completed their pledging period and were inducted on the same night. They were not beaten or paddled very badly that night. By comparison, I had the living shit beat out of me. But I was happy they didn't get beat up too badly; they were both good kids, and now AOT had four members in Oceanside Junior High School.

Although there was peace and quiet in the junior high school between the fraternities, by midwinter, things were coming to a head in the high school between AOT and Phi. At the AOT meetings, the older high school members were talking about a brawl with Phi that was brewing up for a while. It always seemed like every year there were tensions between Alpha and Phi, and each year, there was talk of a fight between the two fraternities. The previous year, under President John Jaeger, there was talk of fighting with Phi, but it never happened. Omega Gamma Delta never locked horns with AOT or Phi while I was in Alpha.

In 1979, Tommy Shriver was the AOT president. This year the cause of the problem was desecration of colors. It seems that some Alpha brothers found a burned AOT tee shirt behind the school. It was brought up at the next meeting, and Phi was the suspected culprit. Omega had no problems with Alpha and had no motive to do that. It was also widely thought that the Phi guys who burned the shirt were gutless because they actually purchased a brand-new AOT tee shirt from Sportorama, which was in Baldwin and which was where all fraternity members went to buy colors, and they burned the shirt behind the school, where no one would see them or know exactly who did it. It was decided that the answer to this would be to confiscate the Phi colors off some guy and then desecrate the Phi colors in full view of the whole school.

I can't say if they actually took Phi colors off of a member or if they went to Sportorama for a Phi shirt as well. I was in the junior high, and I was not prepared for what was about to happen. I had heard talk of an AOT-versus-Phi brawl before, and nothing came of it, but this time, it happened. It was a Thursday afternoon when it happened. My first clue that we were at war with Phi came up behind me at the end of the school day. I was at my locker, facing the locker and opening the combination lock, when I felt my head being smashed against the locker once, twice, three times. I saw stars and was instantly delirious. I didn't know what had happened, but I turned around and saw Anthony Aiello standing there, and he was pissed off. He was yelling something at me to the effect that all my Alpha friends and I were all going to get our asses kicked. I thought he was going to smash my skull again, but the principal of the school, Mr. Downes, was passing by and saw what happened. He stepped in and blocked Aiello from attacking me again. He told Aiello he would be charged with trespassing if he didn't leave immediately. Anthony Aiello left, and Mr. Downes took me to an exit on the opposite side of the school that Aiello had left from.

My forehead was sore, and I staggered home. When I got home, I called Ed Oren to tell him what happened. It turned out he was also attacked at his locker at the same time after school like I was, except he was jumped by Phil Stone and Joe Miola. We knew we had big problems now because we were outnumbered ten to one by the Phi members. The other two younger AOT members did not get bothered by anyone. They were younger and also had older brothers. Besides, Ed and I were both extremely hated by most of the Phi members in the junior high. We decided that we should cut school the next day or risk getting jumped.

At first, I didn't know what the reason was that Ed and I got jumped by Anthony Aiello and his cohorts. I figured he didn't need a reason. But I spoke to my friend Eric Haber later that night, and he had gotten the story from Phi guys, and he relayed to me what had happened at the high school that day. It seemed the Alpha brothers had done everything according to plan. They gathered in front of the school on the grassy circle that the buses parked around when picking up and dropping off students. There were about fifteen Alpha members, and they held up a Phi shirt. Each Alpha member grabbed a piece of it, and instantly, they pulled the shirt apart into pieces. The Phi members who were in the lobby ran out to confront the Alpha members, and a big free-for-all brawl broke out under the portico that ran above the front-entrance walkway. Pete Wilhelm actually climbed out the window of the first-floor classroom, which was facing the scene of the brawl. His teacher tried to physically pull him back in the window, but Pete was determined to get into this rumble.

It was pandemonium for about ten minutes. The Phi members in the high school were outnumbered by AOT overall, and the fight was mostly one-sided as well. The Phi guys deserved an A for effort, though. A much-smaller number of them faced off with the Alphas, and according to witnesses, the Alphas won the fight. The only Alpha member who was injured during the fight was Jimbo Rector. Jimbo was hit in the face with one of those heavy wire-mesh outside garbage cans that you see in public parks and schools. Phi member Umberto Califani had picked up the garbage can and threw it right into Jimbo's face. Jimbo suffered a broken nose and a deep cut to the bridge of it.

The fact that this brawl had taken place and because a lot of Phi guys took a beating that day, now Anthony Aiello wanted Ed Oren and me to pay for it. Back in the junior high, it was just Ed and I facing somewhere around twenty or more active Phi members. Paul Len and John Kane were literally not bothered at all during this upheaval. But Ed and I had to watch our asses from then on. Things really got bad for us over at Merle Avenue in the junior high.

Ed and I decided to cut school the next day, which was a Friday. We met at the Red Store, which was a deli at the midpoint between our houses. Ed and

I had made crude weapons to carry with us in case we were confronted by any Phi members. Ed had a small section of steel pipe that he clenched in his fist. I made a crude pair of brass knuckles out of band iron. About a minute after we met on the corner of Waukena Avenue and Oceanside Road, a Phi member named Ray Montemera came walking by. Ray went to Boardman Junior High and was headed in that direction. Ed and I talked about whether we should jump him and give back to Phi some of what we had been getting. Ed had his pipe clenched in his fist, and I had my crude brass knuckles in my right hand. As Ray got closer to us, Ed and I stared right at him and locked our eyes on him as he walked by. We turned our bodies as he walked by and never took our eyes off him. He saw we were staring him down, and he avoided making eye contact with us. If he had said one word, or even gave us a dirty look, we were ready to pounce on him in a heartbeat. Neither Ed nor I had the propensity to jump a helpless outnumbered person, and that was why we let him pass; but if he had mouthed off to us, there was no doubt we would have beaten him down to the ground. We had taken enough shit from Phi, and we were very edgy that day.

After Ray passed by, we had to decide what we would do for the day and where we would go. I suggested we go to John Craig's house. John Craig was an adult who lived three doors down from Eddie Oren on Third Street. Michael Lipsky, Scott Cole, and I had become friends with John Craig, and he allowed us to hang out at his house. Although he was an adult in his late thirties and we were teens, we had gained his trust; and we spent a lot of time hanging out with him, and we smoked his pot, as well as shared ours with him. Sometimes he would come home from work, and we would already be hanging out in his den, smoking his weed. His house was always unlocked, and he had no problem with us making ourselves at home there whenever we wanted to.

Ed had known John for years, but Ed was the kid who raked his leaves and cut his grass. He wasn't comfortable going into his house and hanging out, and he said he didn't want to go there. Instead, we went to our shack on Waukena Avenue by the canal. We stayed there for about an hour to ninety minutes until we couldn't tolerate the cold anymore. To make matters worse, it started to snow. We had no pot and nothing to eat. I finally convinced Ed to go to John Craig's house. It was just too cold to be outside, and we had nowhere else to go. I told him we could hang there for the day, smoke some weed if John had left any out, and grab some food since John usually had chips or Entenmann's cake in his kitchen. I told Ed that John usually got home around 3:00 PM so Ed could duck out before that if he didn't want to run into him.

As I expected, we hung out there, stayed warm, smoked weed that was in the ashtray, and munched on cake that was in the fridge. Ed and I decided we had to return to school on Monday, but we would have to be really careful after returning to school. John Craig came home while we were there, and Ed was embarrassed and left right away. I stayed for a while and hung out with John and told him about the problem Ed and I had with Phi and explained that was why I invited Ed to hang out there.

When we returned to school on Monday, we didn't get ganged up on like we thought, but there was tension brewing beneath the surface. I had my biggest problems when I went to my study hall class, which I had switched to from shop class to get away from Billy Sandoval. In addition to Billy Sandoval, another Phi member named Billy Sacreteris was in the study hall as well. Now I was not at all worried about Billy Sacreteris at all. He wasn't scary or tough, and he hung on to the coattails of the Sandoval's. In fact, I had a fight with Sacreteris in seventh-grade music class, and I punched him out with two hard hits to the face, and he never said shit to me ever again. But now he had Billy Sandoval sitting right next to him in study hall, and I was all alone with no friends in that class to watch my back, so Sacreteris got the nerve to start fucking with me again. I let it go day after day because I couldn't deal with Sacreteris when he had Sandoval with him all the time.

The two of them were taunting me day after day, and I was getting really tense just to go in the class. Finally, it came to a head when Sacreteris said something that really pissed me off, and I turned to them—they sat behind me in the back of the room—and I told him he was a punk without Sandoval to keep him safe. Sacreteris said something about not needing Sandoval's protection, and that he could kick my ass anytime he wanted with no help. That was the breaking point for me. I got up out of my seat, walked to the back of the room and right up to Sacreteris. As he stood up, I punched him twice in the face and dropped him back into his seat. I was pumped up, and my adrenaline was flowing; I turned to Billy Sandoval, who sat right next to Sacreteris, and dared him to step up and take a swing at me. Now I want to be clear about this; under normal circumstances, I would never have challenged Billy Sandoval, mostly because he was the type of guy to pull a knife or swing a bat or something like that. But in that moment, I was pissed; I had enough of their shit, and with the adrenaline pumping, I was primed to fight him, win or lose. He looked me right in the eye, without getting up, and said, "So you're feeling tough today, Freddy? Take a walk over to the Phi corner downstairs, and we will see how tough you are then with all of us."

With that one statement, he took the wind right out of my sails. I came back to the realization that it wasn't me against Sacreteris or me against Sacreteris and Sandoval. It was me against twenty or twenty-five Phi members in the junior high. As I walked back to my seat, I looked back and saw Sacreteris sitting in his chair, holding his face with both hands, and Sandoval was grinning at me. He didn't stand up to fight me because he saw I was angry and pumped up; he also knew that after I calmed down, I would no longer be in a fighting mood.

He was like a vicious dog; he knew when to back off and when to attack. Now I had all of Phi pissed at me for punching out Sacreteris. It didn't matter that he asked for it and he deserved it. He was their fraternity brother, and I wasn't.

As I expected, I had to deal with Anthony Aiello again. He decided that I had to fight someone in Phi to settle this thing. He came up to me a few days later and said that he decided that Jerry Fantelli and I would make a fair fight. We were the same size and weight. I was never the kind of guy who could fight on demand. I needed to be pissed off enough to swing at someone. But I knew if I didn't agree to this fight with Jerry Fantelli, then I would never be done with this situation. Even with my agreeing to the fight, there was no reasonable assumption it would be over; but if I didn't agree or show up, then these guys would harass me until the end of the year. So I had taken Anthony Aiello up on his word that no one from Phi would show up for this except for him and Jerry Fantelli. I also took him up on his word that he would not interfere or jump in if I was winning. I showed up after school behind the school near Merle Avenue as I had agreed, and I found Anthony Aiello already there, and he was alone. He said Jerry Fantelli would be along in a minute or two. After ten minutes of waiting, he didn't show up. When he didn't show up, it pissed of Aiello. He had been embarrassed by Fantelli, and now he was looking for him. Aiello just said that we no longer had any problem and that now he was going to throw Fantelli a beating for making him and Phi look bad. That was really the last of my problems with Phi and Anthony Aiello that year.

With the end of the year now closing in, it was time for two things: elections of new officers and ninth-grade honorary inductions. The ninth-grade honoraries took place the first week of May, and we inducted three ninth graders in Jimbo Rector's basement. Two of them were my good friends from Oceanside Junior High: Billy Young, whom I had known since the second grade, and Pat Kapps, whom I had met in homeroom in the eighth grade. The third inductee was Pat Torino, who went to Boardman Junior High. Our number of freshmen was increasing, and I was relieved to no longer be all alone with only Ed Oren in AOT in my grade level. Earlier in the year, Mike Canella from Boardman had dogged and gotten into AOT, so now there were six of us in the ninth-grade class of Oceanside AOT, and things were looking good for the future.

Then we had elections. The two brothers nominated were Guy Schiavone and Rich Brandon. I remember wanting Guy to win. He was personable and well liked by everyone in AOT. I recall that Rich Brandon didn't like me or Ed Oren much, and his whole clique within the fraternity felt the same. They had been pushing for Ed's expulsion from the fraternity for most of the school year. Ed was always in trouble with his parents and was perpetually grounded the whole school year. That meant he could not go out at night to attend fraternity meetings. I had spoken with President Tommy Shriver about Ed's situation earlier in the year, and Tom had given Ed a waiver from attending meetings as long as his dues were always paid every week. Ed had been giving me his dues money to pay for him every week without fail. The issue of Ed not attending meetings was brought up from time to time, but he was never brought up for suspension or expulsion.

Now after the elections of 1979 for the class of 1980 school year, Rich Brandon was elected AOT president, and Guy Schiavone was elected vice president. At the end of the meeting, after it had adjourned and the brothers were leaving, Stan Zanetski called me over to him. I went to see what he wanted, and he said to me, "Oren is out, ostracized."

I said, "What do you mean? The meeting is over, and Ed's name was not brought up for expulsion."

Stan said, "The first thing Rich Brandon did was to grab the roster book and write *ostracized* next to Oren's name."

When an AOT brother was expelled from the fraternity, the word *ostracized* was written next to his name in the Oceanside AOT roster book.

I said, "That is against the fraternity's rules and bylaws. He can't single-handedly decide to kick him out without at least bringing it up for a vote."

Stan said, "What's done is done. It's Rich Brandon's fraternity now, and he says Ed Oren is out, so tell him tomorrow to give you any AOT colors he has."

With that, the conversation was over. I was upset; Ed was my best friend, and I liked being in the same fraternity with him. Now the fraternity I loved had just kicked out my best friend, and without even giving him a fair hearing as the bylaws required. The next day at school, Ed came up to me at my locker, and he was really happy. He said, "Fred, I have great news. I did well in all my classes this year, and my parents have lifted my punishment. I can go to meetings now, and I will be at every one."

I said, "Ed, they expelled you from AOT last night."

Ed said, "But I thought as long as I paid dues each week that they wouldn't kick me out."

I said, "That was an arrangement with Tommy Shriver. He stepped down as president last night, and Rich Brandon was elected the new president."

When I told him that, Ed knew there was nothing he could do about it; he knew as I knew that Brandon didn't like us, and he would have tried to get me kicked out too if I had missed too many meetings. But I went to every one. Ed was really bummed out about getting expelled from AOT. He had dogged his whole summer away, got jumped and harassed by Phi all year long, and now, just as he was able to start participating, he was kicked out without a trial or a vote.

I promised Ed I would try to get him back in. An expelled brother who wanted to be readmitted to the brotherhood had the right to address the fraternity and give his story, and then his application for re-admittance would be put to a vote. But this would have to wait until next year.

The summer after ninth grade, I convinced my good friend Leo Black to leave Alpha Sigma Phi and join AOT. Leo had been a Phi member all throughout eighth and ninth grade. I was actually surprised that I was able to convince him to join Alpha. We had conversed a little about fraternities, and Leo had commented that he thought AOT was a better fraternity than Phi. I asked Leo why he stayed in Phi, and he told me that he never attended any Phi meetings. He had been in for almost two years and maybe went to three or four meetings in that time. Apparently, they liked having Leo in Phi, and just having him seen wearing a Phi tee shirt a few times a week was good-enough reason to keep him on as a member.

But when Leo joined AOT, he didn't actually quit Phi first. I had invited Leo to sleep over at my house, and I knew there was an AOT meeting at Tommy Farnswell's house right down the block from mine. There were inductions taking place that night. When Leo and I were hanging out at my house and smoking some weed, I asked him if he was interested in going to the Alpha meeting at Tommy's house to get inducted, and he said yes. I told him he was required to wear a shirt and tie, and since he didn't have one, I gave him a collared flannel shirt and a tie to wear. Considering the formal attire required to attend an AOT interview, I must say he looked really shabby with a flannel shirt, a mismatched tie, jeans, and work boots. Not to mention he had a full beard. Leo had many nicknames during the time I knew him, such as Big Leo and the Boss, and we also sometimes called him Abraham Lincoln because of his beard. I didn't think he would have shaved if I asked him to, so I didn't bother to tell him he was required to shave.

I was really motivated to get Leo to leave Phi and join AOT. He was one of my very best friends in junior high, and I thought he was Alpha material. So I left out a few details when I invited him to interview. Unfortunately, Leo paid a heavy price for those details being ignored. When they saw Leo with a full beard and wearing a flannel shirt, they started saying he looked like a lumberjack. Leo caught the attention of the Alpha brothers from the minute he showed up. They were pissed at the way he looked. They thought he was disrespectful. They were pulling him around by his beard. A lot of the Alpha brothers were telling him he should have shaved before coming to the interview and were pulling at the hair on his face. I could see by the grimaces he made that he was in pain. I noticed that when they were taking him around the room for his beating, his face was bleeding out of the hair follicles from where big chunks of his beard had been pulled out. They worked him over pretty good, and after his paddling, they picked him up and threw him into the canal in Tommy's backyard. There had been some discussion about blackballing him because he was in Phi, but when all the ninth graders spoke up for him and I told them Leo was leaving Phi for AOT, they passed him on his interview. About two weeks later, Leo convinced his younger brother Eric to also quit Phi and come into AOT.

Afterward, back at my house, while smoking pot, Leo had told me that the beating to get into AOT was much worse than when he got into Phi and that he would have shaved if he had known they were going to pull half his beard out. Now another one of my good friends was in AOT, but I missed Ed Oren and wanted to get him back in. First thing when we started high school next year, I would make it a priority to get Ed back into AOT.

Oceanside AOT 1978 in front of Oceanside High School

Oceanside AOT Senior Dinner in 1978

CHAPTER ELEVEN

Spooky Time

Few fraternity presidents have had the reputation to even come close to matching Joe Furino, a.k.a. Spooky. Joseph Furino, who was known as Spooky during his high school years, was no doubt the most effective, efficient, respected, and feared president that Valley Stream Alpha ever had. In fact, there was none in any other Alpha chapters, except for Oceanside's Billy Weitzman, who had the clout, fear, and respect that Spooky had during his time as president of Valley Stream AOT.

Joe had an older brother who had been sergeant at arms in Delta Phi Sigma fraternity in the mid-1970s. Joe and his brother were dark-skinned Italians and living in what was once a nearly-all-white town of Valley Stream; as such, Joe's older brother had gotten the nickname Spooky. Joe had been called Little Spooky when he went into seventh grade. When his brother graduated and moved on, Joe was then called Spooky, by the time he was in ninth grade. By the time Joe was old enough to get into a fraternity, his brother's fraternity, Delta Phi Sigma, had closed its Valley Stream chapter. All the younger brothers of the Delta Phi Sigma members were now going into AOT, and Spooky took the same path, with his older brother's blessing.

In 1977, Joseph Furino was in ninth grade. The current AOT president in 1977 was John Marceda. John's older brother Joe had been a Delta Phi Sigma member as well. John was a junior in high school. He and his fellow juniors had to take ownership of AOT early, after all the seniors from the class of '77 had quit or abandoned the fraternity. John had asked Joe's older brother Anthony for permission to bring Spooky into AOT. Spooky's older brother gave his blessing since all the younger brothers of all of his old Delta Phi Sigma friends were going into AOT as well. As Spooky said about his choice of fraternity, "Omega was out of the question."

Spooky was given a three-week dogging period. He had a particularly tough pledging period. In 1977, the traditions for dogging were still strict. Crew cuts were mandatory, as were a green tie and red suspenders, Hell Night, and the Hell Night hell ride. The Valley Stream chapter at that time still ran pledge classes based on three degrees. Joe would endure all three degrees during the next three weeks. The first week was the first degree of pledging. The dogs were always on their knees in front of the president and other officers in a dark, candlelit room. After the interview, Joe and the other dogs were welcomed to the pledge class by the president, who shook their hands, and then on down through all the officers. The last introduction made was the pledge master, who shook their hands and then gave each a hard, stinging slap in the face.

Every day during the duration of his pledging, Joe and his fellow pledges were required to bring buttered bagels and coffee to the AOT brothers in the park behind the school in the early morning before school started. Each dog was required to take no more than five orders from AOT brothers for coffee and bagels, which meant Joe and each of the other pledges with him had to bring breakfast for five Alpha brothers each morning without failure. In addition to the food, the dogs had to always bring plenty of cigarettes each morning and carry enough gum to go around all day long. In Joe's words, "Looking back on it, every morning was tough."

Joe pledged with his best friend at the time, Robert Carmen. Robert didn't make it into AOT, and he quit dogging after the second week. But up until he dropped out of the pledge class, Spooky would go to Robert's house every morning to make the coffee and butter the bagels. Having Robert around to share the burden of dogging helped Spooky to get through his pledge period, although he was disappointed that his friend didn't make it into AOT with him.

Another aspect of dogging Joe and his fellow pledges had to deal with was dogfights. When Alpha had pledges at the same time as Omega, both fraternities would pit their dogs against each other in dogfights. Joe had to fight an Omega dog named Vito Carino.

The second week of pledging was the beginning of second degree. At this point, all the dogs, including Joe, had been required to get crew cuts, and the second degree consisted of the dogs being forced to eat nasty concoctions that the AOT brothers made from their refrigerators and kitchen. The concoctions were harsh and nasty, and Joe and his fellow pledges had to endure eating live goldfish and drinking these horrible mixtures every day for the duration of second degree.

Third degree was Hell Night. Joe took a bad beating on his Hell Night, but he was exempted from the hell ride. The hell ride would have taken him far out into eastern Long Island to be abandoned with no money. They would have taken him either dressed in a woman's dress or in his underwear, but Joe came from a strict Italian household, and his father was an old-world Italian immigrant. He would not permit his fifteen-year-old son to be out all night, nor would he allow him to be dropped off forty miles from home with no money. Joe's older brother went with him to the Hell Night. Joe's brother Anthony was well known, respected, and feared in Valley Stream. When he walked into the AOT meeting and told President John Marceda that his little brother was not going on a hell ride, which was the last word on that. But Joe paid for it with a severe beating and paddling. To make up for the loss of the hell ride, President Marceda ordered Joe's paddle shots more than doubled from forty to eighty-five. In Joe's own words, "I couldn't sit on the toilet for a week. I had more colors in my ass than a rainbow."

Joe was a true Greenie and loved AOT right from the beginning. President John Marceda had been friends with the Furino family for years. John's older brother Joe had been in Delta Phi Sigma with Spooky's older brother Anthony. John had taken Spooky under his wing to get him adjusted to fraternity life and to keep him out of trouble, as he had promised Joe's older brother he would. Joe's ninth-grade year was uneventful, and he had no trouble that year. As a sophomore the following year, the first major incident took place.

By the time Spooky was in tenth grade, his older brother Anthony had already graduated from high school and had taken to hanging out with bikers, mostly motorcycle club members. One Friday night, there was a biker party just off Central Avenue. Because of the close relationship between the Furino's and the Marceda's, AOT members were invited to this party. Joe left fairly early and was walking home with two girls he knew from school, Sue Mistretta and Lisa Quartoraro. When they went their separate ways, Spooky blacked out. The next day, he woke up to find his father smacking the shit out of him. His father thought he was on drugs because he was so lethargic and dopey. Joe's father brought him upstate that day to get him away from what he thought were his druggie friends.

The next day, the girls saw Spooky's sister Maryanne at Green Acres Mall and asked Spooky's sister how he was recovering from the beating he received in the jumping. Maryanne didn't know what they were talking about and asked them what had happened. The girls told Spooky's sister that when they went their separate ways, they looked back and saw three guys from Valley Stream North Alpha Sigma Phi jump Spooky, beat him senseless, and take his Alpha sweater. The girls even recognized who they were. John Van Craken was the ringleader, and his cohorts were Michael Stone and John Verducci.

When Sue and Lisa saw what was happening to Joe, they ran back to the party to tell Joe's Alpha brothers. The girls saw John Marceda, and John, in a furious fit, went out looking for the Phi guys who jumped Spooky. He probably should have first helped Spooky to get home safe and tell his parents what happened. But John's first instinct was to avenge his younger fraternity brother's assault. Somehow Joe managed to stumble home, but he had no memory of what happened to him the night before.

His family owned a farm in Plattekill, New York. Joe's father took him there to dry out and sober up. Joe's sister Maryanne brought Sue and Lisa back to her house so they could tell her mother what they saw happen to Joe the night before.

After finding out what happened to Joe, his mother called his father upstate to tell him that Spooky had been jumped by three older guys. His father took him back home and brought him to the hospital. He had a concussion, several broken ribs, and a broken nose. It would actually be a year before Spooky had plastic surgery to fix his nose. But now there was the issue of catching up with the three pricks who jumped Spooky and took his Alpha sweater.

The next night, John Marceda caught up with John Verducci in the pizzeria next to the Malverne Movie Theater. In the ensuing brawl that broke out between the AOT and Phi guys in the pizzeria, John Marceda had thrown a glass ashtray at Verducci and hit him in the chest and broke a rib. John was arrested for assault that night.

The next Saturday night, Spooky's brother Anthony went looking for the guys who jumped his little brother. He went with Jimmy Pesaro, John Marceda, and Gary Zarcola to North Park near Valley Stream North High School to look for the guys. John Marceda was AOT president in Valley Stream AOT in 1978, and Gary Zarcola was his vice president. Jimmy Pesaro was a big, muscular guy covered with tattoos, and he was a black belt. The former Delta Phi Sigma's whom Joe's brother Anthony ran with had moved up to running with biker gangs. These guys just did not play, and they were pissed.

They found the guys who jumped Spooky in the park sitting in a parked car drinking beer. The Phi guys started mouthing off right off the bat. Anthony Furino told them they had to return his brother's AOT sweater to him. The Phi guys were continuing to wise off and refused to give the sweater back. Jimmy Pesaro leans into the car the Phi guys were in and opened his jacket to show them he was brandishing a weapon. He gave them two days to produce the sweater and return it to Spooky's brother. The Phi guys saw the gun, and John Marceda told them that Pesaro was not fooling around; he meant business, and they should be afraid of him.

Spooky's brother wanted to beat the shit out of all of them right there and then, but he made a deal with VSN Phi; they were to drop the charges against John Marceda for throwing the glass ashtray at Van Craken, and in turn, Spooky's family would not press charges against John Van Craken, Michael Stone, and John Verducci for the vicious assault on Spooky. In addition, they had to return the Alpha sweater to Spooky's brother within the next two days. The sweater was returned, all charges were dropped, and the incident was forgotten.

In March 1979, in Spooky's junior year, he had gone with a group of AOT brothers to the Valley Stream movie theater on Sunrise Highway to watch the movie *Animal House*. *Animal House* was a hilariously funny fraternity movie, and all the high school fraternities were trying to copy Delta Tau Chi and their antics. Also at this theater was a group of Omega Gamma Delta members from Valley Stream Central. After the movie, everyone was riled up and rowdy. A fight broke out between the AOT members and the Omegas. Spooky jumped right into the fray; but in the ensuing chaos, an Omega named Billy Jones tapped Spooky on the shoulder, and as he turned his head, Jones coldcocked him in the face. The following Monday afternoon, Spooky waited for the bus from BOCES technical school to return to the high school. He knew Billy Jones would be getting off it. As it turned out, Spooky hit the trifecta. Billy Jones, Dave Romero, and another Omega member whose name Spooky can't recall were all getting off the bus at the same time.

These three Omega members were all seniors, and Spooky was a junior. Spooky charged at them from behind and did a flying tackle with his arms outstretched. He took all three down in one tackle. As they all went tumbling to the ground, Spooky threw Billy Jones a vicious beating. The other two were dazed from the takedown and did nothing while Spooky pummeled Jones. When Spooky was finished with him, he was bleeding profusely from the face, his eyes were closed; he had been beaten until his body was limp. These three guys were the only three active seniors in Omega that year, and this triple beating took all three of them out of the picture for the rest of the year. They all dropped out of Omega after that incident.

Spooky was suspended from school and sent home. He was told he had to return with his mother. Spooky returned with his mother the next day to meet with the Valley Stream Central High School principal, Dr. Glen. Dr. Glen told Spooky and his mother that he was being expelled from school for the remainder of the year. They were told that Spooky would have to appear before the Board of Education for the incident and that they should hire a lawyer. The Furino's couldn't afford to spend thousands on a lawyer for this, but Joe had an idea. Joe Furino had already enlisted in the United States Marine Corps. He went to his sergeant and explained the situation, and his sergeant went with Spooky and his mother to meet with the superintendent of the Valley Stream Central District. The sergeant explained to the superintendent that Joe had signed up to join the marines and he needed his diploma to get in the Marine Corps. He asked Dr. Glen and the superintendent to come up with a punishment that was more commensurate with the offense. They settled for a thirty-day suspension from school, and Spooky was able to take tests and complete his schoolwork from home for the month that he was out of school so that he could graduate on time.

After the thirty-day suspension was over, Spooky's mother had to go with him to sign him back into school. All the students in the hall applauded when Spooky walked into school with his mom. He had gained a lot of clout with that beating he put those guys through that day. Although he attacked them from behind, it was one against three, and that evened the odds. Also, Tolliver had attacked Spooky from behind, and Spooky felt that he needed payback—one good turn deserved another. While Spooky was out on suspension, Delta Phi Sigma started back up in Valley Stream Central High School. Although this was an attempt to re-charter Spooky's older brother's fraternity, Spooky thought the guys starting it back up were "a bunch of jerk-offs," in his own words. He wasted no time in banning Delta Phi Sigma from Valley Stream Central. The five guys who tried to restart Delta Phi Sigma were told not to wear colors in school or be seen wearing them anywhere around town or risk having the colors taken right off their backs. Within a few days of Spooky's return to high school, Delta Phi Sigma was dead and gone.

In the 1978 school year, John Marceda was president of Valley Stream AOT, and he had a large number of active members. There were about seventy-five AOT members during John Marceda's year as president, and he had formed a close relationship with Oceanside Alpha and the president of Oceanside AOT at the time, John Jaeger. The following year, when Spooky was a junior, the fraternity was beginning to shrink a little bit. The president and the vice president in the 1979 school year were Michael Janelle and Jack Vorstack. Perhaps they had been less than enthusiastic about running AOT, and they didn't put the same high priority on fraternity affairs that John Marceda did the year before. With the end of the school year coming up, Janelle and Vorstack decided to retire early from AOT. It was already well known that the brotherhood wanted Spooky to be the next president, and actually holding an election was just a formality. But Janelle and Vorstack were only too happy to step down early and pass the fraternity on to Spooky and the junior class.

In the first week of April 1979, elections were held, and Spooky was unanimously elected president of Valley Stream Alpha Omega Theta. His other officers were Tommy Black, who was elected vice president; Todd Slope was elected treasurer, Richard Lopez was elected secretary, and Steven Nitch was elected sergeant at arms. This was the crew that helped Spooky to build a dynasty in Valley Stream that would be long remembered and long talked about for many years.

At the time Spooky took over the fraternity, the membership of AOT had dwindled down to roughly forty members. Taking into consideration the seniors who had just became inactive two months before the end of the school year, as well as a less-than-stellar year for new inductions. Spooky's first priority was to increase the roster of active members and get meeting attendance up as well.

—

As soon as he took over as president, Spooky held a pledge class in April of 1979. They started with eighteen pledges and gave them a two-week pledging period. Two weeks later, they inducted fifteen of them. In September of 1979, Spooky held another pledge class, and again they inducted roughly fifteen new members. And so it went all year long, with new pledges being inducted at least once or twice a month. By October of 1979, the fraternity was up to seventy-five members. By January 1980, Valley Stream AOT had grown to almost one hundred members; by March of the school year, Valley Stream Alpha had an active roster of 125 members. It was unprecedented in the history of the Valley Stream chapter. It was also unprecedented in the history of any AOT chapter; in fact, none of the many fraternities that existed in Nassau County had ever grown that large and powerful. Getting pledges was easy since everyone wanted to be in Spooky's Alpha. Omega Gamma Delta's membership drives suffered during Spooky's run as AOT president.

This wasn't just a fraternity anymore. It was a private army, and all the members were soldiers loyal to Spooky, and he ran a tight ship. Valley Stream AOT under the leadership of Spooky owned Valley Stream in 1980. Another fraternity that had existed in Valley Stream Central since the late 1950s was Kappa Delta Nu, and during Spooky's reign over Valley Stream Central, they had shrunk down to less than five members. Spooky ordered the Kappa Delta Nu Chapter disbanded and forbade them to wear colors anymore. As Spooky described the way things were during his year as president of AOT, "People listened to me when I was president. Nobody fucked with me. I did whatever I wanted to do."

Early in the school year, they were holding a meeting in Spooky's basement. All meetings during Spooky's year were held in his basement because it was a very large room and could hold a lot of guys. Usually, sixty or more members attended the meetings in Spooky's basement. According to Spooky, they never had meetings with less than sixty guys when he was president, and sometimes more than that would show up for meetings.

Spooky remembered issuing fines in the form of a shot with a paddle to maintain order during meetings. "I always made an example out of somebody at a meeting. I gave my vice president a shot one time. There was always some guy in the meeting that got a shot, because they wouldn't shut the fuck up. I'd be talking, and they'd be talking over me. Once you give somebody a shot, everybody quiets down.

"We used to have meetings every other week, and there was so many people in the meetings, there was all little cliques, and everybody was bullshiting, bullshiting, bullshiting. The meeting would start, we'd say the pledge of allegiance, something like that, call the meeting to order, and they would still be speaking above me. I'd give them a fair warning, but you had to make an example of someone. It was never somebody who was a big guy. It was always some guy who was an idiot. It was always the scrawny guy that got the shot. I'd tell him he's getting a shot. He'd say 'But I didn't say anything.' I'd say, 'Get up, you getting a shot.'

"Sometimes it was so funny. They wouldn't get up. They'd say, 'No, I'm not getting up. I'm not taking a shot.' I remember one time, it was Chris Cangelose. He wouldn't get up, that fuckin' guy. The sergeant at arms just hit him right on the front of his legs while he was sitting. It was funny. We used to pee in our pants at shit like that."

At one such meeting, after things settled down, the discussion turned to the Iranian hostage crisis, which had been going on for a few weeks already. AOT brother Jimmy Burns suggested a walkout to protest the Iranian hostage crisis. It was originally planned to be only AOT members to walk out of classes that day. Word got around the school what was planned, and at the agreed-upon time, when the Alpha brothers walked out of class at 9:00 AM, their classmates followed. Virtually 90 percent of the school walked out of classes that day to protest the hostage crisis. It was so dramatic an event that TV news stations showed up, and it was broadcast on the evening news that day. It was in the newspapers as well. The student body of Valley Stream Central then marched over to Valley Stream South High School and instigated a walkout there as well. It was an event that really pissed off the Board of Education and was one of the things they held against Spooky when he was expelled for beating the shit out of the three Omega members that day.

During Spooky's time as Valley Stream AOT president, they had plenty of parties and brew-ups. The difference between parties and brew-ups was parties were planned in advance; usually, there was a band or a DJ, and they were open to non-fraternity members who paid admission to get into the party and consume whatever beer was being served. Brew-ups were impromptu gatherings that happened spur-of-the-moment and usually were just among fraternity brothers. Sometimes brew-ups were held in a park or schoolyard and sometimes at someone's house when their parents were not home. With an active roster of 125 members, there was plenty of partying and drinking going on that year. Every year, AOT would march in the Memorial Day Parade, and after the parade, they would go to Valley Stream State Park and have a fraternity BBQ. Some of the most memorable times during Spooky's time in AOT were the Memorial Day BBQs.

In Joe's words, "Memorial Day for Alpha was a big day. Every year that I was in AOT, on Memorial Day, we went to Valley Stream State Park. We got kegs of beer. Everybody chipped in."

Occasionally, AOT fought with Valley Stream Central Omega Gamma Delta. AOT always had the last word and won every fight and altercation.

The Valley Stream South and Valley Stream North Omega Gamma Delta chapters never helped Valley Stream Central Omega. Although there were three chapters of Omega all in the same town, they never stood up to the one chapter of AOT while Spooky was president. Omega took a backseat to AOT in Spooky's time.

Spooky became a legend in Valley Stream; he took his beating as a younger guy and gave many beatings as he got older. He was involved in many brawls. He was feared throughout Valley Stream. He was respected by future generations of Alpha guys for the next decade. Many times in the years after he had graduated high school, Alpha guys went to him for advice on strengthening the fraternity. Not only did future AOT brothers of Valley Stream go to Spooky for help, but during his presidency, Spooky was approached quite a few times by other Alpha chapters for assistance. Valley Stream Central AOT helped various AOT chapters while Spooky was president, beginning with a group of AOT members from South Hempstead. They had been members of what was then referred to as Rockville Centre Alpha, which was the Mu Nu Chapter.

In 1980, the shit began to come to a boil with Oceanside Alpha Sigma Phi. Oceanside Phi hated Alpha, and that meant every chapter of AOT, not just the Oceanside chapter. Rockville Centre AOT was a small chapter by the standards of other Alpha chapters, but they had always been a tight group. Rockville Centre AOT had usually maintained a roster of thirty or so members. They had traditions of doing civic service and charitable work. When Oceanside Phi started going into Rockville Centre and jumping Alpha guys, the president and officers of Rockville Centre AOT didn't know how to respond to it. They weren't accustomed to brawling, and the president, Matt James, wanted no part in gang warfare. He was college-bound and didn't want these problems on his record if the troubles continued. That caused a split in the Rockville Centre chapter's ranks. All students from Rockville Centre and South Hempstead went to Southside High School. The Rockville Centre chapter was made up of students from Rockville Centre and South Hempstead.

The South Hempstead AOT brothers wanted to fight back against Phi, especially since it was their neighborhoods that were getting infiltrated by Phi the most. The Rockville Centre AOT chapter president, Matt James, preferred to close the chapter down to avoid further fighting with Alpha Sigma Phi. The South Hempstead brothers, who preferred to be called South Hempers, made a trip to Valley Stream in search of Spooky to get his blessing to build a new chapter out of the remnants of Rockville Centre AOT. Spooky took a liking to these South Hempstead Alpha brothers right away. He admired their dedication and their determination to keep AOT in Southside High School. He also respected their willingness to stand up to Oceanside Phi even though they were hopelessly outnumbered.

So with Spooky's arbitration ruling, Rockville Centre Alpha was no longer recognized by Valley Stream, and South Hempstead Alpha was given the Mu Nu Chapter designation that had belonged to Rockville Centre AOT for more than twenty years.

Spooky helped the South Hempstead AOT guys with problems they had with Phi. "They were good guys. I liked those guys," Spooky said of the South Hempers he had taken under the wing of Valley Stream AOT. To make the point well known that South Hempstead AOT had the clout of Valley Stream behind them, Spooky and his crew had taken to hanging out in South Hempstead quite often. Anytime Phi came around looking for trouble, they had to deal with dozens of Valley Stream Alphas who would come in multiple carloads to back up their new South Hempstead brothers. Spooky had some recollections about the times he stood up for his AOT brothers from other towns.

"Whenever Oceanside or South Hempstead needed me, I was there for them, 100 percent. However many guys I could bring with me, I'd bring them. I piled them into my car, and we showed up.

"We were all brothers, that's why people in Oceanside and South Hempstead knew me. I was there, there was no chickenshit ('Oh I can't go'). However many guys we could get (who wants to go). It was volunteer only. If you wanted to come help these guys, you gotta get in the car. We would go with three or four carloads and go down and help them.

"Whatever we could do, we would do. I was invited to a couple of Oceanside and South Hempstead meetings. I went, showed up. They were always very nice to me."

In 1981, Oceanside Alpha had problems with Oceanside Phi, and even though Spooky had graduated already and was technically no longer president, he still rallied the Valley Stream AOT members to go to Nathan's in Oceanside to confront Phi and back up the Oceanside brothers. Oceanside Phi retaliated by going to Burger King in Valley Stream, and there was another fight. After being vastly outnumbered and effectively beaten back, the Phi members retreated to their cars and beat it out of Valley Stream as fast as they could go. In their haste to get out of Dodge, they accidentally left behind one of their guys. At Spooky's insistence, the Valley Stream Alpha's showed mercy to him and didn't kill the guy. The cops picked him up and took him out of the area.

Also in 1980, Freeport AOT was reconstituted by younger brothers of guys who had been members of the Freeport Zeta Chapter years before. Freeport AOT, known as Zeta Chapter, had been defunct for about two or three years. The Freeport members who reopened the Zeta Chapter had also gone to Valley Stream to get the blessing and the OK for their charter from what was considered to be the Grand Chapter of Alpha Omega Theta Fraternity. Freeport had a lot of other fraternities at the time. They had Omega Gamma Delta, Delta

Gamma Rho, and Alpha Theta Gamma. There was a lot of competition to recruit members, and there was instant friction with Delta Gamma Rho, who didn't want AOT coming back into Freeport.

The Freeport chapter of AOT held keg parties every Saturday night in a vacant lot beside the beer dock, right next to the bridge that separated Freeport and Baldwin. They charged $5 or $10 per person for all the keg beer they could drink. Valley Stream AOT was always given free entry to these parties. This helped the Freeport Alphas to gain respectability, show the strength of AOT, and recruit more members. In their first year after reopening the Zeta Chapter, they had recruited forty members. That's not too shabby for a new chapter.

Here are Spooky's thoughts on helping the other Alpha chapters: "The other chapters said that Valley Stream Central was the grand chapter, and we had to help, I had to help. It was my responsibility to help them."

Spooky had also launched a new chapter of AOT in a town that never had a chapter of Alpha Omega Theta. Spooky started Rosedale AOT in 1980. They started with ten to fifteen charter members; they lasted about two years. After the founding members graduated from high school, the Rosedale chapter folded; there was nobody to carry on from the original members.

The last function Spooky presided over was Valley Stream Alpha's participation in the Memorial Day Parade. Fraternities had always marched in the Memorial Day Parade in Valley Stream. In Spooky's senior year of 1980, it would be the last time fraternities would be allowed to march. Things were changing, and the public perception of fraternities was becoming intolerant. Spooky recalled sitting on the hood of his Barracuda while the officers of AOT rode in the car. The Barracuda was yellow with black stripes and was called the bumblebee. Spooky held an AOT paddle while sitting on his car hood for the whole parade while the full brotherhood of Alpha Omega Theta marched behind them.

Although Spooky had a close relationship with the other Alpha chapters and went to their meetings regularly, Spooky never invited other AOT presidents to his meetings in Valley Stream, and his reasoning was "I never had presidents of other Alpha chapters come to my meetings. I never invited them. I didn't need them, I handled everything myself. There was no reason for me to ask them for anything. I had the biggest guys, the most guys. My brother was a monster who ran with biker gangs."

Joe continued to help future AOT classes in Valley Stream for years after he graduated. By 1985, Omega Gamma Delta had grown to be bigger than AOT, and the Alpha members from that time asked Spooky for help and ideas to bring AOT back to the glory days of Spooky's reign. Spooky attended AOT meetings from time to time whenever he was asked to help. He never said no when asked for help or leadership advice.

When asked why he still attended AOT meetings years after graduating, Spooky had this to say.

"I hate people that come up with excuses. I hate excuses. I don't believe in them. If you say you're gonna do something, do it. We were brothers. I loved the fraternity. The fraternity was a lot of fun."

Five years after graduating high school, Spooky ran into Van Craken at a nightclub in Island Park. Spooky's sister recognized him and pointed him out to Spooky. Spooky goes up to his table and shakes his hand. Van Craken didn't recognize him at first. Spooky says, "Remember me? You took my sweater from me many years ago." Michael Stone was also at the table. Those guys shit their pants because it was just the two of them, and Spooky was with about ten of his friends. Spooky's sister asked him not to have these guys jumped, and he said, "No problem." Joe was not bent on revenge for a jumping that happened five years ago; he just wanted to see how they liked being surrounded by a larger number of tough guys with no one to back them up. He looked Van Craken in the eye and told him, "It's a small world we live in, always remember that. There's no place you can hide forever." With that, Spooky shook hands with both Van Craken and Stone and then went back to his table with his friends. Van Craken and Stone left the place immediately after.

When we discussed the topic of the AOT books and official documents, Spooky became annoyed at the thought that some future generations of Alpha brothers had kept documents that had been passed down for decades.

Spooky's thoughts on the AOT documents: "I didn't keep anything. I passed my stuff on at the end of the year like I was supposed to. Those little thieves that took it afterward, they felt. 'Why should I pass it on? I want to keep it.' Then years had gone by, they got married, and threw it away. All the shit that can never be replaced was thrown away."

Joseph Furino enlisted in the marines at the age of eighteen. He rose to the rank of sergeant and served his country with honor and distinction. The leadership skills he learned presiding over Long Island's largest AOT chapter, as well as being the de facto leader of any multichapter AOT gatherings, helped shape his character and future. Joe Furino is now the owner of Pinnacle Construction in Franklin Square, New York, and is still highly respected by his friends and fraternity brothers.

I first met Joe at an AOT brew-up in the summer of 2006. While I was developing the AOT Web site, which resides at alphaomegatheta.com, Joe was one of the first guys to step up and offer me help with the Web site. He was also an integral part of organizing the Grand Chapter reunion in 2007. Without his help, that reunion never would have happened. I consider Joe to be a true Greenie and a good friend, and I am honored that Joe considers me a friend and a brother.

Joe "Spooky" Furino

Pledge in the center of picture on his Hell Night

Joe "Spooky" Furino and his crew circa 1980

Chapter Twelve

My Sophomore Year

September of 1979 was the start of my sophomore year. My high school days got off to a rather rocky start and would set me on the wrong path through most of my high school days. Two significant things happened to me by the first day of school. First, on the first day of high school, my friends and I showed up bright and early to smoke some pot before first period. Like a bunch of dumb asses, without knowing anything about the school, we lit up in the teachers' parking lot behind the school, in full view of some of the classrooms as well. It was Leo Black, Michael Lipsky, a guy named Ron Doherty, and I who were passing around a pot pipe. It was a chamber pipe, which meant that the center of the pipe had a hollow chamber that you could fill with pot, and it would filter the pot you smoked out of it. After that, you could smoke the chamber weed, and it was supposedly stronger.

Like a bunch of idiots, we were standing there in the parking lot, passing around the pot pipe, when a guy in a suit came up to us out of nowhere. He demanded to know our names. We asked who the hell he was. Well, he was Thomas Marciano, the principal of Oceanside High School. We were cold busted right in the act. He brought all of us to his office and took our names and demanded to know who had the pot. We all denied having any, so he took Ron Doherty and demanded that he strip to his underwear. Ron folded like a cheap tent and gave Marciano the pot he had on him. That saved the rest of us from a strip search. Marciano didn't call the cops on us, but we were all suspended and had to be picked up from school. So I was off to a great start in my new school, suspended on the first day before first period.

The next thing that happened actually started at orientation, the day before school started. We went to orientation, but just to hang out. It was Leo Black,

Brian David, Kenny Grimes, and I. We were near the north entrance on Brower Avenue when we noticed a ten-speed bike that was leaning against the fence, unlocked. We commented that whoever owned that bike was not going to find it there when he came out. Who leaves a bike unlocked? All of a sudden, Kenny Grimes jumped on the bike and rode away. Leo turned to us and said, "He better not be taking that bike to my house."

Well, he did take it to Leo's house. When we got to Leo's about twenty minutes later, we found Kenny taking the bike apart in Leo's backyard. Leo got pissed and told Kenny to get the bike out of his yard. When Kenny picked up the bike frame and took it to his house, Brian David and I took the two rims from him to fuck with him. I didn't give it a second thought until two days later, when a detective from the Nassau County Police Department's Fourth Precinct showed up at my house and told me the bike had been reported stolen by none other than Phi member Anthony Aiello. This detective, whose name I can't recall, told me that he wanted to take a statement from me and that I had to give him the bike rim. I did both. He said after he collected all the parts that Aiello would get his bike back.

I figured that would be the end of it, or at least my part in it. I was wrong. Although Kenny Grimes was charged with the theft of the bike, Anthony Aiello never got the bike back. It seems that the detective who took the rim from me then told Aiello that the rear rim had not been recovered, and the bike would not be returned to him until all the parts were recovered. I heard through the grapevine that Aiello was pissed and looking for me. That was just what I needed—to have that gorilla looking to beat the shit out of me again. And I didn't even have the rim anymore.

I knew I had a big problem, so I asked Leo if he had an old bike I could take the rim from to give to Anthony Aiello. Leo gave me a rim with a flat tire, so I was taking it up to the gas station on Long Beach Road to fill it up. As I passed Oceanside Junior High School, I saw Alpha brothers and Omegas playing football on the field. They played every Saturday. Right behind the field, sitting on the steps of the junior high's gym, was Anthony Aiello and all his Phi brothers. I figured since I had the rim that was for him and that since there were Alpha brothers nearby, he wouldn't lay a hand on me. I was wrong.

I walked right up to Aiello and said, "Anthony, I am sorry about your bike getting stolen by Grimes. Here is a rim to make up for the one missing from your bike." Without saying a word, he took the rim from me and swung it right at my face. I saw it coming and covered my face with both forearms and turned my back. I got struck right in the back of my head with the rim. I was dazed and staggered. I felt the back of my head, and I knew I was bleeding. When I turned to him, he punched me in the face. I was afraid that all of the Phi guys were going to jump me. All of a sudden, all of the Alpha brothers and the Omegas came to my defense. The pulled me out of the fire and told Aiello they were not going to let him and his Phi friends attack me all-on-one.

Aiello told the Alphas that I was responsible for the theft of his bike and that the police would not return the bike without the rear rim and that the police told him they had not recovered it, which was not true. I did give the rim to the detective and was no longer in possession of it, but for whatever reason, the bike was not returned to Aiello. The Alpha brothers told me that to make it right and to keep the peace, I had to either recover the lost rim, which was not possible after giving it to the detective, or get Aiello a new bike.

I didn't have the money or the means to get him a new bike, so I was still screwed. I told my friend Mike Lipsky about my predicament, and he said, "No problem. I'll steal a bike for you to give to Anthony Aiello." Which on the surface sounds stupid—to steal a bike to replace a stolen bike—but I didn't have the propensity to steal a bike, and Mike had no problem doing it. If I didn't get a replacement bike for Aiello fast, I was in serious shit.

He actually opened up someone's garage on Perry Avenue and rode away with a brand-new ten-speed bike. He rode it to my house and left it for me. I wasted no time in riding it to Aiello's house. I quietly left it in his driveway and bolted out of there before anyone came out of his house. The last thing I needed was another confrontation with him. But the bike must have satisfied him because I never heard about it again. These two events got me off to such a bad start in high school that my entire sophomore year was a big waste of time.

By the first week of school, we were ready to start bringing up names for interviews to hold inductions the next week. The first meeting was held, and the new AOT president, Rich Brandon, didn't make it because he didn't know where the meeting was being held. He had dropped out of school and was finishing up high school in night school, so he was out of touch with us when we planned the first meeting of the year. The meeting was held with the vice president, Guy Schiavone, presiding. There was a quorum present of three officers and enough brothers to hold the meeting. We had a lot of guys coming into the high school from both Oceanside Junior High and Boardman Junior High who wanted to get into AOT, so we started bringing up names and voting on them. We planned on holding inductions the next week to replace all the seniors who had graduated and gone inactive the previous year. During this meeting, I brought up Eddie Oren's name, and Guy Schiavone then said that he remembered Ed being a great dog when he pledged, and he felt that as a past brother who pledged to get into AOT, he deserved a chance to apply for readmission to the fraternity and speak his piece to the brotherhood. Guy told me to have Ed come to the next meeting.

I told Ed the next day that his name had been passed to come down for an interview the next week. I explained to him that there were three ways it could go if he came to the meeting and asked for re-admittance into AOT. First, they could allow him back in with no sanction, which was not likely. Second, they could vote him down and not allow him back into the fraternity, which was a possibility with Rich Brandon in charge. Third, they could allow him back into AOT with a full night of hazing and paddling, which I thought was a likely possibility. Ed had expressed a willingness to go through the whole honorary induction, take a beating and a paddling all over again if it would get him back into AOT. At this time, Ed had friends who were sophomores besides me in AOT, and I thought he had a good chance to get back into Alpha.

The following week, the meting was held in Leo Black's backyard. Leo lived on Foxhurst Road, and he had a very large and long backyard. It was perfect for inductions—plenty of space for a running start to paddle the inductees. We had a huge turnout of interviews that night. Including Ed Oren, we had fifteen honorary interviews and five pledges from Oceanside Junior High. Twenty potential replacements for all the seniors we lost last June after they graduated. It was second week of school, and we already were probably going to regain the lost members. All inductions after this were going to make us larger than before. I was impressed with the turnout.

The first thing to happen was a squad car from Nassau County's Fourth Precinct stopped in front of Leo's house when they saw the large number of guys in fraternity jackets gathering. They then noticed the inductees because they were all wearing ties. The cops got out of their car and warned us not to hold inductions. They promised that if even one baseball bat got swung at anyone, they would make arrests. We assured them we were only holding interviews and there would not be inductions. Of course, after the cops left, we did hold inductions.

Shortly after the cops left, Rich Brandon arrived. He came into the backyard, and he was visibly annoyed. He immediately became confrontational with Vice President Guy Schiavone about him presiding over the meeting last week and for holding inductions without consent of the president of the chapter. This caused plenty of drama that night. We had twenty guys in the front all waiting to be interviewed for possible membership in AOT, and Rich Brandon wasted close to an hour on petty bullshit. He accused Guy of attempting to usurp presidential authority and suggested that if he wasn't happy being vice president, then he should resign the office. That pissed off Guy really bad, and he did just that. He said he wasn't quitting the fraternity, but that he no longer wished to serve as an officer and had no time to attend meetings since he was now working full-time. Guy walked out of the meeting, and the next order of business was electing a new vice president to replace him. This tied up the meeting even more, and the inductees had to wait. John Corano was elected as the new vice president.

Now we were ready to get to the interviews, or so we thought. Now that Guy had left the meeting, Rich wanted to flex his presidential muscle and said that all the interviews were being sent home because he was not present at the last meeting and did not authorize names being brought up for interviews. There was a very negative reaction from the brotherhood in regard to sending these guys home. It was argued that since we already had them here at our meeting, we should strike while the iron was hot and induct them, because if we sent them home, there was a good chance some or all of them might not come back next week. Some would go over to Omega Gamma Delta if they felt slighted by AOT for wasting their time, especially the pledges. It was getting really hard, almost impossible, to get young guys willing to pledge for three or four weeks, and these five guys would probably not come back if we sent them home.

Finally, after much debate and unanimous sentiment among the brothers present, Rich Brandon consented to holding inductions that night. Now there was another issue he threw into the mix that nearly caused a revolt among the brothers. Rich stated that the interviewees would be beaten, paddled, and then voted on. Now the quorum of brothers was up to full boil. If any of the interviews got downed after being beaten and paddled, they would go back to school and tell everyone that AOT beat the shit out of them and then blackballed them. This was an induction tactic of Alpha Sigma Phi, and most of us did not want the guys we brought down to AOT to risk getting beaten and then blackballed. Guys started threatening to tell their friends they invited to go home and not allow them to be interviewed. After more drama and bullshit, Rich Brandon relented and allowed them to be voted on first, and then we would haze only those who passed their interviews.

Just as we were ready to commence with the interviews, Rich looked around and said, "And by the way, who the fuck brought Ed Oren down here tonight?"

"I did," I said.

He looked at me and said, "He's not getting back in, and that's final."

I said, "Guy told me to bring him tonight. Guy said Ed would get a chance to address the brotherhood and ask for re-admittance to the fraternity."

He said, "Guy isn't here anymore, and he is no longer an officer. There's no way Ed Oren is getting back into this fraternity while I am president, and that's it."

I said, "According to the rules and bylaws, Ed has a right to tell his side of the story and let the guys here vote on his re-admittance."

Apparently, quoting bylaws to President Brandon got him aggravated. He said, "Look, I'm going to down him, and I know a few others that don't want him back in."

He looked around and said, "Who else is going to down him?"

I saw three or four of the seniors all give a thumbs-down, and I knew it was over for Ed. That was it. Brandon had kicked him out without a trial or a vote on expulsion, and now Ed wasn't getting a fair hearing before the brotherhood. He wasn't even given a chance to address the brotherhood and explain why he had gotten kicked out of AOT last year. I was thoroughly disgusted, and I said, "Well, I will go out front and send him home then."

"Stay here. You are not dismissed to leave this meeting. Let him stand out there until the meeting is over, and then you can tell him to go home," Rich Brandon said.

Now I was pissed. I was a younger member of AOT, and I never spoke out of turn at a meeting before. I always kept my mouth shut and avoided getting fined, which was usually one or two paddle shots from the sergeant at arms. But I wasn't going to let my best friend get fucked over and have the added insult of being made to be the last one to go home. For what?

"Bullshit," I said. "I'm telling Ed to go home."

As I walked toward Leo's front yard up the side of his house, I was confronted by the sergeant at arms, Greg Gosinski.

He said, "Turn around and go back into the backyard."

"No," I said.

As soon as I said no, the motherfucker threw a front-stomp kick right into my stomach. I doubled over and couldn't breathe. I couldn't believe it. Not only did I have assholes from Alpha Sigma Phi to worry about, but now my own fraternity brothers were hostile and assaulting me as well. Greg Gosinski was a senior and a football player, and I was a skinny sophomore. He had no cause or right to kick me like that. It was the job of the sergeant at arms to administer fines with a paddle shot. I would have taken my shot if so ordered, but this was pure bullshit, and I was pissed enough to walk out. As I was getting up, my friend Pat Kapps helped me up.

I was saying, "Fuck this shit. I quit this fucking fraternity. I don't need this shit to be assaulted by an asshole like Greg Gosinski."

Pat said, "I know those guys are assholes, Freddy, but they are seniors, and this is their year. Let them have their year. Don't do anything stupid like quitting. Look what happened to Ed. They kicked him out and won't let him back in. Just go back into the meeting, show up at the meetings every week so they can't throw you out, be patient, and wait until next year. Next year, this fraternity will belong to us."

Pat had calmed me down, and I understood his logic. Greg Gosinski was still blocking my path to the front yard, and I am sure the scumbag would have hit me again, so I went back into the meeting. As it went, we interviewed the five pledges, paddled them all, and sent them home with instructions to show up the next day to begin dogging. We also inducted fourteen of the fifteen honoraries who showed up for induction. Ed was made to wait until the end of the meeting before he realized they were not going to even interview him. He realized this as everyone was leaving and Greg Gosinski motioned to him with the point of a finger to move on.

The next day, Ed was pissed off, and of course, he was pissed at me as well. He was mad that his time was wasted and that I didn't do enough to get him the respectful treatment he thought the fraternity should have shown him. Ed was my best friend throughout junior high and high school, but my membership in AOT was a point of aggravation to him the entire time. He always felt that I should have quit the fraternity after the way he was treated, but the way I saw it, getting kicked out was an issue between him and the fraternity. Guys get kicked out all the time. Fraternities have rules and bylaws, and members are obligated to follow them or get thrown out. I tried my best to keep him in, and I tried to get him back in after he was kicked out, but it was not my obligation to quit because he couldn't get back in.

Despite my continued membership in AOT, Ed and I continued to hang out all through our high school years, and we hung out with a guy named Dave Weitz. Dave wasn't in a fraternity, but his younger brother Brian would later get into Phi after trying unsuccessfully to dog for AOT.

As I said before, I was a big pot smoker, but the three of us started moving up to stronger stuff that year. A strong psychedelic drug called mescaline was becoming widely available around town. I remember the first night I took some. I was home in bed sleeping, and I heard little rocks being tossed at my window. I woke up, and I saw Ed and Dave below my window. They told me they had gotten some mescaline and asked me to come out. I got dressed and slipped out of my house on what would be the first of many late-night mescaline trips.

I took what looked like a tiny cylindrical red dot. The first hour, we walked around thinking we had gotten sold bullshit because nothing was happening, but it came on suddenly and powerfully. Everything became super intense. Colors became brighter, sounds became louder. Cars passing by look like bright-colored streaks and made a *whoosh* sound as they went by. Also, everything became unbearably funny. We spent the whole night walking around laughing our asses off at every little thing. Mescaline, or mesc, as we called it then, was to become a pretty regular thing. It was really cheap, only $3 each. As the year progressed, I was doing nothing but smoking, drinking, and dropping mesc. Later, I started getting LSD, which was much stronger than mesc.

Oceanside High School at that time had what they called an open campus, which meant that students were free to leave school grounds when they didn't have a class. Not just for lunch break but also for any period we had free. This led to a lot of class-cutting. When a bunch of AOT guys gathered in the lunchroom or the lobby, if we all had a free period, we would wind up cutting out for two or three periods, or even cutting the rest of the day and going somewhere for a brew-up. Usually, we would go to the house of someone whose parents weren't home and drink beer.

On one occasion, I saw a bunch of my Alpha buddies carrying another one of our Alpha brothers to the swampy creek that ran beside the school. It didn't look right, so I ran over to see what was going on. I saw Steve Maged lying on his back unconscious right next to the sewer pipe that was at the end of the stream. The Alpha guys said he had taken them to his house for a brew-up, and he wound up drinking a whole bottle of vodka. He had passed out while walking back to school, and they had to carry him the rest of the way. That was why they took him to the swamp. They didn't want him or themselves to get in trouble for drinking. When I walked over, Steve started vomiting while he was still unconscious. I immediately thought about Jimi Hendrix choking to death on his own vomit, and I said we had to turn Steve onto his stomach so he wouldn't drown in his own puke. Apparently, Steve was on an empty stomach when he drank the vodka, so the vomit looked like clear green seawater. It wasn't long before the bouncers from the school found out and came over to the swamp to see what was happening. They called an ambulance to come and take Steve to the hospital to pump his stomach.

For me, cutting class became such an everyday routine that I was basically going to school just to hang out and socialize. I think I had teachers who didn't even know me by face. I was a name on their class list that never showed up. I went every morning to get breakfast in the cafeteria and then went outside to smoke cigarettes or weed and then see if anyone was going on a brew-up somewhere. I was getting into the worst habits, and they were not because of the fraternity. My entire sophomore year was wasted, and I got incompletes in every class. I went to summer school and scored enough credits to avoid getting left back, but I was so out of control nobody could change my ways.

As far as the fraternity was concerned, I hung out mostly with Ed, who was a former AOT member, and Dave, who was not in any frat. But I did attend every AOT meeting and went to any brew-up that I could get in on. I enjoyed the frat very much, but Ed and Dave were my closest friends at that time. The three of us also hung out with Leo Black a lot that year.

AOT had a lot of inductions in 1980. Mostly sophomores were getting into AOT. In fact, the frat became bottom heavy. There was a disproportionate number of sophomores in AOT compared to juniors and seniors. By the end of the school year, we had about thirty sophomores, twenty seniors, but only ten juniors. We were already beginning to see that the next year was going to be a problem because AOT was not going to have enough seniors in 1981. Although I didn't like Rich Brandon's way of running the fraternity, I have to admit his year was the last year of the classic AOT of the late 1970s. He had a large chapter, plenty of new inductions throughout the year, and good parties.

He ran a tight ship, and there was strong brotherhood during his term of office. Things really began to fall apart after this year.

There was almost a brawl with Phi behind the high school one night, but he reached an agreement with the Phi president, and the tension settled down. Everybody from AOT and Phi had met in the back of the high school on separate sides of the field. Rich Brandon and John Corano went to the middle of the field to parley with the Phi president and vice president. They negotiated a peace treaty, agreeing not to let any brawls or jumping's take place between AOT and Phi in 1980. It was also determined that graffiti was a major source of tension between our two fraternities, so we agreed to cease spray-painting our fraternity symbols on any public buildings around Oceanside. I remember Rich announcing at the next meeting that anyone caught spray-painting AOT's logo or Greek letters anywhere in town was subject to expulsion from the fraternity. The fraternities were just starting to become gang-like, and his year was the last traditional year of fraternities being Greek-letter clubs. Spray-painting tags and graffiti was making us look bad in the town, so we attempted to curtail defacement of public property even though it didn't last long.

There were two parties I remember from when Rich Brandon was president. Actually, the first one was an event that fell apart. I remember the planning stages of a party we were going to have at one of the firehouses in Oceanside. This was the first party that would actually be in a rented party room instead of someone's backyard. This was to be held at the firehouse near Angelo Lombardo's house. He had gone over there with Rich Brandon to put a deposit on the room. After the room was rented, they told us at the next meeting that they had told the firehouse that the party was a going-away party for a friend going into the military. They knew we never could have gotten the room for a fraternity party. They had it all planned out; we had six kegs of beer, three Budweiser, and three Miller. We were all told not to show our fraternity colors until the party had been going on for more than an hour. The plan was that after we had a hundred people in the party room, we would show our colors and hang our banner. The night of the party, somehow the firehouse got wind of the fact that it was a fraternity party, and they locked us out. I also believe they kept the deposit.

After that happened, we still had six kegs of beer that had already been paid for, so we had the party two weeks later at Guy Schiavone's house. We didn't have money to pay a band, so Guy set up his stereo speakers in the windows pointing into the backyard and blasted music all night. Alpha members were admitted free if they wore colors; everyone else paid admission to get in. The party was a blast, but things started getting out of control after it. Someone had cut up a Phi sweater and hung it from the trees that night, and that pissed them off pretty good. They had threatened to bring in out-of-town Phi guys. Right after that, Alpha guys started getting jumped around town, and it was obviously out-of-towners. The guys were driving up and down Long Beach Road looking for anyone wearing Alpha colors. Guys had been jumped or chased for two or three weeks in a row. We assumed it was Island Park fraternities, and we suspected Island Park Phi, but we never knew for sure who they were; they didn't wear colors when they came into Oceanside.

One night, Billy Young, John McCann, and I were walking across Long Beach Road when all of a sudden, two cars came screeching up to us, and we saw about eight guys getting out with baseball bats. We scattered in three different directions, and trust me, I ran for my life. Eight guys with baseball bats was a recipe for serious injury or death. I ran across Long Beach and cut through Nathan's parking lot and bolted as fast as I could.

The jumping's were getting all of us edgy, and at the next meeting, we discussed what to do about it. It wasn't safe to be on Long Beach Road and wear Alpha colors. These guys always seemed to show up, and they always found guys walking alone or in small numbers. At the time, we suspected it was Island Park Phi, but it could have been Island Park Omega for all we knew; but most likely, it was Phi.

We decided to set a trap for them. Since they had been cruising Long Beach Road every Friday night, we thought we could catch them. We had a mandatory gathering at Burger King on Long Beach Road that Friday night. We had about forty to fifty AOT members gather in the back of the building so they wouldn't be seen from the street. We had two decoys, of which I was one, stand on the sidewalk in front of Burger King wearing AOT jackets. Lo and behold, these same guys who had chased Billy, John, and me two weeks before came pulling into the parking lot at Burger King when they saw us standing in front. As they pulled up, all of the Alphas came charging out from behind the building. Those eight guys ran back to their cars and bolted out of there just before they got swarmed on by forty or more guys. It was a very cool thing to see, and the jumping's of Alpha members by Island Park Phi stopped after that night. We weren't as easy as they thought we would be.

Later on in the school year, Ed Oren started having serious issues with his parents. They were trying to keep him under lock and key for another year, and he was rebelling against them big-time. He started running away from home and living on the streets. He slept at my house or Dave Weitz's house when we were able to sneak him in, but he also spent a lot of nights sleeping in people's tool-sheds. He was breaking into cars at night, stealing radios and anything else he thought he could sell. It was a vicious cycle with Ed and his parents. They would try to keep him a prisoner in his house, he would run away, the cops would eventually pick him up and take him home. His parents would promise to compromise with him so he wouldn't run away again, but they always did something to cause him to sneak out in the dead of night and run off again.

At one point, they put him in a juvenile drug rehab center that was in Valley Stream called Bridge. The place tried to brainwash the kids who were put there into forgetting their friends, not listening to their favorite music, and giving up on smoking pot. My Alpha buddy Leo Black had been sent there by his mother too. A lot of good it did him also. We would sneak out at night and go to Leo's house and toss rocks at his window. He would come out at two in the morning, and we would smoke weed with him. Eventually, his mother gave up on Bridge; it didn't stop him from smoking pot. But at the end of our junior year, Leo's mom moved to Arizona, and Leo and his brother Eric had to go.

Now Ed was in Bridge, and his parents were trying to break him like breaking a dog of bad behavior. Ed was too stubborn, and it wasn't going to work with him. Ed had tickets to see the rock band Rush at the Nassau Coliseum, and his parents were telling him they were not going to let him go. That was enough to cause him to run away again. The whole situation with Ed became an emotional drain on me. His parents were constantly coming to my house unannounced, thinking they would find him there.

In late April, it was time to plan the Senior Dinner. As was the Oceanside chapter's tradition, we elected a junior to head the committee to find a place to hold it and collect money from the brothers to pay for it. Steve Maged was elected to head the Senior Dinner committee, and he rented the party room at Beefsteak Charlie's in Hewlett. Beefsteak Charlie's was a franchise restaurant back in the late seventies, early eighties. Steve put a lot of effort into the party. When we got there, they told us to separate according to who had proof of age and those who were underage. Those who had proof sat at the tables set up in a square form in the center of the room. Those who didn't have proof sat in the booths around the room. I sat in the booth until they had finished checking IDs, then I moved over to the big table where they were serving beer by the pitcher.

Everybody got a steak, potato, and veggies. As the beer consumption went on, the guys were getting rowdy. I went to the men's room to take a leak, and I found Angelo Lombardo stomping on the bathroom sink and separating it from the wall. He was hammered drunk and was laughing his ass off as he trashed the men's room. When we left the restaurant that night, we found the tires on most of the Alpha guys' cars slashed. I think the restaurant management did that to get back at us for all the damage that was caused, but we never knew who did it. At the next meeting, Steve Maged was pissed because Beefsteak Charlie's threatened to sue him for the damages. He demanded to know who caused damage. That whole thing blew over as well when Beefsteak Charlie's found out that Steve was a minor. They had no business renting a party room to him and serving beer to his underage friends, and they decided to drop the whole thing. That was the last time we had a decent Senior Dinner.

After the Senior Dinner, the next thing was a time-honored tradition of marching in the Memorial Day Parade. Oceanside had allowed the town's fraternities and sororities to march in the parade for years, although the parade organizers were beginning to say they wanted fraternities and sororities banned from marching. We had been told not to show up this year, but all the fraternities and sororities showed up anyway. With all of us there, I guess it was too much trouble to refuse us from marching; so we got to march in 1980, but this tradition would soon come to an end.

Another ritual of the fraternity was to go have an all-day brew-up in Eisenhower Park in East Meadow after the parade. I had gone to Eisenhower Park after the parade every year. This particular year, we shared a lot with Omega. It was a beautiful sunny day, and everyone was having a good time drinking, smoking weed, and even serving some BBQ. The peaceful quiet of the day was shattered when a stranger came to our lot, jumped on top of a picnic table, and started pontificating about something. I was a few tables away, and I was curious as to what all the fuss was about, so I went over to see what was going on. As I got close to the table, I saw he had a bloody mouth, and there were about five people sitting at the table he was standing on. When I got close enough to hear what it was all about, I realized he had been beaten up and wanted us to help him out. He was saying stupid shit like, "I don't know any of you, and you don't know me, but I'm white and so are you. Those niggers on the other side of the softball field punched me out and took my money. They asked me if I wanted to buy weed, and as soon as I took out my money, they punched me out and stole it. We gotta go over there and kick their asses. You guys gotta help me."

Well, I knew I wanted no part of this guy and his problems, whatever they were, and the other AOT guys at the brew-up felt the same way. We told the guy he was crashing a private party and to move on, "Forget the lousy twenty bucks they took from you and go home." None of us were interested in that shit. He was a stranger to us, and he probably deserved whatever he got. He did leave our lot, but he found some other dumb fucks from the next lot who were willing to go with him to the softball field where black guys were playing. I didn't realize what was going on until the shit hit the fan really fast. This guy and eight or ten morons he got to go with him started walking across the softball field to confront the black guys who had a softball game going on. When the black guys realized they had trouble coming their way, they called out all their friends from lots surrounding the softball field.

In a matter of a minute, the field was swarmed with at least two hundred black men. They were pissed, and they started crossing the field and coming right toward our lot. This asshole and his friends came running back to us and begged for help. Within the next minute, mounted cops on horseback came charging onto the field and separated the two sides of the softball field. We were very tense for about ten minutes until the cops calmed the situation down. It turned out the guy who claimed he was robbed had actually tried to rob the black guys selling him the pot. He tried to grab the weed and run. They caught him, beat his ass, and took his money. Like I said, he deserved what he got; but now he was dragging us into his bullshit, and he was a total stranger to all of us. By the time we realized what it was all about and what an incident this shithead had just caused, he had to worry about getting his ass kicked by the Alpha guys as well. We were telling him to get the fuck off our lot before we jumped him as well. The cops wound up taking him away for some violation, and the shit calmed back down. I gotta say that was one of the scariest things I ever saw. It would have been Custer's Last Stand for us. We were outnumbered at least fifteen to one. Thank God there was no riot that day.

A short time before Memorial Day, my friendship with Ed Oren had finally gotten me into serious shit. As I said, when Ed was a runaway, he was breaking into cars and stealing anything he thought he could sell. One night, Ed and Dave Weitz came to my house, around two in the morning as usual, and they had mescaline, as usual. But they also had a bunch of stuff they had just taken from the car of a guy named Dennis Kravitz, who lived around the block from me. They had taken his eight-track stereo, a box of eight-track tapes, and a pellet gun. What I didn't realize was that a woman who lived across the street from Dennis Kravitz had seen them, and for some strange reason, she thought Ed Oren was me and she thought Dave Weitz was Ed Oren. So she told Dennis Kravitz that Ed Oren and I had broken into his car and stolen his stuff. I shouldn't have let them leave the stuff in my room, but I never thought I would get nailed since I didn't break into anyone's car or take anything.

I told Ed that I would ask around school to see if anyone wanted to buy the eight-track player from him. Well, Kravitz and a few of his buddies got wind of the fact that I was trying to sell the car stereo. One time, I was coming home late, around one in the morning, and I saw a Camaro parked across the street from my house with Connecticut plates on it. I noticed it right away and knew it didn't belong to any of my neighbors. As I walked up my front walkway, I was still looking over my shoulder at this Camaro when suddenly, Steve Diamante, one of Kravitz's friends, came out from behind the pine tree in my yard. He grabbed me and told me I was going with him. I struggled with him to break free when I got whacked in the back of the head with a billy club. It was the guy who owned the Camaro who cracked me in the head; the son of a bitch came up from behind while I was grappling with Diamante. I saw stars, and those two guys dragged me away from my house and put me in the backseat of the Camaro. They drove to Peter Jervis's house on Arrow Street. These guys were all friends with Kravitz, but Kravitz never showed his face or had the audacity to get involved with this. He let his friend Diamante and his cousin from out of town do the dirty work. I always hated Kravitz; he was a bully with younger kids, but a punk otherwise.

Once we were at Jervis's house, they started demanding to know where they could find Ed Oren. I told them I didn't know and wouldn't tell them if I did know. They called the cops on me, and a patrol car came and took me to the Fourth Precinct. I demanded that charges be pressed for kidnapping, unlawful imprisonment, and assault with a weapon against those guys. The cops laughed at me like it was all a big joke, what those assholes did to me.

I had no excuse for my friends breaking into cars and taking shit, nor did I have an excuse for keeping the stolen stuff in my room. But the worst thing I did was to try to help a friend in need, that was it. Those guys—Steve Diamante, Peter Jervis, Diamante's cousin from Connecticut, and Dennis Kravitz—by working in cahoots were guilty of serious crimes as far as I was concerned. Kidnapping, abduction, and assault with a weapon, almost fracturing my skull, were vigilantism, and the cops never should have tolerated it. My own lawyer told me to forget about pressing charges against them or risk pissing off the judge in my upcoming case. So I had to let the whole thing go.

The whole incident caused me to be sent to live with my father in Hicksville in the hopes that he could get me under control. I remained in Oceanside until the end of the school year, and in late June, I moved to my father's house in Hicksville. I started summer school in Bethpage High School to get the credits that I didn't earn in Oceanside High School so that I could go into the eleventh grade in Bethpage the next year.

The last thing I did with the fraternity before I moved was to go on an AOT camping trip to Wildwood State Park in Wading River. I was bummed out about moving and becoming an inactive member, and I was looking forward to this weekend camping trip. I knew nothing about camping and had no gear at all. Not even a sleeping bag. Before I went on this trip, my father told me, "At the first sign of trouble, call me, anytime, day or night, and I will come out there to pick you up. Whatever you do, don't get into trouble out there in Riverhead."

I figured, *How much trouble could we get into in the woods?* I was wrong. We all met on a Friday night to drive out to Wading River. I walked to the house we were meeting at. I had no tent or even a sleeping bag. I didn't give a shit. I just wanted to go on a trip with my fraternity brothers. When I arrived, they saw I had no gear and asked what I had brought for the trip. I smiled and pulled out a sandwich bag filled with twenty rolled joints, and I said, "I brought weed."

"Good man, Freddy, you're riding shotgun with me. Sit up front and light one of those up," Guy Schiavone said.

We went in two cars. I went with Guy, and we had John Corano and Danny Baldano in the backseat. The whole drive there, we cruised the Long Island Expressway, going at top speed, drinking beer, and smoking weed all along the way. The other car was driven by John McCann, and he had Paul Sorvino, Angelo Lombardo, and another guy whose name I just can't remember. We got to the campsite late, and we all crashed soon after we got there. The guys had set up a tent, but I slept in the backseat of Guy's car that night.

The next day, we went to a nearby supermarket to get food and beer. It was like the scene from *Animal House* when Boone stuffs all the food into Pinto's sweater. We walked out of there with packages of bacon, sausages, chicken wings, hamburger meat, and anything else we could fit under our shirts. I actually didn't take anything; I was too nervous to do that shit, but I bought stuff they couldn't fit under their shirts like eggs, hamburger and hot dog buns, and beers. I don't know how they were able to walk out of that supermarket with so much stuff under their clothes, but they did. We went back to the campsite and cooked breakfast. The rest of the day, we drank beer and smoked weed. Later that night, after dark, we heard some commotion from the campsite next to ours. The people in that site were inviting us to meet them in between the campsites and party with them. I remember they had a bunch of ugly girls with them, and the guys were dull as all hell. I thought it was a waste to smoke my weed with them. I was glad when they went back to their campsite after about an hour of partying with us.

When we went back to our campsite, we realized that our friend Danny Baldano wasn't with us. We started getting nervous that he could be lost in the woods in the dead of night. We started fanning out and looking for him. We really were worried that he was lost in the woods somewhere. When we went back to our campsite after about thirty minutes of looking around, we found Danny in the tent getting a blow job from one of the ugly chicks from the other campsite.

After we realized he slipped away intentionally, Angelo Lombardo got a very rude idea. He said the chick was going to blow all of us, and we should just follow his lead. This sounded like trouble to me, and I stayed outside of the tent, but I poked my head in just enough to hear what was going on. Angelo, John, and Guy all went into the tent in their underwear and pretended like they were surprised to find this girl in their tent. She was startled, and Danny jumped up and pulled up his pants. I thought the whole thing was rude. The dude was getting a blow job; they should have left them alone. But no, the three of them start telling this girl that they were going to go get her boyfriend from the other campsite and bring him to the tent so he could see what his girlfriend had been doing for the past hour, unless she consented to blow all of us. The girl freaked out, got pissed off, and said no fucking way would she take all of us on. She and Danny left the tent, and Danny screwed her somewhere in the woods. He came back about a half hour later. He was annoyed with Angelo, Guy, and John, but not really pissed off; after all, he did get laid.

About twenty minutes after Danny came back, we started hearing commotion from the other campsite again; this time, it wasn't so friendly-sounding. The girl had told her boyfriend that she had been held against her will and raped by all of us. This was getting really ugly. They were coming to our campsite to start trouble. These guys weren't tough at all, and they soon realized that they faced a serious ass-kicking if they didn't go back to their campsite.

Before long, the park rangers showed up and, soon after that, the Suffolk County police. This girl was still claiming she had been gang-raped, and it was beginning to look like we were all going to be charged with a crime. I could hear my father's voice as he told me before I left, "At the first sign of trouble, call me, at any time, day or night, and I will come out there to pick you up. Whatever you do, don't get into trouble out there in Riverhead."

I was really starting to get scared over this. I was there; I saw that what happened may have been stupid and rude, but nobody raped that girl. In fact, she went with Danny of her own free will into the woods to have sex. She had to make up a story to explain to her boyfriend why she had been gone for an hour and a half.

Then Guy Schiavone said to the cops, "I haven't had sexual intercourse tonight, and I demand a physical exam to prove it, and she should have one too. If she claims we all raped her, then there will be evidence on her body to prove that."

Suddenly the girl started saying she just wanted to forget the whole thing. Now Guy, Angelo, and John were going nuts. They started accusing her of lying, making a false statement, ruining our reputations. The cops soon realized she had made the whole story up, but they were telling us we had to leave the campsite.

Now Guy, John, and Angelo were arguing with the cops, demanding a refund for the campsite. The cops were threatening to arrest us if we didn't leave the campgrounds immediately. After John McCann told the cops that his cousin was a detective in the Suffolk County Police Department, they gave us fifteen minutes to vacate the campgrounds or be arrested. I was scared shitless. I just wanted to get out of there, and these guys were verbally abusing the Suffolk County police to no end. I don't know why they didn't actually arrest us, but they wound up escorting us out of the campgrounds all the way to the Long Island Expressway and warned Guy that we would all be spending some time in the county jail in Riverhead if we didn't get on the expressway, leave, and not come back.

I was dropped off in front of my house in Oceanside around three in the morning, exhausted and filthy from two days of not showering and wearing the same clothes.

At this point, I was actually ready to move to Hicksville with my father. I was tired of hanging out, tired of the fraternity, and I needed a change of scenery. I began summer school in Bethpage High School in July and earned the credits I needed to pass into the eleventh grade when school started in September.

Oceanside AOT, 1982

Oceanside AOT circa 1970

Oceanside AOT circa 1978

Oceanside AOT Senior Dinner, 1978

Chapter Thirteen

My Junior Year

The last thing I did before moving to my father's house in Hicksville was to tell the new AOT president, Steve Maged, that I was moving and had to become an inactive member of the fraternity. Usually, there was a $20 charge payable to the fraternity's treasury to become inactive earlier than your graduating year. Steve was cool with me and waived the fee and told me I was always welcome back in Alpha Omega Theta if I ever moved back to Oceanside, or if I was able to attend a few meetings during the next year.

I lived in Hicksville, but due to the way the district lines were drawn, I lived in the Bethpage school district and went to Bethpage High School. I found drastic differences between Bethpage and Oceanside immediately. First, I had trouble making friends in Bethpage for a few months. The students were cliquish, and most had known each other since elementary school. Also, I was a metal-head, and it showed in my appearance. I wore a dungaree jacket with *Black Sabbath* painted on the back. There were virtually no metal-heads in the school. Most were into mellow music like the Grateful Dead, the Doors, and the Rolling Stones. I was a bit of an oddity for a while, except for a girl named Diane Roth, who had a crush on me—and she was not shy about showing it. She waited for me at my locker between almost every class. I dated her for a little while, but we didn't have much in common, and it didn't last more than a month.

While I was trying to fit in at Bethpage High School, there was an upheaval going on in Oceanside between Alpha Omega Theta and Alpha Sigma Phi. The first day of school, the new Phi president, Frank Aiello, Anthony's older brother, had called out the AOT president, Steve Maged, to a fight. Frank was the toughest guy in the senior class and, therefore, in the school; and Steve Maged just wasn't willing to fight the guy. This was causing some friction within AOT as well since some of the brothers in the junior class thought the fraternity as a whole was losing face. It was believed by many that Steve had an obligation to fight Frank even if it meant getting his ass kicked. There was no shame in losing a fight, especially to a guy like Frank Aiello, who was a black belt in karate and had a reputation for wining his street fights; but Steve Maged was looking like a wimp, not worthy of being AOT president. Steve tried to shift the responsibility of dealing with Frank Aiello and Phi as a whole to AOT as a whole. He agreed to a brawl between Alpha and Phi to take place on the field at Elementary School #5. When everyone showed up at School #5, they found the police already there, and the crowd was dispersed. Some within AOT suspected that the seniors and, more specifically, the higher officers actually tipped off the cops so that the brawl would be prevented. The AOT seniors were the first to run when they saw police, and this pissed off the juniors in AOT.

Before everyone scattered, AOT and Phi agreed to meet on the field at the high school in an hour. When the Alphas got to the field at the high school, they saw all of the Phi members had gathered, but half of AOT didn't show up. None of the seniors showed up either. The AOT juniors and sophomores knew they were outnumbered two to one, and they decided to leave the area. But before they left, they decided to call an emergency meeting of the younger brothers the next night.

The meeting was mandatory to all juniors, sophomores, and the few members who were in the junior high. The meeting was also closed to AOT's seniors, and all members were instructed not to tell the seniors about the meeting under the penalty of expulsion from the fraternity. At the meeting, the juniors made their case for impeaching the officers and throwing the officers out of the fraternity as well. The debate was intense, and the meeting ran for hours, longer than most meetings would go. The case was made that AOT was suffering a loss of face and reputation as a result of the actions of Steve Maged, Danny Baldano, and the other officers.

Every year in September, it was recruiting season for AOT, and we always had plenty of new recruits at the start of each new school year. But this year, the student body seemed to be waiting out AOT to see if AOT could survive Frank Aiello's Phi. Recruits who might have joined AOT were going to Omega instead. There was a massive loss of new blood, and it had to be stopped. A new regime was needed to show that AOT was still viable and still strong.

The final decision of the brotherhood was that President Steve Maged and Vice President Danny Baldano were impeached and expelled from the fraternity. The remaining officers were impeached, but not expelled. The rest of the seniors were given choices of how they wanted to end their association with AOT. First, they could quit the fraternity; second, they could remain active members but had to submit to the junior officers running the fraternity; third, they could save face by going inactive, technically remaining brothers in good standing but no longer allowed to participate in fraternity affairs. Most of the seniors took the third option. Some of them had older brothers who had been in AOT, and they didn't want to embarrass their older brothers by getting kicked out of AOT.

So the officers were impeached, and most of the seniors went inactive and moved on; now the juniors were in charge of Oceanside AOT. Pat Kapps was elected president, Billy Young was elected vice president, Jon Truman was elected secretary, and Bobby Bradley was elected treasurer. The troubles with Alpha Sigma Phi were about to get worse.

Phi smelled blood in the water, and the sharks started circling. They knew that AOT had internal upheaval and had lost members. The fraternity was now even smaller, and Phi wanted to deliver a deathblow. Frank Aiello now warned the Alphas to no longer wear colors anywhere in Oceanside. Soon they were demanding the dissolution of the Oceanside chapter of Alpha Omega Theta Fraternity. They also were demanding the Alpha constitution and all fraternity books and documents be turned over to them.

Between Frank Aiello and his brother Anthony, they had the whole AOT chapter in dire straits. Nobody was able to challenge either one of them, and with the full force of Phi behind them, they were unstoppable. The Alphas had to take the fraternity underground for a few months. The new junior officers had been confident that they could turn things around and bring AOT back to the top spot in the school's social structure, but they were now under siege.

To get a breather and quiet things down, the junior officers announced the Oceanside chapter of AOT had officially closed. They had actually gone underground and still held meetings. Phi started demanding the AOT books be turned over to them. To make matters worse, the ruse of pretending to close the Oceanside chapter was so effective that the inactive members from the Oceanside chapter called an emergency meeting and demanded the current members all attend. I had been getting bits and pieces of what was going on in Oceanside while I was living in Hicksville, and I was curious to know what was happening, so I went to the emergency meeting. I had to take a bus from what was then called the Mid-Island Shopping Plaza to Roosevelt Field Mall, then transfer and take the N15 bus to Oceanside. The whole trip took about two and a half hours, including a lot of walking.

I got to the meeting, and there were about ten or twelve of the AOT alumni present and about thirty active AOT members attending. AOT president from 1977 Phil Gerardi was pissed and wanted to know why the chapter was closed. Pat Kapps and Billy Young explained the situation with Phi and how we just didn't have the manpower to stand nose to nose with them at this time. The plan was to wait it out until Memorial Day at the end of the year, and AOT would show up to march, thereby showing the chapter was still around. Phil and the others agreed that this was OK for a short-term strategy. In the meantime, Phil wanted the AOT briefcase that held all of the AOT books and documents to hold for us. This ensured that the suitcase would not fall into the hands of Phi. It also gave AOT president Pat Kapps an excuse to not give up the books. Phi was told that the older inactive AOT members took the books from us, which actually was true.

Phil was really cool with us and offered to let us hold meetings at his apartment in Long Beach if we needed a place to hold meetings. Before long, we were having brew-ups in Phil's apartment on the weekends. There were anywhere from ten to twenty of us drinking and swigging on a jug of Kentucky moonshine he had. It was harsh stuff. One shot and most guys would pass out.

The troubles with Phi seemed to fade out after a few weeks. AOT had caught a breather and had room to reorganize. Although I was still living in Hicksville and did not attend meetings, they continued holding meetings and actually started recruiting again. The chapter was beginning to slowly rebuild and rebound.

I was just beginning to make some friends at Bethpage High School. Mr. Henrich, the teacher in my English class, had taken a dislike to me and another guy in my class named Bill Mansfield. He had put us seated next to each other in the back of the room. Mr. Henrich was a real asshole and one of the worst teachers I ever had. He had formed his opinions based entirely on how we dressed and the long hair we had. Close to the end of the year, Mr. Henrich had told Bill and me to stop coming to his class. He promised to not report us for cutting if we didn't get caught by anyone else. Like I said, he was a poor excuse for a teacher. Bill and I became friends, and he invited me to hang out with his crowd. They all hung out and drank at an elementary schoolyard a block away from Bill's house. The town was so mellow that the cops never seemed to show up, and the place would sometimes have twenty people partying in the schoolyard. I found all the guys from Bethpage to be very cool to hang with, and I had a lot of good times partying there.

I was actually surprised to find that they had no fraternities in Bethpage at all. I had been around fraternities all my life, and I had believed that all towns had them. I didn't think they had an AOT chapter, but I thought there was some kind of Greek system there. When I realized there was none, I started thinking the area was ripe for colonization. I started wearing my Alpha tee shirt to school frequently. The school didn't know what the shirt meant, so I was never told not to wear it on school grounds. The students also didn't know what the tee shirt represented either; but one day, I was walking down the hall, and some guy came up to me, looked at my tee shirt, gave a thumbs-up, and said, "Alpha, yeah man, AOT rules."

I was surprised to have someone recognize an Alpha shirt, so I said, "Are you in AOT?"

"No, but I know a lot of guys in AOT. Do you know Spooky?" he said.

This was the first time I ever heard the name Spooky; it's pretty ironic that I first heard the name of Valley Stream's legendary president all the way over in Bethpage, where nobody even knew what a fraternity was. But I said to him, "No, I don't know who Spooky is. Who is that?"

"Wow, you never heard of Spooky? He is the president of Valley Stream AOT at Valley Stream Central High School. He has a massive chapter with well over a hundred members. When I saw you wearing an Alpha shirt, I thought you must be from Valley Stream too."

"No, I'm from Oceanside," I said.

"When did you move to Bethpage?" he said.

"I moved here at the beginning of the summer. I can't believe there are no fraternities here. We should start an AOT chapter in Bethpage High School," I said.

"I am into it. Let's try to recruit some people, and we can get Spooky and the president from Oceanside to induct and approve the new chapter," he said.

After that initial conversation, I never had any constructive progress with the guy, whose name I cannot remember. He seemed to have a harder time making friends at Bethpage High School than I did, and he was never able to recruit anyone. My efforts were less than astounding as well. The first person I approached with the idea was a guy I worked with at an after-school job in a machine shop in Hicksville. His name was Lou Evan. I talked to him about my fraternity and told him I wanted to launch a chapter of it in Bethpage, and I asked him if he would be interested. He told me that he was being recruited by Bill Mansfield into a gang he was trying to start that they called the Nightstalkers. This changed my whole perspective on the situation. The town was way too mellow for a gang, and I was curious as to why they were trying to start one.

I was friendly with Bill, and I asked him about the Nightstalkers. It seemed that the only friction in Bethpage was occasional altercations with a neighboring school district. It seemed that there was some kind of half-assed club in Island Trees called Usinc. The guys from Island Trees would occasionally start fights or jump someone in Bethpage. This was my leverage to get an AOT chapter going, I thought. I pitched the idea to Bill that if he could recruit at least ten guys to start an AOT chapter in Bethpage, then they would be a part of a brotherhood that stretched across Nassau County. They would have friends from six or seven towns who would back them up and put these douche bags from Island Trees in their place. Bill was intrigued. He asked what he would have to do to get into AOT. I told him that I would bring him to a meeting in Oceanside and that he would get smacked around by all the members, followed by a paddling.

Bill had never heard of such an induction method, and he couldn't believe that guys in Oceanside routinely volunteered for such abuse all for the pleasure of wearing fraternity colors.

I had only one run-in with these douche bags called Usinc; it was, ironically, at a punk rock nightclub in Valley Stream called Exit 13. It was called Exit 13 because it was right off of Exit 13 on the Southern State Parkway. I had gone there with Bill Mansfield and a guy we called Moose. His nickname was totally a goof; he was a skinny, wormy guy with Coke-bottle glasses. Moose had a car, and we didn't, so he went with us that night. I was never into punk rock much, and I really found the place to be a bore, but it was filled with these assholes wearing white tee shirts with the word *Usinc* in black iron-on letters on the front of the shirt.

I was sitting in a chair against the wall, annoyed by the simplistic bullshit punk music that was assaulting my eardrums, when out of nowhere, some guy wearing one of those stupid-looking shirts came up to me and told me to stop looking at his girlfriend. Let me tell you, I was ready to go home twenty minutes before this shit started, and I had no idea of who this asshole's girlfriend was. For all I know, I may have made eye contact with some chick for two seconds without knowing it, and this douche bag was now annoyed.

I told him I didn't know who his girlfriend was, and I wasn't staring at anyone. To his credit, my friend Bill Mansfield rushed right over when he saw a situation happening. It didn't take long before we were surrounded by at least twenty of these Usinc shitheads. They pretty much told us to leave or get jumped by all of them. After we got into Moose's car, I had a brainstorm. I reminded Bill that we were in Valley Stream; the heart of Alpha Omega Theta Fraternity was Valley Stream, I told him. Even though I didn't personally know anyone from Valley Stream, I knew that Valley Stream AOT stood by and supported other AOT chapters. I was sure that if they found out that some half-assed gang from out of town set up shop and claimed a nightclub in Valley Stream as their clubhouse, Valley Stream AOT would not take kindly to that. I told Bill and Moose that this guy named Spooky was the president and that he had over one hundred members in his private army. All we had to do, I told them, was to drive down the main strips in Valley Stream until we saw someone wearing an Alpha jacket or sweater. I could prove my membership in Oceanside AOT and was sure we could convince the Valley Stream Alphas to go over to Exit 13 and take over the place.

As it were, Moose was not at all into any kind of confrontation and wanted no part in getting guys together to kick the Island Trees' assholes out of the nightclub. He was the driver and refused to drive around Valley Stream so I could locate AOT members, and he immediately got back on the Southern State parkway and drove us back to Bethpage. I always wondered what the scene would have been like if we had found some AOT members and confronted the Usinc assholes that night. Just like twenty of them surrounded us, it would have been fun to see them surrounded by forty, fifty, or even sixty AOT members pissed off that these out-of-towners had the nerve to set up shop in the heart of Alpha Omega Theta.

I wanted also to impress Bill Mansfield with the brotherhood of AOT. I was sure that he would be totally into it if he saw fifty guys wearing Alpha colors. I assured Bill it was on the up-and-up and that in order to get the Valley Stream and Oceanside chapters interested in establishing a Bethpage chapter, we would need no less than ten members to start. Compared to Oceanside AOT, which had about fifty members, and Valley Stream AOT, which had more than one hundred members, ten to start a chapter was a real lowball number, I thought, but possible since there were no other fraternities in Bethpage. Bill pitched the idea to some of the crowd he ran with, and no one was interested, no one at all. And so that was the end of the idea of Bethpage AOT.

I still had plenty of good times hanging out with the Bethpage crowd. The whole time I was in Bethpage High School, I never saw even one fight. There just seemed to be no friction at all in that town. We had a few cool road trips. I remember going with Bill and maybe three other guys to see the Rolling Stones at JFK Stadium in Philadelphia. And again, we drove all the way to Philadelphia to see the Who at JFK Stadium.

Although I was away from the bullshit fighting and trouble that was always going on in Oceanside, the drugs were still easy to get in Bethpage too. It didn't take long before I found more than one connection to get mescaline. Right across the street from the high school, there was a gas station, and the attendant sat in a Plexiglas shelter and sold microdots of mesc from there. I also found a deli in Hicksville near my house that was a virtual drug store. Guys hung out there and sold weed, mesc, coke, and who knows what else. During my junior year, I was taking so much mescaline that I was dropping hits probably three or four times a week. I had gotten so comfortable with tripping out that I was taking the stuff early in the morning and passing the whole day at school on a mesc trip. I would then go to work after school and then home to eat dinner with my family. Despite the intense nature of psychedelic drugs, I had developed an ability to keep a straight face, and very few people were ever able to spot that I was tripping out.

One day, while I was at school, a friend of mine named Phil Nolan came up to me and said, "Hey, Fred, you're from Oceanside, aren't you?"

"Yes, I am," I said.

"Oceanside is in the paper today," he said. He had a *Newsday* in his hand.

"What happened in Oceanside?" I said.

"They found a guy murdered behind a shopping center. Did you know this guy John Dodd?" he said.

I grabbed the paper from him and read the article; I couldn't believe what I just read. John Dodd was the change-maker in the game room at Nathan's. John was openly gay and also had a nasty habit of propositioning the teen boys who hung out at Nathan's. He had been threatened and beaten up a few times, but now he was dead.

"Yeah, I knew him," I said.

Soon I would find out just how close I had come to getting involved with the events surrounding John Dodd's murder.

When I lived in Hicksville, I was going to Oceanside on most weekends to hang out with my friends Ed Oren and Dave Weitz. Dave's house was a place where we spent a lot of time hanging out. A few weeks before John Dodd was murdered, Dave Weitz had gotten a connection to get pharmaceutical-quality quaaludes. They came in plastic trays like cold medicine. Theses quaaludes were super-strong; as soon as you swallowed it, it took effect. They were so strong that everyone who took one would pass out within thirty to forty minutes.

One Saturday afternoon, Dave and I had taken the bus to Roosevelt Field Mall, and we took quaaludes. Dave and I had been taking them, and we had developed the stamina to not pass out after taking them. The whole day was a blur, and the only thing I remember was getting off the bus in front of Nathan's, which was across the street from Dave's house. Dave had asked me if I wanted to go in to his house to hang out and smoke some weed. I was really tired and ready to crash, and I didn't want to fall asleep at Dave's house, so I headed home. The decision to go home and not enter Dave's house that night saved me a world of trouble.

As it were, I started walking home, and when I got to the corner of Windsor Parkway and Oceanside Road, a car pulled up to me. The window rolled down, and it was Jennifer Marks. Jennifer was in Delta Pi Delta, and I had known her since junior high. She saw me staggering home and offered me a ride. I always liked Jennifer, and I am sure I was way too stoned on ludes to make a move on her. I don't remember much of what happened while I was with her, except for sitting in her car a block away from my house and smoking a joint with her. Then I went home and crashed for the night and slept well into Sunday afternoon the next day. The next day, I went home to Hicksville without seeing Dave or going back to his house, so I had no idea what happened the night before.

When Dave went into his house that Saturday night, a massive shit storm was about to brew up. Dave's house was always a cool place to hang out. His parents were separated, and his mother never complained about kids drinking or smoking pot in the house. People came by Dave's house constantly. When Dave went into his house, he found his brother Brian hanging out with two of his Phi buddies, Tom Pepino and Michael Osterland. They were all fucked up from the quaaludes, and they were drinking beer and smoking pot. Dave became angry at his brother for having these guys all getting fucked up in the house, and he told them all to get out. In the process of kicking them out, Dave got into a fight with Osterland in his backyard. Dave pinned him down on his back and punched him in the face a few times. After that, he made Pepino and Osterland leave his house.

Now what Dave didn't know was what had happened about thirty to forty minutes prior to kicking them out. Apparently, Brian Weitz, Michael Osterland, Thomas Pepino, and Joe Sandoval had tried to break into the smoke shop in the shopping center next to Nathan's. They had a dumb idea that they could break in through the roof and climb through the heating ducts. When they found they could not get in, they climbed back down into the alley behind the shopping center. There they found John Dodd sleeping on the concrete slab the big generator was mounted on. John would regularly get drunk at the Tucker Inn across the street from Nathan's and then sleep it off behind the shopping center.

When they saw him passed out back there, Osterland looked at the others and said, "It's John Dodd. Let's kill him."

"No, leave him alone, he's not bothering anyone," said Brian Weitz.

Brian never thought they were serious about killing him. He thought they were really going to beat the shit out of him, which he also wanted no part of. After that, they all went back to the Weitz house to hang out, drink, and smoke. About a half hour later, Brian's older brother Dave came home and kicked Osterland and Pepino out of the house. What Dave and Brian didn't realize was that after kicking those two out, they decided to go back and actually kill John Dodd. And they took the murder weapon from Dave Weitz's backyard. They each grabbed an end of a large sparkling rock that was a decorative garden piece. They walked it across the street, each holding an end. It was a Saturday night, and Nathan's was always packed with people on a Saturday night. These two assholes walked right by dozens of people unnoticed that night, but it did get them caught very quickly. People did remember seeing them go back there that night. They were both arrested within two days of the murder.

After Dave and Brian went back into their house and after Pepino and Osterland left, they found Joey Sandoval crawling out of Brian's closet on his hands and knees. Apparently, Joe had passed out in Brian's closet, and he staggered out the back door, presumably headed home since Osterland and Pepino were already gone when he regained consciousness. Whether or not Joe Sandoval had been involved with John Dodd's murder is only speculation, but in fact, it was only Osterland and Pepino who did the killing.

They carried the rock all the way across the street and placed it on top of the generator right beside John's head. The generator stood about four and a half feet tall. That's how far it dropped after they pushed it off the ledge of the generator, and it went crashing down on John Dodd's head. He instantly went into convulsions, and the two animals beat, stomped, and punched John to death.

As I said before, John was openly gay, and he did make rude sexual passes at teens hanging out at Nathan's, myself included; but in no way did he deserve to be murdered in such a brutal fashion. I had seen John sleeping it off behind the shopping center many times, and I never bothered the guy. More than once, he offered to blow me, and I just said, "No, thanks. Not interested." John was an alcoholic, and most of the time, it was the beer talking. He was always shitfaced drunk when he made passes at the kids hanging out around Nathan's.

As I had said before, I had just missed getting caught in all that bullshit by a few seconds. If I had gone into Dave's house instead of going home that night, I would have been involved with the altercation with Pepino and Osterland. Instead, I hung out with Jennifer Marks.

I had found out about John Dodd's murder from the *Newsday* about two days after it happened. I then found out the aspect of it that connected Osterland and Pepino to Dave and Brian Weitz the next weekend when I saw Dave. I could not believe that shit had gone down and that the murder weapon was taken from Dave's backyard. I had enough problems of my own, and I was grateful that this ugly shit was not affecting my life. I didn't need to be connected to a brutal murder.

The common thread between Michael Osterland, Thomas Pepino, Joe Sandoval, and Brian Weitz was that they were all in Alpha Sigma Phi. When the *Newsday* reported on the arrests of those guys, it also mentioned their fraternity affiliation. Fraternities were getting on the bad side of the school, the police, and the general public for the past few years; but news like that was the first nail in the coffin of the fraternity system, not only in Oceanside but in all the neighboring towns as well. People were now regarding fraternities to be nothing more than sophisticated gangs with fancy names. It didn't really matter that Alpha Sigma Phi was the worst of the bunch; all fraternities were being lumped into one category.

Pepino and Osterland were tried separately. Osterland copped a plea to voluntary manslaughter and received a seven- to fifteen-year sentence. He was out in eight years. Pepino went to trial and fought to the end and was found guilty of third-degree murder and received a fifteen-to-life sentence. Joey Sandoval and Brian Weitz were charged with attempted burglary. Sandoval got a slap on the wrist, and Brian, who was a juvenile, was given an eighteen-month sentence at a juvenile detention center in Hawthorne, New York. Eighteen months was the maximum sentence he could receive, being less than sixteen years of age at the time.

By this time, some of the guys I knew in Bethpage knew about the fraternity aspect of this murder, and they were turned right off to bringing a fraternity to

Bethpage. It's just as well; like I said, the town was just too mellow for the kind of conflict that was going on in Oceanside.

The bad reputation that Phi was getting was also being noticed by their own president, Frank Aiello. Frank saw the implications of presiding over a bunch of criminals. He found out that they were planning to do the same thing to Omega what they did to AOT earlier in the year. In Frank's own words, "In '81, after we told AOT they couldn't wear colors, I realized that I had a lot of friends in AOT, and it was more about a few guys we didn't like. Phi still wanted to pursue trouble, and they wanted Omega next. I had no enemies in Omega and told the members who wanted to fight them next, 'You're on your own.' Within a week, I took my cousin and about fifteen members and started the Counts. We hung out with AOT on the weekends for the last year of my high school days and had some good parties at the high school and School #4. We also went pool jumping, and the few Phi members left and the other rogues got beaten up at the high school on the baseball field while at least forty of us [Counts] watched and laughed. Mike Delacatta's father was in the original Counts. It was red-and-black colors. That was why I used the Counts for the new frat. I thought it was a reincarnation of what I wanted Phi to be. Good guys out to have fun with respect."

This turn of events was a shock to everyone in Oceanside. No one ever expected Frank Aiello to resign as president of Alpha Sigma Phi and quit the fraternity. But even worse for Phi, he took about one-third of its active members with him when he quit and reestablished the Counts. Frank quickly built up the Counts with recruitment drives and offered an olive branch to AOT. The president of AOT in 1981 was Pat Kapps, who was a junior, and he remembered being approached by Frank to flip the entire chapter of AOT into the Counts.

"The Counts thing kind of started when there was a split in Phi between the Sandoval's and Frank and Joe Aiello. I think Frank just got fed up with all their constant bullshit. He decided to start his own frat. He began recruitment with the guys in his karate class. Frank was a teacher. At the same time, it was kind of when Alpha was in a rebuilding phase. We had kicked out most of the seniors and were basically left with mostly juniors. Frank had proposed that we join his new fraternity together with what was left of Alpha to form the Counts. At a meeting, we ran it past a few guys. Some guys liked the idea, and some didn't. We mulled it over for a few days, and then at a meeting at Mike Shriver's house, we were going to put to a vote whether to disband Alpha and join the new frat. I myself was kind of riding the fence. Before the meeting, John Rector and I had a long talk about what Alpha meant to each of us and all the shit we went through, so during the meeting, I decided that we were not going to disband. Some guys did leave, though, to join the Counts. Mike Triado, Lonny

Truman, Eric Black, and I think a couple of others. Frank was actually waiting outside the meeting for an answer. When we told him, he was actually pretty cool about it, and we became allies in the war against Phi. After that, Phi was never really the same."

This was a very interesting turn of events, to say the least. Frank Aiello had been a catalyst in the near dissolution of AOT in the first weeks of the 1981 school year. And now he was leaving Phi, taking a big chunk of its membership with him, and also attempting to convince AOT to combine with his new fraternity. Although AOT did lose a handful of members, we were not affected in the way Alpha Sigma Phi was affected. They were now the smallest fraternity in Oceanside after having been the biggest. That's a big slide downward in less than one school year. Although AOT did not dissolve to join the Counts, a new feeling of brotherhood and partnership developed between AOT and Frank Aiello's new social club, the Counts. This new partnership made the AOT/Counts connection a force to be reckoned with. It also caused another unforeseen effect. Omega Gamma Delta had started to become close allies with Alpha Sigma Phi. This would have serious repercussions in the next year. I was still living in Hicksville during all of this, and I had no idea about the Counts being formed until the next year, when I moved back to Oceanside.

As spring approached, I got a phone call in my house in Hicksville from my good friend Leo Black. I will never forget what he said to me.

"Fred, it's Leo. Tommy Farnswell is dead," he said.

"What? How can that be? He is only seventeen years old. How can he be dead?" I said.

"He was found dead in his garage with the car running. No one knows if it was suicide or accidental yet," Leo said.

I was in shock. I had never lost a friend before. I was only sixteen years old and never thought at that time in my life that I could lose a friend like that. Tommy Farnswell came from a strict Catholic family. It was not thinkable that he would kill himself. I was told later on that due to the fact that he was found under the dashboard with greasy hands and tools spread out all over the place, it was ruled an accident. They determined that he had been working on his car and didn't think to open the garage door.

By this time, Tommy's younger brother Ricky was already in AOT as well. There was a huge outpouring of grief and sympathy for the Farnswell family from the bothers of Alpha Omega Theta. We all attended his wake and funeral. There must have been more than forty of us, and we all wore Alpha sweaters to the wake. I was told by Ricky Farnswell that Tommy was buried with his AOT sweater. I was shocked and saddened by Tommy's death, and I still think of him a lot to this day. We dogged for AOT together; we discovered beer, pot, and girls together; we had grown up together; and I miss him still.

The final event of the 1981 school year was the Memorial Day Parade. As usual, we were told we would not be permitted to be in the parade; and as usual, we thought it was all talk and that we would be allowed to march if we just showed up. This year, they meant business. We gathered at the staging area at School #1 on Foxhurst Road. We saw Nassau County police form a human chain in front of us, and they said anyone trying to march would be arrested. A few guys tried to get past them, and sure enough, all the cops broke out into sprints, chasing everyone wearing a fraternity sweater. The cops scattered AOT, Omega Gamma Delta, Alpha Sigma Phi, and the Counts in about five minutes. That was it. No more marching in the parade for any fraternities or sororities anymore. This was the town and police's way of telling us that our presence in Oceanside was no longer wanted. It was the beginning of the end.

Rockville Centre AOT group picture, class of 1977

Oceanside AOT brew-up in Eisenhower Park, 1982

CHAPTER FOURTEEN

My Senior Year

I began my senior year still attending Bethpage High School. Although I was still smoking weed and taking mescaline regularly, I had stabilized my grades and was passing my classes. I made it through my junior year without needing summer school. I was doing all right with classes in the beginning of my senior year as well, but I was bored shitless. My best friend in Bethpage, Bill Mansfield, had graduated last year, and I now had no one in school to hang out with. I was friendly with a lot of people, but not friends on a hanging-out basis. I started thinking about moving back to Oceanside.

By this time, I was thinking about my last year in AOT and my friends Ed Oren and Dave Weitz. I had been out of touch with AOT for so long I didn't know who the officers were, or if I was even still in the fraternity anymore. But I asked my dad if I could finish up my senior year in Oceanside. He agreed, but I knew he was disappointed. In hindsight, I should have stayed in Bethpage High School; there was nothing but more trouble waiting for me when I returned to Oceanside High School, as I would soon find out.

My first day back, I went to the lobby before first period and went to the Alpha bench to see who was hanging out. I saw Pat Kapps first, and he was surprised to see me. He invited me to come to the AOT meeting that night. I was surprised to find that they hadn't kicked me out while I was gone. Although the fraternity was not a high priority for me, I was curious to see the state of the frat, so to speak. I went to the meeting that night and saw quite a few changes. Billy Young was AOT president, dues were raised from 50¢ to $1 a week, and there was a shitload of new faces. There were a lot of new guys whom I didn't know; I was almost feeling like the new guy, except that I was actually the senior member in the entire fraternity. I had been a member since early in the eighth grade, and none of these guys had been in any earlier than late May in the ninth grade, and most of them had waited until high school to get into the fraternity.

I wound up cutting all classes on my first day back, and before long, I was back to my old habits of my sophomore year. I was simply hanging out at school all day and not attending classes. In Bethpage, if a class was skipped, they always put in a cut slip with the main office. In Oceanside, they seemed to have no idea I was even a student there. No one ever questioned me about cutting classes.

I was also surprised to find major changes in the status quo between the fraternities. Frank Aiello had resigned as president, quit Phi, and formed the Counts, which I had not known prior to returning to Oceanside. Alpha Omega Theta was now very closely allied with the Counts. As a result of this new shift in the fraternal power structure, Alpha Sigma Phi had become closely allied with Omega Gamma Delta. I was amazed to find that AOT was now semi-confrontational with Omega Gamma Delta. There had never been issues with Omega as long as I could remember.

My senior year was mostly a blur, probably the year I remember the least of all my high school and junior high years. I was still friendly with everyone in AOT, but I spent most of my time hanging out with Ed Oren and Dave Weitz. Dave Weitz's house was a way station for passersby. We hung out in Dave's room constantly, smoking weed, drinking beer, and tripping on either mescaline or LSD. On any average Friday or Saturday night, people would always stop by Dave's to hang out. They were mostly pirates, which was what we called Omega guys. Omegas were called pirates because of the skull and crossbones on their crest, and AOT guys were called Greenies for our green and red colors.

Dave was friendly with most Omega members, and as such, I was also on good terms with all the pirates in Oceanside in my senior year. I had known most of them since junior high, and many of them passed through Dave Weitz's house regularly. Although I spent most of my senior year stoned and out of touch with fraternity issues, the year was turbulent for all the fraternities. There were constant fights and brawls between the fraternities, and even between neighboring towns.

At this time, Dave was drifting into much-stronger drugs. He was getting heavily into cocaine and Valium abuse. I had occasionally taken Valiums, but only tried coke a few times, and I never liked the stuff at all. It was just as well because Dave became a hardcore cokehead, and he would later take to smoking crack. Dave's first big downfall came when he tried to rob D and D Stationery Store wearing panty hose over his head and pointing a starter pistol. The owner recognized him right away and also knew the gun was just a cap gun, and he took it from Dave's hand and threatened to kick his ass.

In the days that followed, Dave was zonked out on Valium for three or four days at a time and he was impossible to be around. One night, he was calling me to hang out, and I was with an Omega guy named Scott Stone. Scott got the idea to send Dave on a wild-goose chase to meet us somewhere far from where we were hanging out. He told Dave to meet us at Dirty Dick's in Long Beach. Dirty Dick's was what everyone called a sleazy bar on Long Beach Boulevard called Dick's. It was a total dive, and Scott thought it was hysterical to send Dave over there. Dave did go there that night, and as we suspected, he got into conflicts with people there and got arrested. While he was being taken in by the Long Beach police for creating a disturbance on the boardwalk, he confessed to the attempted robbery of D and D Stationery. He was sure they were already looking for him, but the truth was that the owner of D and D never reported the crime, and nobody was looking for Dave. But because he confessed to it, he was arrested. Dave wound up going for what would be the first of many stints at drug rehab.

Ed Oren by this time was notorious to the police in Oceanside. He was still a runaway and still stealing anything he could to support himself. Ed wasn't getting into heavy drug use like Dave was, but his issues were becoming serious as well. I couldn't have him over at my house. My family knew the police were looking for him, and they didn't want him in the house. Ed slept at Dave's house when Dave could sneak him in, but he spent a lot of time sleeping in people's tool-sheds. Although we still hung out, my friendship with Ed was fading out. Ed was bitter that I didn't help him as much as he thought I should have when he was a runaway living on the streets, and he was still insulted that I never quit AOT when they kicked him out and wouldn't let him back in. Before the end of my senior year, Ed and I were no longer friendly, and the last time I saw him was when we went to see the Who at Shea Stadium in 1982.

I myself was beginning to have problems with the high school's bouncers. Nowadays, most schools hire professional security companies, but back in the day, they hired school alumni to bounce in the hallways. These guys were usually working as bouncers at bars and nightclubs at night and bouncing the high school during the day. Two of the bouncers that year were AOT alumni Mike Labrazzo and Kenny Zimmerman. You would think I should have had no problems with them since they were AOT, right? Wrong. These two guys were great with the other AOT members, but they put me through slow torture the entire time I was in school that year, especially Labrazzo. It seemed like everywhere I went, there they were. I was constantly being harassed by these guys.

I knew I was having a major problem when one day, some young kid came up to me and asked if I was Fred Gross. I said yes. He said, "I heard I could get some good drugs off of you." I looked over my shoulder and saw both Labrazzo and Zimmerman trying to act natural and not make eye contact with me. I told this kid that I didn't sell drugs, which was true, and I also told him to go back and tell Labrazzo and Zimmerman to get off my ass. If I was going to get caught doing something, it was not going to be getting set up by a sophomore for the school bouncers. These problems would get worse when one day, while I was at home, my uncle Greg came up to me and said he was told by Labrazzo that I was a big cocaine dealer in the school. Although my uncle was in Omega, he and Labrazzo were both class of 1974 and knew each other well. I told Greg that I was lucky to scrape up enough money to buy a dime bag of weed, and that coke was way out of my league and price range, which was totally true. I didn't like the stuff, and I couldn't afford it, either. I then confronted Mike Labrazzo and demanded to know why he deliberately lied about me selling coke in school to my uncle. His reply to me was that he felt that I was not true "Alpha material," as we used to say, and that it was a mistake for me to be in AOT. He said that I didn't "look like a traditional Greenie," and that back in his day, they never would have let me into AOT. He was acknowledging that he was trying to get me kicked out of school, and he was willing to make shit up to make that happen.

I was determined to not give in to Labrazzo and Zimmerman. I didn't want them to have the satisfaction of knowing that they muscled me out of school. But my grades and lack of attendance were catching up to me. I found myself in the dean's office. The dean was Frank Dapolero. He was an old Omega alumnus, and I probably already had a strike against me in his book for being in AOT. He let me know that I had no chance of passing the grade and advised me to drop out. The sound of it scared me. I didn't want to be a high school dropout, but I knew it was coming really soon. And when the time came, it was I who hanged myself.

I will never forget the day. It was my eighteenth birthday, January 10, 1982. I planned to party hard that day. I went to school with weed and four blotters of LSD wrapped in tinfoil. My whole plan was to hang out at school, smoke some weed with friends, drop a hit of LSD later in the afternoon, and maybe do some drinking legally for the first time later that night. I got to school before lunchtime, and I saw my good friend Leo Black. Leo had moved to Arizona the year before, and he was back visiting for a few weeks. He wasn't enrolled in Oceanside High School anymore, and he was just there to hang out. I invited Leo to smoke a joint with me behind the school. We went out behind the cafeteria, thinking it was a secluded spot; but right after we lit up, we got pinched from two directions, and guess who the two bouncers were? That's right, Mike Labrazzo and Kenny Zimmerman. They blocked us from running away, which I would have done for sure if I had a clear escape route. They knew Leo was trespassing, and they just told him to get off school grounds and not come back. If am not mistaken, that was the last time I saw Leo Black ever again. Then the two of them each grabbed one of my arms and dragged me into Dean Dapolero's office. I was sitting on a chair in front of the secretary, thinking about the weed and

LSD I had on me. I put my hand in my pocket and pinched the tinfoil that the LSD was wrapped in and started rolling it into a ball between my fingers. I rolled it as small and tight as I could get it to go. Then I casually dropped it on the floor and kicked it under my chair.

I assumed that nobody would notice it, or that it would look like a gum wrapper someone dropped. As casual as I was to try not to be noticed dropping it, the secretary did see me drop it, or at least she noticed something under my chair. While I was in Dapolero's office, I figured I would just admit to having a half-smoked joint on me, thinking I wouldn't get in too much trouble for that. While I was in his office, his secretary came in and dropped the little aluminum ball on his desk and told him I had dropped it on the floor. He proceeded to unwrap it in front of me. When he had it open, he started touching and fingering the blotters. He asked me what it was. I calmly told him that if he kept touching it he would find out for himself in an hour or two. He dropped the blotters to his desk, realizing he didn't know what he was touching; I told him he better wash his hands because that was blotter LSD, and it could seep through the pores of his skin. The fucking prick had me arrested on my eighteenth birthday.

By this time, there was no longer any reason to stay in school. My friend Dave Weitz was going to night school to finish up high school, so I decided that was the way to go for me. Omega member Scott Stone was in our class, and the three of us started hanging out a lot in our senior year and after night school. Ed Oren was in jail at this point. The same guys who jumped me in front of my house last year had caught up to Ed and pulled the same vigilante bullshit. They grabbed him off the street and turned him over to the cops.

In my senior year, Billy Young was AOT president, and he did throw a few good AOT parties. There were always brew-ups at School #4 on Oceanside Road every Friday and Saturday night. And on more than one night, Billy managed to actually rent a hall at the firehouse on Oceanside Road near Boardman Junior High School. It was the first AOT party that I went to that wasn't in someone's backyard. Vinnie Nagazzo, who was a student in Oceanside High School (but he actually became a member of Freeport AOT), helped make arrangements to rent the firehouse party room. Vinnie's father was a member of the South Hempstead Fire Department, and he signed for the hall rental. It would prove to be a big mistake later on. The first of the parties at the firehouse was a closed party for AOT members only and was thrown for the Oceanside chapter's inactive members. The party was a success and was attended by the whole Oceanside chapter and about twenty to twenty-five inactive Oceanside AOT alumni. There were no fights or incidents, despite threats from Alpha Sigma Phi to crash the party. In anticipation of that possibility, AOT president Billy Young hired two professional bouncers to work the door and throw out anyone not invited.

The party went over so smoothly that the firehouse personnel told us we were welcome back anytime; it was a big mistake on their part. They should have left well enough alone. Another party was booked about two months later. This was a semi-open party, which meant non-AOT members could attend, but with an invite only. This was to attempt to minimize the potential for trouble. It turned out that the AOT guys were the biggest trouble that night.

John Rector, who was a junior, was in a band, and his band played at the party. There was plenty of keg beer, and even a bar serving liquor and shots. I was drinking more than usual that night and doing shots one after another. They were free, and I was going with the flow, doing shots with everybody who invited me to do one. If I had just drunk, I would have been fine, but I did something stupid. I decided to drop a tab of LSD.

From past experience, I knew that if I took LSD first and then started drinking after the LSD kicked in, I could drink one after another without feeling even a little bit drunk. But I would find this evening that dropping a tab of acid after becoming heavily intoxicated on beer and booze was a really bad idea. When any psychedelic drug kicks in, it amplifies every sensation. So when I was staggering shitfaced drunk, the LSD amplified that and made me dizzy and disoriented beyond belief. The room spun, and I'd never felt that dizzy before. I walked out for fresh air and started walking home. I puked my guts up as I walked every step of the way home. I spent the rest of the night on the floor of my bathroom, worshiping the porcelain god. I am sure it was a great party, but I missed most of it.

As it were, after I left, midway through the night, the dance floor in the party room was drenched in beer and water. People were doing knee slides all over the floor. Sometime after that, the AOT brothers kicked in the doors to the garage that the fire engines were in, and they all started climbing all over the fire engines. The whole party was a drunken, rowdy mess, and AOT was not welcomed back after that. No more parties at the firehouse again.

Oceanside AOT president from 1982 Billy Young, said of his only regret of the year, "Baumann Buses was getting rid their old buses, and I think they were selling them off for like two hundred bucks. We had that much in the treasury, and I wanted to buy a bus to turn it into a party bus. The only reason we didn't buy it was because we didn't have any place to park it. John McCann had a CDL license, and he was going to be the driver."

All throughout the year, there were tit-for-tat issues with Phi members. Someone would spray-paint AOT on a building, and someone from Phi would come along and spray-paint AOT SUCKS on top of it, or vice versa. One day, Billy Young was eating pizza with his girlfriend at a pizzeria on Long Beach Road when he saw Pete Quesada and Billy Sandoval go behind the pizzeria with spray paint cans in their hands. After he finished eating his pizza, he went out behind the pizzeria and confronted the two of them. They stopped dead in their tracks, and Billy Young took the spray paint from them. He then proceeded to cover up all the AOT SUCKS graffiti they had painted on the building; he then spray painted PHI SUCKS while they watched and did nothing to stop him.

AOT had the upper hand in its dealings with Phi in Oceanside. AOT vice president Sal Sina would routinely wear Phi tee shirts to school just to piss them off. He was brazen and not afraid of any of them, and he challenged any one of them to do something about it. One night, AOT president Billy Young and vice president Sal Sina found themselves surrounded by Phi president John Sandoval, his younger brother Billy, and a few other Phi members. Billy Sandoval pulled out a can of Mace and tried to mace Sal Sina. Billy Young picked up a wire-mesh garbage can and threatened to smash Billy Sandoval in the face with it. Billy Young offered to put down the garbage can and have it out with Billy Sandoval if he put down the Mace, but Sandoval knew he could not win a fight with Billy Young, so he refused to put away the Mace. After a brief standoff, a bunch of other AOT guys showed up and evened the odds. Billy Young fought Phi president John Sandoval, and Sal Sina fought Billy Sandoval; a brief free-for-all ensued between the AOT guys and Phi until the Nassau County police showed up and the crowd scattered.

The issues with Phi came to a head again at Nathan's one night when the AOT brothers went to confront them. They were tired of the constant bullshit with Phi and wanted to have it out once and for all with the worst members of Phi. AOT member Billy Vulmer went up to Phi vice president Bob Stone; he calmly put his arm around him and acted like he wanted a chitchat, but without warning, Billy tightened his grip around Stone's neck with his left arm and punched him in the face with his right hand. Billy Vulmer proceeded to pummel Bob Stone to the ground. At that moment, AOT president Billy Young attacked Phi president John Sandoval, and AOT vice president Sal Sina attacked Billy Sandoval at the same time. Then AOT brother Eric Eisenhower and his brother, who was not an AOT member, both tag-teamed Phi member Ricky Romero. Eric and his brother were both literally built like sumo wrestlers and had a combined weight of close to six hundred pounds, if not more. They both pressed Ricky Romero up against a car and literally smothered him with their body weight. They cleaned house and put those Phi guys in their place. Alpha Sigma Phi had found out once and for all that they had no leverage over AOT. They were no longer a threat and were more of a nuisance than anything else after that.

Surprisingly, there were also some confrontations with Omega Gamma Delta in 1982. There was supposed to be a brawl on the football field at the high school one night, but it really turned into a few individual fights between the AOT and Omega members who had personal issues. There was never really any animosity between AOT and Omega, and an all-out brawl just was not going to happen. As it turned out, a few guys who didn't like each other had to duke it out to settle scores.

The biggest fight of the year did not involve AOT, but it sure did affect us. It was a fight between Oceanside and Baldwin. More specifically, Oceanside Omega teamed up with Oceanside Alpha Sigma Phi and went into Baldwin to attack Baldwin Omega Gamma Delta. One Friday night, I was hanging out at Dave Weitz's house, drinking beer and smoking weed as usual. Then there came a knock at the window. Dave opened it, and it was Omega president Ed Sarcozzi and Omega members Mel Summers and Kenny Tyrell. Ed Sarcozzi asked Dave to let them all in the house. They all went around the backyard, and Dave let them in the back door. When they came into Dave's room, Ed Sarcozzi told us the cops were looking for them, and they needed a place to hide out. When we asked them why they were hiding from the cops, they told us they had just come from a big brawl at Burger King in Baldwin. Ed told us that Oceanside Omega had teamed up with Oceanside Phi and they attacked members of Baldwin Omega Gamma Delta. He also told us that Phi member Billy Sandoval had baseball-batted a Baldwin guy. He ran up behind the guy and swung the bat full swing and struck him in the back of the skull.

Ed told us that he thought the guy might even be dead. He said it was a bad scene, and people were screaming when they saw the guy lying facedown in the parking lot with blood gushing out of the back of his head. Then all the Oceanside Omega and Phi members jumped back into their cars and bolted out of there as soon as they realized someone was seriously injured.

I was perplexed on many levels. I could not believe that Omega Gamma Delta would partner with Alpha Sigma Phi for any reason. It wasn't a natural relationship. I also didn't understand why Oceanside Omega would attack members of Baldwin Omega when they were members of the same brotherhood. I asked Ed Sarcozzi why he had Oceanside Omega attack members of the same brotherhood from another town and in cahoots with Phi as well. Ed told me that the Baldwin Omegas were assholes and they deserved to get jumped; furthermore, he felt he had more in common with Phi members who were from the same town as him than with fellow Omega brothers from Baldwin.

What had happened was that tensions had been brewing between Oceanside Omega and Baldwin Omega for a while. Oceanside Omega member Mel Summers was actually a Baldwin resident, but because of the way the district lines were drawn, he went to Oceanside High School. But he lived in Baldwin, and he started having problems with Baldwin Omega members. They harassed him and started fights with him whenever they saw him hanging out in Baldwin. They were taking town rivalry over fraternal brotherhood and were busting his balls for being an Oceanside High School student. They didn't care that he was also in Omega. After some attempts to work things out between the presidents of Oceanside Omega and Baldwin Omega, things got worse. The situation degenerated to the point of the alliance between Oceanside Omega and Oceanside Phi and the plan to attack Baldwin Omega members at Burger King on Grand Avenue.

Now the shit had really hit the fan. Someone was seriously injured as a result of this fraternity fighting. The guy did fully recover, but the police and local school districts had had enough of fraternities. In the days after the fight at Burger King, the police rounded up members of Omega and Phi from Oceanside. It didn't take long before eyewitnesses picked Billy Sandoval out of a lineup, and he was charged with the attack. Taking a full swing at the back of someone's head should have been prosecuted as attempted murder and gotten him a long stay in jail, but as it were, he got off with a slap on the wrist. That slap on the wrist would cost a young lady her life at the hands of Billy Sandoval just a year later. He had been seeing a woman who was married and a neighbor of his; but when she tried to break it off, he abducted her, raped her, and strangled her in her own car. He then set fire to the car to try to cover up the crime. He was convicted of second-degree murder, first-degree manslaughter, first-degree rape, and first-degree robbery and is currently serving thirty years to life sentence in Green Haven Prison, Upstate New York.

This brawl and its disastrous consequences led to the rapid demise of the fraternity system in Oceanside, Baldwin, and Rockville Centre. The Nassau County Police Department came to Oceanside High School and met with members of the school's fraternities in the cafeteria and told them all that the police were now regarding the fraternities to be gangs, and they were going to crack down on fraternity members wearing colors or hanging out in large groups around town.

The meeting with the police department did little or nothing to stifle the fraternities. But the meeting with the high school principal did slow us down quite a bit. I was hanging out at the high school in the cafeteria one day, although I was not a student anymore apart from attending night classes at the same school. While sitting with a few AOT members, we suddenly heard an announcement on the PA.

"Will the following students please report immediately to Mr. Marciano's office."

A list of about fifteen names was read out, and we all instantly realized that all the names they were calling to the principal's office were all AOT members. Although my name was not on the list of AOT members summoned to Thomas Marciano's office, I was intrigued to know what was going on. I wasn't a full-time student anymore, so they couldn't kick me out of school, so I went into Marciano's office with the others.

Although I was no longer a full-time student in Oceanside High School and I was not called or required to go to Principal Marciano's office, I knew AOT was about to get harassed by the school administration; and I was curious to see what was happening, so I went with them to the principal's office. When we got there, it was just like Dean Wormer's tirade at the end of *Animal House*. He started pontificating about how it was all over for the fraternities and that the high school was not a democratic institution, but rather, his personal domain to rule as he pleased. He proceeded to tell us that the fraternity system had come to an end in Oceanside High School. He informed us that from this point forward, membership in any fraternity meant expulsion from high school. This would be final and beyond appeal.

We tried to engage Marciano in rebuttal. We told him he was violating our rights to associate freely, but he would not budge. He insisted that any known member of the fraternity would be thrown out of school. One thing that I noticed was that they had called only about fifteen AOT members to the office; but if they wanted to expel all of us, why did they call a small number of members to the office? It was because they were really clueless as to how many members we had and who was a card-carrying member of the fraternity. I had been a member of Alpha Omega Theta since I was in eighth grade; I was the most senior member in AOT, and the high school had no idea I was a member. We had at least fifty members in 1982, maybe more, and they had a list of fifteen names; what a joke.

Marciano went on to tell us that we had to turn in our fraternity colors to him to demonstrate the chapter had been closed. He informed us that each person in the room was obligated to comply or be expelled. He reminded all present at the meeting that if we had intentions of going to college or the military, an expulsion was a serious smudge on our permanent records. We inquired why we were getting this treatment and not the other fraternities. Marciano assured us that the other fraternities in the school would be getting the same treatment as us, but we were first to be called in.

It occurred to me that Thomas Marciano had violated our rights on many levels. What he did was unlawful in my opinion. But we were teenagers, and we had no idea how to defend ourselves legally. I found out from my friend Ed Sarcozzi, who was president of Oceanside Omega Gamma Delta, that Marciano tried to use the same leverage on the Omegas as well, a few days after he pulled that shit on us. The Omegas blew that shit off like it was nothing. Omega Gamma Delta was a fraternity that had an alumni association that managed the affairs of the combined chapters of the fraternity as a whole. Representatives from Omega Gamma Delta's national office showed up at the high school with lawyers in tow and informed Marciano that the school and the district faced a lawsuit if the Omegas were singled out for expulsion due to the fraternal affiliation.

As for us in AOT, we gave Marciano a few old crusty tee shirts as a show of sincerity that we were disbanding, but we still held meetings and continued to recruit new members. As for me, I was tired of all the fraternity bullshit; I was glad that high school was coming to an end for me, and I really had no feeling of nostalgia in respect to the fraternity. I did want to see it continue after my class graduated, but I really wanted to move on and not look back as well.

The only thing that remained for me as a matter of unfinished business was the Senior Dinner. As a subordinate member of Alpha Omega Theta fraternity, I paid my Senior Dinner fee each and every year since I was in the eighth grade. Now I was a senior, and the younger members were supposed to be honoring us with a Senior Dinner. I couldn't help noticing that nobody was bringing this up or discussing it in any way. In all my years in AOT, I never spoke up at meetings, except for the one night that I tried to get Ed Oren back into the fraternity. Other than that one time, I kept a low profile and avoided being fined by whoever the sergeant at arms was at the time. But now I was annoyed, and I wanted my fucking Senior Dinner. I paid every year; now these younger guys had to treat me and the other seniors, as our tradition had always been.

Despite the fact that we were operating underground and all the fraternities were having major issues with the school district and the Nassau County Police Department, I brought up the Senior Dinner at meetings, and I was persistent in letting these guys know they had an obligation to throw us a party. It really looked like they were trying to get out of it. No one was showing interest in heading the Senior Dinner committee. I was pushy and insistent that I wanted my Senior Dinner, and I started attending all the meetings to keep pushing this on the younger AOT brothers. Finally, they put together a Senior Dinner committee and promised to throw us a party.

Each year prior to this one, we always went to a restaurant and rented the party room. This year, the party they threw us was in Michael Shriver's backyard. I know now they did the best they could under the circumstances, but at the time, I was pissed about the way they threw the Senior Dinner for the outgoing AOT class of 1982. They had their mothers make trays of baked ziti and baked chicken. The food they served was ice-cold and dry, and the rotgut Schmidt's beer they served was undrinkable.

I took my paper plate of half-eaten food, along with an almost-full bottle of Schmidt's, and dumped them in the garbage. I walked out before the thing was over and never looked back. I had many good times with the fraternity, but I also had a lot of reasons to look forward and leave AOT behind without even a single thought. I had my future in front of me and no reason to worry about my fraternity anymore. AOT belonged to the next generation now.

Oceanside AOT, 1978; in Memory of Danny Carmeinke

Oceanside AOT circa 1979 in front of Oceanside High School

CHAPTER FIFTEEN

The Last Days of AOT

There were many factors that led to the demise of the Long Island chapters of Alpha Omega Theta Fraternity. In fact, those same factors led to the dissolution of all the other fraternities in Nassau County as well. The hazing practiced by fraternities was always an issue, many years and decades before the infamous hazing incident of a young football player from Mepham High School at football camp in 2003. Alpha Omega Theta Fraternity, as well as the many other fraternities in Nassau County, had originally been formed as athletic social clubs in the 1940s and 1950s. By the 1970s, these fraternal organizations began to act and function as gangs with fancy Greek names.

The Oceanside chapter had been under pressure to disband since 1981 from the school administration and the Nassau County Police Department. When the problems between AOT and Phi began to come to a full boil in 1981, the Nassau County Police Department sent representatives to Oceanside High School, and mandatory meetings were held in the school cafeteria. Attendance at these meetings by members of AOT and Phi was required. The police department warned that they were now regarding the fraternities to be gangs in actual fact and would begin harassment of fraternity members when they were seen in groups of more than three and wearing colors on the street. This threat had little or no effect on fraternity membership at the time.

Fraternities had been embedded in the social fabric of Oceanside for decades. It was not something that could be simply undone with threats. After all, the school system in Oceanside had halfheartedly been trying to dislodge the fraternities for decades. As far back as 1965, when a shoving match between a member of Omega Gamma Delta and a member of the Gents led to the accidental death of the Gents member when he was shoved into the wall and fractured his skull, the school administration in Oceanside had banned fraternities and social clubs and had been trying to keep them and their colors out of sight in the school itself. Ever since the brawl that took place in 1979 in front of the school between AOT and Phi, the school had been more aggressively pursuing ways to break up the fraternities. Popularity and support for fraternities had been eroding for quite a few years in all the towns that had fraternities. AOT had already faded out in Garden City and Uniondale by the 1980s. The once-respectable Rockville Centre AOT chapter had folded in 1980 and was reformulated as South Hempstead AOT (the South Hempstead crowd being the only ones in the Mu Nu Chapter in Southside High School who wanted to fight with Oceanside Phi).

In 1981, the problems with Phi had forced the Oceanside chapter of AOT to go underground for half the year. The reemergence of Oceanside AOT in the latter half of the school year was coupled with an alliance with a reformulated, old-time Oceanside social club, the Counts, which in turn caused an alliance between Alpha Sigma Phi and Omega Gamma Delta. All of this led to an escalation of the brawling in Oceanside, as well as cross-border fights in Rockville Centre and Baldwin.

The split in the ranks of Rockville Centre AOT caused the chapter to shrink by half overnight. Although the Mu Nu Chapter re-chartered as South Hempstead AOT, the chapter was not viable enough to last; and within two years, it had folded.

In 1982, in Oceanside, the AOT chapter members, as well as other fraternities' members, were threatened with permanent expulsion from school by Principal Thomas Marciano. This extreme measure by the school administration was a direct result of the massive brawl that took place in Baldwin at Burger King between Oceanside and Baldwin fraternities. The rumble involved upward of fifty members of two Omega Gamma Delta chapters from Oceanside and Baldwin and Alpha Sigma Phi from Oceanside. It was a brutal free-for-all with bats, two-by-fours, axe handles, and bottles. Oceanside Omega and Phi had joined forces and attacked Baldwin Omega in the parking lot of Burger King on Grand Avenue. The incident left one Baldwin student lying facedown with a fractured skull and left for dead by the Oceanside fraternity members who had invaded Baldwin that night and by Phi member Billy Sandoval, the guy who had swung the bat at the back of the guy's head.

After that incident, 1982 was the last year for Omega Gamma Delta as a fraternity in Baldwin, and the next year was the end for Baldwin AOT as well. Sometime in between, Baldwin's third fraternity, Delta Gamma Rho, had folded as well. The Baldwin school administration, the First Precinct, and the students in Baldwin had all had enough of the fraternities. The sight of a kid who almost died because he wore the wrong colors and was in the wrong place at the wrong time was enough to cause Baldwin students to abandon their fraternities.

It appeared as though there was a concerted effort between the Oceanside and Baldwin school districts, in collusion with the First and Fourth precincts of the Nassau County Police Department, to put massive pressure on fraternity members to force closure of the various fraternity chapters. Threats of expulsion were somewhat effective since high school seniors who were college-bound or planning to join the military did not want an expulsion on their permanent records. It didn't really cause anyone to quit the fraternity in Oceanside, as far as I know. But it did drive the fraternities underground for a few years.

In Oceanside, the fraternities still had meetings and recruited new members, but they kept it out of the view of the school administration as much as possible. After my class had graduated in 1982, AOT was passed on to the new president, John Rector, popularly known as John John. In 1983, they had a good year led by John Rector. They had a fairly large and viable fraternity without any major incidents that year. John John kept it under the radar during his tenure as AOT president. After what happened in Baldwin the year before, all the fraternities in Oceanside had good reason to let things cool down. The following year, AOT was passed on to President Michael Shriver, the younger brother of 1979 Oceanside AOT president Tommy Shriver.

Once again, the shit would stir up. It can be said that Michael Shriver's year was the last solid traditional year of AOT in Oceanside. He had a large chapter, and AOT had become the largest fraternity in Oceanside High School during his year as president. Omega Gamma Delta was dwarfed by comparison. One day, a brawl had spontaneously broken out between AOT and Omega Gamma Delta members in front of the school. Things had been so quiet for so long that the school had actually assumed that the fraternities had disbanded. In fact, none of them had disbanded.

The sheer lack of knowledge of the Oceanside school district about the fraternities that had been around for decades was evident in newspaper articles written about the fraternity brawl in 1984. In prior years, the fighting was usually between AOT and Alpha Sigma Phi, but this time, the incident was between AOT and Omega Gamma Delta. In response to this question, "Are high school fraternities a thing of the past?" Victor Lacrosse, superintendent of the Oceanside Union Free School District was quoted as saying, "They come and go about every three years." Additionally, Victor Lacrosse said, "Oceanside High School has been fraternity free for three years."

In the same article, Oceanside High School principal Richard Cramer erroneously stated the colors of Omega Gamma Delta were black and orange, when anyone working in Oceanside High School should have known the Omega colors were black and gold.

Fourteen members of AOT and Omega were suspended from school as the result of the free-for-all brawl that erupted under the portico in front of the school. The cause of the fight was a black-and-gold scarf that Alpha members had taken from an Omega member. Since wearing fraternity jackets, sweaters, and tee shirts was not allowed, frat members had taken to wearing scarf's that had their fraternity colors. The scarf that was taken from the Omega member was shredded into dozens of pieces by the Alpha members. After the Omega member that had the scarf confiscated by AOT members went to tell his Omega brothers, a confrontation took place, which was over pretty quickly and ended with only one kid getting a broken nose. But the effects of the skirmish shook the fraternity system in Oceanside to its foundation.

All the students involved in the brawl were suspended for five days from school. After that, the school cranked up its efforts to disband the fraternities. This time, they didn't just threaten the fraternity members. This time, they contacted the parents of each identifiable fraternity member. They informed the parents as to the seriousness of their son's continuing membership in an unsanctioned fraternity. Parents were now brought into the loop to work with the school administration and police department to get their kids out of the fraternities. The tactic of getting parents involved produced the kind of immediate results the school was looking for. According to Oceanside High School Principal Richard Cramer, "The fraternities are not resurfacing with the same power they maintained in the past years. We're told that after this weekend, a number of people declared themselves out of their group. We plan to take steps to make sure these groups stay dismantled."

In addition to that, Superintendent Victor Lacrosse had this to say, "We intend to be as severe with them as we have been in the past. Moreover, in the future, anyone involved in a fraternity fight will be automatically suspended, face criminal charges and possible expulsion pending a superintendent's hearing."

Further showing his absolute ignorance in regard to the continued existence of fraternities in Oceanside, Victor Lacrosse said this: "Oceanside High School has been fraternity free for three years."

This was laughable in the face of the pure fact that fraternities had been a part of the social structure of Oceanside High School uninterrupted since 1940. Omega Gamma Delta had its Oceanside chapter founded in 1940, Oceanside AOT came into existence in 1957, Alpha Sigma Phi hit the scene in Oceanside High School in 1968, the Counts, who had been a social club in the 1950s and 1960s, had disbanded around 1965 and then made a comeback in 1981. Apart from a few other fringe fraternities that didn't last long, the "big three" fraternities had existed unhampered and uninterrupted in Oceanside from the year of each of their inceptions.

Now pressure was being put on the presidents of both AOT and Omega to declare their chapters closed once and for all. President Michael Shriver was brought before the school board in a superintendent's meeting to press him into declaring the Oceanside chapter of AOT closed. Facing his own expulsion and that of other AOT members, Michael complied with the demands of the school board under duress. After formally declaring the chapter closed, the AOT suitcase containing all the chapters' books and documents dating back to 1957 were taken by various members of the chapter as souvenirs. To this day, we still have not recovered any of the Oceanside chapter's documents, and no one from the chapter class of 1984 has admitted to taking or possessing the books.

After Michael Shriver capitulated to the school board, soon the other fraternities would follow AOT into oblivion. But it would still take another two years before the fraternities would finally die out in Oceanside for good.

After Michael Shriver "officially" declared the Oceanside chapter closed, the younger members tried to pick up the pieces and keep it together. Under the leadership of new AOT president Frank Montanez and vice president Skip Purcell, Oceanside AOT carried on in secret all through 1985. Although the chapter class of 1985 was a dedicated bunch who did their best to keep AOT alive, they were unable to turn back the tide that was now burying Alpha Omega Theta and the fraternity system.

The following year, AOT was passed on to new president Donald Carmeikle, who was the younger brother of my old friend Danny Carmeikle. By this time, fraternity membership was at an all-time low in Oceanside. Once upon a time, membership in AOT had anywhere from fifty to seventy-five members. By the time of Michael Shriver's presidency, AOT averaged about forty-five members. During the 1985 school year, while Frank Montanez was AOT president, the fraternity had shrunk down to about thirty active members. In the final year of Alpha Omega Theta in Oceanside, while Donald Carmeikle was president, the fraternity had dwindled down to fewer than twenty members. Even though fighting had all but ceased and the two rival fraternities no longer existed, students just didn't want to join fraternities anymore. Alpha Sigma Phi and the Counts had faded out the prior year, and the last two standing were AOT and Omega Gamma Delta, but both of these two once-massive fraternities were mere shells of what they had once been. Multiple chapters of both had disappeared over the recent years, and now these two were ready for extinction as well. In AOT, the last year of operation was 1986, and most of the chapter's active members were high school seniors. There was literally no one to pass the fraternity on to at this point, and the chapter died when this class graduated. The next school year of 1987 was truly the first year Oceanside was "fraternity free" since 1940.

All things considered, the pressure from the school, pressure from the police, and the constant fighting between rival fraternities had led to the collapse of the fraternity system, which had been in Oceanside for decades. The same can be said for the chapters in Baldwin, Freeport, and Rockville Centre. The schools had finally succeeded in making fraternity membership unappealing to students. Kids were losing their desire to join a club that required them to take a vicious beating and paddling as a prerequisite to membership. Additionally, joining a fraternity usually led the new fraternity member into becoming instant enemies with the members of other rival fraternities. Students just didn't want to get beaten up to join a fraternity that would require them to fight other fraternities. It had finally lost its luster. By the end of the 1986 school year, all the fraternities were dead and gone from Oceanside. The year 1987 was the first year since 1939 that saw Oceanside High School without any fraternities at all.

By comparison, a few miles away in Valley Stream, Alpha Omega Theta and all the other Valley Stream fraternities were still going strong. Valley Stream Central AOT alumnus Steve Raff recalled the almost-eerie disappearance of the other AOT chapters literally overnight. In 1985 and 1986, Valley Stream had been in contact with Oceanside AOT. The Valley Stream AOT chapter was aware that Rockville Centre, South Hempstead, Freeport, and Baldwin AOT chapters had all disappeared without a trace, and no word from anyone in those towns was ever relayed back to the main chapter in Valley Stream about the reasons for closure of those chapters. The Valley Stream chapter was determined to maintain contact with Oceanside, the last surviving chapter besides Valley Stream. However, when school started in the fall of 1986, communication with Oceanside abruptly died.

The brothers of the last functioning AOT chapter were mystified as to why entire chapters were folding up so abruptly with no formal closure announcement to the Valley Stream chapter. Steve Raff recalled going on many excursions to Oceanside, Baldwin, Rockville Centre, and even to Garden City to try to see if there were any survivors to the fraternities' mass extinctions. In each town, when they visited the high school dressed in AOT colors, they were astounded to find that there was no trace of fraternities where they were once plentiful. Although students did recognize the colors, they would usually just tell the Valley Stream AOT members that fraternities no longer existed in that town or that school.

By 1988, the Valley Stream chapter realized they were the last ones. Valley Stream AOT had been the first chapter, and now they were the last AOT chapter. They had become the epitome of the AOT motto, "First, last, always." In addition to AOT and Omega Gamma Delta in Valley Stream Central, the other two high schools in Valley Stream, North and South, still had their fraternities as well. Besides Valley Stream, West Hempstead was one of the last towns to have fraternities also. These last bastions of fraternity membership would soon become a powder keg of violence.

The troubles began in Valley Stream in 1986, coincidentally, the same year that fraternities faded out in Oceanside. AOT brother Steve Raft, from the Valley Stream Central class of 1988, recalled the beginning of a rivalry that would become intense and violent over the next few years:

"It was a Saturday afternoon in mid-October 1986. I was with my friend Claudio (an AOT brother) spending the afternoon at Central High School for Saturday recreation when a ninth-grade brother came running up to me to tell me about some kids that kept driving by the high school. He thought there might be trouble and asked that we come outside. As I followed him out, I saw three kids I didn't recognize running into the school through another door. I ran after them with Claudio, only to find them in the basement of the school, beating on another ninth-grade brother. Although we were outnumbered, Claudio and I immediately jumped in. The physical exchange was intense but brief. Amazingly, I came out fine, but the same could not be said for Claudio's nose. The melee ended as quickly as it had started, with the three boys running out of the school. We didn't recognize any of them and spent the whole week trying to figure out who these guys were. For some reason, we decided that they were from Valley Stream North High School. Come Monday, we began making plans to avenge Claudio. We spread the word to show up in front of Central at 10:00 PM on Friday. About fifty to sixty people showed up in thirteen cars. This group consisted mostly of AOT, with three guys being in Omega. This was the start of a year-long alliance with Omega as we teamed up against Phi and their likes in West Hempstead, Island Park, and Valley Stream North."

Prior to this incident, there had been no real interaction or altercations with AOT from Valley Stream Central and Alpha Sigma Phi from Valley Stream North since the time Spooky was AOT president. This was the first time the AOT members of this time, from Valley Stream Central, had been involved with Phi. On that thought Steve Raff had this to say.

"For almost all of us, this was our first trip to Valley Stream North in search of Phi. In the two years I had been in AOT, there had been no interaction whatsoever between AOT and Phi, but that was all about to change as we got in our cars and headed north. It's funny to mention that this was 1986, and cell phones did not exist, so some of us actually used CB radios to keep in touch as we headed out on our search-and-destroy missions.

"On the way to North, we kept getting separated at red lights because there were just so many cars. I was in the last car with Chris Argo, and we had no CB. We got separated from the pack and decided to head for North HS on our own. We parked the car in front of the school and found nobody. We decided to walk out onto the dark football field behind the school and wait. Then, out of nowhere came a monster crowd of kids charging toward us, and I saw my life flash before my eyes. Fortunately, it was the lunatics we had come out there with. We all shared a laugh and then went back on the prowl.

"After finding nobody around the school, we got back into our cars and headed toward Franklin Avenue. Again, I was with Chris, thirteen cars back. As the first car reached Franklin Avenue, the traffic light turned red. Then I saw the light turn green, but nobody was moving. I suddenly realized that something was happening up front, and everybody started piling out of their cars and running toward the corner parking lot. Chris pulled over, and we ran up to the crowd, but in a matter of thirty seconds, the action was already over. I saw kids from North running in every direction. Those that could not run were crawling. The rest were getting pounced on. I won't mention names, but I witnessed several beatings being dispensed to the North kids that we all assumed were Phi boys.

"Afterward, we all went back to our stomping grounds. All of us were unscathed, and it seemed a pretty good night. That Monday back at school, we spoke to kids from North that attended BOCES, only to find out that the parking lot was not filled with Phi boys. Turns out, we beat North's football team. Those guys were weak. No wonder they had such a shitty record that year."

This incident, which began with a few out-of-town kids jumping a couple of young AOT members in Central High School, had escalated into a full-scale invasion of Valley Stream North for revenge. These two events led to a state of war between Valley Stream Central and Valley Stream North that lasted a few years. In this war, sides were chosen and alliances were forged. The historic rivalry between AOT and Omega Gamma Delta had finally been put to rest. Now the two fraternities banded together, held joint meetings and co-hosted parties in order to maintain solidarity in Central High School in the face of Alpha Sigma Phi from Valley Stream North and their allies from West Hempstead and Island Park.

Steve Raft's views on the subject of war and alliances: "Long story short, that turned out to be the start of a very long year for us, where it was hardly safe to be out alone. The jumping's on both sides were frequent and sometimes relentless. There were some very ugly moments and some humorous ones as well. The most memorable was when a friend's car broke down in West Hempstead while we were out looking for Phi boys. His car was very well known, and he feared it being destroyed if discovered. So $20 and four cans of spray paint later, a 1970 Chevy Nova went from being a yellow car with black stripes to a black car with yellow stripes. Would have made it green with red stripes, but that would have been too obvious, and besides, we couldn't afford enough spray paint for that kind of makeover. Eventually, the Nova made it home safely, as did we. Wish that could have been the case every time."

And Steve's final thought on the subject of fraternities in general, Phi in particular, fighting, and the redeeming social values of Alpha Omega Theta Fraternity: "I don't want to give the impression that being in a fraternity was all about fighting and typical high school buffoonery. While fighting did seem to dominate my junior year of high school, I can't blame these experiences solely on being in a fraternity inasmuch as I can place the blame on some Phi boys who all too frequently went above and beyond the status of "Asshole." A few years after high school, I ran into one of these assholes. Still holding a grudge, he wanted to brawl on the spot, but I was no longer interested. During our last meeting three years earlier, I came out ahead, and I was perfectly content living with that parting memory.

"All the while, I couldn't help but wonder if Phi had ever been anything other than a bunch of assholes. Somehow I doubt it. It's a shame too, because hazing aside; it was the fighting that really brought the fraternities down.

"During the last year I was in AOT, we tried to expand the chapter and contribute to the community, but the negative reputation that had been built up over the recent years was just too much to overcome. Within a decade of my graduating high school, high school fraternities continued to dwindle and disappear, in many cases doing so without a trace of ever having existed. Considering the good that these organizations can do, I think this a sad reality, especially when you consider the nature of the real gangs, which seem to have replaced them. Perhaps on the college level, the original spirit of Alpha Omega Theta can be reborn, and the good times and brotherhood can continue."

The fighting between Valley Stream Central and Valley Stream North would flare up from time to time over the next few years. For some strange reason, AOT and most of the other fraternities continued to thrive in Valley Stream for a few more years. The first casualties were the Omega Gamma Delta chapters in Valley Stream North and South. Constant harassment from Phi in the North led to the closure of the Omega chapters in North and South high schools. The alliance between AOT and Omega Gamma Delta in Central continued to hold strong for the remaining years of both fraternities' existence in Valley Stream Central.

One of the last known presidents of AOT in Valley Stream Central was Chris Smith. Chris had gotten inducted into AOT at the age of fourteen when he was in eighth grade in 1988. By the time Chris has been inducted, pledging had come to an end, and new inductees were brought in with a one-night Hell Night induction. They still called it pledging, but the practice of three- to six-week pledging periods was long over. The so-called pledges were brought in to the meetings and subjected to about two hours of beatings, paddling's, and abuse. When Chris was inducted, the Valley Stream chapter was still a large fraternity with upward of seventy-five members. Chris tells about his induction night

"The night I went down, it was a mandatory meeting. There were about seventy people, there was a hell line of seventy people, and I had to run through. I got my shots over by the Valley Stream train tracks. We had left the guy's house to get shots over there."

Chris one day made the acquaintance of Valley Stream AOT's legendary president, Joe "Spooky" Furino. Chris was a young AOT member, newly inducted into the fraternity. He was walking in his neighborhood wearing an AOT sweater and just happened to pass by Spooky's house; the two of them were neighbors. Spooky saw this young kid walking down the street wearing an AOT sweater, and he was surprised to see an Alpha sweater. In a surprised manner, Spooky said,

"You're in AOT?"

"Yeah, I'm in AOT. Who are you?"

"I used to run AOT in this town. They used to call me Spooky."

"You're Spooky? Wow, I heard of you. They still talk about the time when Spooky ran AOT and there were over one hundred members."

From that chance meeting, Spooky and Chris Smith would become good friends. Chris invited Spooky to the next AOT meeting. It would be the last time Spooky would attend an AOT meeting. But he was thrilled that all these young Alpha members knew who he was, and they were all saying, "Wow, is that Spooky?" They were all impressed; it was like meeting General Patton. Spooky also recalled one evening that he had to help Chris when a carload of rival fraternity members were chasing him.

"I remember one night Chris had a problem. He was being chased by a bunch of kids. He was being chased by a carload of guys, and he couldn't make it home. He lived a couple of blocks from where I lived. So I was outside my house. Chris comes up to my door and says, 'Joey, can you help me out?' I come outside with a bat, and I walked him home. They wanted to take his colors. The car saw me and took off. I got him home safe."

Chris recalled the situation between the Valley Stream fraternities at the time.

"It was big, man, both Alpha and Omega in like '88, '89. Everybody wore sweaters and colors in school, everybody. We always had fights with Phi from North. It was so bad that you couldn't give your sweater to your girlfriend to wear. Phi from the North would come and beat up the girl and take the sweater. It was crazy. If you were leaving a party or someone's house, you couldn't hide your colors. You had to run home sometimes. It was sad, I'm telling you.

"Jumping was a big thing. I was carrying around a bottle of Mace with me. There was constant, constant violence. Guys got beat up bad. Some wound up in hospitals. With Omega, we kept the peace with them. We didn't like each other, but we were in the same school. With Phi from the north and the Knights from West Hempstead, we had problems with them. In Valley Stream South, they had Kappa. Kappa was like our half brothers. We went to each other's meetings. But they weren't organized like we were. We had it to the T."

Chris remembered in 1990, when things were so bad that nobody wanted to be AOT president, the task fell into the lap of Rocco Marceda, the younger brother of VSC AOT president from 1978 John Marceda.

"When Rocco Marceda was a senior in 1990, he was inducted into AOT. Dustin Edgars was the president. He had problems with the cops. He went to that big brawl in the north, he got suspended out of school, his father flipped out because his father was a cop, and Rocco got it handed to him because no one else wanted it. All of our officers had gotten thrown out of school for going to the north that year. At the next meeting, no one wanted to step up, so Rocco said, 'All right, I'll be president.'"

Rocco Marceda recalled being asked to join AOT at a time of serious tension and conflict with Alpha Sigma Phi from Valley Stream North.

"Dustin Edgars was president and brought me into Alpha because they needed people because a lot of the eleventh and twelfth graders quit because of a big fight with North High School Phi, and a lot of people had been arrested.

"John Mas was our sergeant at arms, and he passed away in a car accident in our senior year, and it was a tough loss. We never forgot him. He loved being in Alpha, and he used to watch my back when we took the bus to BOCES in Carle Place. I was the president, and it was just us two and one kid from Omega, Mike Kinz. The three of us had to look out because when we stopped through North High School to drop off students, on the way back, they would try to get on the bus and take our colors. It was crazy."

Chris's take on Rocco's crew as AOT president: "It went from the tough guys of 1990 to not-so-tough guys. Rocco's crew was not the toughest guys, but they were nice guys. They were very well respected. Rocco was a good guy. Everybody liked Rocco."

Chris spoke about the tense situation regarding wearing colors in Valley Stream during his tenure as AOT president.

"When we ran the fraternity, after a while, they started suspending everyone for wearing colors in school. So we all got scared. They were really cracking down. If you wore colors, they threw you out of school. It really got that bad, so we all got scared, so we folded. And then a year later, AOT came back in again but wasn't in full force. We were scared of the cops. If they saw you wearing colors on the street, they would harass you. It was in 1988. The Board of Education came down hard on all fraternities in Memorial, Central, North, and South. If you wore colors, you got suspended. The administration had it with fraternities. We still did wear colors for another three years. We would wear a regular shirt on top of an AOT tee shirt. You couldn't wear jackets anymore, you couldn't wear sweaters anymore. We'd hang out in the park wearing an AOT sweater, and the cops would arrest you. You couldn't wear colors anymore, even outside the school."

Although there weren't many fights when Chris ran AOT, Chris did deal with the repercussions of the big brawl in 1986 that took place between AOT from Central and Phi from Valley Stream North, years after the brawl had taken place. The wearing of colors was banned by all the high schools in Valley Stream after that rumble, and the local police became downright unfriendly to fraternity members or kids wearing colors around town.

Chris did not recall holding elections to pass on the fraternity at the end of his tenure as president. He had actually, formally, and officially folded the VSC chapter of AOT before the end of the school year in 1991, in response to intense pressure from the school and local police; and the following year, the younger AOT brothers picked up where he left off. Joe Ciancia became AOT president in the 1992-93 school year, and Chris recalled passing on all of the books of the Valley Stream AOT chapter to him.

According to Chris, it wasn't about fights when he was president.

"We had great times, we had softball games, we had state-park parties, and we had BBQ's. It was fun, and we had a good time. We had a crew of guys that were serious. We wore colors every day, and every day we wore a different shirt. We were really into it."

During Chris's time in AOT, he saw the end of serious beating of new pledges. Chris told how the inductions became easier toward the end of the fraternity's existence.

"After I got in, those were the last years of getting your ass kicked. Guys that came down were younger brothers of past AOT brothers, and their brothers would bring them down. They were out of school three or four years, and no one would touch their little brothers in front of them. It was bullshit. We didn't blackball a lot people at the end when I was in. Almost everybody that pledged got in. But sometimes these guys went through everything—the hell line, the shots—and they got blackballed. Back in the day, we had a lot of guys transferring to another fraternity. Guys would leave Omega to get into Alpha and vice versa, and they would only have to take ten shots if they transferred."

Chris rose through the ranks of the AOT hierarchy to become president.

"I started out as ninth-grade rep, then I went to sergeant at arms, then I went to vice president to president. Once I became vice president, I started to bring all my closest friends down. I brought all the jocks down, and I made sure the pledge masters didn't touch them. We had three pledge masters, and a couple of times, I had to go in the back and break things up. One time, one of the pledge masters didn't like a real good friend of mine, and he smacked the shit out of my friend. My friend threatened to kick the pledge master's ass, and he was gonna quit pledging. I sat him down and convinced him to finish up the induction. After you get pledged, you get introduced to all the officers. You would pledge for a half hour, then they would shake hands with all the pledge masters and sergeant at arms, and each one would smack them. Each member would have no choice. They would smack them or paddle them. We used to line them up and tackle them like football. It was fun."

On the subject of maintaining order, Chris had this to say.

"I didn't have as many members as Spooky. He had over one hundred, but I had about seventy guys in. We would have meetings, and people would flake out, and we made sure they came to meetings. We would say, 'Listen, you miss two meetings, and you're out of the fraternity.' We had meetings every other week, or sometimes three out of four weeks a month. If you didn't make it to two out of three meetings, you're out. We ran it well. We were serious."

Chris discussed holding meetings and how he had to get creative in locating places to hold fifty to seventy AOT members.

"We used to hold meetings in people's houses and their backyards, but after a while, it got hairy. Then we started doing them at the state park in Valley Stream and Shore Avenue schoolyard. It became too hard to have meetings at people's houses. It was just too loud."

The last known president of Valley Stream AOT was Tom Spinner. The usual problems of pressure from the school, fights with Valley Stream North, and apathy of the student body to hazing all were factors in the demise of the fraternity. But the final nail in the coffin was from the last AOT president himself. Tom had inherited the fraternity from Rodney Bocce in 1996. With a membership roster of forty members, the chapter should have been stable; but because of poor turnout at weekly meetings and low morale among the brotherhood, Tom officially closed the chapter, and none of the younger members ever tried to pick it up or carry on after that. The year 1996 was the last recorded year of any active chapter of Alpha Omega Theta Fraternity.

It is not at all surprising that the last Long Island chapters of AOT and Omega Gamma Delta were the two oldest chapters of each fraternity. The Omega chapter in Central High School was the second Omega chapter founded on Long Island; it was founded in 1939, second only to the Lynbrook chapter founded in 1925. Valley Stream AOT, which had been founded in 1955 in Valley Stream Central High School. The chapter founded by Chick Hackney, brought over from Brooklyn with the help of Joe Brugnolotti and Mickey Percy, was both the first and last Long Island chapter of AOT. Valley Stream Alpha became the epitome of the AOT motto, "Alpha Omega Theta—first, last, always."

Oceanside AOT brother with Tau Delta Gamma girl circa 1986

Valley Stream AOT circa 1987

CHAPTER SIXTEEN

Oceanside AOT Reunion

In June of 2002, I had found the Web site classmates.com, and I started looking up people I knew from back in the day. I don't know what made me think of it, but I became nostalgic for Alpha Omega Theta. I wondered when the fraternity finally folded, and more importantly, I wondered who had the massive pile of paperwork that we called "the books." We had accumulated more than twenty-five years of documents that we kept in a green suitcase that was brought to each meeting. In my sophomore year, we had so many documents that we had to get a second suitcase to keep them in.

I posted this thread on a class-mates message board online in the Oceanside section on June 2, 2002:

> I was a member of the green-and-red frat, also known as Alpha Omega Theta, from the years 1978-1982. I dogged in junior high, got hassled a lot by Alpha Sigma Phi in Merle Ave. We had a suitcase of books and paraphernalia, the book we all signed had signatures going back to the guys that started it in 1957. Some of the signatures were marked "killed in Vietnam." When the frat disintegrated around 1984, someone took possession of the books. I am curious where they might be, and if anyone would be interested in a late 1970s Alpha reunion, we used to call 'em brew ups.

On February 15, 2003, I received a reply from Chip Hawkins from the class of 1961. Chip's reply was intriguing, and I would later establish communication with Chip. Chip and I still correspond to this day. Here is what Chip said in his reply to my posting:

Fred,

This is the only thread I have seen about AOT in all the years since high school. I have often wondered whatever became of us all. I was asked to dog in 1958 and actually was sworn in, in 1959. I don't remember all of the founding members, but Dan McMillan comes to mind. I wish I had some info for you on the books. It was pretty nostalgic to even see the name Alpha. I hated the reference as the "Christmas Tree" club. Wicked memories of hell night. Bob Petrocelli came across the yard at about forty mph running with a paddle in his hand and hit me so hard my lights went out. Thanks for letting me just remember.

On September 29, 2003, Mitch Wexman, class of 1978, added to the thread:

I was in AOT from about 1976-1978. I still have my Alpha Omega Theta Homewreckers, Inc. t-shirt. I remember getting a few paddles with a baseball bat sliced down the middle and being passed around the room taking kicks and open-handed punches by many. Interesting sociology experiment. It was all fun.

And Chip's reply to Mitch on September 30, 2003:

You know the characteristics of a true war story is one-upsmanship so it probably doesn't surprise you that you're in store for a "can you beat this?" I think Alpha started in '57 or '58. I missed the first go round of dogging in '58 and was a proud pledge in the latter school year of '58. It was of the era where not a lot was lost in the translation, things being pure and all that. Society and the school administration had little effect on the dogging process. So, if you don't mind my telling you that if you hadn't been hit by Bob Petrocelli ('59-'60) bearing a "screamer," you hadn't been hit. A "screamer" was a 6" x 24" oak paddle with 1-1/2 holes closely drilled in it to cut down wind resistance. Its trajectory was from across the room with two full 360 turns incorporated to gain full momentum. The scrotum was released and unprotected due to the grabbing of both ankles with both hands to maximize the stretching of the skin across the buttocks. Ever since then I have no idea where the books are.

In the midst of the activity of this thread, which was getting multiple replies, I had actually found another thread announcing an Alpha Omega Theta reunion at the Knights of Columbus in Oceanside. I posted this to the thread I had started:

> It would be great if we could at least get copies of the original AOT books to use for a Web site dedicated to Alpha Omega Theta. We were a long and proud Oceanside tradition. We should get a permanent web presence. Also I hear there will be a reunion at

> Saturday August 21 7:00 PM-12:00 PM
> Knights Of Columbus
> 2985 Kenneth Place Oceanside, NY 11572
> $70 Per Person
> Full Bar and Buffet
> Featuring Music of the Mystic

> A little steep, but worth it. I hope the Mystic plays good tunes. I remember great parties with local bands like the Untouchables in Pete Wilhelm's backyard, and Ed and the Crunchy Frogs (yep that's what they were called) in Tommy Shriver's backyard. AOT parties were a wild time, people barfing on the front lawn, peeing in the neighbor's shrubs. Let's hope this one lives up to the wild times of the past.

As you can see by my last post, I was already beginning to think about a reunion and documenting the history of Alpha Omega Theta Fraternity on a Web site. I was amazed that a Google search turned up nothing about Alpha Omega Theta. It seemed that there was nothing on the Internet in respect to AOT or any of the other fraternities and sororities from Nassau County. I did a Web search and found that the domain name space alphaomegatheta.com was available, so I registered the name prior to the August 2004 reunion. I didn't do anything with the domain name at first. I wanted to get feedback from other AOT members at the reunion before building an AOT Web site.

I hadn't thought about AOT in more than twenty years, but now that a reunion was coming up, I was excited to see everyone. I bought two tickets for me and my wife, and I wondered whom I would see there. My wife had no idea what this reunion was about. She is from El Salvador, and she has no idea what a fraternity is, or why we were getting together. She thought it was some kind of high school reunion. After I found out about the reunion on classmates. com, I later noticed a banner announcing the reunion hanging on Farmer Joel's on Oceanside Road, and the sign in front of Johnny Russo's Bar and Grill also announced the AOT reunion.

As the day of the reunion arrived, I didn't know if it was formal or casual attire. I decided to wear slacks, black shoes, and a collared shirt. To my embarrassment, I saw everyone wearing jeans and tee shirts. In fact, they were wearing AOT tee shirts. When I walked in the door, the first person I saw checking names was Guy Schiavone. I immediately recognized and remembered him, and he remembered me as well. I was happy that the cost of a ticket included a free AOT tee shirt. I hadn't owned or worn colors since 1982, and I was happy to see the AOT crest again. I quickly ran out to my car to throw my collared shirt into it and change into my new AOT tee shirt. The shirt had a small crest on the left side instead of a full-sized shield taking up the whole front. The shirt provided me with what I needed to start the AOT Web site. But first, I wanted to float my idea past some of the other Alpha brothers.

I stepped into the hall, and I was thrilled to see so many guys I knew. I saw Pat Kapps first, and we chatted for a few minutes before he led me to where Billy Young was. I had known Billy Young since the second grade. After a few minutes of catching up with Billy, he told me that Pete Wilhelm was at the reunion. He brought me over to Pete, and it was overwhelming to see him again. I grew up living next door to the Wilhelm's, and I had not seen any of them, including Pete, after our families sold our houses in Oceanside in the early 1980s. Pete was the guy who brought me into Alpha. I was disappointed to find that John Jaeger, the AOT president in 1978 when I was inducted, would not be attending. John had suffered a debilitating stroke about a year before and was still rehabilitating. I had always looked up to John when I was a younger AOT brother, and I was saddened to hear of his health problems. Before the band started playing, we all lined up for a group picture.

My wife and I milled around the rest of the evening, eating, drinking, and chatting with people. Phil Gerardi, AOT president from 1977, was walking the floor with a video camera and making a short movie. He went up to each brother to get a few comments. I spoke to Bubba Howe about starting a Web site for Alpha Omega Theta. The Web page he had paid to have made for him to announce the reunion sucked, and it had no features at all. The only thing you could click on was the link to e-mail Bubba. Bubba had paid a lot of money for the Web page, and it wasn't even a real domain name. It was a page on someone else's Web site. I pitched the idea of our own domain, which would live at alphaomegatheta. com, and Bubba loved the idea. I got a lot of positive feedback from the Alpha brothers I discussed my ideas for the new AOT Web site with.

As the night progressed, I met a bunch of guys at a table who were all from Rockville Centre Alpha from the late 1960s. Right after meeting them, I realized this party was a dress rehearsal for an even bigger event. I saw that there was a good showing of Oceanside AOT members from the 1970s and a few from the 1960s. But except for the five guys from Rockville

Centre AOT, there were no members from other chapters of Alpha, and definitely none of the earliest members from the 1950s in attendance. At that moment, I came up with the idea to hold another reunion, except the next one would be an open invite to all members of AOT from every chapter that ever existed.

Right after the party ended, many of us went across the street to Johnny Russo's Bar and Grill to continue having a good time. I am not usually a big drinker these days, and I didn't get too hammered that night either, but the reunion was so much fun I wanted to hang with old friends for as long as they were hanging out. My wife was a bit bored by all of this since she didn't know anyone, but she kind of had a good time too.

I was told by Billy Young that everybody would be meeting tomorrow at Johnny Russo's for a BBQ. I was supposed to work the next day, but I figured what the hell; I never got a chance to hang out with high school fraternity buddies, so I played hooky from work and went to Johnny Russo's. Bubba Howe showed up, and I discussed the AOT Web site in more detail with him. He was very interested in seeing this project get off the ground. He asked me what I needed to get started, and I told him I needed as many photos as possible to give the Web site appeal, something for people to look at. Bubba and Billy Young both promised to send me the pictures they took at the reunion, which they both did a few weeks later.

After an hour of hanging at Johnny Russo's, it came up in discussion that Jerry Branco, who was the owner of Branco's Clam Bar and Grill in Freeport, and also a Freeport AOT alumni from 1963, had invited AOT brothers to free beer at Branco's if they wore their AOT colors. Needless to say, we headed on over there right away. I had met Jerry a few months before the reunion in a bagel store in Freeport. I saw him wearing an AOT tee shirt one day, and I was surprised to see an Alpha shirt for the first time in more than twenty years. I introduced myself to him as an Oceanside AOT alumnus, and Jerry instantly gave me the Alpha grip. He introduced himself as a Freeport AOT alumni and treasurer in his senior year of 1963. We talked about the upcoming reunion. I still see Jerry all the time around Freeport as he is still a Freeport resident. I frequent Branco's Clam Bar every summer, and Jerry was also nice enough to give my son Joseph his first job there busing tables.

We went over to Branco's. It was a beautiful sunny summer day, and throughout the day, about ten or twelve different Alpha members stopped by Branco's. True to his word, Jerry instructed the barmaids to give free bottled beer to anyone wearing an Alpha shirt until 5:00 PM.

It was at this little get-together that I first met a Rockville Centre AOT member from the class of 1977 named Greg Colarossi. Greg had been sergeant at arms in his senior year, and at some point in the years that followed, after the dissolution of Rockville Centre Alpha, the last members of the chapter offered Greg the books from the AOT Mu Nu Chapter to keep. They thought he was a good choice to keep the books without disposing of them carelessly. They were right. The documents Greg has are the most complete I have seen of any AOT chapter.

Greg was telling us that an older Rockville Centre AOT president from 1968 named Mark Fordham had offered him $1,000 for the remnants of the Rockville Centre AOT books. Greg turned down his offer and decided to keep the books. A wise choice since those books would later provide a vast amount of insight into the history of an Alpha chapter which I would use on the website.

I had a great time that whole weekend, and I had gotten great inspiration from the AOT brothers to document the life and times of Alpha Omega Theta Fraternity on a Web site where it will live forever. I started in the simplest manner. I took the AOT tee shirt they gave me at the reunion, and I put it on a flatbed scanner. I scanned the AOT shield and saved it as a background. I then used FrontPage to build a simple home page, with the Alpha shield right in the center and a heading that says "Welcome to Alpha Omega Theta.com" at the top of the page. Nothing fancy; it was simple, but just perfect. I wanted to test the water before going to a professional hosting service, so I hosted alphaomegatheta.com on a UNIX server in my house. I installed a simple program for showing thumbnail pictures, and I uploaded all the pictures from the reunion that Bubba and Billy sent me. The site got visits by a few Oceanside AOT members, but not a mad rush like I thought. Also, because I hosted the site at home, it went down frequently. Both computers that were hosting the Web site, the UNIX server that ran the Apache Web server and the Windows ME PC that ran the thumbnail program, were in my young daughter's room, and she would frequently turn these computers off. I was always getting guys telling me they could not get to the Web site.

After about nine or ten months, I got bored with it and stopped trying to keep the site up and running. Thanks to Billy Young, who constantly bothered me to bring the AOT Web site online again, I decided to do it again, and to do it right this time. I did a Web search and located a hosting company that offered hosting for less than $15 a month. I paid in advance for six months of hosting, and I uploaded the Web site home page to the new hosting service. The hosting service was well worth the money. They offered all sorts of extra features to add to the Web site, such as a message board, a guest book, a photo gallery, a chat room, and more. I installed all of those features, and then I got to work getting the word out that the AOT Web site was back and better than before. I decided the time was right to get the word out to all the other AOT chapters about the new AOT Web site. I went to classmates.com and posted an announcement and a link to the AOT Web site on the message boards of

Oceanside, Baldwin, Freeport, Uniondale, Rockville Centre, Valley Stream, and Garden City.

The hits started coming in right away. AOT brothers from all the chapters started signing the guest book and registering screen names on the message board. I started asking the visiting AOT members to send any old pictures they had, and then I got a flood of old pictures sent to me from all different years, decades, and chapters. As I write this book, the AOT photo gallery has close to twelve hundred photos on it.

I had reached out to Chip Hawkins, whom I had met online at classmates.com two years earlier, to tell him about the Web site and to try to reach some of the senior AOT alumni from his time. At first, Chip didn't respond to me, but I was persistent. Chip was the earliest AOT member from Oceanside I had ever communicated with, and I knew he had a wealth of knowledge about the founding and the founding members of Oceanside AOT. My persistence paid off, and Chip did reply to me after three or four annoying e-mails from me via classmates.com. At first, Chip said he didn't have much info to share and he didn't keep in touch with many old AOT brothers. But I continued to pick his brain, and he sent me a list of the earliest Oceanside AOT members from the classes of 1958 to 1961.

I decided to post this list of names on a page dedicated to the earliest members of Oceanside AOT. Then the idea caught on. I started getting lists of names e-mailed to me for various years, and later, I started adding names from other chapters. Currently, the AOT Alumni Directory is a work in progress. I may never have a 100 percent complete list for every chapter and every year, but the current listing is pretty extensive for most chapters, and I still get new names sent to me from time to time to add to the AOT Alumni Directory. I can personally thank Valley Stream AOT brothers Mike McNamara, class of 1966, and Anthony Ratobala, class of 1971, for providing an almost—100 percent roster of names from the Valley Stream Central chapter between the years 1961 to 1973. I later did research at the libraries in the towns that had AOT chapters, and I photocopied yearbook pictures to link to the names in the directory. The AOT Alumni directory is one of the more popular aspects of the Web site, next to the photo gallery.

A few months after the AOT Web site going online, I went into Johnny Russo's Bar and Grill, which was renamed John's Union Park Café. I heard that AOT alumni hung out there, so I went there looking to meet a few people to spread the word about the AOT Web site. It was there that I met the Oceanside AOT president from 1968, Billy Weitzman. I saw him sitting across the bar from me, and I recognized him from the pictures Bubba had sent me from the reunion. I asked the bar owner, Johnny Russo, who was an AOT alumnus from my class of 1982, if the guy sitting across from me was in AOT. Johnny told me that he was Billy Weitzman and that he had been an AOT president. I asked Johnny if Billy was approachable. Johnny said yes, definitely. In fact, Johnny said, "If you tell him you were in AOT, he will probably buy you a beer. Billy loves meeting guys that were in AOT."

So I went and introduced myself. "Hi, my name is Fred. I remember seeing you at the AOT reunion in 2004."

"You were in AOT? What year?" Billy said.

"I was in from 1978 to 1982," I said.

"Did you hear that there is a Web site for AOT now? Some guy set it up a month ago," Billy said.

"Yeah, I am the guy. I set it up, and the reason I am here is to find some AOT members to spread the word about the Web site," I said.

"You put up that Web site? That's great, how much did it set you back?" Billy said.

"Not much. It costs less than $15 a month," I said.

Bill reached into his wallet and put $50 on the bar in front of me and said, "Take this to help with the cost of hosting and managing the Web site."

"That's not necessary. It's not costing that much, and I paid for six months in advance with the hosting service," I said.

"Well, did anyone kick in to help you pay for it?" Billy said.

"No," I said.

"Well, in six months, the rent will be due on the Web site again. Did you plan to keep on paying for it out of your own pocket?" Billy said.

"I hadn't thought that far ahead," I said.

"Well, take this fifty bucks, and when the Web site needs to be paid up again, come see me, and we will find other AOT brothers to kick in to keep it going," Billy said.

"Actually, I had an idea to print up some new AOT tee shirts and sell them to raise money to pay up the hosting cost for the next year," I said.

"Now you're talking. Do you have someone to make the tee shirts?" Billy said.

"Yeah, there is a tee shirt silk screen factory next to my father's office in Hicksville. He will give me a discount since he does business with my father," I said.

"Get the tee shirts made, and I will split the cost of them with you, and you can sell all of them to raise money to keep the Web site going," Billy said.

With that conversation, I had made the acquaintance of a good friend. I ordered fifty AOT tee shirts to be made, and Billy Weitzman made good on his offer to pay for half of them. After I received the tee shirts, I offered to give half of them to Billy, and he refused. He took one tee shirt for himself and told me to sell the rest. I found Billy to be a hell of a guy and generous. The one tee shirt he took for himself he gave to an AOT brother from his class of 1968 at a summer BBQ. Angelo Termani was admiring Billy's AOT tee shirt, and Billy literally gave Angelo the shirt off his back. When I found out that Billy had given away his only AOT tee shirt, I insisted that he take another one for himself. Not long after, Billy gave that shirt away as well. As we had discussed, I sold the tee shirts and used the money to pay for the AOT Web site's hosting for the next year.

A few weeks after becoming friends with Billy, he gave me a VHS videotape that contained about ten minutes of Super 8 video footage from an AOT party that was thrown in 1968. The event was a party for graduating senior AOT brothers, which started our Senior Dinner tradition. They held the affair at a place called Joe Terzo's Pizzeria on Woods Avenue in Oceanside. In the mid-1970s, Joe Terzo's would become Alias Smith and Jones Tavern.

I took the video home and watched it. I was enchanted by the charm of this video and how it was a moment frozen in time. In the middle of the tumultuous 1960s, here was a tight brotherhood of clean-cut young men who represented the best qualities of young Americans. The video was originally silent, but someone had added music to it. With the Beatles song "Yesterday" playing in the background, the video started with Billy Weitzman coming into the room wearing a jacket and tie and smoking a cigar. All throughout the video, Alpha brothers could be seen wearing green-and-red Alpha sweaters with skinny black ties. Everyone in the video is smiling, laughing, and appears to be having a great time. The brotherhood is obvious and strong in that room that day. I posted the video on the AOT Web site, and it quickly became a favorite feature to the Alpha brothers visiting the Web site.

At the suggestion of the Oceanside AOT president from my year, Billy Young, I added a memorial page for all of the AOT members from all the chapters who passed away. It is a sad page to view, but we honor them by remembering them. Occasionally, I still get notice of an AOT brother who has passed away, and I add the name to the "In Memory of" page.

During the first year of the AOT site being online, I reached out to numerous AOT members from all chapters and all years. I had made the acquaintance of Valley Stream AOT president from 1980 John Morella. John found the Web site from a flyer I posted on a light pole in the parking lot outside the game room in Nathan's in Oceanside. In my conversations with John, he advised me to look for and reach out to Joe Furino, a.k.a. Spooky. Spooky was the Valley Stream AOT president from 1980. John Morella had told me that Spooky was a dedicated AOT brother, and that he was sure Spooky would be of assistance with the new Web site. John told me to look up Pinnacle Construction as Spooky is the owner of the company.

I went online to yellowpages.com and looked up Pinnacle Construction and called the number listed. I spoke to Spooky's receptionist, and I told her I was a member of Joe Furino's high school fraternity and I was looking for him. I left her my phone number, and twenty minutes later, Spooky called me. I introduced myself and told him about the AOT Web site. Spooky was immediately interested. He offered to meet me somewhere for a beer. He asked me if I needed money for the site, and I said no. I told him I was looking for old photographs and also to network with as many AOT members from all the chapters as possible. Spooky told me he had some pictures from high school he wanted to get posted on the Web site. We agreed to meet at Branco's Clam Bar in Freeport for a few beers. In the midst of this meeting arrangement, I had also mentioned to Jerry Smith that I was going to meet Spooky at Branco's, and he told me that he was coming as well and bringing a few other AOT members from Valley Stream Central 1956 and '57. Jerry Smith was the first vice president of Valley Stream AOT and one of its founding members. When my friend Billy Weitzman heard that some of the founding members of Valley Stream AOT would be meeting us at Branco's, he decided to come, and he brought Charlie Termani, who was treasurer when Billy was president of Oceanside AOT in 1968. Greg Colarossi, who had been sergeant at arms in Rockville Centre AOT in 1977, also came to the brew-up.

It was a beautiful summer day that I first met Joe Furino, a.k.a. Spooky, at Branco's Clam Bar. I also met Jerry Smith, Bobby Playa, and Bill Trishone. Jerry had been a founding member and vice president, and he brought along Bobby Playa, who had been in the first dogging class for VSC AOT and later the treasurer in 1957. Bill Trishone was from the class of 1957 and had been the only president in the Valley Stream North chapter of AOT who didn't last more than one year. We all came from different years and different chapters of AOT, yet we had a common bond, and we had a great time drinking that day and toasting AOT. We had such a good time that Spooky invited all of us out to dinner at a restaurant in Westbury called Café Bacci.

The whole idea of bringing together members from every chapter was beginning to gel. It was all coming together better than I had imagined. Very soon after this, the possibility of forming the first new chapter of AOT in thirty years would present itself.

Past presidents of Oceanside AOT

Group picture from AOT reunion 2004

Group picture from AOT reunion 2004

CHAPTER SEVENTEEN

Canadian AOT

In the summer of 2006, I had created a MySpace page for an AOT profile. I was looking to reach out to college-age men who would be interested in forming a chapter of Alpha Omega Theta Fraternity in their schools. On June 1, 2006, I got a message to the from a young man in Calgary, Canada, who found us and had interest in forming a chapter in Canada. Here is a thread of the conversation that went back and forth between Greg Flange, a student at the University of Calgary, and me.

Greg's first contact with me:

> Howdy,
>
> I saw your post in the Delta House group. I'm curious about starting a Fraternity at the University of Calgary.
>
> > Cheers,
> > Greg

My reply to Greg:

> Hi Greg,
>
> Have you looked over the Alpha Omega Theta website yet? It's at www.alphaomegatheta.com. Are you still interested in starting a chapter? If so, we can definitely offer a charter if you have a few friends to start it up.

You can reply to me direct at webmaster@alphaomegatheta.com or through MySpace.

> Fred Gross
> Alpha Omega Theta webmaster
> Freeport NY

After our first exchange, I was trying to gauge Greg's level of interest in AOT. In the next exchange, I offered Greg more info on Alpha Omega Theta Fraternity.

Fred

Before I commit to anything, I need to talk to my buddies first. Can you let me know anything in regards to cost? Also, where do you have chapters, and how many alumni do you have?

> Greg

* * *

Hi Greg,

Have your friends checked out the Alpha Omega Theta website? I see we have been getting a lot of hits coming from Canada since you found us. You can get a listing of most of the Alumni from most of our chapters on the alumni page at www.alphaomegatheta.com/AOT_Alumni_Names.htm

I can also send you a detailed history of AOT if you like.

> Fred
> webmaster@alphaomegatheta.com

* * *

Fred

Anything you can tell me about your brotherhood would be beneficial in making our decision.

> Thanks
> Greg

At this point, I sent Greg a written history of Alpha Omega Theta Fraternity and informed him that there would be no charge to him and his crew for any induction fees or start-up costs, and this was the reply I got:

Dear Sir,

After long debates with some of my friends, we have decided that we would indeed like to start a chapter of Alpha Omega Theta.

How do I go about becoming a brother of Alpha Omega Theta? If you need to know more about me, here is a bio:

I am a student at the University of Calgary pursuing degrees in Political Science and Sociology (with a concentration in Crime Deviance and Social Control), and minors in Canadian Studies and Religious Studies. I have been involved in both student politics (in 2004 and 2005 I ran in the Students' Union election for president, being narrowly defeated the second time), and Canadian politics, including being a local party strategist and working in the last federal election as an assistant to one of the Prime Ministerial Candidates while he was in Alberta. I have also worked for the Gauntlet Undergraduate Newspaper (http://gauntlet.ucalgary.ca/) as an illustrator/writer for 2 years. I served as an illustrations editor for a semester.

I have also been the president of the U of C Irish Club, the Vice President of the U of C Canadian Club, a committee member for the Calgary Red Cross and Amnesty International. I am active in the Canadian Political Science Association, the Council of Canadians, and the Monarchist League of Canada.

I am currently the Tyler for the Knights of the Royal Black Preceptory of the British Empire encampment 640, and the lecturer for Loyal Orange Lodge 2980 (http://orangenet.org/outram/). I have also made an application to join Concord. 124 Masonic Lodge (http://www.freemasons.ab.ca/cfh.html). In addition, I am also on the Calgary Committee for the Parland Institute, a Canadian political think tank (http://www.ualberta.ca/~parkland/).

If you feel that I am suitable for membership in your fraternity, please feel free to contact me. I am eager to get a chapter going as soon as possible so that we can be granted sanction by the U of C Students' Union by the Fall so that we can participate in Frosh week events, especially clubs week, which will give us a booth to recruit new members.

So what do you need me to do at this point?

Cheers,
Gregory P. Flange
Calgary, Alberta, Canada

At this point, it looked like Greg and his buddies had decided to go forward with forming an AOT chapter at the University of Calgary. Now it was time to work out the details of how to proceed.

Hi Greg,

That is great news, I am glad that you chose AOT. I will confer with the Alumni that are involved in the website and new chapter development.

We will send you a charter for your chapter, copies of other chapters' bylaws, which you can use as a guide to writing your own bylaws, and a letter of agreement to form a chapter of Alpha Omega Theta. Please give me an address to where I can send you the documents you will need to get started. I would like to get them mailed to you as soon as possible.

We will put you on a fast track to being a full-fledged chapter. You and your friends won't have to settle for colony status. All we ask in return is to try your best to bring us a good name and reputation in your university, that you bring in enough new members to maintain, and pass on a functioning fraternity when you graduate. And lastly, that you make an effort to spread Alpha Omega Theta to other schools.

As I stated earlier we are not asking for any money for your application or charter, nor will we ask for any dues be paid to us. The only cost will be if you order colors and a banner from us. Of course you can choose to get colors and a banner from a local source and we will not have any problem with that. Just make sure the colors are consistent with our shield, that they are only Green and Red if you order them from your own source.

Please send all future e-mails to me at webmaster@alphaomegatheta.com.

The only question I have is how many charter members do you have to start this chapter with you?

Thanks again. I look forward to the start of a great new chapter of AOT. I am sure you are the right guy to build it.

Fraternally yours
Fred Gross
AOT Class '82
Alea Iacta Est

Once I had a firm commitment from Greg and his crew to launch a new chapter of AOT at the University of Calgary, I inquired as to the university's rules and requirements for fraternities to obtain recognition from the school. This was his reply:

Hello Fred,

The University doesn't require us to be incorporated. However, we can be recognized by an act of parliament; however, that is more of just a honourary thing. I have some friends in a Senator's office so maybe they could help us be recognized as a legal Canadian entity. (Actually under Nafta agreements I think the NY corporate charter may be recognized, but I'm not entirely sure.)

At the U of C there are currently 3 Fraternities (and one "business Frat") and 2 Sororities. They are treated like any other club. The U of C does not officially do any of the recognizing. In fact a few fraternities have existed on campus with no recognition (Chi Gamma and Delta Upsilon, I believe). To become "sanctioned" we need recognition from the Students' Union. In order to do so we need 12 active U of C Undergraduate members and 8 members, who can be anybody. Here is the link about starting a Fraternity at the U of C: http://www.su.ucalgary.ca/55.0.html. We will have limited benefits from the SU. I already have my Alcohol-awareness training, so we will be covered on the SU's insurance and allowed to have events that involve the serving of alcohol by SU staff. Other than that they won't give us funds for events like other clubs, in exchange for allowing us to pick members, be single gendered, and they will overall leave us alone.

Also, if we are granted a charter, would it be possible to put a Canadian Flag on the website with the American Flag? That'd be great.

Thanks, and I look forward to our next e-mail correspondence.

Cheers,
Greg

Greg's reply to my inquiry about the University of Calgary's requirements to recognize AOT as a legitimate fraternity on campus was informative and straightforward. It appeared as though Greg had a plan to get all his ducks in a row and put together a crew large enough to satisfy the U of C Student Union's requirements to recognize AOT. At this point, we were ready to go forward and grant them a charter. Before issuing a charter, we wanted to get all the charter members to sign a letter of agreement to spell out what we expected of each other in this endeavor.

Hi Greg,

Let me know when you have your charter members ready and how many there are. I have a letter of agreement and a Charter for your new chapter. I will e-mail you the letter of agreement for you to read and show the others. If everyone is OK with it, I will then snail mail you a paper copy, which you all would sign and return to me.

After we receive the signed letter of agreement, we will issue a charter and all the documents that go with it. I am looking forward to it.

Fraternally yours
Fred Gross
Oceanside AOT
Class of 1982
Alea Iacta Est

Greg replied that they were ready to roll.

Hello Fred

Sounds good. We're still in the process of trying to organize a good group of guys to form the foundation for the Brotherhood in Calgary.

It may take a week or two, but I will let you know as soon as I am sure of the founding members. If we could see the constitution/letter, that would help because some of our friends are a bit unsure at this point, and I'm sure those documents would help turn them around.

Thanks,
Greg

As we had discussed, I sent Greg two copies of the letter of agreement between the charter members at the University of Calgary and the Grand Chapter of AOT. Additionally, I sent a copy of the Charter of Calgary AOT for them to view and provide me feedback on anything they wanted changed. They were hard copies sent via regular U.S. Postal Service. They were supposed to read it and discuss it among themselves. They were then supposed to have each charter member sign both copies. One copy they would mail back to me, and the other copy they would keep for their own chapter records. When I didn't get a reply from Greg, I inquired as to the status of the agreement.

What's up Greg,

Are you making any progress with recruiting charter members? I will be ordering more AOT tee shirts and tank tops. Do your guys want any?

Fred Gross
Oceanside AOT
Class of 1982
Alea Iacta Est

*　　*　　*

Fred, Howdy,

My sincerest apologies for not keeping up regular contact with you. I've just started a new job and I work long hours (however the money is good so I won't have to work in the fall, which means I can devote more time to the fraternity!).

I'm still finalizing members. I'd much rather spend a bit more time ensuring we have a solid group of men, rather than haphazardly throwing together a group that won't last a semester.

A few guys who are interested are working up north in the Oil fields for the summer, and a few others just got shipped off for military training; on the other hand, a few others have just come back from overseas. I should be able to have everything settled soon. At the very latest I will know by mid-July (15th), with the conclusion of the Calgary Stampede (which essentially turns the city into one huge beer garden).

I will move as fast as possible on this, as I too am eager to get Alpha Omega Theta running. However, like I said, I want to do this right.

At this point the constitution looks fine (other than the part about the flag, which we would just change to "Queen and Dominion" for Canada, or something acceptable and appropriate for all involved parties).

I will let you know once I have a solid membership cemented; until then, here are some names of definite members:

Gregory P. Flange
Salvatore Leon (who is willing to donate his apartment for fraternal activities)
Brandon Jackson (working in the North for six weeks on, one week off)
Jason Chin (doing military training)
Jack Moses
Jonathan Moses

There are a few more; however, I want to make sure they are definite before I pass on their names.

In anticipated Fraternal Brotherhood,

Greg

*   *   *

Hi Greg,

I'm thrilled to see you guys are ready. As for the language about the flag, please realize that we in the USA are taught to revere the flag first, so it seemed like the right language to pass on. You can change the line to your own best interpretation. Let me know how you want it to read and I'm sure it will be fine for us as well.

———

Remember that when you write bylaws that they are for your chapter only, so you can add almost anything you need that will satisfy your crew. You should make writing bylaws your first order of new business at your first meeting as a chapter.

Great idea about officers serving in multiple offices. That's what it's all about, working on issues and finding solutions that serve your best interest.

Seven is a good number to start with. Most of our chapters were started with six so you are doing great. Give the other guys one last chance to be charter members. Let them know you are definite and have a date for launching the new chapter. Maybe a few more will come on board. The ones that don't will have to be your pledges if they want to join later.

I will re-mail you a Word-formatted version of the Beta Alpha Charter and you can edit section 4 E to suit your need. Print it on pastel green paper with dark red font.

Print 2 copies of the charter and of the letter of agreement. Have all seven charter members sign both and mail both copies of both documents to me at

Alpha Omega Theta Fraternity

Please let me know if your seven guys want tee shirts for the induction. I am ordering some and would like for all of you to have colors (or colours?) to be seen with.

Let me know

Fred Gross
Oceanside AOT
Class of 1982
Alea Iacta Est

After some debate among the Calgary recruits to determine if their charter would have a reference to revere the Canadian flag or the Queen of England, they all agreed to sign the document.

Fred,

I've got one of the guys printing up the documents right now at work, so I'll just send the documents to you. As for the pledging rules, I can't say whether or not recruits will go for it. After talking to friends in other frats from across Canada, I've been told that the U.S. frat system and culture is completely different. In the U.S. it has much more weight and importance. So we'll have to wait and see how we will handle the recruits.

Have a great Fourth of July!

Greg

Now that the documents were almost ready to be mailed back to AOT on Long Island, we had some discussion on minor details of running the local Calgary chapter. I also reiterated and reminded them of their agreement to recruit enough members to make their chapter viable, as well as their agreement to attempt to spread AOT to neighboring universities.

OK Greg,

Try to get them printed on green paper with red font. But it's not critical.

If you want, I can print them out and send them to you, then you can return signed copies to me. That way your first documents are authentic. I'm meeting my guys tomorrow for a Brew Up and I'm sure I can get them to sign first. Let me know what works for you.

If you guys want to have meetings every two weeks that's up to you. Those are the things you will need to work out in your chapter bylaws. I will send you chapter bylaws from Rockville Centre and Freeport AOT's. You can use them as an example, and then create your own rules. Bylaws usually dictate the rules for meetings, fines for breaking the rules, initiation fees, weekly dues, etc.

You guys may want to collect initiation fees from each other and use it to start your chapter treasury.

As for the shirts. It's fine if you want to make your own. I just want to be sure the shield artwork is consistent. Other than that, feel free to order shirts, sweaters, sweatshirts, or whatever from anyone you can get them made by. Just be sure the shield is correct, and the colors are correct. Medium to dark green background, dark red letters, except for stationery, which can be light green paper.

I am going to see all my guys tomorrow at another Brew Up and possibly again Thursday when an AOT brother's band is playing at another AOT brother's restaurant. So I will get my guys ready for your guys. I will send you the stuff you will need.

Let's make a good effort to recruit enough members over the summer so you can go to the fall semester as a recognized fraternity by your student union.

You may want to make pledging shorter just for this summer to attract enough members. That's just a suggestion. What did you think of the pledging rules and agreements? Do you think new recruits will go for that at the U of C?

Lastly, please try to have a digital camera when we have the induction. We would like pictures for the website and a group picture of all of you after your induction is complete. Have the group pic taken by an uninvolved person, like someone's girlfriend or something. After induction all will be given an option of getting an AOT e-mail address, password for the Brothers Only section, and when you are ready, will add content to the site for the U of C Chapter page.

We are getting new polo shirts with the AOT shield embroidered. They will be real nice.

We have decided that we will give you and the other six charter members one shirt each as a gift from us.

I have all the documents that you will need to get started ready for you. We are just waiting for the signed charter and agreement letter to arrive. As soon as we have them we will make arrangements with you for a conference call with all of you on your side and my guys over here.

Will you be looking to have your own banner made? Or do you want me to price one for you?

Also, what do you think will be your time frame to apply to the Student Union for membership?

Fred Gross
Oceanside AOT
Class of 1982
Alea Iacta Est

Now that all the details had been worked out on the charter, we now had to work out the details of the initiation of these charter members. Spooky from Valley Stream had ordered a few dozen polo shirts with the AOT shield embroidered. The polo shirts were ordered as an enticement to get AOT alumni to come to our brew-ups and help organize the upcoming AOT reunion. Spooky had paid for these out of his own pocket and insisted on giving the polo's away for free to AOT brothers. Spooky generously offered to give the officers of the new Calgary chapter each one free polo shirt as well.

Hey Fred,

Almost ready to mail the document. I just need to grab two more signatures. I will mail it rush to get it there faster. Sorry for the delay. Polo's would be great! Thank you. I have no idea where to get a banner, so if you could price that out for us, that would be great. Also, were you ever able to find anything about pins? I found a supplier who could make them for about $4cdn each, but we would need to place an order for at least 100.

As for the students' union, we would have to have a formal meeting with them and pass a review board. However, the next review board won't be until the fall. I imagine the earliest would be late August. I will find out for sure and let you know.

I'll e-mail you once the documents have been mailed.

Thanks,
Greg

After the agreement was finalized with the guys in Calgary, Canada, we began discussing when we could do a formal induction. It was decided that we would have a conference call between New York and Calgary and administer the oaths of brotherhood to the charter members of Calgary AOT. Valley Stream AOT president from 1980 Joe "Spooky" Furino, offered the use of his office for the conference call on our end and the Canadian AOT recruits would meet in Salvatore Leon's apartment in Calgary.

Greg,

Which Saturday? This Saturday or next? I will tell the guys that this Friday is off. Let me know if you can do it this Saturday or next Friday or Saturday. If we do it Friday I will work it out for 8:30 PM NY time.

If it's this or next Saturday, what time will work for you? I think I can get them together almost anytime for a Saturday. Let me know.

> Fred Gross
> Oceanside AOT
> Class of 1982
> Alea Iacta Est

After some back-and-forth banter on the subject of getting everyone together on the same evening, we finally agreed on the upcoming Friday night.

Fred

OK, I just came back from wing night with some of the guys. We discussed it and it looks like this Friday will work best for everyone. So let's go ahead with July 28th. The absolute earliest I can get everyone together though is 7:30 PM Calgary time. That's the absolute earliest I can get anyone to show up (due to work commitments).

So let's do it this Friday (July 28th). Sorry for all the confusion. We will meet at Sal's apartment. We will have a speaker phone.

> Thanks,
> Greg

*   *   *

Greg,

I confirmed with Spooky, we are on for Friday. We will call you at the number you gave at about 7:30 PM your time.

I sent a packet to you. Hopefully you will receive it by Friday. If you don't receive it by then you can access all docs on the website. I will create a username and password for you to get into the documents.

> Fred Gross
> Oceanside AOT
> Class of 1982
> Alea Iacta Est

Greg replied, acknowledging our phone conference that Friday night and also provided some interesting info on the possibilities of creating two more new AOT chapters at neighboring universities.

Fred

Yes we are on for this. I have mailed the documents to you today. My apologies for not getting everything together sooner but Stampede takes a lot out of you. The good news is that Stampede also brought about an increased interest in Alpha Omega Theta (by the way, the website assisted greatly in this, thank you). Not only do more guys want to join, but there is possible interest in starting chapters in New Brunswick, Canada, and at the University of Northern British Columbia. I'll try my best to follow up with these. We won't be able to have all 11 guys there. 4 are out of town and won't be back until the fall, so we'll have to initiate them then. And one or two guys may need to work. I think all the guys that are in line for officer positions will be present.

Talk to you tomorrow,

> Greg

On July 28, 2006, the following was posted on the AOT website by me, Fred Gross, Webmaster of the fraternity website:

At 9:30 PM New York Standard Time (7:30 PM Calgary time), Joe "Spooky" Furino (Valley Stream Central AOT President 1980), Bill

Weitzman (Oceanside AOT President 1968), John Marceda (Valley Stream Central AOT President 1978), and myself, the AOT website webmaster, Fred Gross, administered the Oaths of Brotherhood and the Oaths of Office to the first officer class of the Beta Alpha Chapter of Alpha Omega Theta Fraternity at the University of Calgary in Canada. Thanks to Joe "Spooky" Furino for allowing us to use his office to have the conference call, and for sending beautiful new AOT polo shirts to the charter members. Thanks also go out to Greg Flange for making this all come together on his end. Greg was inducted as the first president of his new chapter. Bring us a great rep on your campus, our new AOT Brothers. The new chapter's first officer class is as follows:

> Gregory P. Flange—President
> Salvatore Leon—Vice President
> Jack Moses—Treasurer
> Sam Yi—Secretary

These gentlemen have promised to get busy and induct new Brothers right away. They plan to have more than 20 new Brothers by next month. The plan is to bring the membership up to the numbers required for membership in the University of Calgary's Student Union. Greg is a resourceful guy and will no doubt acquire full membership for the U of C Chapter of AOT in the Student Union. Good Luck, Brothers, and Alea Iacta Est.

The reaction from many of the AOT alumni in New York upon hearing that a new chapter of Alpha Omega Theta had been founded was shock and pleasant surprise. After the official founding of the AOT chapter at the University of Calgary, President Greg Flange communicated a desire to create a meaningful induction ceremony to replace the vicious hazing that used to be inflicted on inductees. Here is what he had to add:

Fred

As soon as we're able to get back together we will all sign the book. But we've not all been together since the package arrived.

By the way, is there any special meaning behind our grip? And since the discovery that the Frat was not born on Christmas Eve, what do the colours stand for now?

I know the Kappa Sigma Initiation is based on the Masonic ceremony of the Blue lodge. Zeta Psi also has a very Masonic-style induction. Some parts of it are similar to the movie *The Skulls* (based on Skull and Bones), where pledges are buried alive in a coffin then "reborn" as full members. The inductee is then ceremonially instructed on the importance of secrecy and brotherhood. These ceremonies are used to instruct members of the Fraternities' values, secrets, and to reinforce the bonds of brotherhood by bringing outsiders into the brotherhood. (I know in the '80s and before all of these, frats also had Hell nights the night before the ceremony, but for legal liability issues have chosen to no longer allow them.)

With your blessing I would like to write up a short ceremony for inducting new members into the fraternity. Such a ceremony would add an air of gravity to the oaths, as well as act as a tool to reinforce the values of the Red and Green. Because our virtues seem to be primarily based on the code of chivalry, I was thinking of a ceremony along the lines of the first degrees into the Knights of the Royal Black Preceptory, Knights of St. Johns, or the Knights Templar (think along the lines of the initiation seen in *The Kingdom of Heaven*) would be the most appropriate.

While we most likely can't get away with any sort of hazing, we can add mental stress to an initiation. Members would have no idea what they were walking into and would be kept unsteady throughout the ceremony.

I stress that if we were to create some sort of initiation ceremony we would not be changing anything, but instead adding to it. Such a ceremony would act to reinforce our oaths and highlight our most important values.

What do you think?

Cheers,
UofC AOT
Class of 2006
Alea Iacta Est

Greg's suggestion to create a ceremonial induction ritual was an excellent idea since hazing and Hell Night was now out of the question. It showed me

---

that he was a great thinker and planner. I really had a good feeling that he was the right man to lead the new Calgary chapter of AOT.

Greg,

I think you have a great idea. In fact I was going to recommend that you come up with your own ideas for induction, as the only experience I have contained a serious beating and paddling.

As a chapter of AOT you now enjoy a large degree of autonomy. As long as the principles of the shield are upheld and the history is passed down, you guys are free to implement your own rituals. I am sure you will come up with something good.

About the grip and colors, I asked John Stefano about the colors and he said that they chose Green and Red because the Christmas season was coming on the date that they founded AOT. That's what he says and he was there so I guess we have to take his word for it. I didn't ask about the grip, but I will try to get in touch with him to ask. If we don't find out I think you can make your own interpretation.

Did the shirts get there yet? We can always have more made for new guys, but Spooky isn't going to send them free. What are your plans for reaching your goal to get into the student union?

If you guys want to make a big splash when the semester starts, I suggest parties. Let people get to know AOT is there now.

Fred Gross
Oceanside AOT
Class of 1982
Alea Iacta Est

Greg updated me on their receipt of the polo shirts we sent them, as well as his newly written induction ceremony, which he sent to me for approval.

Fred,

I received the shirts today. They're great. Thanks to everyone for them. I'll pass them on to the other brothers ASAP.

Right now we're planning a party for sometime in the next month.

We should be having another initiation in a week or so. I have written up a rough draft of an initiation for the Frat, and I just wanted to know what you guys thought of it. I'm completely open to criticism, advice, or anything you think could be added to it (or taken away). I did some research and came across the 9 worthies, who were apparently considered the epitome of knighthood in the 1300s. Since the 30 traits of the Frat seem to all be based on chivalry, I thought that the 9 worthies would be a good foundation for the ritual. That, and drinking with swords and blindfolded scared freshmen! The ritual is somewhat based on a couple other initiations: Templars, the Royal Black Preceptory, the Knights of the Rosey Cross, Masonry, Orangeism, the Knights of the Order of St. John (Hospitaller), and some other organizations that I'm familiar with.

So what do you think?

Greg

After reading the ceremony Greg wrote, I was quite impressed and gave him a seal of approval. I also inquired as to the level of commitment from his charter members since one of them had seemed kind of negative in his opinion as to whether AOT was going to work out in Calgary in an e-mail he sent me.

Greg

You've got me convinced. You are a natural at this. I like it. You definitely did your homework on Knighthood and knighting.

The only small detail is the skull and crossbones. They are actually the symbol that stands at the top of one of our competitor fraternity's shield. They were called Omega Gamma Delta and they only have one or 2 high school chapters left out of 20 or so they had in their heyday. Their Grand Poobah was arrested for paddling a teen in the woods last year. A 70-year-old pervert paddling a teen bare-assed in the woods. It pretty much ended them and killed their website. If you look at the recent pictures of Oceanside 1970 you will see a few guys wearing black-and-gold sweaters; that was Omega. They were a segregated fraternity for white Christians only. That's why AOT was always better.

I would suggest an Alpha shield or a knight's helmet at the pages header.

Other than that, it's very cool. I like it a lot.

Let me know when you guys induct a few brothers and tell me how it went with this procedure. I am curious. Sal seems to think the other two officers are doubtful about starting a frat. Are they on board? And the other guys that signed the agreement? Will they honor what they signed?

> Fred Gross
> Oceanside AOT
> Class of 1982
> Alea Iacta Est

Greg reassured me as to the commitment from his crew.

Fred

Yes all the guys will honour their agreements, I'm still talking to them and that's who we're initiating in the next week or so. As for Sam and Jack, they're in 100%. I just talked to them today. I'm very close to both and know they'd tell me if they weren't in.

You'll have to take whatever Salvatore says with a grain of salt. He doesn't really know anyone other than myself, so he needs to get to know the other guys before he gets used to them. Ben generally gives out a perception of not caring and being very reserved, but underneath he's different. Sal is more than a little on the nerdy side, but don't worry. I know the others will warm up to him. Everyone just needs to spend some more time together, that's why this party will help with that. Don't worry, everyone is in. It's more a matter of getting everyone in line and getting them used to each other and what the other guys are really like.

Things may move a little slower in the summer because we all have other duties and jobs, but once the fall semester starts everything will fall into place. Also I've pulled some strings and the Clubs coordinator is willing to let us become a sanctioned frat before the next semester.

We'll send pics as soon as I can get some.

As for the Skull and crossbones, I used it because of its ominous presence and because it has served as a symbol for the past 3,000 years to remind men of their own mortality. As a symbol, it's one of the most common, and essentially every secret society and fraternity I know uses it as a tool and symbol in one way or another. Besides, it sounds like Omega is dead. It's time for Alpha to rise. Perhaps we need to find a new "omega." There's nothing that can bring together a group of guys better than an enemy.

Greg

Although the letter of agreement they had signed with us stated that the Calgary chapter would submit meeting minutes and updated rosters to us back on Long Island, I found right from the start that updated info was not coming from them unless I inquired.

Hi Greg,

How's everything? Sal told me you have more pledges. That's fantastic. How are you dogging them? What does a brother in training have to do to get into Beta Alpha AOT?

Sal says the 2 other possible chapters have cooled off. Any chance of regenerating interest?

Also, we are meeting this Friday to discuss the upcoming all—chapter AOT convention. This party depends on attendance at this Brew Up and the response from AOT brothers if we secure a date.

I hope you guys will consider a pilgrimage to NY for this event. If it happens.

You guys are doing great. Everybody here is thrilled. Good idea about the Green-and-Red sashes.

Fred Gross
Oceanside AOT
Class of 1982
Alea Iacta Est

Greg wrote to me to tell me that the proposed two other chapters had fallen through and he showed little interest in trying to get those guys back on board. He spoke a little about their pledges and a party that ended in a big brawl, just as ours used to go on Long Island.

Fred

Sorry I haven't been in contact much. I don't know what happened to the other chapter enquiries . . . once school starts people have short attention spans. As for pledges, we have one right now that we kept, we generally just make him work at parties, etc. We are initiating him tomorrow night.

I don't think any of us have any funds to go to New York. Right now I'm on a ramen noodles diet and Sal has $60 for the next 2 weeks, that has to cover beer and food. So we're not in a spot financially to go. I would love to, however, but I'll have to live it through pictures.

I was just reading on the website about the 1981 fights. We had a similar situation at the last party "Frosh Slosh 2." Some party guests decided to do coke, or PCP (we're not sure which), unbeknownst to us. One guy decided to slap his girlfriend around in the bathroom. When we heard her yell, every brother ran to help her. The guy's buddies attacked us. It ended up being a fifty-man brawl, Alphas and our supporters, vs. Druggies and Townies. People were literally thrown through walls. Jason corralled them into the backyard, but he didn't know we had nailed all the gates shut to stop people from sneaking in. The coked-up guys were so scared they knocked down the fence. The guy who started the fight by beating up his girlfriend stepped on a board with a nail in it, which went right through his foot, and he was running around like that. Eventually they all ran away. No Alphas or our supporters were injured. But then the cops came. 5 cruisers, 1 paddy wagon, the Police "HAWKS" helicopter and the SWAT team! They sent the Swat team to break up our party because it was so huge. The party has become a legend in campus history. None of us were arrested, but the cokeheads were eventually picked up and thrown in the drunk tank (so I heard). The walls in our house are still fucked.

Just thought I'd let you know that Alphas are keeping up the old traditions. Jerry has a bunch of photos, try emailing him, or accessing his FaceBook site.

Cheers,
Greg

I tried to reassure Greg about gaining new recruits through throwing good parties. I also began asking him to provide some input for a Calgary AOT section I wanted to add to the AOT Web site. I also reminded him once again about getting Calgary AOT membership into the U of C Student Union and to try to restart the new chapter recruitment that seemed to be going well prior.

Hey Greg,

Sounds like you guys had a real night to remember. Its parties like that which will bring you new members. People want to be in the frat that parties the hardest.

That article was e-mailed to me by a guy that was in Oceanside AOT at the very end. It was the constant fighting with the other 2 frats (Omega Gamma Delta and Alpha Sigma Phi) that was the downfall for all of the frats.

You say this pledge is one you kept, did you drop others? How many members so far?

Anyway, I know I keep asking this, but I really want to get the U of C section up and online. It will help you to look top notch to potential pledges and the university. I really want to see you guys get recognized by your student union, a web page and affiliation with a Grand Chapter will look great for you. Have a meeting and come up with some ideas for the U of C section, I will put them up on the site. Otherwise I will just upload a new website and write a short intro for your page.

I am still interested in those other chapters. If they were interested before, they may still be. School starting may have distracted them, try to encourage them, let them know we are here to help them get started also. And once they get started, they will have plenty of freedom to conduct their chapter however they see fit.

The AOT party will be six to eight months away, so you always have the option of coming if your money situation changes.

About the repairs to your walls make the pledges fix it.

> Fred Gross
> Oceanside AOT
> Class of 1982
> Alea Iacta Est

I then received an e-mail that piqued my curiosity in the seriousness of Greg and his crew to continue to be committed to AOT in Calgary.

Howdy Fred,

On Friday night we held another initiation. Robert was initiated into the brotherhood. We also held elections. Jerry Moses ran uncontested for President and won. The rest of the new officers are as follows:

> Jerry: President
> Robert: VP
> Sal: Secretary
> Temple: Sergeant at arms
> Greg: Treasurer
> Jason: Pledge (Dog) Master
> Scribe: Vacant
> Tyler: Vacant

Also there will be a TOGA party this Saturday.

Have a happy Canadian Thanksgiving.

> Cheers,
> Greg
> Treasurer

After I received this e-mail, I had my first indication that the crew we recruited at the University of Calgary was bored with their new toy and was giving it to their younger brothers. I had explained to Greg, when he took on this responsibility, that he and his fellow officers were supposed to serve in office until right before graduation and then hold elections among the juniors to fill the offices for the upcoming year. Greg had been chapter president for less than four months, and he had already called elections to pass on the fraternity to the newest members. Greg had been an integral part in putting all of this together, and on the surface, he seemed to be gung ho and tireless in his efforts. But all of a sudden, without rhyme or reason, he got bored with it and walked away from the cause.

Additionally, the new president and vice president were not even students at the University of Calgary. Greg's chapter was chartered at the University of Calgary and was supposed to only be inducting members from the U of C student body. Most of the new recruits they inducted were students at a two-year technical school called the Southern Alberta Institute of Technology. I quickly established communication with Jerry Moses and Robert Roselle, the new president and vice president, respectively. I found them to be eager to carry the mantle of AOT. I was disappointed in Greg and Sal for passing it on like a toy they got bored with, but I was still willing to work with Jerry and Robert.

At this point, I had heard no further info from Greg or anyone else over there about AOT gaining membership in the University of Calgary's Student Union, and I suspected they had not tried to accomplish this task, which was an integral part of our agreement. Coincidentally, one of the Calgary AOT members had sent me a link to a student campaign page on FaceBook for a candidate running for president of the U of C Student Union. I decided to test the water, and I communicated with her through her FaceBook page. I introduced myself and inquired as to the status of AOT's membership in the Student Union. Here is some of my correspondence with University of Calgary Student Union presidential candidate Susan Wagner:

Hello Fred,

I sent an email to your club this evening outlining how I intend to "give back" to your frat. I'd love to talk to you further about what I can do for you next year . . . can we meet in person this week?

Susan

Now I had the attention of one of the two leading contenders for Student Union president at the U of C, and I decided to pitch AOT to her and see if she was willing to help us out.

Hi Susan

That would be rather difficult. I live in New York. I am the webmaster of the Grand Chapter of AOT, which is located on Long Island.

I would certainly appreciate any help you can give to the local chapter of AOT in the U of C.

We sanctioned them as a chapter last summer, and we were really hoping they would attain recognized status on campus and with the Student Union.

Our highest-ranking member is Greg Flange, who is Treasurer of the Beta Alpha Chapter of AOT.

If I can be of any assistance in the matter, I can be reached at webmaster@alphaomegatheta.com
Our fraternity website is at www.alphaomegatheta.com.

> Thank you
> Fred Gross
> AOT webmaster

After my posting on Susan's FaceBook page and subsequent e-mail correspondence, I got an e-mail from Susan's opponent, Alma Sanchez. Here is what she had to say:

Hi Fred,

I noticed that you posted on Susan Wagner's group page regarding the Beta Alpha Chapter. My name is Alma Sanchez and I am also running for the position of SU President of the U of C. Part of my platform includes a change in the way that the SU deals with clubs on campus. I noticed that your Fraternity is not listed on the SU Clubs list; I feel that it is important that all students who are involved in clubs have the support of the SU. I would be in full support of making a Beta Alpha Chapter an official SU club, which allows for various benefits (travel and conference funding, equipment rentals, food and beverage funding, and room bookings). The students are my top priority. Please let me know if you have any questions. Thank you for your time.

Alma

So now I have both contenders in this election wanting to get a lock on AOT votes. I went with it and sent her a "what can you do for us" type of e-mail.

Hello Alma,

I would certainly appreciate any help you can give to the local chapter of AOT in the U of C.

We sanctioned them as a chapter last summer and we were really hoping they would attain recognized status on campus and with the Student Union.

Our highest-ranking member on campus is Greg Flange, who is Treasurer of the Beta Alpha Chapter of AOT. Please get in touch with Greg as I know he has an interest in seeing the Beta Alpha Chapter succeed at the U of C.

If I can be of any assistance in the matter I can be reached at webmaster@alphaomegatheta.com
Our fraternity website is at www.alphaomegatheta.com.

Thank you
Fred Gross
AOT webmaster

Now at this time, I thought I was being clever. I now had the attention of the two candidates for the Student Union presidency, and both showed interest in helping AOT gain recognized status with the Student Union. Obviously they were both thinking of gaining votes in their election, but I figured if the members of AOT wanted recognition in their school, they would get behind the candidate who offered them a fast track to Student Union membership. I was in for a rude awakening when I received angry correspondence from Greg Flange a few days later. I sent Greg this message informing him of my contact with Susan Wagner. For some reason, I actually thought he was still on board with making AOT a recognized and respected fraternity on the U of C campus. I was in for quite a shocker with his response to my correspondence with Susan and Alma.

Greg,

From Susan Wagner, what do you think?

"For AOT to become a club on campus Greg can contact the Club Chair Dan Dixon. I don't start until May 1st, but Greg can get the ball rolling this year if he wants to. It's really up to him and it falls under the Operations and Finance commission."

Fred

This was Greg's reply to the correspondence that had been going around.

Fred

I really wish you would of talked to me prior to doing whatever the hell you did. I was out of town due to a family emergency. First of all we don't have enough members to be a sanctioned club. Second, even if we did, we don't want to because we would lose all freedom we have (including the right to consume alcohol as a group). Third, U of C is *very anti-Greek*. Whoever said whatever to you was because it was election time. However I now have to deal with whatever agreements you tried to make. I know all of the people you contacted. They all *hate* fraternities. You have done untold damage to my reputation and position I held on the U of C campus, both as someone involved in the clubs committee, and at the University newspaper.

You had no right to use my name in any of your conversations in apparently the way you did. Please do not contact me about this anymore.

Greg

I knew that Greg was no longer committed to AOT, if he ever really was, but his tirade seemed childish and asinine to me, considering that he knew what my expectations of him and his new chapter were from the very beginning.

Greg

You told me from day one that you wanted to be legitimate on campus. I know I did not misunderstand that because you told me so yourself.

If you had actually told me what was going on instead of ignoring me then maybe this wouldn't have happened.

—

If you are done with then so be it.

Later on and good luck

Fred

After the falling-out between Greg Flange and me, the new Calgary AOT president Jerry and I decided to assign a new chapter designation to his chapter and transfer the chapter from the University of Calgary to the Southern Alberta Institute of Technology. The SAIT chapter was designated Beta Beta. Greg Flange and the two or three members he brought into AOT from the U of C had walked out and left the guys from SAIT to try to keep it going on their own. Greg began posting horrid, vile shit about me on public message boards on Facebook and MySpace. Here is some correspondence with new chapter president Jerry Moses on the new developments:

Jerry,

I see on Greg's MySpace profile that he now has Zeta Psi listed as his Greek organization. Is that a frat at U of C or is he starting all over again? Not that I really care, I just didn't know if you knew that.

Considering this guy's childish tirade to trash me on public boards, which he did again today, I have to ask what's the status of the chapter members that are from U of C? Are they joining your chapter? Are they going to try to revive Beta Alpha without Greg? Or are they loyal to Greg. I don't want to micromanage, but I think that is very important to determine at this time?

Is Robert still behind this effort? What kind of disruption can and is Greg causing to your efforts?

Fred

I found Jerry to be easy to approach, and he assured me that he was on board and willing to give his best efforts for AOT in Calgary.

Fred

Robert is very much behind this effort. Greg's affect on our situation is minimal at best. There have been several people showing interest in the FaceBook AOT group as of late. I'm not sure exactly where they came from (I think they are Greg's friends), but I have been wary and they have not been offering me the respect I deserve. I think Greg isn't used to not getting things his way, and so he decided to be a big baby about things.

Jerry

I replied to Jerry, asking him to pull all the disgusting shit Greg wrote about me on a FaceBook group set up for Calgary AOT. I also inquired as to the status of Greg's crew from the U of C AOT chapter.

Jerry

I see how he responds. He is throwing a cyber tantrum.

I can't stop him from flaming me on the public boards, but I'd appreciate it if you delete his posts when they trash me. If I was you, I would kill Greg's pseudonym from the group and only let card-carrying members into the group. That's just my suggestion.

I am 100% with you and Robert if you are committed to the effort. I will step back for a while and let you do your thing. You can feel free to contact me whenever you want, and please send an updated roster when you add members.

I just want to know what's the status of the U of C members? What are they going to do? Will they Go with you, go with Greg, or try to give Beta Alpha another try without Greg? Please let me know.

Your tee shirts and chapter books were shipped yesterday; you should have them in a week or ten days. Let me know when they arrive.

Fred

The flaming by Greg Flange stopped after a week; Jerry and Robert took up the task of trying to make a legitimate club out of AOT at the Southern Alberta Institute of Technology. To their credit, I can say that they sure did try their best, but the culture at SAIT was anti-fraternity. I did receive some correspondence from someone at SAIT in reference to AOT's application for recognition by the school. We were told that due to the gender-exclusive nature of fraternities—as in they only allow males to obtain membership—the application was denied.

Jerry and Robert fought the good fight to gain recognition and respect for AOT, and they did regularly throw parties, keggers, and even a few toga parties. They did recruit new members and took the chapter membership up to about ten members, but with the lack of support from the school, their chapter was never able to become viable. They still wear their AOT colors and still throw a party every now and again. Jerry has promised to try to bring AOT with him to the University of Victoria when he finishes his two years of study at SAIT and transfers.

As to the future of the Canadian branch of AOT, only time will tell.

CHAPTER EIGHTEEN

Grand Chapter Reunion 2007

On the evening of July 28, 2006, Joe "Spooky" Furino, Billy Weitzman, John Morella, and I had all gathered in Spooky's office at Pinnacle Construction to induct the charter members of the new chapter of AOT in Calgary, Canada, via conference call. After the induction, as we were leaving Joe's building, I had a conversation with Joe that would begin the chain of events for the next year, leading to a reunion bigger and better than the one held for Oceanside AOT two years before.

We were standing on the corner outside Joe's building on Franklin Avenue in Franklin Square, and I asked Joe if he thought an AOT reunion inclusive of all chapters of Alpha and covering all years of the fraternity's history would be feasible. Joe told me that he thought it was a great idea. I told Joe about the AOT reunion in Oceanside two years earlier and that it drew 125 people just from Oceanside. This time we would be inviting members from every chapter of Alpha Omega Theta. This party had potential to be huge. As far as we knew, Valley Stream AOT had not yet held a reunion, so there was great potential to get a big crowd from the many years of Valley Stream AOT; and Joe's involvement in this reunion would draw Valley Stream AOT members like a magnet.

At this point, it was just an idea, but we decided that we would hold a few meetings to discuss the concept further. We had to pick a location for the reunion, we had to find other AOT alumni willing to work on the reunion committee, and we needed to get a fairly accurate idea of how many would actually attend. And this was just the tip of the iceberg. After taking the idea to people I knew from Oceanside AOT, I was surprised to find that the idea got a lukewarm response from a lot of guys I knew. Some of them felt that the Oceanside AOT reunion had only been two years earlier, and they were not ready for another big party.

I was sure that if I got all the other chapters on board for this reunion, the Oceanside guys would come to it as well. The next step was to gauge the interest of the members from the other chapters. In the two years that the AOT Web site had been up and running, I had accumulated more than 150 e-mail addresses in my AOT address book. I started by sending a mass mail to them and then posting an announcement of a potential AOT multichapter reunion on the AOT Web site. In my e-mail, I asked everyone to reply to me with a yes or no as to whether they would attend a reunion. The results I got were a cross-reference of all the AOT chapters, and it provided me a foundation to build a reunion on.

Before any decision had been made about whether or not to hold a reunion, an extraordinary thing happened. We found the original Brooklyn members who started Alpha Omega Theta Fraternity in 1946. There was actually a long, tedious process that led to the Brooklyn Alpha brothers.

About eight to ten months after the AOT Web site went online, I had gotten an e-mail from Peter Martin. Peter had been sent a link to the AOT Web site by another Baldwin AOT alumnus from 1960 named Ray Coni. Peter had told me that he was the first president of Baldwin AOT and one of its founding members. I was always a history buff, and Pete presented a chance to research the history of the Long Island chapters of AOT. I always had a burning curiosity about Brooklyn AOT. We were told upon induction that the fraternity was founded in Brooklyn in 1948, but nobody I ever knew in all my years in AOT had ever met a member from Brooklyn, and it was widely believed that Brooklyn Alpha was either defunct or never really existed.

I asked Peter Martin what he knew of Brooklyn AOT, and to my delight, he actually had met a few of them back in 1958 at Baldwin High School. The brothers from the Long Island chapters were playing a game of softball after working on a new constitution, and a carload of Brooklyn AOT members had come to meet them and check on the status of the Long Island chapters. Unfortunately, that was the only time he met Brooklyn AOT members, but it did confirm that they did exist and they did take an interest in the growth of the Long Island chapters.

Having taken the Brooklyn aspect of the research as far as it could go with Pete, I decided to start at the beginning of his experience in AOT and pick his brain. Pete was a great interview subject, and he remembered everything. I began by asking Pete how he had gotten involved with becoming a charter member of the Baldwin chapter of AOT and who recruited him. Pete had been dating a girl from neighboring Freeport who had an older brother in Freeport AOT. Through his girlfriend's brother, he had been recruited to pledge for Freeport AOT's chapter.

I further inquired if Pete remembered the names of any of the Freeport AOT members who had recruited him. Pete, in fact, did recall quite a few names of some of the Freeport AOT members. I had taken down about five names from Pete and immediately began research on classmates.com to see if I could locate profiles for any of them. I was disappointed to see that none of the names Pete had provided could be located on classmates.com, but I did see one similar name. There was a woman listed for the class of 1958 named Cindy Sepino. Pete had given me the name Ron Sepino from the class of 1960 to search for. I had a hunch she was his sister, so I took a shot and sent her a message via classmates.com, introducing myself and explaining about the fraternity Web site and my quest to locate early members of Alpha Omega Theta Fraternity. Although Cindy never did actually reply to me, she did forward my contact info to another Freeport AOT alumnus, Rocky Clarke from the class of 1957. Rocky immediately contacted me and introduced himself via e-mail.

Rocky also was a wealth of information. Rocky had been the Freeport chapter's first secretary and one of its charter members in 1956. Rocky had kept the meeting minutes from the first ten Freeport AOT meetings, and he sent me scanned copies. He also helped me trace the origins of AOT back one more step to Valley Stream.

It seems that the charter members from Freeport AOT were very friendly with the Valley Stream AOT members through interschool wrestling. Rocky had been friendly with most of the original Valley Stream members. He had given me a list of names to further research from Valley Stream AOT, and I went to classmates.com once again to investigate.

Once again, I found the sister of the AOT member I was searching for. I had gotten a reply from Cheryl Argenti, the sister of Valley Stream brother Arnie Argenti, informing me that her brother Arnie had passed away two months prior. I conveyed my sympathies to her on behalf of AOT. She assured me that Arnie would have loved the AOT Web site if he had gotten a chance to see it before he passed away. I had not found any other names that Rocky had given me of Valley Stream Central AOT members from 1956 on classmates.com. It seemed like I had hit another dead end. Then I found a thread of conversation on the Valley Stream Central message board of a popular website. It was titled "1955-1957 Wrestling Teams."

As soon as I saw the topic, I was curious. I remembered that Rocky said that most of the Valley Stream Central AOT members were on the wrestling team, so this message board thread could provide me with some information. The thread was started by a guy looking for members of the wrestling team from 1955 to 1957. The last response of the thread was left by a guy named Anthony Hackney. Here is the post he left.

Mike, you are missing the boat if you are not in touch with Jerry Smith. Jerry is the president of "Friends of Long Island Wrestling" and can be reached at xxx-xxx-xxxx (cell) and xxx-xxx-xxxx (home) and xxx-xxx-xxxx (office). Jerry will bring you up to date on the whereabouts of ALL OF THE WRESTLERS. I am in touch with Jerry on at least a weekly basis. Good Luck and regards, Chick Hackney.

At the time I read the message, I had no idea who Chick was, but I did recognize the name *Jerry Smith* in Chick's post. Jerry was one of the names given to me by Rocky, and he was identified as one of the early Valley Stream Central AOT members.

I read and reread the posting several times before I got the nerve to actually call Jerry Smith. I was worried that he would hang up on me, but he was very nice and quite surprised to get a phone call inquiring about Alpha Omega Theta Fraternity. The conversation went like this.

"Hello, is this Jerry Smith?" I said.

"Yes, it is, who are you?" Jerry said.

"Jerry, you don't know me, but I got your phone number off of a posting on classmates.com. I hope I am not bothering you," I said.

"No, that's OK. What can I do for you?" Jerry said.

"Well, to get right to the point, were you a member of Alpha Omega Theta Fraternity?" I asked.

There was about twenty to thirty seconds of silence before he responded. I had thought he had hung up on me for a moment. But then he replied. "Wow, I haven't heard that name or even thought about Alpha Omega Theta in decades," Jerry said.

"So you were in AOT. Can you tell me about the guys that started the fraternity in Valley Stream? Who started it? Who brought it from Brooklyn? What year did it start in Valley Stream?" I asked.

"Well, I was one of the founding members. In fact, I was the chapter's first vice president. We started AOT in Valley Stream High School in 1955, two years before it became Valley Stream Central," Jerry replied.

"We were always told that AOT started in Brooklyn and was then brought to Valley Stream. Is that true? Can you shed some light on that?" I asked.

"Yes, it's true, Alpha Omega Theta was a fraternity founded in Brooklyn, but it was fading out by the time we were recruited to found the Valley Stream chapter," Jerry replied.

"Well, how did AOT come from Brooklyn to Valley Stream? Who did it?"

"Well, that would be Chick Hackney. Chick was the guy. His family moved to Valley Stream in 1955, and he came to school wearing a green-and-red sweater. At the time, the only fraternity in Valley Stream High School was Omega Gamma Delta. A new fraternity was just what Valley Stream needed, and Chick provided an opportunity to build one. So I hope that answers your question. Chick was the connection. Chick was the guy responsible for bringing AOT to Long Island."

The conversation lasted about fifteen minutes, and Jerry gave me Chick's phone number and told me to call him the next day. The next day, before I could call him, Chick called me. Jerry had given him my cell number.

We had an interesting conversation about how he recruited Jerry and eight other guys to start Valley Stream AOT back in 1955. But I was also interested in learning about the origins of Brooklyn AOT. Anthony Hackney, a.k.a. Chick, was the first person I spoke to who actually was a card-carrying member of Brooklyn AOT. I was thrilled to be conversing with him. Chick was a junior in high school when his family moved to Valley Stream. He was one of the younger members and didn't have firsthand knowledge about the origins of the fraternity, but he was able to tell me everything about the Brooklyn members who pushed him to form a chapter in Valley Stream.

According to Chick, Joe Brugnolotti, Mickey Percy, and Jim Stack were instrumental in urging him to recruit charter members and inducting them in a ceremony in Brooklyn. This had given me a whole new direction to look into. I now had names of actual Brooklyn AOT members, and I learned through Chick that Brooklyn AOT had been run out of Brooklyn Manual Training High School.

I thought I had great leads to follow, but I soon hit another dead end. The only resource I had for researching was classmates.com, and I found none of the names Chick had given me on that Web site. About one month prior to this, I had done a search on the New York State, Department of State Web site for records of incorporation of Alpha Omega Theta Fraternity, and I had found those documents that had been filed in 1948, the exact year we had been told the fraternity started. I had given a copy of that document, with the names of the original guys who signed the charter of incorporation, to Greg Colarossi. Greg was an alumnus from the Rockville Centre chapter from 1977, and he was a private investigator by trade. Greg had tried locating the guys who signed the charter of incorporation but found all of them either deceased or simply beyond locating. Just when we had given up on finding any Brooklyn AOT members, we now had new leads. I contacted Greg and gave him the names that Chick had given to me, as well as Chick's phone number so he could interview him.

For a few weeks, Greg had limited results. He did determine that Jim Stack had passed on years before but was unable to locate the other two. He finally determined that he had incorrect spelling for Joe Brugnolotti and he had the wrong first name for Mickey Percy. It seemed that Mickey's real name was Albert and that Mickey was a nickname. Now Greg was able to locate both of them. He first found Joe Brugnolotti living in North Carolina, and ironically, Mickey Percy was still living in Brooklyn.

We found that neither Joe nor Mickey were founding members of Brooklyn AOT, but they were instrumental in bringing AOT to Long Island. However, they both provided a long list of Brooklyn AOT member names to further research; and before long, Greg located John Stefano living in Melville, New York. John Stefano was one of the four founding members of AOT. Shortly after Greg located John Stefano, we met for lunch with him at Phil Gerardi's restaurant, the Fishery, in East Rockaway.

Greg, Billy Weitzman, Phil Gerardi, and I all met John one afternoon, and it was a fantastic lunch I will never forget. John was picked up by Greg in Melville and driven to the Fishery. We spent an hour and a half listening to stories of how he and three of his friends founded AOT in 1946 and, also, how surprised he was to find how the fraternity had grown all over Nassau County in the years that followed.

Shortly after that, Greg found Ed Carroll and John Sposito, two of the other founding members of the fraternity. Sadly, one of the early members, John Cangin, had passed away some years ago. Now that we had located three of the four founding brothers of Alpha Omega Theta, we had men of honor to toast at the reunion. In essence, we had a theme for the reunion. We would be celebrating the sixtieth anniversary of the fraternity, and we would be celebrating with the founding members of AOT and other alumni from the Brooklyn chapter as well. The prospect of meeting the founding members from Brooklyn AOT was intriguing to many of the alumni from the Long Island chapters.

Over the next month, Greg continued to locate about five or six other members from Brooklyn Alpha. Although some of the Alpha guys I knew from Oceanside seemed to be uninterested in the prospect of a multichapter reunion, Spooky and I continued to discuss the concept. Spooky and I went to Chateau Briand in Westbury to look into a price for a banquet room. The place was opulent and high class. It was a black-tie—required catering hall. Spooky had his daughter's sweet sixteen party there and had attended many affairs at Chateau Briand, so he was partial to having the reunion there. I was also impressed with the classiness of Chateau Briand and was also leaning toward wanting to hold the reunion there.

After our visit to Chateau Briand, we had decided that we would plan a reunion for the next spring. When I floated the idea past Phil Gerardi, he suggested that the Knights of Columbus was the place to hold the reunion. We had the last one there in 2004, and the prices were about twenty dollars a plate cheaper than Chateau Briand. He felt that cheaper prices would be better received by the Alpha brothers than a high-class black-tie party with an expensive per-head ticket price. As an extra measure, I went and got a price from the Coral House in Baldwin, just so I could show the reunion committee that we priced around. They were almost as expensive as Chateau Briand but offered a much-smaller room, which would hold much fewer attendees.

We decided to have a meeting to invite anyone who had suggestions to attend. I sent out an e-mail and posted an announcement on the AOT Web site inviting AOT brothers to come to the reunion meeting and to have suggestions on a venue. We met in mid-October 2006 at John's Union Park Café, and we had about eight guys show up. All in attendance, except for Spooky and I, voted to have the reunion party at the Knights of Columbus in Oceanside. The guys liked the idea of being able to wear jeans and tee shirts instead of proper attire. We also agreed on a DJ instead of a band since a lot of people complained that the band was too loud at the last reunion, and people who hadn't seen each other in years had trouble conversing.

After the decision had been made to throw this party, the next step was to go reserve the party room at the Knights of Columbus. Spooky offered to put up the deposit money to get started. I personally guaranteed Spooky's money so if the event failed to happen; I was responsible for refunding his money. I met Spooky at John's Union Park Café a week later to get the money for the deposit. Right after that, Billy Weitzman and I went over to the Knights of Columbus to reserve the room. I put the five hundred that Spooky gave me down on the room as a deposit, and we reserved Saturday, April 14, 2007. We were required to ensure a minimum of 150 attendees to the Knights of Columbus. If the party attracted any less than 150, we were required to still pay for 150 guests. The total tab on the party was close to $5,000.

I was sure this would be easy—to draw a minimum of 150 AOT members from a half-dozen chapters spanning sixty years to a party celebrating the sixtieth anniversary of the fraternity with the founding members from Brooklyn. In fact, I was sure we would bring more than the minimum. I envisioned a room with between 250 to 300 guests. I was wrong. It wasn't easy at all. In fact, it was pure hell for six months promoting the event and trying to get guys to buy tickets. It was even harder to get guys to volunteer to be on the organizing committee. For the first five months, it was I and I alone who did most of the legwork.

I did get some help from Spooky early in the effort. During the discussion phase of the reunion, Valley Stream 1957 alumnus Bobby Playa had given me a Valley Stream Central alumni directory book. It contained the names, addresses, phone numbers, and e-mail addresses of hundreds of Valley Stream Central alumni. I used that book matched against the AOT alumni directory lists for every year AOT had an active chapter in Valley Stream Central. Using that book to find contact info for dozens of Valley Stream AOT alumni, I created a list of AOT members to get a mass-mailing invitation.

I wrote a creative invitation and made copies. Spooky offered to send the invitations out to the entire Valley Stream AOT alumni on behalf of the reunion committee. I did a mass mailing to Oceanside AOT members using the lists that were made by the organizers of the Oceanside AOT reunion in 2004. I regularly did mass e-mailings to all the guys in my AOT address book as well.

Soon after, I set up a PayPal link on the AOT Web site so guys could get their tickets with an online transaction.

Despite the kitchen-sink approach, the tickets sold at a snail's pace. We held committee meetings once a month, and each time, it was only Spooky, Billy Weitzman, and I who would attend. I was apprehensive that only a handful of tickets had sold, but Billy and Spooky kept telling me to wait until after the holidays. People were focusing on the holidays in November and December, so we could expect a rush in ticket purchases in January.

Well, January came and went, so did February, and still I had only sold a handful of tickets to the reunion. I was really getting nervous; the reunion was two months away, and I had collected only about $600 of the almost $5,000 I needed to settle that bill with the Knights of Columbus. I started to pound the pavement. I went to John's Union Park Café to talk to AOT guys hanging out there, as well as to the owner, John, who was an Oceanside AOT alumnus. I went to see the organizers of the previous AOT reunion to seek help in locating people they had gathered for the last reunion.

Everywhere I turned, people were bullshitting me to death. Everybody claimed they were definitely going to the reunion and would buy tickets later. People were saying they would pay at the door. No one understood that the Knights of Columbus needed payment in full one week prior to the party with a final head count. There was no way I could count on or allow payment at the door on the night of the reunion.

This situation came to a full boil one day when I literally was hung up on and had a door slammed in my face both in the same day. One Saturday afternoon, I called an Oceanside alumnus from 1977 who had expressed an interest in the reunion months prior. I called him, and as soon as I said "Hi, Jimmy, this is Fred Gross," the fucking prick hung up on me without a good-bye, or even having the decency to tell me he wasn't interested. Later that night, I was invited to go to the home of an Oceanside AOT alumnus from 1971 named Frank Rector to work on the reunion. The problem was that I was invited by Jon Truman, not Frank Rector. Jon was invited to a party at Frank's house that night, and he in turn told me that they were just going to hang out to drink a few beers and that Frank was interested in helping to gather his fellow class of 1971 AOT members for the reunion.

When I was pulling up to Frank's house, I got a call on my cell from Jon Truman telling me he wasn't going to make it that night. He had just gotten back from Atlantic City and was too hung-over to go out again. I figured since I was already in front of Frank's house, and since I had spoken on the phone to Frank about two weeks prior, he wouldn't mind if I knocked on his door.

About two weeks prior to this night, I had gotten a call from Billy Weitzman. He was at Farmer Joel's on Oceanside Road getting breakfast when he ran into three AOT guys. They were Tommy Shriver, Oceanside AOT president from 1979; Frank Rector, Oceanside AOT vice president from 1971; and Mike Franzizi, Oceanside AOT treasurer from 1975 and also the owner of Farmer Joel's. Billy told me they were all excited about the reunion and they wanted more fliers that they could pass out to their guys. Billy had passed the phone to Frank, and he asked me for fliers that he could pass out.

I figured that since Frank had asked for fliers, I had a good excuse to knock on his door even if Jon Truman wasn't going to be there. Well, I was not well received. It seemed that Frank was having a family affair that evening, and I appeared like a crasher. When I told him Jon Truman had invited me and reminded Frank that he himself had asked for fliers a few days before, it still didn't change the awkwardness of the moment. He was pissed at me for showing up on his doorstep, he was pissed at Jon for inviting me, and even more pissed at Jon for not showing up to the party that he was invited to. I stood there on the front porch, on one of the most freezing nights of the year, and had the door closed on me. I walked away steaming mad. I had had enough and wanted no more of this reunion, and I was now intent on killing the event.

I alone had signed the contract with the Knights of Columbus, and as such, I was financially liable for the cost of the affair in the event that it failed to happen. I called the banquet manager to inquire about canceling the party. I was told that the night I had booked was a prime Saturday evening during wedding season. It was explained to me that if they could not rebook the room on short notice, less than two months, then I would be held accountable for the full cost of the party even if it didn't happen. If I was lucky and they did manage to rebook the room, I would still forfeit the deposit paid for reserving the room and date, in which case I would still be personally responsible to reimburse Spooky for the money he put up as a deposit.

Now I was in deep shit. About seven weeks to go until party night, only about $750 collected toward a $5,000 dinner tab, and I was getting very little interest and no help from anyone other than Spooky and Billy Weitzman. Spooky had done the mailers from his office, and Billy passed out a few fliers, but I was mostly on my own.

I wrote a sternly worded e-mail and sent it to all in my AOT address book. In a nutshell, I told everyone that the event was in danger of cancellation unless a huge upswing in interest was shown by the AOT brothers ASAP. I called a reunion committee meeting to be held at John's Union Park Café and asked anyone interested in saving this event to show up. This was my last chance to salvage this situation and avoid being financially liable for a failed event.

Given the poor response over the past few months and the shitty treatment I had gotten from more than a few people, I really was not optimistic about this. I was sure that the meeting would be another disappointment, with only two or three guys showing up. But this time, it was different. On the night of the meeting, I was running about twenty minutes late. I was in no particular hurry since I was sure nobody would show up anyway. Then Billy Weitzman called me on my cell phone.

"Freddy, where are you? Everyone is here, and they are waiting for you," Billy said.

"Really? How many are there?" I said.

"There are about fifteen guys here including a Brooklyn AOT guy," Billy said

"Which Brooklyn guy?" I asked.

"His name is Mickey. He has an AOT tattoo on his arm," Billy said.

"Yeah, that would be Mickey Percy. I can't believe he came down," I said.

"He is a great guy, and he seems thrilled to meet us. Listen, Mickey is psyched for this reunion. He says there is a bunch of Brooklyn AOT guys that can't wait for this party. We are gonna make this happen. There is no way this is getting cancelled, so get over here right away," Billy said.

I now had a sense of urgency as I hurried over to John's Union Park Café to meet the guys who showed up to salvage this party. When I got there, the first person I saw was Billy Weitzman. He was at the bar drinking with Mickey Percy. He introduced me to Mickey, although we had spoken on the phone before. All the guys got together, and we took a table in the back room. There was a pretty good cross section of AOT members from different years, chapters, and decades at that table.

Paul Labrazzo, from Oceanside class of 1979, was there. He is the younger brother of Mike Labrazzo from the class of 1974. Trey Smits, vice president from the Rockville Centre chapter class of 1968, was there. Jon Truman from my chapter and class of 1982 showed up as he promised. Guy Schiavone happened to be drinking at the bar that night and came over to the table to toss some ideas around since he had worked on the previous reunion. Greg Colarossi from Rockville Centre AOT class of 1977 was there. Steve Theo, who was Oceanside AOT president in 1970, showed up also. Of course, Spooky was there as usual; he never missed a meeting or gathering whenever we had one. And Spooky brought one of his guys, Dave Basilio from Valley Stream AOT class of 1980.

All in all, we had a great turnout, but more important was the fact that everyone who showed up wanted to contribute to turning this thing around and making it a night to remember.

We sat at the table and ordered food and drinks. Then we got down to business. They wanted to know what was the status of the reunion and how much more we needed to collect. I told them that I had only collected about seven hundred and change toward the total bill of just under five thousand. I reminded everyone that we needed to collect enough to pay for a minimum of

150 plates no later than one week prior to the reunion date. There were also other mundane details to work out, such as decorations and awards for the founding members of AOT.

I laid it on the line for them and simply told them that if I didn't have at least a little more than half the money within the week, I would have no choice but to cancel the event. Now I knew I was on the hook with the Knights of Columbus, but I wanted everyone to know this could be cancelled due to lack of enthusiasm and funding. At that moment, Greg Colarossi stood up and pulled out a wad of cash. He handed it to me and said he was buying a block of twenty tickets. With the tickets priced at $55 dollars each, he handed over $1,100 to put into the kitty. His plan was to sell the tickets to people he knew and take some pressure off me. When he put that much money into the reunion fund, other people started opening up their wallets right there at the table. Dave Basilio bought two tickets, the owner of John's Union Park Café bought two tickets, Steve Theo bought two, Mike Labrazzo bought one, and Jon Truman bought four and promised to sell ten more for the committee. Spooky had put up the deposit, and with that, he owned a block of ten tickets that he planned to give to his crew from Valley Stream AOT class of 1980. Billy Weitzman had bought two tickets weeks prior.

I walked out of that meeting with almost $1,400. That gave us a little less than half of what we needed, but now I was in a comfort zone. I was feeling for the first time that this was going to come off as planned.

The next day, I got a call from Phil Gerardi. Although he had been lukewarm to the idea of another reunion, he was now ready to help out with this one. Phil knew a lot of AOT guys spanning a ten-year time period. He assured me that he was going to make phone calls and go door-to-door to collect from all his crew. Suddenly, it all seemed to be coming together. Phil was calling me every other day with money and checks he collected and names to add to the guest list. I started receiving checks from AOT guys from all over the country in the mail. The PayPal link started to produce results as well. Guys were buying tickets, and they were going pretty fast. Just as planned, we had collected from 140 guests. Although that was ten people short, we had collected enough money to pay for 150 guests, as promised, to the Knights of Columbus. And still we continued to book more guests.

About a week before the reunion, I paid the Knights of Columbus the balance of the bill, and I went to look into having plaques made to award the Brooklyn founding members at the reunion. I by chance went to a place called Olympic Awards in Oceanside on Long Beach Road and inquired about plaques. I gave the man behind the counter the inscriptions to etch into the plaques. When he saw they were in reference to Alpha Omega Theta, he said, "Hey, I was in AOT, class of 1963."

"What's your name?" I asked

"Bob Harden, but I was called Rob back then," he said.

"Well, Bob, you are invited to this thing as well, and tell any other guys you know from AOT they are invited too," I said.

I had gotten a great feeling buying the plaques from a fellow Greenie. It was a good sign that this thing was gonna be great. Phil Gerardi had taken responsibility to get balloons to decorate the tables. Mike Labrazzo had taken the task of ordering banners to hang at the reunion. He ordered two banners, one large and another medium saying, "Welcome brothers to the sixtieth anniversary of Alpha Omega Theta." I also made up some paper certificates to give to all the attendees who had been presidents of their chapters. I also went and rented a projector to connect to a computer, through which I ran a continuous slideshow of over twelve hundred photos depicting sixty years of AOT from all the various chapters. The slideshow ran all night long. I had requested that the Knights of Columbus decorate the tables with green tablecloths, red napkins, and red roses as centerpiece.

During the time I was recruiting guests for the reunion, I had gotten confirmations from members representing various chapters and years of AOT. When Phil Gerardi saw the list of confirmations I had gotten on my own, he realized that almost all of them were early AOT members from the 1950s and 1960s. All of the AOT brothers I had succeeded in bringing on board were early AOT brothers whom he did not know, and he realized the potential of the event if he could get his crew from 1970 to 1978 to attend as well. The possibilities for a real broad cross section of members from various years, decades, and chapters were great. To his credit, Phil single-handedly recruited and collected from at least forty guys. His participation put us over the top, and to this day, I am grateful for his help during that very difficult and frustrating time.

One group of AOT alumni that had been eluding me was the founding members from the Valley Stream Central chapter. I had e-mail and contact info for most of them, but all were noncommittal except for VSC 1957 alumni Bobby Playa, who was the first person to send a check back in November. I was most interested in Chick Hackney, who was the founding member and the guy who brought AOT to Long Island. Chick had been avoiding giving a definite answer. It turned out that Chick had a family reunion also planned for the same weekend; but as luck would have it, Chick's family affair was rescheduled for another weekend, and he contacted me to confirm his attendance about two weeks prior to the reunion. Once Chick had confirmed that he was coming, I then got a flood of confirmations from his other Valley Stream AOT charter members. Jerry Smith, Fred Gifford, John Cisco, and VSC 1956 alumni Jack Bruno, who was from the first pledge class of VSC AOT.

Now we had the original Brooklyn members, plus the original Valley Stream Central members confirmed to attend. I felt like I had accomplished most of what

I wanted to do. The shortfalls and disappointments were the lack of participation of some entire chapters. Uniondale and Amityville AOT did not produce one single guest. Rockville Centre AOT had only three guys show up, and none of them was Greg Colarossi either, despite the fact that he bought a block of twenty tickets. Greg had sold most of his tickets to Brooklyn AOT members when he had trouble getting Rockville Centre AOT members to buy them. Greg was a private investigator by trade, and he had a great opportunity to work in Sierra Leone guarding diamond miners as they transported diamonds from the mines to the capital city. The contract assignment forced him to miss out on the AOT reunion even though he had worked on it. Also, Rockville Centre AOT president from 1968 Mark Fordham, had bought a block of six tickets, although Mark lives in Florida and apparently could not make it. Only two of the four tickets he paid for were actually used by attending guests that night.

Additionally, I was frustrated in my attempts to attract members from the Middletown chapter in Connecticut to the reunion. Although I had made e-mail contact with about eight different Connecticut AOT members, I had no luck in getting any of them to attend. Middletown AOT 1971 Alumni Bob Vince was the only one who actually bought tickets to the event. He purchased two tickets, but he didn't show up at the party. I think he was disappointed at the lack of enthusiasm by his fellow Connecticut AOT alumni.

I personally was annoyed and bothered at the lack of enthusiasm from the early founding members from Oceanside AOT. I had managed to contact at least five of them, and I got noncommittal responses until the last minute, and none of them showed up. The senior-most members from Oceanside who attended were Chip Hawkins from class of 1961 and Rudy Rubala from the class of 1960.

Two days prior to the reunion, I was given contact info for Oceanside AOT alumnus from 1983 Joe Keller. Joe Keller was the editor for a local newspaper called the *Herald*. I contacted Joe at the *Herald* and told him about the reunion. He had prior commitments and could not attend, but Joe arranged to have a photographer from the *Herald* to document the event.

On the night of the reunion, I went to the Knights of Columbus about an hour early to start setting up the room. I set up the computer and projector for the slideshow. Phil Gerardi worked with the person he bought the red and green balloons from to fill the balloons and place them on the table settings. Paul Labrazzo set up the banners. Prior to going to Sierra Leone to work on the security project, Greg Colarossi had taken several old photos from the Brooklyn years and had them blown up to poster size. They were pictures taken at black-tie ballroom dances in the 1940s. We positioned those poster-sized pictures around the room. The room was well set up and decorated to be as green-and-red—with as much AOT nostalgia in the room—as possible. I even brought my young, then—twelve-year-old, son Joseph with me to help me to set things up. I put an AOT tee shirt on him, and he was thrilled to be there.

People started showing up at seven o'clock on the dot. Phil Gerardi had ordered about two hundred new AOT tee shirts that said "Grand Chapter Reunion 2007" under the crest. He sold them at the door for $10 each. By the end of the night, he had almost sold every one of them. We had Phil's wife, Donna, and Greg Colarossi's wife, Margo, who was an alumnus of Oceanside Delta Pi Delta, working the door and checking people in and selling the tee shirts.

I had created a master guest list to check people in. I had a separate list for each chapter and each year for each chapter. So when someone came in, they told what chapter and year they were in, then their name would be checked off on the list. Although we had a few no-shows of people who paid, we also had a lot of people show up who didn't reserve a ticket in advance, wanting to pay at the door. Although we needed to pay the Knights of Columbus in advance and we told everyone there would be no admittance at the door for anyone who didn't pay, we didn't want to turn anyone away, either. We had collected from 140 people prior to the reunion, and on the night of the party, we had another fifty people show up and pay at the door. It really was amazing.

We invited the founding Brooklyn brothers—John Stefano, Ed Carroll, and founding Valley Stream brother Chick Hackney—as guests of honor. Each was also given a free admission for a spouse or guest. Chick flew in to New York alone and didn't bring a guest. John Stefano and Ed Carroll brought their extended families with them. The Brooklyn AOT tables at the reunion had at least twenty-five guests with them. The Brooklyn AOT members' attendance was really the whole buzz about this party. AOT members from every chapter were curious to meet them. No AOT members after 1956 had ever had any contact with Brooklyn AOT, and they were very well received at the reunion.

Brooklyn members Mickey Percy and Joe Brugnolotti were driving into Oceanside looking for the Knights of Columbus when they pulled into the parking lot at the Lincoln Shopping Center to ask directions. They saw some women in the parking lot and asked which way to the Knights of Columbus. The ladies looked into the car and asked, "Are you guys from Brooklyn AOT?"

"Yes, we are," Joe and Mickey said.

"Wow, it's great to meet you guys. Everyone is excited that Brooklyn AOT is coming to this party," the ladies said.

"You were expecting us?" Mickey and Joe said.

"We sure are. We were Delta Pi Delta Sorority from Oceanside, and we are going to the reunion too," the ladies said.

With that, the ladies got into their car, and Joe and Mickey followed them over to the Knights of Columbus. On the way over, Mickey turned to Joe and said, "Hey, Joe, those young ladies were expecting us. We're celebrities here tonight."

That encounter really made their night. Joe and Mickey were impressed that people on the street knew about this party and were anticipating Brooklyn AOT members attending. It really made them feel welcome. During the first hour, as guests arrived, the photographer that Joe Keller sent from the *Herald* showed up and took great pictures of the party. The next issue of the *Herald* had an article about the reunion written by me, with the photos taken by the photographer.

About an hour into the party, we had the DJ stop the music, and I gave a speech thanking the original founding members from Brooklyn AOT for attending, as well as Chick Hackney. I invited all of them up to the DJ booth so we could give out the plaques to each one of them. The whole party of almost two hundred gathered around the DJ booth to watch the awards being given out. After I had finished speaking, Billy Weitzman took the microphone and thanked me for working so hard on this event, and he also chastised those who broke my balls during the organizing of the reunion. Phil Gerardi said a few words and then handed the microphone to John Stefano, who addressed the party. He told us how surprised he and his fellow Brooklyn AOT members were to see how many chapters had spawned from the one they planted in Valley Stream in 1955. He also asked how many in the room were past AOT presidents. John offered thanks to all in attendance who had been AOT presidents.

In addition to the plaques I gave to the AOT brothers of honor, I had also given each one a copy of the Alpha Omega Theta constitution in a plastic folder. Paul Labrazzo had replicas of the AOT patch made up to sell at the reunion. It was a nice copy of the same patch that we used to have sewn on the front of an AOT sweater. Paul had a few of them put into a twelve-inch picture frame, and he gave one to each of the honored brothers.

I was surprised and humbled when Paul gave one to me, and right after that, Oceanside 1961 AOT brother Chip Hawkins stepped up and gave me a present wrapped in gift paper. I opened it, and to my delight, it was a brand-new AOT paddle that Chip had made specially for me. It was an old-style paddle from the 1950s. It was an eight-inch-wide, one-inch-thick oak paddle with a handle carved into it. It was painted green and red and had the letters *AOT* painted on it. I had spent so much time working on this thing and hadn't asked for or expected anything for myself, but I was thrilled that both Paul and Chip thought of me. I keep both the paddle and the AOT crest patch on and next to my desk.

After the awards were given out, the music resumed and the party continued. I finally had time to relax and mill around. I walked the floor with my wife, Mina, and we spoke to people. We chatted with John Stefano and Ed Carroll. Greg Colarossi's wife, Margo, had come into the party from working the door, and I asked her to film my wife and me walking around the party with my camcorder.

I am sure I got to speak to each and every AOT brother who attended that night. The food was served buffet style, and I barely had time to eat one small plate of food. The bar was open all night, and I don't think I had more than two beers. But I had a great time. It was truly a wonderful night. The dance floor was full most of the night, and the DJ played a nice mix of music from every decade spanning the 1940s to the present. Everyone loved the slideshow. It played all night, and I could hear people's surprise whenever someone saw a picture of themselves from high school on the big projector screen.

Not many of my AOT brothers from Oceanside class of 1982 came, but I made a lot of new acquaintances. I particularly enjoyed meeting the Valley Stream AOT guys from the late 1980s to mid-1990s. They were the youngest attendees, and they partied like they were back in high school. As the party came to a close at 11:00 PM, about twenty to thirty people went across the street to John's Union Park Café to continue the festivities. I went there as well and drank with the guys for a few hours more.

The AOT sixtieth-year reunion was one of the most memorable moments in my life. It was a rough ride to get it going, and it was a thankless job until after the reunion was over. In the days and weeks after the party, I continued to get e-mails from thrilled partygoers, and I received a heartfelt apology from Frank Rector on the night of the reunion for the unfortunate incident on his doorstep a month before. This e-mail I got from Peter Martin, the first Baldwin chapter president of 1958, sums it all up nicely:

I don't know what motivated you to set this up, but I'm extremely glad that you decided to invest so much of your time and energy. I would rank this as one of those defining events in my life that not only stirred up a lot of terrific memories but also helped my adult (supposedly more) mature mind put the whole AOT experience in perspective. It was great to meet so many Brooklyn guys.

AOT jackets at 2007 Grand Chapter Reunion

Valley Stream AOT brothers at reunion 2007

Valley Stream AOT brothers

Oceanside Delta Pi Delta ladies under the AOT banner

EPILOGUE

This book is the culmination of sixty years of Alpha Omega Theta's history, four years of Web site development, two fraternal reunions, and a year of writing and research. The author, Fred Gross, was a member of the Oceanside Kappa Theta Chapter from 1978 to 1982. This book was made possible with the kind and generous assistance of many Alpha brothers spanning six decades and multiple chapters.

Despite the turmoil and violence, I look at the time I spent in Alpha Omega Theta Fraternity to be an amazing and fantastic time in my life. Regardless of the school districts' position and banning of fraternities and the public perception of us, I can say with pride that Alpha Omega Theta Fraternity turned young men into outstanding adults. Our combined rosters of every chapter have produced doctors, lawyers, accountants, contractors, businessmen, proprietors, military men, athletes, and even Hollywood stars.

Fraternity membership was a right of passage, which, sadly, no longer exists today on Long Island but unfortunately has been replaced with gangs—who are extremely more violent than anything the fraternities ever were and commit acts more heinous than anything the fraternities ever did. I do not personally know, or have been told, of any AOT member who became a hardcore criminal as a result of his time in the fraternity. On the contrary, AOT turned out men of good character consistently.

If you are a college-age man and enjoyed reading about the life and times of Alpha Omega Theta Fraternity, you can learn more about our noble brotherhood at www.alphaomegatheta.com. Contact us at webmaster@alphaomegatheta.com if you are interested in chartering a chapter of AOT at your college.

ACKNOWLEDGMENTS

Fred Gross would like to personally thank the following AOT brothers for their contributions to this book, the Grand Chapter Reunion, and the AOT Web site since the AOT Web site went live almost four years ago.

Joe "Spooky" Furino—Valley Stream Central AOT President 1980
Spooky has an undying love of Alpha Omega Theta. Joe supplied the polo shirts that were given out at the reunion committee meetings. Joe also supplied the financing to publish this book

Billy Weitzman—Oceanside AOT President 1968
Billy has been a great friend and has been generous with material support for the AOT Web site and the Grand Chapter Reunion in 2007. You are a true Greenie, Billy.

Pete Martin—Baldwin AOT Chapter's First President 1958
Pete has been a true inspiration to me since he reached out to me after he found the AOT Web site. It was Pete who suggested documenting the history of AOT while those of us who lived it are still around. Pete provided great stories and has amazing recollections.

Joe Brugnolotti—Brooklyn AOT 1951
Joe was the driving force behind the founding of the first Long Island chapter in Valley Stream. Every card-carrying member of every chapter of Alpha Omega Theta owes a debt of gratitude to Joe.

Al "Mickey" Percy—Brooklyn AOT 1951
Mickey was one of the Brooklyn brothers responsible for planting the AOT flag in Valley Stream. Brother Mickey's claim to fame was his short part in the

classic Jack Lemmon movie, *The Out of Towners*. Mickey was a mounted cop for the NYPD, and he was seen in the movie chasing Jack Lemmon on horseback through Central Park.

Anthony "Chick" Hackney—Valley Stream Central's First President
Chick was the guy who moved from Brooklyn to Valley Stream and was the catalyst who made it all possible. Despite his modesty, Chick was "the guy" who planted the Alpha flag on Long Island for the first time in 1955.

Bobby Plaia—Valley Stream Central AOT Secretary 1957
Bobby showed up at every reunion meeting; he was the first guy to send a check for his reunion tickets and also provided me with his Valley Stream Central Alumni directory, which made it possible to locate so many people from the Valley Stream chapter for the reunion in 2007.

Bill Trichon—Valley Stream Central AOT 1957
Bill was generous enough to give me the original Brooklyn chapter candleholders used during initiations in Brooklyn AOT. Thanks, Bill. I still keep them on my desk.

Tony Rattoballi—Valley Stream Central AOT 1971
Tony provided great info for both the AOT Web site and this book. Tony never tires of telling Alpha stories.

Rocky Clarke—Freeport Secretary AOT 1956
Rocky provided meeting minutes from the first ten AOT meetings in Freeport, giving a glimpse into the beginnings of the Freeport chapter. Rocky also helped me to locate the original Valley Stream members.

Rich Edlin—Rockville Centre President AOT 1967
Rich was a great inspiration and gave me great insight into the early years of Rockville Centre AOT and the philanthropy that they practiced unselfishly.

Mark Ford—Rockville Centre AOT President 1968
I can't thank you enough for your generous contribution to the Web site and to this book, Mark.

Chip Hawkins—Oceanside AOT 1961
Chip was the first piece of this puzzle. Chip had great memories and was willing to share them with me. Chip provided great info on the earliest AOT brothers from Oceanside. Chip was also kind enough to present me with a brand-new

1950s-style AOT paddle at the reunion in 2007. I still keep it next to my desk, Chip. Thanks, bro.

Phil Gerardi—Oceanside President AOT 1977
Phil has been a great help in gathering info for the Web site, as well as recruiting and collecting money for the reunion in 2007. Phil told some good stories, which were used in this book. Thanks, Phil.

Billy Young—Oceanside President AOT 1982
Billy provided plenty of old photos and great ideas for the AOT Web site, as well as good stories for this book. Billy is one of my oldest friends.

Greg Colarossi—Rockville Centre Sergeant at Arms AOT 1977
Greg put his skills as a private detective to work and unselfishly researched members of the Brooklyn chapter of AOT. Greg's success at locating many of the Brooklyn chapter members enabled us to finally bring the two branches of AOT together at the Grand Chapter Reunion in 2007.

Paul Librizzi—Oceanside AOT 1979
Paul jumped right into the reunion organizing committee and provided both of the banners that we hung on the walls at the reunion.

Mike Librizzi—Oceanside AOT Secretary 1974
Mike was a ball-buster to me when he worked as a bouncer at Oceanside High School, but he made up for it by providing material support for the AOT Web site when it went online, and he was one of the first to send a check to attend the AOT reunion in 2007. You're alright by me bro.

Steve Raff—Valley Stream AOT 1988
Steve contributed great material about VSC circa 1980 to this book.

Patrick "Mike" McKenna—Valley Stream AOT 1966
Mike provided great information for the development of the AOT Web site, particularly the Alumni Directory for VSC AOT.

Chris Smith—Valley Stream AOT President 1992
Chris provided great stories for this book. Thanks, bro.

Jerry Bracco—Freeport AOT Treasurer 1963
Jerry has always made AOT brothers from all chapters welcome at Bracco's Clam Bar in Freeport. He was also kind enough to give my son a summer job.

Lastly, I thank my family. My lovely wife, Mina, who always stood by me and supports my projects; my son, Joseph, who is now at the tender age I was when I was inducted into the fraternity; and my beautiful daughter, Brandi, who is the light of my life.

I also want to mention my mother and father, Fred Gross Sr. and Lorraine Volpe, who no doubt will be surprised when they read this book, and my two sisters Kerrie and Lesley who never experienced fraternities and sororities when they went to high school.

See you all at the next AOT Grand Chapter Reunion.

Alea Iacta Est
First Last Always

INDEX

C

Calgary Alpha Omega Theta-Beta
  Alpha Chapter 266, 280, 295-6
Cangin, John 30-1, 34, 301
Carmeikle, Danny 7, 160-2, 239, 244
Carmeikle, Donald 244
Carmeinke, Danny 7, 160-2, 239, 244
Carroll, Edward "Ed" 7, 16, 18, 21-2,
  24-5, 27-8, 301, 309-10
Catapano, Ray 77
Caylen, Andy 165-6
Ciaffalo, Mike "Snitchy" 122
Ciancia, Joe 251
Cisco, John 47, 58, 307
Clarke, Rocky 57, 59, 61, 63, 66, 298-9,
  318
Colarossi, Greg 126, 258-9, 263, 300-1,
  305-6, 308, 319
Condon, Jimmy 124-5
Coni, Ray 297
Corano, John 139, 141, 198, 203, 208
Counts, the 62, 91-3, 97, 224-6, 229,
  241, 243-4
Cronin, Jeff 74-5
Cue Club 90

D

Delta Gamma Rho 109, 190-1, 241
Delta Phi Delta 17, 28
Delta Phi Sigma 181
Delta Pi Delta 13, 28, 133, 221, 309
Delta Sigma Phi 181
Dodd, John 221

E

Ed and the Crunchy Frogs 256
Edgars, Dustin 250
Edlin, Richard 79, 89

F

Farmer Joel's 146-7, 256, 303-4
Farnswell, George Thomas "Tommy" 134-
  8, 141-4, 150-2, 155-6, 159, 164, 225
  Alpha Omega Theta, member of
  137-8, 150-2, 156, 164
  death 225
  Gross, Fred, friendship with 134-6,
  138, 141, 159
"fleas" 114
Fleishman, Larry 123
Fordham, Mark 259, 308
Franzizi, Mike 304
Freeport Alpha Omega Theta-Zeta
  Chapter 54, 57-8, 71, 75, 84
  beginnings 58-9, 61
  chapter designation changed 61
  charter members 57-8, 62, 298
  dissolution 109
  membership 62
  relationship with
    other AOT chapters 57-8, 75, 298
    other fraternities 109, 191
  reopened 109, 190-1
Freeport High School 57-8, 60-1, 71
Freeport Speedway 58
Furino, Joseph "Spooky" 106, 181, 192-
  4, 218-19, 246, 296
  Alpha Omega Theta
    chapter president of 181, 185-9,
    191-2, 219, 246, 249, 262
    involvement in, grand chapter
    reunion of 296, 301-6
    legacy in 189-90, 218, 249
    life after 191-2, 249
    membership in 181-7, 190, 192
  Alpha Sigma Phi, run-ins with 183-
  6, 188, 192
  nickname, origin 181
  Smith, Chris, friendship with 249, 252